#23

LATINOS
IN SCIENCE,
MATH, AND
PROFESSIONS

LATINOS IN SCIENCE, MATH, AND PROFESSIONS

DAVID E. NEWTON

Facts On File
An imprint of Infobase Publishing

Latinos in Science, Math, and Professions

Copyright © 2007 by David E. Newton

All rights reserved. No part of this book may be reproduced or utilized in any form or by any means, electronic or mechanical, including photocopying, recording, or by any information storage or retrieval systems, without permission in writing from the publisher. For information contact:

Facts On File, Inc.
An imprint of Infobase Publishing
132 West 31st Street
New York NY 10001

Library of Congress Cataloging-in-Publication Data
Newton, David E.
    Latinos in science, math, and professions / David E. Newton.
        p. cm.—(A to Z of Latino Americans)
    Includes bibliographical references and indexes.
    ISBN 978-0-8160-6385-7 (acid-free paper)
    1. Hispanic Americans in science—United States—Biography—Dictionaries. I. Title.
II. Series.
    Q141.N46 2007
    509.2'273—dc22   2006016769

Facts On File books are available at special discounts when purchased in bulk quantities for businesses, associations, institutions, or sales promotions. Please call our Special Sales Department in New York at (212) 967-8800 or (800) 322-8755.

You can find Facts On File on the World Wide Web at http://www.factsonfile.com

Text design by Annie O'Donnell
Cover design by Salvatore Luongo

Printed in the United States of America

VB CGI 10 9 8 7 6 5 4 3 2 1

This book is printed on acid-free paper.

With appreciation to Ann Raker and
members of the New England Old English Sheepdog Rescue,
on behalf of all those sheepies who are not able to say
"please" or "thank you."

CONTENTS

LIST OF ENTRIES

Abel, Carlos A.
Acrivos, Juana Luisa Vivó
Acuna, Mario
Aguilera, Renato J.
Alcalá, José Ramón
Alderete, John F.
Alvarado, Raul, Jr.
Alvarez, Luis Walter
Alvarez, Rodolfo
Alvarez-González, Rafael
Alvariño, Angeles
Amaya, Maria
Arrendondo, Patricia
Avila, Vernon L.
Ayala, Francisco J.
Baca Zinn, Maxine
Baez, Albert V.
Bañuelos, Rodrigo
Barbosa, Pedro
Barona, Andrés, Jr.
Barrera, Cecilio
Benacerraf, Baruj
Bernal, Ivan
Bernal, Martha
Berriozábal, Manuel
Bustamante, Carlos J.
Cabrera, Lydia
Calderón, Alberto P.
Calderón, Calixto P.
Calvillo, Evelyn R.
Candia, Oscar A.

Cardona, Manuel
Cardús, David
Carmona, Richard H.
Casals-Ariet, Jordi
Castro, George
Castro, Gonzalo
Castro, Max
Castro, Peter
Catalano, Carlos
Cavazos, Lauro F.
Chang-Díaz, Franklin
Cifuentes, Inés
Cintron, Guillermo B.
Córdova, France Anne
Cortinas, John V., Jr.
Cota-Robles, Eugene
Cuatrecasas, Pedro
Cubero, Linda Garcia
Dallmeier, Francisco
De La Cancela, Victor
de la Mora, Juan Fernández
Delgado, Jane L.
del Moral, Roger
Díaz, Fernando G.
Díaz, Henry F.
Diaz, Luis A.
Diaz, Nils J.
Díaz, Robert J.
Duran, Benjamin S.
Escalante, Jaime
Escobar, Javier I.

Estévez, L. Antonio
Fernandez, Louis Anthony
Fernandez-Baca, Jaime A.
Fernández-Pol, José A.
Ferreyra, Guillermo S.
Figueroa, Orlando
Finlay, Carlos Juan
Fischbarg, Jorge
Foyo, George
Garcia, Carlos Ernesto
Garcia, Catalina Esperanza
García, Celso-Ramón
García, Héctor P.
Garcia, Jose Dolores, Jr.
García, Julio H.
Garcia, Marcelo H.
García, Oscar N.
Garcia-Luna-Aceves, J. J.
Garzoli, Silvia L.
Gigli, Irma
Gilbert, Fabiola Cabeza de Baca
Gómez, Cynthia A.
Gomez, Frank A.
Gomez-Cambronero, Julian
Gómez-Pompa, Arturo
González, Elma
Gonzalez, Paula
Gonzalez, Rafael C.
Gonzalez-Lima, Francisco
Guerrero, Jorge
Gutiérrez, Ana Sol

AUTHOR'S NOTE

This book reviews some of the most important figures in the physical and social sciences and in the field of invention who have contributed to U.S. culture from the Spanish-speaking world. The book uses the word *Latino* in its title to describe these individuals, although a number of comparable terms have also been used for these men and women. One sometimes sees the terms *Chicano* and *Chicana, Hispanic, Iberian, Mexican American, Cuban American,* or *Dominican American,* for example. Each term is more or less different from the others, a difference that sometimes has considerable significance to individuals to whom it may (or may not) apply.

For example, some people argue that the term *Hispanic* refers only to those individuals whose culture can be traced directly to Spain itself. Similarly, the terms *Latino* and *Latina* are sometimes reserved for individuals whose roots are in Latin America and not specifically in Spain. Although differences in terminology may seem to be insignificant points of semantics, they may be far more than that to some people. In fact, some people contacted for inclusion in this book declined to be listed because they did not define themselves as *Latino* although they were, in fact, Spanish-speaking or from a Latin American country or met the author's criteria for inclusion on some other basis.

To be clear, the basis for inclusion in this listing of important Latinos in the sciences is that an individual (1) come himself or herself from a Spanish-speaking country, such as Spain, Mexico, or Cuba, or have an ancestry that can be traced to such a country; (2) have lived for some significant period of time in the United States; and (3) have achieved some prominence in one of the physical sciences, mathematics, social sciences, or the field of invention.

The list of individuals included in the book is by no means complete. Many outstanding Latino scientists have not been included for a number of reasons, including the author's inability to obtain a complete set of biographical data, the individual's unwillingness to be listed, or lack of space to include all qualified men and women.

If there is any lesson to be learned from the biographical sketches that make up the core of this book, it is the admiration and respect due so many Latino scientists, mathematicians, and inventors. While it is true that some men and women came from well-to-do families in which a college education and professional success were taken for granted, a remarkable number of the scientists described here struggled to overcome prejudice, poverty, lack of English-language skills, and other deficits that would probably have deterred many of their contemporaries, both Latino and Anglo. They are men and women of whom all Americans can be proud.

INTRODUCTION

The United States has long been described as a great "melting pot," a country that owes much of its national character to the contributions of peoples who have come from around the world and brought with them their own customs and traditions. *Melting pot* may not be the most appropriate term for American culture. To a considerable extent, many men and women who have come to the United States have chosen to retain at least some portion of the cultural heritage. Thus, immigrants from the Dominican Republic often become American citizens with as much commitment to their adopted land as any native-born American. But many Dominican Americans also treasure and retain customs and practices important in their native lands.

However one defines the rich mixture that makes up the U.S. population, there is no question about the contribution that Spanish-speaking men and women have made to American history from its very beginning. In the East, Spanish explorers such as Juan Ponce de León, Hernando de Soto, and Álvar Núñez Cabeza de Vaca planted the flag of Spain in parts of Florida, claiming the land for their kings and queens. In the West, a fluid and shifting border between the two young nations of Mexico and the United States ensured that a southwestern culture would be strongly and permanently Hispanic in character. In later centuries, Spanish-speaking populations have continued to arrive and spread throughout the United States, bringing touches of the Dominican Republic,

Peru, Argentina, Mexico, Cuba, and dozens of other Hispanic nations wherever they settled.

And there is hardly an aspect of American culture that has not been influenced by the rich traditions of Spanish speakers. In every part of society, from the arts to politics to sports to the sciences, Spanish speakers have become famous and made their mark on the fields in which they worked.

During the 19th century, the contribution of Latinas and Latinos to the sciences reflected to some extent the state of science itself in this country. The United States had long had a solid tradition of interest in the natural sciences: geology, geography, botany, and the other "useful arts and sciences" whose understanding could be used to improve the quality of life in this new country. So it is not surprising that the earliest Latina and Latino scientists were interested in problems of disease (Juan Carlos Finlay), useful herbs and food plants (Ynés Mexía), healthful nutrition (Fabiola Cabeza de Baca Gilbert), and cultural history (Lydia Cabrera).

By the beginning of the 20th century, however, American scientists were becoming more interested in the pure and abstract sciences. The early decades of the century saw the rise of robust professional scientific associations, specialized schools and colleges of science, federal funding for pure research, and other elements of a mature scientific profession in the United States. Some Hispanics made important contributions to the early development of the physical, biological, and social sciences in the United States. Somewhat surprising, however, is the relative paucity of Spanish surnames among the great leaders of American science between 1900 and 1950. How does one explain that phenomenon?

One explanation, of course, is that, until recent decades, Hispanics probably made up a relatively small fraction of the U.S. population. Exact data to support that conclusion are difficult to find since the U.S. Bureau of the Census did not inquire about Hispanic origins until 1970. Yet, it is intuitively clear that the greatly increased immigration of Spanish-speaking people from South and Central America, Mexico, and the Caribbean over the last half century has greatly increased the pool from which scientists come in this country.

At least equally important, however, has been another factor: low expectations and limited educational opportunities for people of Hispanic heritage. Latinos had to struggle not only with their academic subjects but also with the lack of incentives provided them in order to achieve success in their fields.

That situation has clearly begun to change. As recently as 1991, 4.5 percent of all bachelor's degrees in science and engineering were earned by Hispanics, 3.1 percent of all master's degrees, and 3.2 percent of all doctorates. By comparison, Hispanics at the time made up just over 9 percent of the general population in the United States. Slightly more than a decade later, in 2003, the number of Hispanics earning bachelor's, master's, and doctoral degrees had increased to 7.2 percent, 5.2 percent, and 4.1 percent, respectively—changes that significantly exceed increases in the Latino population itself. Doors have begun to open, and more and more Latinos from the United States and other parts of the world have begun to form a significant core of prominent workers in the physical and social sciences.

Abel, Carlos A.
(Carlos Alberto Abel)
(1930–) *immunochemist*

Carlos Alberto Abel is a medical researcher who has specialized in the chemical components of the immune system. In recent years, he has focused on a study of the human immunodeficiency virus (HIV), its chemical structure, and its biological function.

Abel was born in Buenos Aires, Argentina, on May 7, 1930. He received his bachelor of science from Manuel Belgrano College, in Buenos Aires, in 1949, and his M.D. from the University of Buenos Aires in 1957. For two years, he served as a physician in the pediatric section of the Children's Hospital in Buenos Aires before relocating to the United States and beginning an internship at St. Joseph's Hospital in Providence, Rhode Island. He then served as a resident at the University of Maryland Hospital in Baltimore from 1960 to 1966.

Over the next four years, Abel served in a number of research positions, including research fellow in immunology at the Scripps Clinic, in La Jolla, California (1966–69); research fellow at the Arthritis Foundation in New York City and at the Wellcome Trust in London (1969); and visiting scientist at the University of Oxford (1969–70). In 1970, he accepted an appointment as assistant professor of biophysics and genetics at the University of Colorado Medical Center, in Denver. He was later promoted to associate professor, a post he held until 1984. During the same period, Abel was a member of the immunological section of the National Jewish Hospital in Denver.

In 1984, Abel left Denver to become senior scientist at the Geraldine Brush Cancer Research Institute, in San Francisco, a post he held until 1992. He then resigned that position to form his own consulting business in immunological medicine. Abel's research has focused on the chemical characteristics of lymphocytes, white blood cells that play an essential role in the immune system, and the functions they play in immune responses. He has become very interested in the study of HIV and has served on the University of California Task Force on AIDS.

Further Reading

"Abel, Carlos Alberto." In *American Men & Women of Science,* 21st ed., edited by Pamela M. Kalte and Katherine H. Nemeh, vol. 1, 7. Detroit: Thomson Gale, 2003.

"Carlos Alberto Abel." In *The Hispanic American Almanac,* 3d ed., edited by Sonia G. Benson, 1. Farmington Hills, Mich.: Thomson Gale, 2003.

Acrivos, Juana Luisa Vivó
(Juana Luisa Adolfina Vivó)
(1928–) *physical chemist*

Juana Luisa Vivó Acrivos is an internationally recognized authority on a number of topics in the field of physical chemistry, including X-ray absorption spectroscopy, in which the way X-rays are taken up by materials is used to study their properties; organic and cuprate superconductors, materials consisting of carbon compounds and/or copper that conduct an electric current with essentially no resistance; metallic-ammonia systems; and X-ray and electron diffraction studies, in which the properties of a material are studied by the way in which X-rays and/or electrons pass through them.

Born Juana Luisa Adolfina Vivó on June 24, 1928, in Havana, Cuba, she was the daughter of Lilia Azpeitia and Adolfo Vivó. She was educated at the University of Havana, where she received her B.S. in 1951 and her D.Sc. (Doctor of Science) in 1956. Concurrently, she was awarded her Ph.D. in physical chemistry, with a minor in mathematics, from the University of Minnesota, in Minneapolis. Also in 1956, she was married to Andreas Acrivos, a native of Greece who was later to become famous as one of the world's foremost authorities on fluid mechanics. Between 1956 and 1962, she completed two postdoctoral programs, one at Stanford University, in Stanford, California (1956–59), and one at the University of California at Berkeley (1959–62).

Upon completing her postdoctoral studies, Acrivos was hired as assistant professor in the department of chemistry at San Jose State University, in San Jose, California. She was later promoted to associate professor (1967), full professor (1972), and upon her retirement, emerita professor (2000). In addition to these assignments at San Jose State, Acrivos also served as the National Science Foundation Woman Professor of Chemical Biodynamics at San Jose from 1987 to 1988; visiting scientist at Stanford University from 1971 to 1975

and 1980 to 1987; visiting fellow at Trinity College of Cambridge University, in Cambridge, England, in 1983; visiting fellow at Lucy Cavendish College of Cambridge University in 1990; and visiting scientist at the Cavendish Laboratory at Cambridge University in 2000. She is now retired.

Acrivos is the author of more than 100 papers in peer-reviewed journals and coeditor of *Physics and Chemistry of Electrons and Ions in Condensed Matter* (with N. F. Mott and A. D. Joffe). In addition to her fellowships at Cambridge, she has been given San Jose's Meritorious and Professional Performance Award three times (1984, 1986, and 1987), the Dean's Award for Exemplary Research (1976), and Phi Kappa Phi's Distinguished Academic Achievement award (1980). In 1975, she was elected a University Fellow at San Jose State.

Further Reading
"Acrivos, Juana Luisa Vivo." In *American Men & Women of Science,* 21st ed., edited by Pamela M. Kalte and Katherine H. Nemeh, vol. 1, 23. Detroit: Thomson Gale, 2003.
"Vivó Acrivos, Juana Luisa Adolfina." In *Who's Who among Hispanic Americans, 1994–95,* 3d ed., edited by Amy Unterburger, 872–873. Detroit: Gale Research, 1995.

Acuna, Mario
(Mario Humberto Acuna)
(1940–) *space scientist*

Mario Humberto Acuna has served in a number of roles at the National Aeronautics and Space Administration (NASA), including principal investigator and coinvestigator, instrument scientist and project scientist for the *Explorer 47* and *50, Mariner 10, Pioneer 11, Voyagers 1* and *2,* and Viking missions. In 1986, he was chosen to be principal investigator for the Mars Observer Magnetic Field Investigation, later the Mars Global Surveyor Mission. This mission's spacecraft arrived at Mars in

September 1997, and Acuna is now analyzing data transmitted to Earth by the *Mars Global Surveyor* about Mars's magnetic field.

Acuna was born in Córdoba, Argentina, on March 21, 1940. He attended the National University of Tucumán, in Tucumán, Argentina, where he earned his bachelor's degree in humanities and economics in 1963 and his M.S.E.E. (Master of Science in Electrical Engineering) in 1967. During the period from 1963 to 1967, Acuna was employed by the Argentine National Space Research Commission at the University of Tucumán in several cooperative space research projects with NASA's Goddard Space Flight Center (GSFC). He was also involved in a series of upper-atmosphere space research projects conducted with high-altitude balloons and meteorological satellite tracking stations.

The mid- to late 1960s was a period of unrest in Argentina, when military leaders routinely interfered with the operation of the nation's system of higher education. Acuna decided his prospects for continued graduate studies would be better in the United States, so he left Argentina in 1967 and took a job as head of the Electronics Systems Division at the aeronautical company Fairchild-Hiller Corporation. He remained with Fairchild-Hiller until 1969, when he was appointed design engineer for research and development at NASA's GSFC in Greenbelt, Maryland. Acuna has continued his affiliation with GSFC ever since, where his primary interest is in the development of instruments for the measurement of geophysical magnetic fields as well as plasmas, electromagnetic waves, gamma rays, and X-rays. During his early years at GSFC, Acuna pursued his doctoral studies at the Catholic University, in Washington, D.C., earning his Ph.D. in space science in 1974.

Acuna is the author of more than 140 scholarly papers and is in demand as a speaker at meetings and conferences on topics related to planetary exploration, magnetic fields and plasmas in the solar system, and instrumentation for space research. His work has been honored with a number of awards, including the Schneebaum Memorial Award for Engineering Excellence, the NASA Medal for Exceptional Scientific Achievement, the Exceptional Service Medal, the Award of Merit, and the Distinguished Service Medal, all NASA honors, the last being the agency's highest honor. He has also received the Outstanding Engineering Achievement Award of the Catholic University Alumni Association and the Outstanding Technical Contribution Award given by the Society of Hispanic Professional Engineers. In 2003, he was awarded a Presidential Rank Meritorious Award for his service to the U.S. government.

Further Reading

"Acuna, Mario Humberto." In *American Men & Women of Science,* 21st ed., edited by Pamela M. Kalte and Katherine H. Nemeh, vol. 1, 24. Detroit: Thomson Gale, 2003.

SpaceRef.Canada. "NASA Scientist's Career Spans Agency History." Available online. URL: http://www.spaceref.ca/news/viewpr.html?pid=15942. Posted on January 18, 2005.

Aguilera, Renato J.
(1957–) *immunologist*

Renato J. Aguilera's research focuses on two areas: learning more about the genetic basis for the production of essential chemicals involved in the formation of lymphocytes, a type of white blood cell, in the body's immune system and the development of a vaccine that can be used against viruses such as the human immunodeficiency virus.

Aguilera was born in El Paso, Texas, on December 22, 1957. His father is Mexican, and his mother, a second-generation Mexican American. Although born in the United States, Aguilera grew up in Ciudad Juárez, Mexico, just across the Rio Grande from El Paso. He has written that his father was very proud of being Mexican and wanted Aguilera to grow up in Mexico and speak only Spanish. As a result, Aguilera remained in Ciudad Juárez until he was a teenager, an experience he still treasures because, he says, it taught him to appreciate his Mexican heritage.

When he reached the age of 15, Aguilera moved back across the river to El Paso, where he finished high school. His high school years were difficult, primarily because he spoke English poorly. He continued to work hard, however, and eventually graduated with senior honors in English, political science, and history. Still, it was the sciences and mathematics that interested Aguilera most, and when he enrolled at the University of Texas at El Paso (UTEP), he decided to major in biology. He received his B.S. from UTEP in 1981 and his M.S. in biology, with a specialization in immunochemistry, in 1982. Aguilera then enrolled at the University of California at Berkeley, from which he received his Ph.D. in immunology in 1987.

After completing a two-year postdoctoral program in immunology at Berkeley, Aguilera accepted a job as assistant professor in the department of molecular and cellular biology at the University of California at Los Angeles (UCLA). He was promoted to associate professor in 1997 and in 2002, was appointed professor in the department of biological sciences at UTEP, a post he continues to hold today. In addition to his teaching and research responsibilities, Aguilera has served as member of a number of important committees, including the board of directors of the Society for Advancement of Chicanos and Native Americans in Science, the leadership committee at the Jonsson Comprehensive Cancer Center, and the board of scientific counselors of the National Institute of Environmental Health Sciences. He has also been codirector of the Minority Access to Research Careers Program at UCLA, director of the graduate program in biology at UTEP, deputy director of the Border Biomedical Research Center at UTEP, and director of the RISE (Research Internships

in Science and Engineering) Scholars Program at UTEP.

One of Aguilera's primary fields of interest is the study of infectious diseases among people living in the border community of Mexico and the United States. He and his colleagues are interested in learning more about infectious agents present in the area, particularly those that might be used in a biological attack against the United States. Their mission is not only to expand research in this area but also to increase the number of trained specialists who can improve the health of individuals living in the border community.

Further Reading

"Aguilera, Renato J." In *Who's Who among Hispanic Americans, 1992–93,* 2d ed., edited by Amy Unterburger, 10. Detroit: Gale Research, 1992.

Athey, Susan. "Profile: Dr. Renato J. Aguilera." National Institute of General Medical Services, Minority Programs Update (Winter 1999). Available online. URL: http://publications.nigms.nih.gov/mpu/winter99/#profile. Downloaded on February 20, 2005.

Society for Advancement of Chicanos and Native Americans in Science. "Dr. Renato Aguilera." SACNAS Biography Project. Available online. URL: http://64.171.10.183/biography/Biography.asp?mem=25&type=2. Downloaded on February 20, 2005.

Alcalá, José Ramón
(1940–) *anatomist*

José Ramón Alcalá is a leading researcher on the structure and function of the membranes that make up the lens of the mammalian eye. His research has led to a better understanding of the cause, nature, development, prevention, and treatment of cataracts, a condition that results in a cloudiness of the lens and diminished vision. He has developed methods for using experimental animals in the research on human ocular (eye) disorders and diseases.

Alcalá was born in Ponce, Puerto Rico, on May 1, 1940, to Aurea Estela Ruiz, a registered nurse, and José Antonio Alcalá, a civil engineer. His father died when Alcalá was eight years old, and his mother remarried a year later. When his stepfather, a member of the U.S. Army, was transferred to Fort Leonard Wood, Missouri, in 1956, Alcalá left the school he was attending in Santurce and finished high school at Waynesville High School, adjacent to Fort Leonard Wood. He then went to the University of Missouri, in Columbia, where he received his B.A. and M.A., both in zoology, in 1964 and 1966, respectively. He undertook his graduate studies at the University of Illinois, earning a Ph.D. in anatomy in 1972.

After receiving his doctorate, Alcalá accepted an offer to teach and do research at the Wayne State University School of Medicine, in Detroit. He served there as assistant professor (1972–78) and associate professor (1978–87) of anatomy, associate professor (1986–88) and full professor (1988–90) of ophthalmology, and professor of anatomy and cell biology (1987–92). In 1992, he left Wayne State to join the faculty at the Ponce School of Medicine, in Ponce, Puerto Rico, where he was chair and professor of anatomy (1992–96) and professor of anatomy (1996–97) before retiring in 1997.

Alcalá is the author of 36 scientific articles and three book chapters. One of his articles on the protein composition of bovine (cattle) lens membranes is among the most frequently cited articles in its field, still receiving mention in other papers as often as 10 times a year. Among the honors he has received are the Distinguished Service Award of the Association of Black Medical Students in 1985 and the Distinguished Service Award of Wayne State's Office of Minority Recruitment in 1987. He is a member of nine professional societies, including the American Society of Mammalogists, the Society of the Sigma Xi, the Association for Research in Vision and Ophthalmology, and the International Society for Eye Research.

Further Reading

"Alcala, Jose Ramon." In *American Men & Women of Science,* 21st ed., edited by Pamela M. Kalte and Katherine H. Nemeh. vol. 1, 74. Detroit: Thomson Gale, 2003.

"Alcala, Jose Ramon." In *Who's Who among Hispanic Americans, 1994–95,* 3d ed., edited by Amy Unterburger, 18. Detroit: Gale Research, 1995.

"José Ramón Alcalá." In *The Hispanic American Almanac,* 3d ed., edited by Sonia G. Benson, 638–639. Farmington Hills, Mich.: Thomson Gale, 2003.

Kusinitz, Marc. "Jose Alcala." In *Notable Twentieth-Century Scientists,* edited by Emily J. McMurray, 15–16. Detroit: Gale Research, 1995.

Alderete, John F.
(1950–) *microbiologist*

John F. Alderete specializes in research on the world's number-one sexually transmitted disease (STD) caused by the parasite *Trichomonas vaginilis,* an organism that increases one's risk for catching human immunodeficiency virus. He has also been active in a variety of programs designed to encourage Latinos and Latinas, blacks, Native Americans, and other minorities and nonminorities to achieve their educational and professional goals.

Alderete was born of Mexican parents in Las Vegas, New Mexico, on October 28, 1950. He was the third of seven children brought up in a typical barrio (a neighborhood of primarily Spanish-speaking individuals) where many homes lacked basic facilities that most people take for granted. He has written, for example, of having to go into the surrounding countryside with his family on weekends to search for wood with which to cook and heat their home or to sell so the family could earn extra money. During the week, Alderete remembers, he rose at 4:35 A.M. to work a few hours at a bakery

John F. Alderete is professor of microbiology at the University of Texas Health Science Center at San Antonio. *(Courtesy of Dr. John F. Alderete)*

his true love, biology. A year later, he earned his second B.S., this time in biology. While still an undergraduate at NMTech, Alderete published his first scientific paper.

In fall 1974, Alderete took an internship with Tom H. Wilson in the department of physiology at the Harvard Medical School. After completing his term at Harvard where he generated enough data for his second paper, he entered the doctoral program in microbiology at the University of Kansas at Lawrence. He completed that program and was awarded his Ph.D. in microbiology in 1978. After a two-year postdoctoral fellowship at the University of North Carolina at Chapel Hill, Alderete accepted a teaching and research appointment at the University of Texas Health Science Center at San Antonio (UT-HSCSA). He was appointed professor of microbiology at UT-HSCSA and has remained in that post ever since.

Alderete has an impressive professional record, with more than 53 book chapters and op-ed articles and more than 100 peer-reviewed papers to his credit. He has given more than 363 seminars on his research and educational issues throughout the United States and around the world and 135 presentations at scientific meetings. He serves on the editorial board of three journals, *Infection and Immunity, Archives of Medical Research,* and *BMC Microbiology,* and has been a reviewer for more than 46 other journals.

The educational challenges faced by minority students has always been an issue of special concern to Alderete. He has organized and/or participated in a number of programs designed to encourage such students to achieve their maximum potential. For example, he designed a program known as the Saturday Morning Science Camp for minority students, their parents, and teachers, which after more than 15 years was adopted by a community-based organization. He has also sponsored a number of weekend laboratory tours, career days, and mentoring programs, such as providing internships for 38 high school and undergraduate students. In 2004,

before attending junior high school. Throughout high school, he worked full time at a gas station.

Alderete attended elementary school in his own neighborhood with other Latino children. For junior high school, however, he transferred to a different school district of mostly privileged Latino children, where, he has said, he felt as if he had been "thrown into a fire." He graduated from both that school and the same local district high school, convinced that he could achieve whatever he attempted. After graduation from high school, he enrolled at the science-elitist New Mexico Institute of Mining and Technology (NMTech) at Socorro, New Mexico. Uncertain as to what he wanted to do with his life, Alderete decided to major in mathematics. He earned his B.S. in that subject in 1973 but had meanwhile discovered he was awarded the William A. Hinton Research Training Award from the American Society for Microbiology (ASM) for his work with underrepresented minority students in the sciences and was elected Fellow of the Academy of Microbiology of ASM. Alderete helped found a company, Xenotape Diagnostics, that produced the first-ever point-of-care diagnostic for the STD he has studied. He now serves as vice president and chief scientific officer of the company.

Further Reading

"John F. Alderete." Sigma Xi: The Scientific Research Society. Available online. URL: http://www.sigmaxi.org/meetings/archive/meet.2000.nom.ag.shtml. Downloaded on September 8, 2005.

Society for Advancement of Chicanos and Native Americans in Science. "Dr. John F. Alderete—Microbiologist." SACNAS Biography Project. Available online. URL: http://64.171.10.183/biography/Biography.asp?mem=26&type=2. Downloaded on February 4, 2005.

Xenotope Diagnostics. "John F. Alderete." Available online. URL: http://www.xenotope.com/bios.html. Downloaded on November 10, 2005.

Alvarado, Raul, Jr.

(1946–   ) *engineer*

Raul Alvarado, Jr., has worked for more than two decades in the aeronautical and space fields with the Rockwell International and McDonnell Douglas corporations. He has also volunteered for more than 15 years in programs designed to promote opportunities for minorities in engineering, serving most recently as chair of the Society of Hispanic Professional Engineers Foundation, whose purpose it is to increase the participation of Latinos and Latinas in the engineering profession.

Alvarado was born in El Centro, California, on January 5, 1946, to Carmen and Raul Alvarado, of Mexican heritage. He attended Central Union High School in his hometown, concentrating more on athletics and extracurricular activities than on academics. Like many children of Hispanic background, Alvarado received little encouragement from his teachers and counselors and never gave serious thought to attending college until his senior year when a counselor said to him that he had never realized Alvarado had been doing so well in school. Had he known, the counselor said, he could have gotten a scholarship for Alvarado. In spite of that discouraging experience, Alvarado did enroll at Imperial Valley Junior College, from which he received his associate's degree in mathematics in 1966. He then attended Northrop University, in Inglewood, California (no longer in existence as an independent institution), where he was granted a B.S. in aerospace engineering in 1973.

Alvarado's first job after graduating from Northrop was with Rockwell International, at the time a large conglomerate with active space and aircraft divisions. Alvarado served as executive assistant for personnel development at Rockwell from 1981 to 1984 and as project engineer and proposal manager from 1984 to 1989. In 1989, he left Rockwell to take a position as senior engineering scientist in the space station division of McDonnell Douglas. His assignment at McDonnell Douglas, which merged with Boeing in 1997, is to work on the data management system, a computer system that controls the operation of all elements present in the *International Space Station.*

Alvarado first heard about the work of the Society of Hispanic Professional Engineers (SHPE) in 1974, shortly after the organization was formed. Although he had never thought very much about his own Hispanic heritage, he began to appreciate the special contributions it had made to his life and to American culture. He determined to do what he could to expand the opportunities of Latinos and Latinas in the sciences and specifically as engineers. He became increasingly active in SHPE and eventually was elected national president three times, the only person to have been so honored.

Since 1980, he has also been chair of the SHPE Foundation.

Alvarado has also served in a number of other community and educational organizations. He has been a member of the advisory board of the Center for Employment Training in San Jose, California; a founding member of the National Association of Elected and Appointed Officials; and a member of the board of trustees of the Northrop University Alumni Association. He was given the City of Los Angeles Mayor's Award in 1980, the Minority Achievers Award of the YMCA in 1981, and the Society of Career Development for Minorities Award for Outstanding Support for Career Conference in 1988. In 1991, he was named the winner of the Hispanic Engineer National Achievement Award for Community Service.

Further Reading

"Alvarado, Raul, Jr." In *Who's Who among Hispanic Americans, 1994–95,* 3d ed., edited by Amy Unterburger, 28. Detroit: Gale Research, 1995.

Mellado, Carmela. "Helping Dreams of Opportunity Come True." Hispanic Engineer and Information Technology Online. Available online. URL: http://www.hispanicengineer.com/artman/publish/article_39.shtml. Downloaded on March 2, 2005.

Alvarez, Luis Walter

(1911–1988) *physicist, inventor*

Winner of the 1968 Nobel Prize in physics for his research on the bubble chamber (a device for detecting radiation), Luis Walter Alvarez was known for his studies on a wide variety of phenomena, including the isotope of hydrogen known as tritium, at least three different forms of radar, the first atomic bomb, the catastrophic effects of asteroid collisions with the Earth, and the properties of subatomic particles such as the neutron and proton. Alvarez was also a prolific inventor with 22 patents to his credit. For this work, he was

elected to the National Inventor's Hall of Fame in 1978.

Alvarez was born in San Francisco, California, on June 13, 1911. His paternal grandfather had been born in Spain but left home for Cuba at an early age. He later moved to the United States, where he made a fortune in real estate in the Los Angeles area. He then moved to Hawaii before returning to California and settling in San Francisco. Alvarez's father, Walter Clement Alvarez, was a physician who carried out research in physiology during part of each day and maintained a private medical practice for the rest of the day. Dr. Alvarez left San Francisco in 1925 to take a position with the Mayo Clinic, in Rochester, Minnesota. There, Dr. Alvarez worked at first as a research physiologist and later as a clinician. Upon his retirement, he began writing a syndicated newspaper column on medicine, a column that eventually became so popular that Dr. Alvarez became known as "America's Family Doctor." Luis Alvarez's mother was Harriet Skidmore Smythe, whose family was of Irish origin. The Smythe family had left Ireland to found a missionary school in Fuzhou, China. His parents had met each other and married while they were both students at the University of California at Berkeley.

Luis Alvarez attended grammar school and Polytechnic High School in San Francisco before moving to Rochester with his parents. From an early age, he was fascinated not with the medical and biological subjects that made up his father's career, but with the tools and technology he found in his home. At the age of 11, for example, and with his father's help, he built his own radio set, an especially impressive accomplishment since the radio had become a practical invention only a few years earlier. Alvarez also taught himself how to wire electrical circuits before ever having had formal instruction in physics and electricity. By the time Alvarez was attending high school in Rochester, his father had arranged for him to receive personal instruction as an apprentice in the clinic's machine shop.

When Alvarez enrolled at the University of Chicago in 1928, he planned to major in chemistry and mathematics. He changed his mind, however, when he discovered how much he disliked the laboratory work associated with chemistry. Also, he had found a new passion: experimental physics. He enrolled in a course entitled "Advanced Experimental Physics: Light" and found, as he later wrote in his autobiography, "It was love at first sight." He then proceeded to take 11 more physics courses in the next five quarters, and his career as an experimental physicist was confirmed. He was awarded his bachelor's degree in physics in 1932 and then remained at Chicago to complete his master's degree two years later and his Ph.D. in 1936.

While still a graduate student, Alvarez made the first of a number of important discoveries for which he became famous. Along with his adviser, Arthur Compton, and another physicist, Thomas Johnson, he discovered that the number of cosmic rays reaching the Earth's surface varies depending on the direction from which they reach the planet's atmosphere. The three researchers developed an explanation as to how this phenomenon comes about. They concluded that cosmic rays consist of positively charged particles that are deflected disproportionately in different directions.

Shortly after receiving his doctoral degree, Alvarez was offered a position as research associate at the University of California's Berkeley Radiation Laboratory by its director, E. O. Lawrence. He accepted, beginning an association with the university that was to last 42 years. He took two leaves of absence from Berkeley during this long period, once from 1940 to 1943 to work at the radiation laboratory of the Massachusetts Institute of Technology (MIT) and a second time during World War II to work for the Manhattan Project under which the first atomic bomb was developed. His time with the Manhattan Project was spent at the University of Chicago's Metallurgical Laboratory (Met Lab) from 1943 to 1944 and at the Los Alamos Laboratory from 1944 to 1945.

Luis Walter Alvarez was awarded the 1968 Nobel Prize in physics for his research on the bubble chamber, a device for studying nuclear reactions. *(© The Nobel Foundation)*

Alvarez had been at the University of California for only a short time before he had earned a nickname by which he eventually became widely known: "the prize wild idea man." The name was suggested by colleagues who were amazed that Alvarez never seemed to lack for new and very different ideas for research projects. One of the first of these projects was a study of K-electron capture, completed during Alvarez's first year at Berkeley. K-electron capture is a process by which some atomic nuclei pull in an electron from the first orbital around the nucleus and, in the process, change into a different kind of atom. Shortly after his work on K-electron capture, Alvarez made another breakthrough. He studied two simple isotopes, hydrogen-3 (also known as tritium) and helium-3, which often occur together and whose differences had long puzzled scientists. Alvarez made two important discoveries about the isotopes, that tritium is radioactive and that helium-3 is a normal component of natural helium gas.

The onset of World War II interrupted Alvarez's research at Berkeley, as it did the work of most American scientists. He left Berkeley for a new assignment at MIT, where he began work on improving the way in which radar was being used by and against aircraft. Radar had been invented in 1935 by the British physicist Robert Watson-Watt. The technology, whose name is an acronym for *ra*dio *d*etecting *a*nd *r*anging, had proved to be an invaluable tool in detecting aircraft during the early years of World War II. Some historians claim that the use of radar saved Great Britain from defeat by Germany in the early 1940s. But the technology had lost some of its effectiveness as new methods were developed to detect and counteract radar signals.

At MIT, Alvarez worked on three radar projects that increased the system's efficiency and extended the conditions in which radar could be used. One of these systems, code-named Vixen, was developed to make radar more effective in detecting submarines that had surfaced. A second system, ground-controlled approach, used radar signals to permit aircraft to land at night and in poor visibility. The third system, code-named Eagle, involved modifications in radar use that allowed pilots to find targets for their bombs in heavily clouded or overcast skies.

After completing his work on radar at MIT, Alvarez was asked to work on development of the new atomic bomb, first at the Chicago Met Lab site and later at Los Alamos. His major contribution during this period was the development of ignition devices used in Little Boy and Fat Man, the first nuclear weapons dropped on Japan on August 6 and 9, 1945.

At the end of the war, Alvarez returned to Berkeley, where he worked with Lawrence on the development of new particle accelerators, or "atom smashers." As part of this work, he decided to focus on improving one of the most common instruments used in studying accelerator reactions, the bubble chamber. Alvarez introduced the use of liquid hydrogen in the bubble chamber, greatly simplifying the interpretation of phenomena. It was his accomplishments in this area that earned Alvarez the 1968 Nobel Prize in physics. As a result of the improved bubble chamber invented by Alvarez, he and other scientists were able to discover a number of new elementary particles that had never been seen before.

The scientific discovery for which Alvarez may be best known to the general public came about accidentally. In 1980, he decided to travel on a research project to Italy with his son, geologist Walter Alvarez. During this visit the Alvarezes found a band of sedimentary rock with a concentration of the rare metal iridium much higher than normal. The band was found to have an age of about 65 million years. In attempting to explain their discovery, the Alvarezes hypothesized that the band was formed when an asteroid, containing high concentrations of iridium, collided with the Earth. They also suggested that that collision released so much smoke and dust into the atmosphere that solar radiation was greatly decreased. That decrease in radiation, they surmised, resulted in a dramatic loss of plant life, which, in turn, resulted in the death of great numbers of animals on Earth and, most important, in the extinction of dinosaurs.

In addition to the Nobel Prize, Alvarez received a number of honors and awards, including the Einstein Medal, the Michelson Award, and the National Medal of Science. He was awarded honorary degrees by the University of Chicago, Carnegie-Mellon University, and Kenyon College.

He died at his home in Berkeley on September 1, 1988.

Further Reading

Alvarez, Luis. *Alvarez: Adventures of a Physicist.* New York: Basic Books, 1987.

Codye, Corinn, and Bob Masheris. *Luis W. Alvarez.* Fort Bragg, Calif.: Raintree Publishers, 1989.

Garwin, Richard L. "Memorial Tribute for Luis W. Alvarez." In *Memorial Tributes,* vol. 5. National Academy of Engineering. Washington, D.C.: National Academy Press, 1992.

Towers, Peter. *Discovering Alvarez: Selected Works of Luis W. Alvarez.* Chicago: University of Chicago Press, 1987.

Weber, Robert L. *Pioneers of Science: Nobel Prize Winners in Physics.* Washington, D.C.: American Institute of Physics, 1980.

Alvarez, Rodolfo

(1936–) *sociologist*

Rodolfo Alvarez is the third Mexican American to have earned a Ph.D. in sociology in the United States. His special areas of expertise include the study of ways in which institutional discrimination based on class, gender, and race develops and how this discrimination affects the institution's relationship with the general public, the productivity and motivation of the institution's workers, and the institution's ability to recruit, promote, and maintain efficient working relationships with employees.

Alvarez was born in San Antonio, Texas, on October 23, 1936, the son of Ramon and Laura Lobo Alvarez. Upon graduation from high school, he enlisted in the U.S. Marine Corps, reaching the rank of sergeant before receiving an honorable discharge in 1957. He then enrolled at San Francisco State University, from which he received his B.A. in sociology in 1961. Prior to completing his studies at San Francisco State, he spent a year in Europe, studying at the Institute for American Universities in Aix-en-Provence, France. In 1960, he was awarded a certificate in European studies by the institute. Alvarez attended the University of Washington in Seattle for his graduate work, earning an M.A. and Ph.D. in sociology in 1964 and 1966, respectively. Periodically, he has also participated in a number of management training programs, including the Institute for Education Management, sponsored jointly by the School of Business and School of Education at Harvard University in 1973; the executive training program, sponsored by the Anderson Graduate School of Management at the University of California at Los Angeles (UCLA) in 1974–75; and the program in strategic planning in higher education, offered by the National Center for Higher Education, in Denver, in 1981.

Upon receiving his doctoral degree, Alvarez was offered a position as assistant professor in the department of sociology at Yale University. He held that post from 1966 to 1972, before accepting an offer to become associate professor of sociology at UCLA in the fall of 1972. He was promoted to full professor in 1980, a post he held until his retirement from UCLA in 2003. He now holds the title of professor emeritus of sociology. In addition to his positions at Yale and UCLA, Alvarez has served as visiting lecturer in the department of sociology at Wesleyan University in Middletown, Connecticut, and as director of UCLA's Chicano Studies Research Center from 1972 to 1974. In 1973, he founded the Spanish Speaking Mental Health Research Center, of which he became director and principal investigator. Alvarez has been very active in a number of sociological associations and has served as president of Alpha Kappa Delta, the international honor society in sociology; the Association for Humanist Sociology; the Pacific Sociological Association; and the Society for the Study of Social Problems. He is the author of *Discrimination in Organizations* (with Kenneth G. Lutterman, 1979) and *Racism, Elitism,*

Professionalism: Barriers to Community Mental Health (1976).

Further Reading

"Alvarez, Rodolfo." In *Who's Who among Hispanic Americans, 1994–95,* 3d ed., edited by Amy Unterburger, 33. Detroit: Gale Research, 1995.
"Rodolfo Alvarez." In *The Hispanic American Almanac,* 3d ed., edited by Sonia G. Benson, 645. Farmington Hills, Mich.: Thomson Gale, 2003.

Alvarez-González, Rafael
(1958–   ) *molecular biologist*

Rafael Alvarez-González's research focuses on the chemical structure and behavior of fundamental compounds involved in a variety of life processes, such as the enzymes that catalyze the reactions by which molecules of DNA (deoxyribonucleic acid) replicate (make copies of) themselves and synthesize new molecules of RNA (ribonucleic acid). He has also studied the chemical nature and behavior of chromatin, the material that makes up chromosomes; the process of signal transduction, by which cells use chemicals to transmit information into, out of, and through their structure; and the way in which genes are expressed in eukaryotic cells.

Alvarez-González was born in the state of Michoacán, in Mexico, on November 25, 1958. He attended the University of Michoacán, in Morelia, from which he received a B.S. in microbiology and chemistry in 1979. He continued his graduate studies at the University of North Texas, in Denton, which granted him his M.S. and Ph.D. in biochemistry in 1982 and 1985, respectively. Alvarez-González then completed two postdoctoral programs, one at the University of Zurich's Institute of Biochemistry and Pharmacology (1985–86) and one at the biomedical division of the Samuel Roberts Nobel Foundation, in Ardmore, Oklahoma (1987–88).

Upon completion of his postdoctoral studies, Alvarez-González joined the faculty of the University of North Texas Health Science Center, in Fort Worth, as adjunct assistant professor in the department of biochemistry and as assistant professor in the department of microbiology and immunology. In 1996, he was promoted to associate professor in the department of molecular biology and immunology, a post he continues to hold. He has also held a number of other positions at the North Texas Health Science Center, including vice chairman of the department of microbiology and immunology (since 1994), acting chairman of the department of microbiology and immunology (1995–96), associate director of basic research at the center's Institute for Cancer Research (1998–2000), and adjunct associate professor of the School of Public Health (since 2000).

Alvarez-González has published more than 50 scholarly papers and has served as an editor of *Archaea* (an international journal of microbiology), *Cancer Investigation,* and *Molecular and Cellular Biochemistry.* He has been an invited speaker at a number of international conferences held in Canada, Chile, France, Greece, Japan, and Portugal. From 2001 to 2005, he served on the Minority Access to Research Careers (MARC) Study Section of the National Institute for General Medical Sciences and during the last two years of that period, served as chair of the section.

Further Reading

"Alvarez-González, Rafael." In *American Men & Women of Science,* 21st ed., edited by Pamela M. Kalte and Katherine H. Nemeh, vol. 1, 116. Detroit: Thomson Gale, 2003.
North Texas Health Science Center. "Rafael Alvarez-Gonzalez, Ph.D." Department of Molecular Biology and Immunology. Available online. URL: http://www.hsc.unt.edu/departments/molbioim/bio.cfm?id=230. Downloaded on April 4, 2005.

Alvariño, Angeles
(Angeles Alvariño de Leira)
(1916–2005) *marine biologist*

For more than a half century, Angeles Alvariño contributed to science's understanding of the nature and distribution of marine zooplankton, tiny one-celled organisms that drift on the ocean's currents and form the basis of the marine food web. She discovered 22 new marine species of organisms.

Alvariño was born on October 3, 1916, in El Ferrol, Spain, to María del Carmen González Díaz-Saavedra de Alvariño and Antonio Alvariño Grimaldos, a physician. Alvariño exhibited a curiosity about the natural world at an early age and took advantage of the large collection of books on natural history in her father's library. While still a child, she decided that she wanted to follow in her father's footsteps and become a physician, but he discouraged her from pursuing a medical career. He felt that the disappointments of not being able to cure some patients would be too great for her to bear.

When she entered college at the University of Santiago de Compostela, in Spain, Alvariño still planned to become a physician, and she took courses to prepare her for medical school. By the time she received her bachelor's degree in 1933, however, her father's continued resistance to these plans had convinced her to follow another path. When she entered the University of Madrid for her graduate studies, therefore, she chose to major in natural sciences, rather than medicine. After only a year at Madrid, Alvariño's studies were interrupted by the outbreak of the Spanish civil war. The university closed its doors during the worst years of that conflict, and she was unable to continue her studies until it reopened in 1939. She was finally awarded her master's in natural science in 1941. A year earlier, she had married Sir Eugenio Leira Manso, an officer in the Spanish royal navy, whose name she sometimes appended to her own.

After completing her studies at Madrid, Alvariño taught biology, botany, zoology, and geology for seven years at a variety of colleges in the region of El Ferrol. She eventually discovered, however, that she was more interested in doing research than in teaching and in 1948, took a job as research biologist with the Department of Sea Fisheries in Madrid. Soon after she began work with the department, she decided that she also wanted to continue her studies in marine biology at the Spanish Institute of Oceanography in Madrid; however, women were not allowed to attend the institute because they were barred by a two-centuries-old law from traveling on navy ships. In spite of the regulation, Alvariño was admitted to the institute and allowed to continue her research in marine biology. At the same time, she participated in a doctoral program in chemistry from

Angeles Alvariño was, until her death in 2005, considered the world's authority on three groups of marine organisms, the chaetognaths, hydromedusae, and siphonophores. *(National Marine Fisheries Service, SWFSC)*

which she received a doctoral certificate in 1951. A year later, she finally was appointed as a biologist and oceanographer at the Spanish Institute of Oceanography.

In 1953, Alvariño received an appointment as a British Council Fellow at the Marine Biological Laboratory at Plymouth, England. The appointment was an important turning point her in life because it provided her with an opportunity of working with the renowned British marine biologist Frederick Stratten Russell. Russell encouraged Alvariño to focus her research on a then relatively unknown group of marine organisms that included the chaetognaths (arrowworms), hydromedusae (umbrella or bell-like jellyfish), and siphonophores (also a type of jellyfish, the Portuguese man-of-war being perhaps the best known). Alvariño was faced with the challenge of not only discovering more about these organisms but also developing techniques by which they could be collected from the oceans. Upon her return to Spain in 1954, she set about solving these problems.

In 1956, Alvariño received a Fulbright Fellowship to continue her studies at the Woods Hole Oceanographic Institute, in Woods Hole, Massachusetts. Her work there so impressed her supervisor, Mary Sears, that Sears recommended her for a position at the Scripps Institution of Oceanography in La Jolla, California. Alvariño accepted the position offered her at Scripps and remained at the institute until 1969. During her tenure at Scripps, Alvariño continued her studies of chaetognaths, hydromedusae, and siphonophores in oceans around the world, gradually becoming one of the best-known and most highly respected experts in this field of marine biology. She also used her research to complete the requirements needed to obtain her doctoral degree from Madrid (now known as the University Complutense), which she received in 1967.

In 1970, Alvariño resigned her position at Scripps to take a job with the Southwest Fisheries Science Center (SWFSC) of the National Marine Fisheries Service, a division of the newly created National Oceanic and Atmospheric Agency (NOAA). At SWFSC, her continued work with chaetognaths, hydromedusae, and siphonophores took a somewhat new approach. These organisms tend to be relatively sensitive to changes in their watery environment, making them useful as "indicator species," that is, species that detect and respond to relatively small changes in their chemical and physical surroundings. Alvariño's research could be used, therefore, to find marine regions undergoing environmental stresses because of natural or human factors, such as changes in water temperature or salinity. Although she officially retired from SWFSC in 1987, she was given an emeritus appointment, allowing her to continue her studies at the center. Alvariño died in La Jolla, California, on June 10, 2005.

In addition to her research activities, Alvariño held a number of academic appointments during the last three decades of her life, including associate professorships at the National Autonomous University of Mexico (1976), San Diego State University (1979–82), and the University of San Diego (1982–84). She also served as visiting professor at the Federal University of Paraná in Brazil (1982) and the National Polytechnic Institute of Mexico (1982–86). She published more than 100 scholarly articles, books, and book chapters. In 1993, she was awarded the Great Silver Medal of Galicia by King Juan Carlos and Queen Sophia of Spain.

Further Reading

Alic, Margaret. "Angeles Alvariño." In *Contemporary Hispanic Biography,* edited by Ashyia N. Henderson, 4–7. Farmington Hills, Mich.: Thomson Gale, 2003.

DiCanio, Margaret. "Angeles Alvariño." In *Notable Twentieth-Century Scientists,* edited by Emily J. McMurray, 34–35. Detroit: Gale Research, 1995.

Oakes, Elizabeth H. "Alvariño, Angeles." *International Encyclopedia of Women Scientists.* New York: Facts On File, 2002, pp. 5–6.

Amaya, Maria
(Maria Alvarez Amaya)
(1955–) *nursing administrator, researcher*

Maria Alvarez Amaya has worked in both clinical and academic settings for three decades, during which her primary area of interest has been in environmental health problems confronted by women and children, especially among those in the southwestern United States. She is currently director of the Encuentros Project, supported by the National Institute of Environmental Health Sciences of the National Institutes of Health. The mission of the project is to study the exposure of children in the Texas-Mexico border region to lead in the environment.

Maria Alvarez was born in Canutillo, Texas, on March 16, 1955, to Salome E. Escudero and Thomas C. Alvarez, of Mexican ancestry. She attended the University of Texas at El Paso, from which she received her bachelor of science in nursing in 1976. She then attended the Texas Woman's University, in Denton, where she received her master of science in nursing (in maternal and child health) in 1978, and New Mexico State University, in Las Cruces, which granted her a Ph.D. in educational management and development in 1986.

Amaya has been employed as a nurse in one capacity or another since receiving her B.S.N. in 1976. From 1976 to 1977, she was charge nurse in the pediatric unit at the Hotel Dieu Medical Center, in El Paso, and from 1979 to 1987, she worked as a staff nurse in both the labor and delivery unit and the neonatal intensive care unit at the Thomason Hospital in El Paso. From 1992 to the present, she has held a number of other clinical positions, including staff nurse at the newborn nursery of the Vista Hills Medical Center, in El Paso, and in private practice as a prenatal care provider at the Centro Medico del Valle, in El Paso, and at the El Paso City County Health and Environmental District.

Concurrently with her clinical work, Amaya has held a series of academic appointments, beginning as instructor at the University of Texas at El Paso College of Nursing and Allied Health (CNAH) from 1979 to 1984. She was then promoted to assistant professor (1986), associate professor (1992), and full professor (1999) at CNAH. She is now Wakefield Distinguished Professor and a certified women's health care nurse practitioner. In addition, Amaya has served as program coordinator of the parent-child nursing program (1996–99) and the women's health nurse practitioner program (1996 to present) at CNAH. Beginning in 1999, Amaya has also been clinical adjunct faculty member at the Texas Tech University Health Sciences Center, in El Paso.

Further Reading
"Amaya, Maria Alvarez." In *Who's Who among Hispanic Americans, 1994–95,* 3d ed., edited by Amy Unterburger, 30. Detroit: Gale Research, 1995.

Encuentros Project. "Dr. Maria Alvarez Amaya." Binational Community Lead Project. Available online. URL: http://encuentros.utep.edu/About.html. Downloaded on April 4, 2005.

Arredondo, Patricia
(Patricia Maria Arredondo)
(1945–) *psychologist*

Patricia Maria Arredondo is a specialist in the counseling of Latinos, women, immigrants, and individuals from multicultural backgrounds. She is also founder and president of Empowerment Workshops, Inc., an organizational consulting firm in Boston.

Arredondo was born in Lorain, Ohio, on July 16, 1945, the daughter of Eva Zaldivar and Apolinar Arredondo, of Mexican heritage. She attended Kent State University, in Kent, Ohio, from which she received her B.A. in Spanish and journalism in 1967. She then continued her graduate studies at Boston College, where she earned her M.Ed. in counseling 1973, and at Boston University (BU), from which she received her Ed.D. in counseling psychology in 1978. While completing her graduate studies, Arredondo worked as a counselor at Brookline (Massachusetts) High School from 1970 to 1978.

After receiving her doctorate, Arredondo served for one year as assistant professor of education at the University of New Hampshire, in Durham, before taking a similar position at BU. She remained at BU until 1986, also serving as adjunct professor at Tufts University, Simmons College, and the University of Massachusetts, all in Boston, during the same period. In 1985, she founded Empowerment Workshops, a consulting service that offers training in office relationships between the sexes. In 1999, Arredondo returned to academia as associate professor in counseling and psychology in education at Arizona State University (ASU), in Tempe. In 2004, she was promoted to full professor at ASU.

Arredondo has been very active in a number of professional organizations, having served as chair of the Board for the Advancement of Psychology in the Public Interest, cochair of the Latino Professional Network, and president of the American Counseling Association, the National Latina/Latino Psychological Association, the Chicano Faculty and Staff Association of ASU, and the Parents' and Children's Services board of directors of Boston. Among the honors she has received are the Samuel H. Johnson Memorial Award of the Association for Multicultural Counseling and Development, the Libra Scholar Award of the University of Southern Maine, the Kitty Cole Human Rights Award of the American Counseling Association, and the Pinnacle Award for Business Achievement of the Greater Boston Chamber of Commerce. She was awarded an honorary doctorate by the University of San Diego in 1998 and was recognized as a "Living Legend" by the American Counseling Association in 2004.

Further Reading

"Arredondo, Patricia Maria." In *Who's Who among Hispanic Americans, 1994–95,* 3d ed., edited by Amy Unterburger, 54. Detroit: Gale Research, 1995.

Connecticut Counseling Association. "Connecticut Counseling Association Annual Conference." Available online. URL: http://www.ccamain.com/conf_05_cca.htm. Downloaded on April 5, 2005.

Avila, Vernon L.
(Vernon Lee Avila)
(1941–) *biologist, textbook author, educational administrator*

Vernon Lee Avila taught introductory biology courses at San Diego State University, in California, for three decades and was director of the university's Minority Biomedical Research Support program in biology during much of that time. In addition, he served in a number of administrative positions at the National Institutes of Health, the University of Puerto Rico, the Educational Testing Service, and the National Cancer Institute.

Avila was born in Segundo, Colorado, on April 5, 1941, the first of three sons born to Eloy, a coal miner, and Isabell Avila, of Mexican heritage. The Avila family was very poor, although Avila claims he never realized that fact until the advent of television, when he was able to see how other people lived. His experiences in elementary school were not unlike those of other young Hispanics, receiving little encouragement from his teachers to try harder and do better in school.

A turning point in Avila's life, as it was for so many other young people of the late 1950s, was the launch of the first artificial satellite, *Sputnik I,* by the Soviet Union in 1957. Avila has written that that event convinced him that he "had to go to college." He applied to the University of New Mexico, and although his high school grades were not very good, he was accepted. He completed the usual four-year course in two years and 10 months and was awarded his B.S. in biology in 1962. At the time, he assumed that he would spend the rest of his working life as a teacher of high school biology.

That prospect changed, however, when Avila took a summer course sponsored by the National Science Foundation. He did very well in the course and became convinced that he would be able to succeed in graduate school. He enrolled at Northern Arizona University, in Flagstaff, where he earned a master's degree in biology in 1966. He then applied for the doctoral program at the University of Colorado in Boulder and was accepted. He was awarded his Ph.D. in biology in 1973. It was at Colorado that Avila first began to identify himself as a Latino, joining a number of Chicano organizations and taking part in demonstrations to call attention to the unequal treatment of minorities on campus.

After receiving his Ph.D., Avila was offered a job teaching biology at San Diego State University, a position he was to hold for the next three decades until his retirement in 2003. There, he became involved in the university's Minority Biomedical Research Support (MBRS) program, funded by the National Institutes of Health to promote the involvement of underrepresented minorities in biomedical research. In 1989, Avila wrote his first textbook, *Biology: Exploration into Life.* In 1992, he founded his own publishing company, Bookmark Publishers, through which he released his introductory textbook, *Biology, a Human Endeavor.* In 1995, he published yet another text, *Biology: Investigating Life on Earth.* Recently, Avila was chosen by the Educational Testing Service of Princeton, New Jersey, to write the subject area test in biology for its Graduate Record Examination (GRE).

In addition to his teaching and writing activities, Avila has held a variety of administrative positions. He served at the National Institutes of Health in the MBRS program (1987–88), as special assistant to the dean of the College of Sciences at the University of Puerto Rico (1985–87), and as

an expert consultant at the National Cancer Institute (1978–79).

Further Reading

"Avila, Vernon L." In *Who's Who among Hispanic Americans, 1994–95,* 3d ed., edited by Amy Unterburger, 62. Detroit: Gale Research, 1995.

Society for Advancement of Chicanos and Native Americans in Science. "Dr. Vernon Avila—Biologist." SACNAS Biography Project. Available online. URL: http://64.171.10.183/biography/Biography.asp?mem=28&type=2. Downloaded on March 3, 2005.

Ayala, Francisco J.
(Francisco José Ayala)
(1934–) *evolutionary biologist*

Francisco José Ayala is one of the world's leading evolutionary biologists, having significantly advanced human understanding of the mechanisms by which evolution has occurred from the molecular level up. In addition, he has written and spoken extensively on the interaction among science, technology, philosophy, ethics, religion, and national policy.

Francisco José Ayala was born on March 12, 1934, in Madrid, Spain, the son of Soledad (Pereda) and Francisco Ayala, a businessman. He attended the University of Madrid, from which he graduated with a B.S. in 1955, before continuing his studies in theology at the University of Salamanca, where he earned a licentiate in sacred theology and was ordained a Dominican priest in 1960. After completing his work at Salamanca, Ayala decided to continue his studies in the biological sciences at Columbia University in New York City. He earned his M.A. in 1963 and his Ph.D. in genetics a year later.

Upon completion of his graduate studies at Columbia, Ayala took a position as research associate at Rockefeller University, in New York City.

Francisco Ayala holds a degree in sacred theology, is an ordained Dominican priest, and is one of the world's authorities on evolutionary biology. *(Courtesy of Dr. Francisco J. Ayala)*

After one year at Rockefeller, he was appointed assistant professor of biology at Providence College in Providence, Rhode Island. In 1967, he returned to Rockefeller as assistant professor of biology. In 1971, he left the East Coast to take a position as associate professor of genetics at the University of California at Davis, where he remained until 1987. During his tenure at Davis, Ayala also served as associate dean for environmental studies (1977–81), chair of the division of environmental studies (1977–81), and director of the Institute of Ecology (1977–81). In 1987, Ayala left Davis to become distinguished professor of biological sciences at the University of California at Irvine. Two years later, he was also appointed professor in the department

of philosophy, Donald Bren Professor of Biological Sciences, and director of the Bren Fellows program.

Ayala's research has extended over an impressive range of topics, including the development of new methods for measuring the way in which populations adapt to changes in the environment, determining the ways in which genetic polymorphisms (differences of DNA sequences within individuals or groups of individuals) affect the way organisms adapt to new environments, and analyzing the ways in which groups of organisms compete with one another for limited resources. In recent years, an important theme in Ayala's research has been an attempt to better understand the operation of the so-called molecular clock, the relatively regular change in mutations that appears to occur in populations over long periods of time. Most biologists believe that improved comprehension of the molecular clock will improve their understanding of evolutionary history, as well as the times at which various significant events in evolutionary history have taken place.

Ayala has also long been interested in the interrelationship of biology with other aspects of human society. He has written about topics such as ethical behavior as a by-product of evolutionary development, molecular biology and human origins, "progress" as a biological concept, the biological roots of morality, intelligent design, and the teaching of science in U.S. schools. His dual role as professor of biological sciences and professor of philosophy reflects his interest in the range of ways by which humans attempt to understand the world in which they live. He has said that, while he "find[s] science rewarding and enlightening and fulfilling," it does not tell humans "all that is worth saying about the world."

Ayala's honors fill more than a page of his curriculum vitae and include such awards as the 2003 Gold Medal of the Stazione Zoologica in Naples, Italy; a U.S. National Medal of Science in 2001; the 2000 Gold Medal of the National Academy of

Sciences of Italy; the 2000 William Procter Prize for Scientific Achievement from the scientific society Sigma Xi; the 1995 President's Award of the American Institute of Biological Sciences; and the 1994 Gold Honorary Gregor Mendel Medal of the Czech Academy of Sciences. He holds honorary doctorates from the Universities of Athens (Greece); Bologna (Italy); Barcelona, Madrid, Valencia, Vigo, León, and the Balearic Islands (all in Spain); Masaryk (Czech Republic); and Vladivostok (Russia). He has been elected a member of the U.S. National Academy of Science, the American Academy of Arts and Sciences, and the American Philosophical Society. Ayala has written more than 750 scholarly papers and edited, authored, or coauthored 15 books. Among the best known of his books are *Genetics and the Origin of Species* (1997), *Tempo and Mode in Evolution* (1995), *Modern Genetics* (2nd edition, 1984), *Population and Evolutionary Genetics: A Primer* (1982), *Evolving: The Theory and Processes of Organic Evolution* (1979), *Evolution* (1977), *Molecular Evolution* (1976), and *Studies in the Philosophy of Biology* (1974).

Further Reading

"Ayala, Francisco." In *Notable Latino Americans,* edited by Matt S. Meier, with Conchita Franco Serri and Richard A. Garcia, 21–22. Westport, Conn.: Greenwood Press, 1997.

Counterbalance Meta Library. "Francisco Ayala." Available online. URL: http://www.counterbalance. net/bio/ayala-body.html. Downloaded on February 22, 2005.

Jones, J. Sydney. "Francisco J. Ayala." In *Notable Twentieth-Century Scientists,* edited by Emily J. McMurray, 79–81. Detroit: Gale Research, 1995.

Slack, Gordy. "A Good Life." Today@UCI. Available online. URL: http://today.uci.edu/Features/profile_detail.asp?key=44. Downloaded on February 22, 2005.

B

Baca Zinn, Maxine
(Maxine Baca)
(1942–   ) *sociologist*

Maxine Baca Zinn is widely recognized as one of the leading experts on the sociology of gender, race, family, and ethnic relations. She has played an important role in promoting the study of the role of Latina and Latino families in American culture.

Maxine Baca was born in Santa Fe, New Mexico, on June 11, 1942, into a family with a Mexican background and a strong academic tradition. Her mother had earned a B.A. and became a teacher, and her father had completed two years of college before going to work for the federal government. All three of Baca's siblings earned college degrees.

As a child, Baca experienced the same ethnic prejudices familiar to many Hispanics at the time. In a culturally diverse community such as Santa Fe, strict traditions dictated with whom one could associate, what one's academic expectations should be, which courses one should take in school, and so on. Baca Zinn has said that she felt "trapped academically in 'Mexican' classes where the education expectations were lower than those of the white students."

As a student Baca persisted, graduated from high school, and was awarded a scholarship to Texas Western College (now the University of Texas at El Paso). During her second year at Texas

Western, she married her high school boyfriend, Alan Zinn, and moved with him to Long Beach, California. There, she enrolled at California State University at Long Beach to continue her studies. In 1966, she was awarded her B.A. in sociology by Long Beach. After two years of teaching at a Catholic elementary school, Baca Zinn returned with her family to New Mexico and enrolled at the University of New Mexico (UNM), where she began her studies for a master's degree in sociology. She was granted that degree in 1970 and then remained at UNM as an instructor in the New Careers Program (1969–71) and the department of sociology (1970–71).

In 1971, Baca Zinn enrolled in the doctoral program in sociology at the University of Oregon in Eugene. After completing her residency requirements at Oregon, she accepted a teaching position at the University of Michigan at Flint (UM-F) while still working on her doctoral dissertation. She completed that work in 1978, was awarded her Ph.D., and was promoted to assistant professor at UM-F. She remained at UM-F for another decade, serving as associate professor (1980–86) and professor of sociology (1986–90) and faculty associate at the university's Survey Research Center (1979–81). During that period, Baca Zinn was also visiting scholar at Memphis State University's Center for Research on Women (summer 1984), research professor in residence at Memphis State (spring 1987), visiting professor of sociology at the University of California at Berkeley (1986), guest professor of sociology at the University of Connecticut (spring 1988), and distinguished visiting professor in women's studies at the University of Delaware (1988–89). In 1990, Baca Zinn left UM-F to become professor of sociology and senior research associate at the Julian Samora Research Institute at Michigan State University in East Lansing, positions that she continues to hold today.

Baca Zinn's greatest contribution to sociology has been her efforts to integrate the experience of Latinas, in particular, but also of other women of

Maxine Baca Zinn is professor of sociology and senior research associate at the Julian Samora Research Institute at Michigan State University. *(Courtesy of Dr. Maxine Baca Zinn)*

color, into the study and practice of sociology. She has said that her own training involved contact almost exclusively with white males, who had little information on or understanding of the nature and dynamics of Latino and Latina culture. She decided that she would make it her goal to educate the sociological community about this neglected field and encourage more research into the Latina community.

The success of Baca Zinn's efforts is difficult to overestimate and has been widely recognized by her colleagues. She has received outstanding alumnus awards from both the California State University at Long Beach and the University of New Mexico and was given a special recognition for contributions to the Western Social Science Association award in 1988. In 2000, Baca Zinn received both the American Sociological Association's Latino/a Section Distinguished Contributions to Scholarship and Research Award and its Jesse Bernard Career Award. The latter honor recognizes "enlarging the horizons of sociology to encompass fully the role of women in society."

Further Reading

"Baca Zinn, Maxine." In *Who's Who among Hispanic Americans, 1992–93,* 2d ed., edited by Amy Unterburger and Jane L. Delgado, 57. Detroit: Gale Research, 1995.

Stamatel, Janet P. "Maxine Baca Zinn." In *Contemporary Hispanic Biography,* edited by Ashyia N. Henderson, 25–28. Farmington Hills, Mich.: Thomson Gale, 2003.

Baez, Albert V.
(Albert Vinicio Baez)
(1912–2007) *physicist, science educator*

Albert Vinicio Baez's primary field of research dealt with the theory and application of X-rays, especially with regard to the relatively new field of X-ray imaging optics, a process by which X-rays are used to make images of objects. He is perhaps better known today for his efforts in the field of science education, having worked nationally and internationally to promote and improve the quality of science curricula and materials available to students of all ages.

Baez was born in Puebla, Mexico, on November 15, 1912. His father, Alberto Baez, a Methodist minister, decided to move his family to the United States when Baez was still a young child. The family settled in Brooklyn, New York, where Baez's father organized a Spanish-speaking church, and his mother, Thalía, became a social worker at the Young Women's Christian Association (YWCA).

After completing his elementary and secondary education in local schools, Baez enrolled at Drew University, in Madison, New Jersey, from which he received his bachelor's degree in mathematics in 1933. He then continued his studies at Syracuse University and was granted his M.A., also in mathematics, in 1935. Until the onset of World War II, Baez taught mathematics and physics at a series of institutions, including Morris Junior, Drew, and Wagner Colleges in New York City.

In 1942, Baez went to Stanford University in California to offer a course in physics for the U.S. Army. He decided to remain at Stanford and begin a doctoral program in physics. He chose to study X-ray optics under the supervision of the eminent physicist Paul Kirkpatrick and was awarded his Ph.D. in 1950. Baez's work involved the construction of the first X-ray microscope, for which he and Kirkpatrick first coined the term *X-ray optics.*

Upon graduation from Stanford, Baez accepted a post in the physics department at the University of Redlands (UR) in California. At UR, he continued his research on X-rays, attempting to use them to produce holographic images (images that have a three-dimensional appearance). He took a one-year leave of absence from UR in 1951–52 to teach physics at the University of Baghdad in Iraq.

The direction of Baez's career changed dramatically in 1957. In that year, the Soviet Union launched the first artificial satellite, a 184-pound (83-kilogram) metallic sphere that orbited the Earth every 96 minutes. The U.S. public, its legislative representatives, other politicians, most military leaders, and many members of the scientific community were dismayed at the realization of the Soviet Union's technological sophistication in building and launching the Sputnik satellite. Any nation that could place an artificial satellite into orbit, the assumption was, could also deliver bombs from one part of the world (such as the Soviet Union) to another part (such as the United States).

Among the many programs suggested for matching the Soviet "threat" posed by Sputnik was a flood of money for improving science education in the United States. The argument was that the best way to close the supposed technological gap between the Soviet Union and the United States was to offer more and more demanding science courses at an earlier age to U.S. children. As a result, the newly created National Science Foundation (NSF) began to pour hundreds of millions of dollars into efforts to improve the quality of science teaching in the United States.

One program funded by the NSF was the Physical Science Study Committee (PSSC), established originally by Professor Jerrold R. Zacharias at the Massachusetts Institute of Technology to write a new physics curriculum for high school students. Baez attended early meetings of the PSSC as a representative of Stanford and became fascinated by the challenges the group presented for improving science education. He decided to resign his post at Stanford in order to work full time at PSSC, where he remained from 1958 to 1960. At the end of that period, he accepted an offer from the United Nations Educational, Scientific and Cultural Organization (UNESCO) to become director of its newly created division of science teaching, based in Paris. During his tenure at UNESCO, Baez oversaw the development of new science education programs in biology, chemistry, mathematics, and physics in Africa, Asia, Latin America, and the Middle East.

Between 1967 and 1975, Baez was employed by the Encyclopaedia Britannica Educational Corporation, where he was responsible for the development of more than 100 educational films in the field of physics. He also continued to teach at a number of institutions, including Harvard University, Harvey Mudd College, the University of Maryland, the United Kingdom's Open University, the Algerian Institute of Electricity and Electronics, and the National Polytechnic Institute of Mexico. From 1974 to 1978, Baez was also chair of the Committee on Teaching Sciences of the International Council of Scientific Unions. In 1991, Baez's contributions to the field of science were recognized when he (along with Kirkpatrick) was awarded the Denis Gabor Award of the International Society of Optical Engineering. He died on March 20, 2007, in Redwood City, California.

Further Reading

"Alberto Vinicio Baez." In *The Hispanic American Almanac,* 3d ed., edited by Sonia G. Benson, 653. Farmington Hills, Mich.: Thomson Gale, 2003.

Baez, Albert V. *The New College Physics: A Spiral Approach.* San Francisco: W. H. Freeman, 1967.

Bradby, Marie. "Albert V. Baez, Ph.D." Hispanic Engineer and Information Technology Online. Available online. URL: http://www.hispanicengineer.com/artman/publish/article_39.shtml. Downloaded on February 8, 2005.

Sammis, Kathy. "Albert V. Baez." In *Notable Twentieth-Century Scientists,* edited by Emily J. McMurray, 91–92. Detroit: Gale Research, 1995.

Bañuelos, Rodrigo

(1954–) *mathematician*

Rodrigo Bañuelos was the recipient in 2002 of the Blackwell-Tapia Prize, sponsored by the Institute for Pure and Applied Mathematics at the University of California at Los Angeles, the Mathematical Science Research Institute, Cornell University, and Arizona State University. The prize, given once every two years, is awarded to an individual who has contributed to his or her field of specialization and has served as a role model for other mathematicians and students.

Bañuelos was born on June 5, 1954, on a ranch called La Macita in the Mexican state of Zacatecas, to José and Rosalva Bañuelos. For the first 15 years of his life, he worked on his parents' farm, with his aunts and uncles as his only teachers. Then his parents decided to immigrate to the United States, where the family settled in Pasadena, California. In spite of being unable to read or write in English (or any other language), Bañuelos was enrolled at the local middle school and eventually graduated from Blair High School in Pasadena.

Having no plans to attend college, Bañuelos went to work in Pasadena but had the good fortune to become friends with Juan Lara, a student at the University of California at Los Angeles (UCLA) and later an administrator in the University of California system. Lara described the importance of a college education, and convinced by Lara's argument, Bañuelos enrolled in Pasadena City College in 1973. He remained there only a year before transferring to the University of California at Santa Cruz, where he decided to major in physics. Bañuelos eventually changed his major to mathematics and was granted his B.S. in that subject in 1978. He then enrolled in the M.A.T. (master of arts in teaching) program at the University of California at Davis, receiving his degree in 1980. He was also granted a teaching certificate in the same year and began his first teaching job, as a teaching assistant at UCLA in 1980. He also began his doctoral studies in mathematics and in 1984 was awarded his Ph.D.

Upon completing his doctoral studies, Bañuelos accepted a two-year appointment as Bantrell Research Fellow at the California Institute of Technology (Caltech). In 1986, he left Caltech to accept a position as assistant professor of mathematics at Purdue University. He has remained at Purdue ever since, having been promoted to associate professor in 1989 and to full professor in 1992.

Bañuelos's area of expertise is probability theory, with special attention to its applications to other fields of mathematics, such as harmonic analysis, partial differential equations, spectral theory, and geometry. In trying to explain his work to one interviewer, he pointed out that "we are not talking about two plus two equals four. We are talking about things far more sophisticated."

Bañuelos has long been committed to improving the opportunities available to minorities in science and engineering. For example, he has served on the American Mathematical Society's Task Force on Participation of Underrepresented Minorities. He is also interested in and concerned about human rights issues and serves on the Human Relations Commission in his hometown of West Lafayette, Indiana. In 2004, Bañuelos was honored with election to the Institute of Mathematical Statistics for his contributions to research in statistics.

Further Reading

"Bañuelos, Rodrigo." In *Who's Who among Hispanic Americans, 1992–93,* 2d ed., edited by Amy Unterburger and Jane L. Delgado, 61. Detroit: Gale Research, 1995.

Morales Almada, Jorge. "Latino Genious [sic] in Mathematics Receives Award." *La Opinión* (November 7, 2004, 1). Available online. URL: www.msri.org/local/BTapiaEng.pdf. Downloaded on February 22, 2005.

Barbosa, Pedro

(1944–) *entomologist*

Pedro Barbosa is an expert on the interactions between plants and insects, with special emphasis on the role that insects may play on the abundance and distribution of plants in an ecosystem. He is interested in using the information elucidated from his studies to develop strategies for the control of agricultural predators through integrated pest management (IPM) strategies.

Barbosa was born in Guayama, Puerto Rico, on September 6, 1944. He attended the City College of New York, from which he received his B.S. in biology in 1966. He then enrolled at the University of Massachusetts at Amherst, where he earned his M.S. and Ph.D. in entomology (the study of insects) in 1969 and 1971, respectively. After receiving his doctoral degree, Barbosa took a position as assistant professor in the department of entomology and economic zoology at Rutgers University in New Brunswick, New Jersey, where he remained until 1973. He then returned to the University of Massachusetts, where he served as assistant professor (1973–78) and associate professor (1978–79) in the department of entomology. In 1982, he left Massachusetts to assume his current position as professor in the department of entomology at the University of Maryland in College Park.

Barbosa's research deals with one of the most interesting problems in biology: How do plants protect themselves from attack by predators? Whereas animals use a number of mechanisms, many of which involve physical movement such as running away or hiding from predators, plants are immobile and do not have that option.

One of the important discoveries biologists have made is that plants are able to produce and emit certain types of chemicals that are toxic to organisms that attack them. For example, trees that are attacked by insects may protect themselves by exuding chemicals specifically toxic to those insects.

This information can be of great value to agricultural scientists. If the chemical character of these substances can be identified, it may be possible to make them artificially and inject them by means of genetic engineering techniques into plants where they do not occur naturally, thus increasing the resistance of those plants to attack by insects.

Barbosa has made great progress in understanding the defensive mechanisms of plants against insects. In recognition of this work, he has received a number of awards, including the 1986 and 1987 Bussart Memorial Award in Research, the 1989 Science Award of the Institute of Puerto Rico of New York, and a 1993 Ciba-Geigy Recognition Award. In 1997, he was made a fellow of the Entomological Society of America.

Further Reading

Barbosa, Pedro, and T. Michael Peters, eds. *Readings in Entomology.* Philadelphia: Saunders, 1972.

Maryland Agricultural Experiment Station. "Maryland Dividends." Available online. URL: http://www.agnr.umd.edu/maes_exe/dividends/barbosa1.pdf. Accessed on August 2, 2006.

Barona, Andrés, Jr.
(1945–) *educational psychologist*

Andrés Barona, Jr.'s work deals with psychometrics, the science of measuring various characteristics of human behavior, personality, cognitive abilities, interests, and/or aptitudes. He is especially interested in the education of children who are culturally and linguistically different from those who make up majority populations.

Barona was born in Mexico City on July 3, 1945, the son of Luz N. and Andrés Barona. He attended Texas A&M University, from which he received his B.S. and M.Ed. in 1972 and 1974, respectively, and the University of Texas at Austin, from which he received his Ph.D. in educational psychology in 1982. While working for his doctorate at Austin, he was a graduate teaching instructor and research assistant at the university (1977–79) and a school psychologist for the Dallas Independent School District. During his last year of doctoral studies, he was also visiting assistant professor and director of the university's Hispanic Doctoral Training Program.

After earning his Ph.D., Barona accepted a position as assistant professor in psychology in education at Arizona State University (ASU), at Tempe. He was later promoted to associate professor and coordinator of the school psychology program in psychology in education (1988), director of the division of psychology in education (1991), and interim associate dean for graduate programs and research of the university. He is now professor emeritus of psychology in education at ASU.

Barona has served as president of the National Hispanic Psychological Association and is a fellow of division 16 of the American Psychological Association. He won the American Psychological Association's Young International Psychologist Award in 1984 and ASU's Outstanding Research and Outstanding Teacher Awards, both for 1990–91. He is coeditor (with Eugene E. García) of *Children at Risk: Poverty, Minority Status, and Other Issues in Educational Equity* (1990).

Further Reading

"Barona, Andrés, Jr." In *Who's Who among Hispanic Americans, 1994–95,* 3d ed., edited by Amy Unterburger, 63. Detroit: Gale Research, 1995.

College of Education, Arizona State University. "Andres Barona." Available online. URL: http://coe.asu.edu/barona. Downloaded on April 5, 2005.

Barrera, Cecilio
(Cecilio Richard Barrera)
(1942–) *microbiologist*

Cecilio Richard Barerra has had a distinguished career as a researcher, studying the structure and function of small organisms, such as the members of the fungus family, and the nature of enzymes and other chemical compounds of which they are composed. In the latter years of his career, he became a college administrator at New Mexico State University and the University of Illinois at Urbana-Champaign.

Barrera was born in Rio Grande City, Texas, on November 30, 1942, but grew up in his father's hometown of Rome, just a few miles away. His mother had immigrated to the United States from Mexico when she was six years old. Barrera developed an interest in science at an early age, at least in part because he was involved in the agricultural activities of his extended family, where he was constantly exposed to plants and animals in their natural setting. When he applied to attend the University of Texas at Austin, therefore, he decided to major in microbiology, the study of microscopic organisms such as bacteria, fungi, protozoa, and viruses. He earned his B.A., M.A., and Ph.D. in microbiology from Texas in 1965, 1967, and 1970, respectively.

Upon completing his doctoral studies, Barrera accepted a position as a postdoctoral research associate at Clayton Foundation Biochemical Institute in Austin, where he worked until 1975. At that point, Barrera was offered a post as assistant professor of microbiology at New Mexico State University, in Las Cruces, where he remained until 1988. During his last four years at New Mexico State, Barrera served as associate dean of the graduate school. In 1988, Barrera moved to the University of Illinois at Urbana-Champaign (UIUC), where he became associate dean of the graduate college. In this position, Barrera is in charge of the Office for Minority Affairs and of graduate admissions and outreach activities.

Throughout his academic career, Barerra has been interested in the underrepresentation of minority students in the sciences and mathematics and has worked with various organizations to increase the participation of Latinas and Latinos, blacks, and other minorities in the sciences. He was one of the founding members of the Society for the Advancement of Chicanos and Native Americans in Science (SACNAS) and served on its board of directors and as vice president of the organization. For 10 years, he also was director of UIUC's Minority Biomedical Research Support Program and Minority Access to Research Careers program, both sponsored by the National Institutes of Health.

Further Reading

"Barrera, Cecilio Richard." In *American Men & Women of Science,* 21st ed., edited by Pamela M. Kalte and Katherine H. Nemeh, 354. Detroit: Thomson Gale, 2003.

Society for Advancement of Chicanos and Native Americans in Science. "Dr. Cecilio Barrera—Microbiologist." SACNAS Biography Project. Available online. URL: 64.171.10.183/beta/pdf/barrera_cecilio_H.pdf. Downloaded on April 5, 2005.

Benacerraf, Baruj
(1920–) *immunologist*

Baruj Benacerraf was a corecipient of the 1980 Nobel Prize in physiology or medicine for his discovery of the genetic mechanism that regulates a body's response to attack by foreign materials.

Benacerraf was born in Caracas, Venezuela, on October 29, 1920. His parents were Abraham Benacerraf, a Sephardic Jew from Spanish Morocco, and Henrietta Lasry, from French Algeria. Abraham Benacerraf was a highly successful textile merchant and importer who moved his family to Paris when Baruj was five years old, making it possible for the boy to receive a classic French education which, he later described in his Nobel autobiography, was "a lasting influence on my life."

In 1939, as political events in Europe became more threatening, Benacerraf's father decided to return to Venezuela. The family remained in South America for only a short period of time, however, because it had been decided that Baruj should be educated in the United States. They relocated to New York City in 1940 and, at his father's encouragement, Benacerraf enrolled at the Philadelphia Museum of Art's Textile Engineering School (TES). Plans for Benacerraf to follow in his father's footsteps fell through, however, when he quickly decided that a career in business was not what he wanted from life. After two weeks at TES, Benacerraf withdrew and enrolled instead in the premedical program at Columbia University's School of General Studies. He completed the requirements for his B.S. in two years and graduated in 1942.

Following graduation from Columbia, Benacerraf's plans to pursue a medical degree appeared to have been thwarted when he was denied admission by 25 medical schools, including those at Columbia, Harvard, and Yale. He later said that he attributed this disappointment to his "ethnic and foreign background," that is, his Jewish background and Venezuelan nationality.

All was not lost, however, because of the efforts of a single person, George W. Bakeman, then assistant to the president of the Medical College of Virginia and father of one of Benacerraf's closest friends. Bakeman arranged for Benacerraf to be considered for one of the last openings in the college's freshman class. He was accepted for that opening and began his medical studies in July 1942.

The beginning of Benacerraf's medical education corresponded with the onset of World War II, and he was drafted into the U.S. Army only a few months after beginning his studies. He was allowed to complete his medical degree before being activated and was awarded his M.D. in 1945. He was commissioned first lieutenant in the U.S. Army Medical Corps (USAMC) shortly thereafter. After completing an internship at Queens General Hospital in New York City, Benacerraf completed his basic training and was shipped to France for his tour of duty. In 1947, he received his discharge and returned to the United States.

By this time, Benacerraf had decided that he was more interested in medical research than in opening a medical practice, a decision that he later said "was not fashionable." Because he had suffered from bronchial asthma as a child, Benacerraf had become especially interested in immunology and the mechanisms by which allergic reactions occur. He spoke with a number of specialists in the field and was encouraged to seek a position with Elvin Kabat, a young immunochemist at the Columbia University School of Physicians and Surgeons (SPS). He received an interview with Kabat, was accepted for a post at SPS, and began his research there in February 1948. Although he was happy to receive the appointment, Benacerraf had to work without salary and had to support himself financially during his early years at SPS.

Benacerraf later acknowledged the very strong influence that Kabat had on his academic career. He described his mentor as "a hard task-master with rigorous standards and an absolute respect for the quantitative approach to science." He said that he learned from Kabat the importance of intellectual honesty, scientific integrity, and the importance of experimental proof.

At the time, the field of immunochemistry was in its infancy. Scientists had only a broad, general understanding of the changes that take place when the body is invaded by foreign materials, such as viruses, bacteria, pollen, or dust particles. It was known that in such an event, the body's immune system begins to manufacture proteins called antibodies that attack, surround, kill, and/or immobilize the invading materials. The chemical mechanisms by which antibodies are manufactured and how they recognize foreign materials (as opposed to components of the body itself) were entirely unknown.

In 1949, Benacerraf's career took another turn. In that year, his father had suffered a debilitating stroke and moved back to Paris with his wife. Benacerraf decided that he also should return to France to be close to his (and his wife's) family. He sought and was given a research post at the Broussais Hospital in Paris, where he worked in the laboratory of the renowned Bernard Halperin, who had discovered antihistamines, drugs that block the action of histamines in the body and prevent the major symptoms of an allergic reaction. The new assignment also made it possible for Benacerraf to make frequent trips to Venezuela, where he could oversee his father's still-thriving business.

One of the most important aspects of Benacerraf's tenure at Broussais was his opportunity to meet and work with the Italian immunologist Guido Biozzi. Together, the two researchers developed the mathematical equations that describe the amount of foreign material that can be removed by phagocytes (a type of white blood cell) from the liver and spleen.

Over a period of six years, Benacerraf gradually began to regard his work at Broussais as a dead end and to believe that no other opportunities were going to become available to him in Paris. He decided to return to the United States and in 1956 was appointed assistant professor of pathology at the New York University (NYU) School of Medicine. It was Benacerraf's first salaried position in the academic world. Although he continued to spend a modest amount of time managing the family business, he finally had a full-time "home" in the research community.

At NYU, Benacerraf worked on a variety of immunological problems, including cellular hypersensitivity, anaphylactic hypersensitivity, tumor-specific hypersensitivity, and the structure of antibodies. He also began a series of studies, in collaboration with Gerald M. Edelman at Rockefeller University, of the genetic basis of the immune response. These studies eventually led to a Nobel Prize for Edelman in 1972 and for Benacerraf in 1980.

Benacerraf's Nobel-winning discovery resulted from a series of experiments on guinea pigs, some of which produced antibodies when injected with a foreign material and some of which did not. Benacerraf was eventually able to show that the immune response (or lack of it) was due to the presence

Baruj Benacerraf was corecipient of the 1980 Nobel Prize in physiology or medicine for his research on the genetic mechanisms of the human immune system. *(© The Nobel Foundation)*

(or absence) of a gene, to which Benacerraf gave the name *Ir* (for immune response) *gene*. The Ir gene was found to be located in an ancient and poorly understood section of the so-called major histocompatability complex (MHC) portion of chromosome 6. Benacerraf's discovery opened the floodgates for immunochemists, who soon found more than 30 discrete genes in mice, rats, guinea pigs, and rhesus monkeys and were able to develop an essentially complete chemical map of the giant MHC region.

Benacerraf's discovery has had enormous practical consequences. It has provided the basis for explanations about differential sensitivity to certain diseases, that is, the greater tendency of some individuals to contract disorders such as multiple sclerosis and rheumatoid arthritis than other individuals. It has also made possible a better understanding of (and, therefore, improved prospects for therapies for) autoimmune disorders, in which the body's immune system attacks its own cells and tissues.

In 1968, Benacerraf was offered the post of director of the Laboratory of Immunology at the National Institute of Allergy and Infectious Disease at the National Institutes of Health. Only two years later, he resigned that post to become Fabyan Professor of Comparative Pathology and chairman of the department of pathology at the Harvard Medical School. He held the former post until 1991, when he was named Fabyan Professor Emeritus, a title he continues to hold today. In 1980, he was also chosen to be chief executive officer of the Dana-Farber Cancer Institute in Boston and a year later also became president of Dana-Farber, Inc. In 1996, he was named special adviser to the president of the Dana-Farber Cancer Institute, a position he also continues to hold today.

In addition to the Nobel Prize, Benacerraf has been given a number of other honors and awards. These include the 1996 Gold Headed Cane Award of the American Association for Investigative Pathology, the 1996 Charles A. Dana Award for Pioneering Achievements in Health and Education, the 1995 Officier de la Légion d'honneur of the French government, a 1990 National Medal of Science, the 1988 Distinguished Investigator Award of the American Rheumatism Association, the 1988 Margaret Byrd Rawson Award of the American Dyslexia Society, and the 1985 Rous-Whipple Award of the American Association of Pathologists. Benacerraf has also been awarded a number of honorary degrees from institutes such as Gustavus Adolphus University (1992), Harvard University (1992), the Weizmann Institute of Science (1989), Adelphi University (1988), Columbia University (1985), Yeshiva University (1982), the Université d'Aix-Marseille (1982), New York University (1981), Virginia Commonwealth University (1981), and the University of Geneva (1980).

Further Reading

Encyclopædia Britannica. "Benacerraf, Baruj." Available online. URL: http://www.britannica.com/eb/article-9078536. Downloaded on November 11, 2005.

Benacerraf, Baruj. *From Caracas to Stockholm: A Life in Medical Science.* Amherst, N.Y.: Prometheus Books, 1998.

———. "Reminiscences." *Immunological Reviews* 84, no. 4 (July 1985): 7–27.

Metcalfe, Philip. "Baruj Benacerraf." In *Notable Twentieth-Century Scientists,* edited by Emily J. McMurray, 145–147. Detroit: Gale Research, 1995.

Nobelprize.org. "Baruj Benacerraf—Autobiography." Available online. URL: http://nobelprize.org/medicine/laureates/1980/benacerraf-autobio.html. Downloaded on February 16, 2005.

Bernal, Ivan
(1931–) *chemist*

Ivan Bernal's research has focused on studies of the transition metals (elements that make up groups 3 through 12 in the periodic table), the geometric configuration of certain organic compounds, organometallic compounds (organic compounds that contain at least one metal atom), and the structure of organic compounds that contain sulfur.

Bernal was born in Barranquilla, Colombia, on March 18, 1931. He attended high school at the Colegio de San José in Barranquilla, from which he graduated in 1948. He then immigrated to the United States, where he attended Clarkson College of Technology (now Clarkson University), in Potsdam, New York, and earned his B.S. in chemistry in 1954. He continued his graduate studies at the University of Virginia, in Charlottesville, from which he earned his M.S. in physical chemistry in

1956, and at Columbia University, in New York City, where he was granted his Ph.D. in chemical physics in 1963. Physical chemistry and chemical physics are closely related subjects that deal with the physical characteristics and behavior of chemical compounds. From 1963 to 1964, Bernal was a postdoctoral fellow at Harvard University.

In 1964, Bernal took a position as research collaborator at the Brookhaven National Laboratory, in Upton, New York. In 1967, he was reassigned at Brookhaven with the title of chemist, a post he held until 1973. In that year, he accepted an offer to become associate professor of chemistry at the University of Houston, in Texas. He was promoted to full professor in 1975, a post he continues to hold. He also served as associate chair of the department of chemistry from 1975 to 1976.

In addition to his teaching and research assignments, Bernal has served as a consultant on chemical problems to both governmental agencies and industrial corporations. From 1964 to 1967, he was a consultant to the Rockefeller Foundation in Colombia, where he worked on problems of higher education at the country's universities. During the same period, he was a guest lecturer at the Universidad del Valle, in Cali, Colombia. One of his major responsibilities at Cali was to evaluate students who were going to be sent abroad for advanced training. He has also worked as a consultant to the Dixie Chemical Company of Houston (1986–88), the Combustion Research Company of Houston (1987–89), and Triangle Research Laboratories of Houston (1992–93).

Bernal is a prolific author, with more than 365 scholarly papers to his credit. He has served as an external reviewer, visiting professor, and invited speaker for scholarly conferences and organizations in Australia, China, Denmark, Germany, Great Britain, Hong Kong, Italy, Poland, South Africa, and Turkey. He has received a number of honors, including election as a visiting fellow at the Australian National University and Oriel College of the University of Oxford, in England.

Further Reading

"Bernal, Ivan." In *American Men & Women of Science,* 21st ed., edited by Pamela M. Kalte and Katherine H. Nemeh, vol. 1, 507. Detroit: Thomson Gale, 2003.

University of Houston, Department of Chemistry. "Ivan Bernal." Available online. URL: http://www.chem.uh.edu/Faculty/Bernal/. Downloaded on April 5, 2005.

Bernal, Martha
(Martha E. Bernal)
(1931–2001) *clinical psychologist*

Martha Bernal was the first woman of Mexican ancestry to earn a Ph.D. in clinical psychology in the United States. For more than four decades, she conducted research studies on psychological issues faced by the Mexican-American community in the United States and the nature of and reasons for negative stereotypes held by white Americans with regard to the Mexican-American community.

Bernal was born in San Antonio, Texas, on April 13, 1931, the daughter of Alicia Enriquez and Manuel Bernal. Her parents had come to the United States from Mexico as young adults in the 1920s and settled in south Texas. Bernal was raised in El Paso, which, as in much of south Texas, had a strong bicultural heritage. Like many of her fellow students, Bernal did not speak English when she began school, and she learned early on that the dominant Anglo culture disapproved of both her language and her Mexican culture. Against the traditional views of her father (who thought she should focus on being a wife and mother) and the strong objections of her teachers and counselors to the education of young Mexican women, Bernal finished high school, graduating from El Paso High School in 1948. She then entered the University of Texas at El Paso, from which she received her B.A. in 1952. Still battling the preconceived notions and expectations of many of her professors, she decided to continue her studies at Syracuse University, in New York, earning her M.A. in psychology in 1957. She then transferred to Indiana University, at Bloomington, where she was granted her Ph.D. in clinical psychology in 1962.

Unable to find an academic appointment after receiving her Ph.D., Bernal instead sought and received a grant from the U.S. Public Health Service to participate in a two-year postdoctoral program at the University of California at Berkeley. There, she became involved in a program of research that was to command her attention for the next decade, the use of classical conditioning techniques for the treatment of autistic children. In 1965, she received her first academic appointment, as assistant professor and senior psychologist at the University of California at Los Angeles (UCLA). She remained at UCLA until 1971, when she accepted an appointment as associate professor of psychology at the University of Denver, in Colorado.

During her first few years at Denver, Bernal began to become dissatisfied with the direction of her research. At the conferences she attended, she came into contact with a number of individuals who started to awaken her awareness of the problems that women and ethnic minorities face in their everyday lives. She came to feel that her work with autistic children, although of value, might be less important to her than studies of her own culture and the interaction between Hispanics and Anglos in the United States. She decided to design a new direction for her research in which she could attack these questions. She wrote that "After 1979, I wanted to conduct research that had bearing on central issues affecting ethnic minorities. . . . and I struggled for several years to carve out a new minority mental health research area for myself."

One of her first studies in this area was funded by a grant from the National Institute of Mental Health to find out how well prepared clinical psychologists are to deal with psychological issues of minority groups, such as Mexican Americans. Her study found that there were relatively few psychologists of color available to work with individuals from minority groups and inadequate training for Anglo psychologists whose work dealt with such populations. The study became a model for the research, teaching, and training that Bernal carried out over the next 30 years.

In 1986, Bernal left Denver to become research professor at Arizona State University, in Tempe, where she remained until her death on September 28, 2001. At the time of her death, she was no longer actively involved in research, although she was still serving as a member of the American Psychological Association's Commission on Ethnic Minority Recruitment, Retention, and Training in Psychology (CEMRRAT) task force and the university's Committee on Gay, Lesbian and Bisexual Affairs. Among the awards she received during her lifetime were a Distinguished Life Achievement Award from division 45 of the American Psychological Association, one of four Pioneer Senior Women of Color awards of the first National Multicultural Conference and Summit of 1999, the Carolyn Attneave Diversity Award for lifelong contributions to ethnic minorities of the American Psychological Association, and an award for Distinguished Contributions to the Public Interest from the American Psychological Association.

Further Reading

Ballie, R. "Martha E. Bernal Dies at Age 70." *Monitor on Psychology* 33 (January 2002). Available online. URL: http://www.apa.org/monitor/jan02/latina. html. Downloaded on April 6, 2005.

"Bernal, Martha E." In *Who's Who among Hispanic Americans, 1994–95*, 3d ed., edited by Amy Unterburger, 88. Detroit: Gale Research, 1995.

Webster University. "Martha Bernal: Life and Contributions." Women's Intellectual Contributions to the Study of Mind and Society. Available online. URL: http://www.webster.edu/~woolflm/bernal. html. Downloaded on April 6, 2005.

Berriozábal, Manuel
(Manuel Phillip Berriozábal)
(1931–) *mathematician*

Manuel Phillip Berriozábal's area of expertise is general topology, the study of the properties of a figure that remain the same no matter what transformation is made in the figure in a one-to-one manner. In addition to his academic research and teaching, he has been very active in the development of programs designed to assist women and minorities to prepare for careers in mathematics and the sciences.

Berriozábal was born in San Antonio, Texas, on May 12, 1931. His mother was of German descent, and his father had immigrated to the United States from Durango, Mexico, in 1910. The family moved to Independence, Missouri, when Berriozábal was still young, and he began his studies in parochial schools there. At the age of 13, he won a scholarship to De La Salle Military Academy, in Kansas City, Missouri, from which he graduated in 1948 as valedictorian of his class. He then enrolled at Rockhurst College in Kansas City, earning his B.S. in mathematics in 1952.

Berriozábal then began a master's program in mathematics at the University of Notre Dame, only to have his studies interrupted by a tour of duty with the U.S. Army. He returned to Notre Dame in 1955 and completed his M.S. in mathematics in 1956. He then accepted a teaching position at Loyola University (now Loyola Marymount University) in Los Angeles for two years before beginning a doctoral program in mathematics at the University of California at Los Angeles (UCLA) in 1958. He completed that program and was awarded his Ph.D. in mathematics in 1961.

After graduation from UCLA, Berriozábal accepted a teaching post as assistant professor of mathematics at Tulane University in New Orleans, Louisiana. In 1966, he moved across town to become associate professor of mathematics at the University of New Orleans (UNO). He served at UNO in that position from 1966 to 1972 before becoming professor from 1972 to 1976. In the latter year, Berriozábal was offered the post of professor of mathematics at the University of Texas at San Antonio (UTSA), a title he continues to retain today.

Berriozábal has published a number of papers and conducted many seminars on topics in the field of topology. But he has also been very active in the design and operation of programs for women and minorities in the fields of mathematics and science. The first such program was the Prefreshman Engineering Program (PREP) initiated in

Manuel Berriozábal is a specialist in the mathematics of topology problems and has worked to encourage greater participation by Latinas and Latinos in mathematics programs. He founded the Prefreshman Engineering Program (PREP) in 1979. *(Courtesy of Manuel Berriozábal)*

1979. PREP is a mathematics-based academic enrichment program for middle and high school students that runs for eight weeks each summer. When first proposed, the program was not well received by some academics, legislators, and others. One member of the Texas Education Coordinating Board expressed the view that "the Mexican American community is not where engineers come from," and so funds spent on PREP would, he thought, be wasted. Other critics felt that students would not give up vacation time to attend academic classes.

Those critics were proved wrong when PREP became a resounding success. It was eventually replicated on more than 30 college campuses across Texas and eight other states. It has made possible access to mathematics and science programs in higher education that would otherwise have been unavailable to high school graduates. Berriozábal's role in the development of PREP has not gone unnoticed. In 1994, he was given the Hispanic Heritage Foundation's Hispanic Heritage Award in Education and in 2004, the Distinguished K–12 Education Award of the Society for the Advancement of Chicanos and Native Americans in Science. He has also been honored with induction into the Texas Science Hall of Fame (2000), the UTSA President's Distinguished Achievement Award for Excellence in University Service (2003), and the Volvo for Life Hometown Hero Award (2004). In 2001, Berriozábal was also given the Mathematical Association of America's Yueh-Gin Gung and Dr. Charles Y. Hu Award for Distinguished Service to Mathematics.

Further Reading

Bennett, Jennie, et al. "NCTM Task Force on Promising Students." Available online. URL: http://www.nku.edu/~sheffield/taskforce.html. Downloaded on February 10, 2005.

Berriozábal, Manuel P. "The San Antonio Prefreshman Engineering Program: Reaching Out to Educationally Underserved Students and Making a Connection to Science and Engineering Careers." Presentation to the Congressional Subcommittee on Basic Research of the U.S. House of Representatives Committee on Science, July 29, 1999. Available online. URL: http://www.house.gov/science/berriozabal_072999.htm. Downloaded on February 10, 2005.

"Berriozabal, Manuel Phillip." In *Who's Who among Hispanic Americans, 1992–93,* 2d ed., edited by Amy L. Unterburger and Jane L. Delgado, 74. Detroit: Gale Research, 1992.

HispanicBusiness.com. "San Antonio Professor Honored by Volvo as One of City's Greatest Hometown Heroes." Available online. URL: http://www.hispanicbusiness.com/news/newsbyid.asp?id=15957. Posted on May 1, 2005.

Senate of the State of Texas. "Senate Resolution No. 822." Available online. URL: http://www.capitol.state.tx.us/tio/78R/billtext/SR000822F.HTM. Accessed on November 11, 2005.

Society for Advancement of Chicanos and Native Americans in Science. "Dr. Manuel Phillip Berriozábal—Mathematician." SACNAS Biography Project. Available online. URL: http://64.171.10.183/biography/Biography.asp?mem=31&type=2. Downloaded on February 10, 2005.

Bustamante, Carlos J.
(Carlos Jose Bustamante)
(1951–) *molecular biologist*

Carlos Jose Bustamante is interested in the structures of nucleic acids and proteins, two families of biochemical molecules of primary importance in cells. He has developed methods for studying the physical and chemical properties of such materials, one molecule at a time. The ability to manipulate and analyze single molecules of complex substances such as these is a new and very powerful analytical tool for chemists.

Bustamante was born in Lima, Peru, on May 6, 1951. He received his B.S. from the Universidad

Peruana Cayetano Heredia, in Lima, in 1973 and his M.S. in biochemistry from the Universidad Nacional Mayor de San Marcos, also in Lima, in 1975. He continued his graduate studies at the University of California at Berkeley, where he received his Ph.D. in biophysics in 1981. Bustamante then completed his postdoctoral studies at the Lawrence Berkeley National Laboratory, in Berkeley, California, from 1981 to 1982.

In 1982, Bustamante accepted an appointment as assistant professor in the department of chemistry at the University of New Mexico, in Albuquerque. He later rose to become associate professor (1986–89) and professor (1989–90) at New Mexico. Bustamante also served as Searle Scholar (1984), Alfred P. Sloan Fellow (1985), Presidential Lecturer in Chemistry (1986), and State of New Mexico Eminent Scholar (1989) during his tenure at New Mexico. In 1991, Bustamante left New Mexico to become professor of chemistry and a member of the Institute of Molecular Biology at the University of Oregon, at Eugene. Three years later, he was also appointed Howard Hughes Medical Institute Investigator at Oregon. Bustamante changed institutions once again in 1998, when he accepted an appointment as professor in molecular and cell biology, chemistry, and physics at the University of California at Berkeley, a post he continues to hold. He also continues to serve as an investigator for the Howard Hughes Medical Institute.

Bustamante has published more than 175 papers in peer-reviewed journals. In 2004, Bustamante was honored with the Founders Award of the Biophysical Society "for his pioneering role into the new and growing field of single-molecule biophysics," and in 2005 he received the Richtmyer Award of the American Association of Physics Teachers for his ability to convey difficult concepts in science to the general public.

Further Reading

"Bustamante, Carlos Jose." In *American Men & Women of Science,* 21st ed., edited by Pamela M. Kalte and Katherine H. Nemeh, vol. 1, 910. Detroit: Thomson Gale, 2003.

Kher, Unmesh. "Protein Wizard." CNN: America's Best Science and Medicine. Available online URL: http://www.cnn.com/SPECIALS/2001/americasbest/science.medicine/pro.cbustamante.html. Downloaded on April 29, 2005.

Howard Hughes Medical Institute. "Carlos Bustamante, Ph.D." Available online. URL: http://www.hhmi.org/research/investigators/bustamante_bio.html. Downloaded on April 29, 2005.

Cabrera, Lydia
(1899/1900–1991) *ethnologist*

Lydia Cabrera is widely recognized as one of the greatest authorities on Afro-Cuban culture and religion. She was the author of 23 books, most of which were fictional accounts of Afro-Cuban culture developed on authentic ethnographic themes.

Differences of opinion exist about the facts of Cabrera's birth. She herself claimed to have been born in Havana, Cuba, on May 20, 1900, but official documents, including her passport, list the year as 1899 and the place of birth as New York City. In any case, she grew up in Havana the youngest of eight children born to Elisa Marcaida Casanova and Raimundo Cabrera Bosch. Cabrera's father was a prominent lawyer, jurist, and writer who was president of the first Cuban corporation founded in the 18th century, the Sociedad Económica de Amigos del País (Economic Association of the Friends of the Nation). He was also publisher and editor of the Havana newspaper *Cuba y América,* for which 13-year-old Lydia anonymously wrote a column dealing with births, deaths, marriages, and social events. She continued to write the column over a period of three years.

As was the custom with many wealthy Cuban families of the time, Cabrera was educated at home by private tutors. She attended a formal school only briefly but completed the equivalent of a secondary education at home. Among all subjects, art became her favorite, and for a period of months, she continued her studies (against her father's wishes) at the San Alejandro Art Academy in Havana. She had her first public exhibition in 1922, a show that

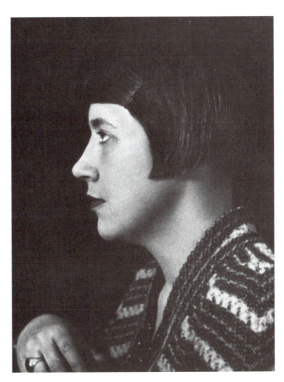

Lydia Cabrera was an authority on the contribution of African blacks to the religion and culture of Cuba. *(Courtesy of the Cuban Heritage Collection, University of Miami Libraries, Coral Gables, Florida)*

received favorable reviews from critics. Although she maintained an interest in art throughout her life, she discontinued her studies and began saving for a trip to Paris.

In the early 1920s, Paris was the center of a renaissance in all fields of culture. Men and women interested in developing new approaches to music, literature, painting, and other subjects fled to the French capital, where any and all new ideas were welcome for consideration and debate. Cabrera was eager to become part of this culture and in 1922 opened an antique store with her longtime companion María Teresa Rojas to earn money needed for the trip.

In 1927, Cabrera had achieved her financial goals and left for Paris. There, she settled in the Montmartre neighborhood and studied at the École du Louvre and École des Beaux-Arts. She found endless opportunities to meet and interact with artists and writers from all over the world. Some of the most influential contacts she made were with Africans who had come to Paris to live and study. Cabrera had long been interested in African culture, especially with regard to the influence it had had on shaping Cuban society. As a young white girl in Havana, Cabrera had been cared for by Afro-Cuban nannies and servants and even as a child had evinced an interest in the culture, customs, and Santeria of her black associates. (Santeria is a religion consisting of a mixture of Catholic religious teachings and traditional African [Yoruba] beliefs first practiced in Cuba by the descendants of African slaves.) Her experiences in Paris whetted Cabrera's desire to learn more about the contributions that Africans had made to the evolution of modern Cuban culture.

The first product of Cabrera's research on this topic was a series of stories dealing with the Afro-Cuban experience, stories that were published in 1936 in French as *Contes nègres de Cuba (Afro-Cuban Tales)* and four years after in Spanish as *Cuentos negros de Cuba.* Cabrera's book quickly became widely popular among students of Cuban culture and especially among Cubans of African ancestry. For the first time, these Afro-Cubans were introduced to the distinctive, fundamental, and important contribution to Cuban culture their ancestors had made.

By 1938, Cabrera had come to the realization that the best place to continue her studies of Afro-Cuban culture was not Paris but her native Cuba. She returned to Havana, therefore, and began to immerse herself in the local Afro-Cuban society. She attended religious ceremonies and community meetings, interviewed individuals, and visited numerous private homes. Her work was remarkable particularly because of the ability she developed to become accepted as a white woman by black individuals, families, and communities, who usually saw her more as a friend than an observer or an interviewer.

In 1954, Cabrera published the book for which she is most famous, *El monte,* through a company she and Rojas established, Ediciones C. R. The title of the book is most obviously translated as "The mountain," but can also be understood as "The wilderness." Her biographer, Edna M. Rodríguez-Mangual, suggests that the latter translation may be more appropriate in the context of Afro-Cuban religion, where it represents "a sacred or magical place where the divine is found." In any case, *El monte* brings together the information and understandings of Afro-Cuban culture and religion accumulated by more than a decade of Cabrera's research.

Cabrera continued her ethnological research after publication of *El monte.* That research led to three more books, *Refranes de negros viejos* (1955), *Anagó: Vocabulario lucumí (El yoruba que se habla en Cuba)* (1957), and *La sociedad secreta Abakuá* (1958). The last of these books deals with the culture of a highly secret society, the Abakuás, who, among other traditions, excluded women. Cabrera's revelation of the group's beliefs and practices was a remarkable accomplishment. According to some observers, it may have been responsible for Cabrera's decision to leave Cuba for the United States in 1960, as a result of threats from the Abakuás. She may also have left, according to other biographers, more because of her opposition to the Castro revolution of 1959, which she strongly opposed.

In any case, Cabrera and Rojas settled in Miami, where Cabrera published nothing for a decade. When she finally renewed her writing activities, she produced more than a dozen books in the ensuing decade. Three of these books were written in Madrid during a two-year visit to Spain.

By the late 1970s, Cabrera's work was receiving recognition in the United States and around the world. She was awarded honorary doctorates by Dennison University, Manhattan College, and the University of Miami. In 1976, a conference in her honor was held at Florida International University, and the proceedings were published as *Homenaje a Lydia Cabrera,* a special issue of the journal *Noticias de Arte.* Cabrera's health began to fail in the mid-1980s, and she was devastated by the death of Rojas, her companion of nearly 50 years, in 1985. Cabrera died in Miami on September 19, 1991. She willed her papers, correspondence, photographs, musical collection, and memorabilia to the Otto G. Richter Library at the University of Miami, where they are available for research and study.

Further Reading

"Cabrera, Lydia." In *Hispanic Americans,* 2d ed., edited by Nicolas E. Meyer, 40–41. New York: Checkmark Books, 2001.

Gutiérrez, Mariela A. *Lydia Cabrera: Aproximaciones mitico-simbólicas a su cuentística.* Madrid: Verbim, 1997.

———. "Lydia Cabrera (1899–1999): Recapitulando en la alborada de su centenario." Homenaje de la Habana Elegante. Available online. URL: http:// www.habanaelegante.com/Summer99/Bustos. htm. Downloaded on February 10, 2005.

Rodríguez-Mangual, Edna M. *Lydia Cabrera and the Construction of an Afro-Cuban Cultural Identity.* Chapel Hill: University of North Carolina Press, 2004.

University of Miami, Richter Library. "Lydia Cabrera." Available online. URL: http://www.library.miami. edu/umcuban/cabrera/cabrera2.html. Downloaded on February 10, 2005.

Calderón, Alberto P.
(Alberto Pedro Calderón)
(1920–1998) *mathematician*

Alberto Pedro Calderón was one of the preeminent mathematicians of the 20th century. Along with his mentor and later colleague Antoni Zygmund, he founded a school of mathematical thought whose goal is to integrate otherwise disparate fields of mathematics, as well as to expand the ways in which mathematical tools can be used to solve practical problems in physics and engineering.

Calderón was born in Mendoza, Argentina, on September 14, 1920. His father was a medical doctor from an old and prestigious Spanish family. Hoping to provide young Alberto with all possible opportunities to fulfill his academic potential, his father sent him to study in Switzerland. Calderón's ultimate goal was to attend the famous Eidgenössische Technische Hochschule (ETH) in Zurich, an institution where many of the 20th century's greatest scientists had been trained. The first step in reaching that goal for Calderón was enrollment at a preparatory elementary school in Zug, Switzerland.

It was during his early years at Zug that Calderón discovered his passion for mathematics. He once told of his being offered an excuse from a school punishment provided that he could solve a problem in geometry. He not only solved the problem, but, he later wrote, "The problem seduced me, and awoke in me an eagerness to solve more and more similar problems. This incident clearly showed me what my vocation was, and had a decisive influence in my life."

Calderón's plans to remain in Switzerland and study at the ETH did not come to fruition, and he returned to Argentina to complete his secondary education. He then enrolled at the University of Buenos Aires, where he majored in civil engineering. He was awarded his bachelor's degree in 1947 and accepted an offer to remain at the university as assistant to the head of electrical circuit theory in the school of engineering.

Arguably the most important single event in Calderón's life occurred in 1948 during a visit to the university by the renowned Polish-American mathematician Antoni Zygmund. Calderón attended a lecture given by Zygmund in which the latter worked through a complex proof of a problem in trigonometric series. At the conclusion of the presentation, Calderón objected to Zygmund that the proof he had offered was "different and much more complex than" the proof in Zygmund's classic book on trigonometric series. Zygmund was puzzled because the proof he had offered was actually identical to the one in his book. He challenged Calderón to suggest a simpler proof, which Calderón proceeded to do.

As it turned out, the confusion about proofs arose from the fact that Calderón was accustomed to reading only the titles of mathematical papers. Then, he knew the topic and the conclusion of the paper, but not the author's sequence of steps in arriving at his or her conclusion. Instead, Calderón devised his own proof which might be, but often was not, the same as the author's.

Zygmund quickly recognized Calderón's extraordinary mathematical intuition and offered him a Rockefeller Scholarship at the University of Chicago, where Zygmund was then professor of mathematics. Calderón accepted the offer and began his doctoral studies at Chicago under Zygmund's supervision. He was awarded his Ph.D. in

Alberto P. Calderón was one of the founders of the Chicago school of mathematics. One focus of his research was to find better ways of applying mathematical principles to real-life physical problems. *(Courtesy University of Chicago)*

1950 and was appointed visiting professor of mathematics at Ohio State University. He left Ohio State in 1954 for a one-year fellowship at the Institute for Advanced Studies at Princeton University in New Jersey and then accepted an appointment as associate professor of mathematics at the Massachusetts Institute of Technology (MIT) in 1955. In 1959, Calderón left MIT to return to Chicago where, except for a second visit to MIT (1972–75), he remained until his retirement in 1985. At Chicago, Calderón served as department chair (1970–72) and Louis Block Professor of Mathematics (1968–72).

Throughout his career, Calderón worked with his mentor, Zygmund, to develop a strikingly different approach to mathematics than was popular at the time. This approach eventually became known as the Chicago school of mathematics, or the Calderón-Zygmund theory of mathematics. One of the key elements of the Calderón-Zygmund approach to mathematics is its commitment to the integration of abstract theory and practical applications. The tendency to focus on complex theoretical questions with few or (more commonly) no known practical applications has long been a major theme in the history of mathematics. Many great mathematicians have devoted their entire lives to trying to find the number of real or imaginary numbers, the size of infinity, the meaning and properties of imaginary numbers, and other questions whose practical significance is not apparent to the average person (or, in some cases, to other mathematicians). Zygmund's own career had been devoted largely to this kind of mathematical research.

But mathematics clearly has applications to the real world as well. It allows one to calculate the velocity and path of moving objects, the expansion and contraction of materials, the rate of chemical changes, and the answers to countless other real-life problems. With his background in civil engineering, Calderón was certainly aware of and eager to develop these practical applications of mathematics. And his genius and skill in dealing with abstract, as well as practical, problems gave him a special opportunity for finding ways of applying a whole range of powerful mathematical tools to the analysis of a variety of physical problems.

In addition to his work in mathematics, Calderón sought to find and encourage talented students from his homeland. In the early 1970s, he returned briefly to Argentina to present lectures and to work with doctoral students in mathematics. He also arranged for some of those students to come to the United States to continue their studies. Calderón also had a special love for Spain. In 1979, he was instrumental in organizing an international congress on harmonic analysis at El Escorial, an annual meeting that is still held there.

During his lifetime, Calderón wrote nearly 80 scholarly papers. Among the honors he received were the Böcher Prize of the American Mathematical Society in 1979, the Mathematical Prize of the Karl Wolf Foundation in 1989, the Steele Prize of the American Mathematical Society in 1989, and the National Medal of Science in 1991. He was also recognized on a number of occasions by the Argentine government, honors that included the Provincia de Santa Fe Prize in 1969, the Konex Prize in 1983, and the Consagración Nacional Prize in 1989. Calderón was elected to a number of prestigious societies, including the American Academy of Arts and Sciences (1957), the National Academy of Exact, Physical and Natural Sciences of Argentina (1959), the National Academy of Sciences of the United States (1968), the Royal Academy of Sciences of Spain (1970), the Latin American Academy of Sciences of Venezuela (1983), the French Academy of Sciences (1984), and the Third World Academy of Sciences (1984). He died in Chicago on April 16, 1998.

Further Reading

Geometry Net. "Alberto P. Calderón." Available online. URL: http://www-history.mcs.st-and.ac.uk/history/Mathematicians/Calderon.html. Downloaded on February 14, 2005.

Guzmán, Miguel de. "The Genius That Only Read the Titles." International Commission on Mathematical Instruction Bulletin, no. 47 (December 1999). Available online. URL: http://www.maths.soton.ac.uk/EMIS/mirror/IMU/ICMI/bulletin/47/Calderon_El-Pais_article.html. Downloaded on February 14, 2005.

Noble, Holcomb B. "Albert Calderón, 77, Pioneer of Mathematical Analysis." *New York Times,* April 20, 1998, p. B11.

Windhausen, Rodolofo A. "Alberto P. Calderón." In *Notable Twentieth-Century Scientists,* edited by

Emily J. McMurray, 292–294. Detroit: Gale Research, 1995.

Calderón, Calixto P.
(Calixto Pedro Calderón)
(1939–   ) *mathematician*

Calixto Pedro Calderón is a mathematician who specializes in problems of mathematical biology, ordinary differential and partial differential equations, differentiation theory, harmonic analysis, and the history of mathematics.

Calderón was born in Mendoza, Argentina, on December 29, 1939, the son of Matilde García and Pedro Juan Calderón. He attended the University of Buenos Aires, from which he received his Licenciatura en Matemáticas (equivalent to a B.S.) in 1965 and his Doctorado en Matemáticas (equivalent to a Ph.D.) in 1969. After receiving his bachelor's degree, he spent one year as a specialist in the Department of Science Affairs at the Pan American Union, in Washington, D.C. He then returned to Argentina where he served as assistant professor at the University of Cuyo, in Mendoza (1966); the University of San Juan, in San Juan; the University of San Luis, in San Luis (1968); and the University of Buenos Aires (1969), while working on his doctoral degree.

After completing his doctoral studies, Calderón was invited to become visiting assistant professor in the department of mathematics at the University of Minnesota, in Minneapolis–St. Paul. He then returned to the University of Buenos Aires, where he worked as assistant professor (1970–71) and associate professor (1971–72), before returning to the University of Minnesota as associate professor (1972–74). In 1974, he accepted an offer to join the faculty of the mathematics, statistics, and computer sciences department at the University of Illinois at Chicago. He served first as associate professor (1974–81) and then full profes-

sor (1981–2000) until his official retirement, when he was named professor emeritus at Illinois. During his tenure at Illinois, Calderón was also visiting associate professor at Rice University, in Houston, Texas (1979); visiting professor at the Institute of Science, in Santa Fe, Argentina (1983); and adjunct faculty member at Oakton College, in Des Plaines, Illinois (1988–present).

Some of Calderón's most interesting work in recent years has been his attempt to find mathematical models that can be used to describe the growth of cancer cells. In these studies, Calderón and his colleagues have attempted to find ways of using mathematics to predict the early stages of cancer cell growth in order to detect tumors while they are still relatively few in number. By doing so, it may be possible to develop therapies that can be used with greater success before the tumors become too large to treat successfully by other methods.

Further Reading
"Calderón, Calixto P." In *Who's Who among Hispanic Americans, 1994–95,* 3d ed., edited by Amy Unterburger, 111. Detroit: Gale Research, 1995.

"Calderón, Calixto Pedro." In *American Men & Women of Science,* 21st ed., edited by Pamela M. Kalte and Katherine H. Nemeh, vol. 2, 11. Detroit: Thomson Gale, 2003.

Calvillo, Evelyn R.
(Evelyn Ruiz Calvillo)
(1943–   ) *nursing administrator*

Evelyn Ruiz Calvillo is a teacher, administrator, counselor, and researcher in the field of nursing, with a special interest in health problems of Mexican Americans. Her current interest centers on the causes and characteristics of the rise of diabetes among Hispanics.

Calvillo was born in Roswell, New Mexico, on February 15, 1943, the daughter of Sarah and

Tom Ruiz, of Mexican heritage. She attended the Hotel Dieu School of Nursing in El Paso, from which she received her diploma in nursing in 1964. She continued with her studies at the University of Texas at Galveston, earning her bachelor of science in nursing in 1983. Her graduate studies were completed at Loma Linda University, in California, where she earned her master of science in nursing in 1986 and at the University of California at Los Angeles (UCLA), which granted her a doctorate in nursing in 1991. She was the first Hispanic to earn this degree in the state of California.

Calvillo's doctoral dissertation dealt with the health beliefs of individuals in various cultures, a topic that continues to interest her. She believes that a better understanding of this question is essential to developing programs that focus on problems of special concern in Hispanic and other cultures. Her research on diabetes among Hispanics is only the latest manifestation of this general interest in health attitudes among various cultures.

In the two decades following receipt of her nursing diploma, Cavillo was engaged primarily in clinical practice, working as a registered nurse at Providence Memorial Hospital, in El Paso (1972–78) and at Clear Lake Hospital, in Houston (1980–83), before becoming director of nursing at Chapman College, in Orange, California (1986–90). After receiving her doctorate, she joined the faculty at California State University, Los Angeles (Cal State LA), as associate professor of nursing. She has since been promoted to full professor of nursing at Cal State LA, where she teaches courses in medical surgical nursing, pathophysiology, nursing research, and professional issues. In addition to her teaching responsibilities, she serves as nurse counselor, a post in which she works with students having academic, social, or other types of problems. She remains active in the field of research and serves as codirector of the Learning Community for Underrepresented Nursing Majors, a project designed to help underrepresented minorities find positions in nursing programs.

In 1994, Calvillo was named one of the "Top Ten Nurses of the Year" in *NurseWeek* magazine. She was also awarded the Dr. Ildaura Murillo Rhode Award for Educational Excellence at the 1995 annual conference of the National Association of Hispanic Nurses.

Further Reading

"Calvillo, Evelyn Ruiz." In *Who's Who among Hispanic Americans, 1994–95,* 3d ed., edited by Amy Unterburger, 113. Detroit: Gale Research, 1995.

California State University, Los Angeles. "Evelyn Calvillo." Faculty: School of Health and Human Services, Available online. URL: http://www.calstatela.edu/faculty/ecalvil/#education. Downloaded on April 6, 2005.

Candia, Oscar A.
(1935–) *ophthalmalogical researcher*

Oscar A. Candia is one of the world's foremost researchers in the field of ophthalmology, the field of study dealing with the anatomy, functions, diseases, disorders, and treatment of the eye.

Candia was born in Buenos Aires, Argentina, on April 30, 1935, the son of Luisa and Francisco Candia. He attended the Colegio Nacional General Manuel Belgrano, in Curuzú Cuatiá, Argentina, from which he received his B.S. in 1952 and the University of Buenos Aires School of Medicine, which granted his M.D. in 1959. Candia then remained at the University of Buenos Aires as an instructor from 1960 to 1963 before immigrating to the United States and joining the faculty of the University of Louisville in Kentucky as research associate from 1964 to 1965 and assistant professor from 1965 to 1968. In 1968, Candia joined the faculty at the Mt. Sinai School of Medicine in New York City, becoming associate professor of ophthalmology (1968–77), associate professor of physiology (1978–84), and full professor of ophthalmology and physiology (1984–present).

Candia's primary field of interest involves the mechanisms by which fluids and electrolytes (such as sodium and potassium ions) are transported across the epithelial layer of the eye, the external layer of cells that cover the eye. This research is expected not only to lead to a better understanding of the physiological and chemical changes that take place in the eye but also to possible treatments for a variety of ocular (eye) diseases. For example, a condition known as dry eye affects millions of people. The condition results from a decreased flow of fluid in the eye, causing problems with one's vision. Candia's research may suggest mechanisms by which the production of fluids in the eye can be increased, with consequent relief from the symptoms of dry eye. It may also be helpful in dealing with more serious diseases of the eye, such as cataracts and glaucoma.

Candia has been active in a number of professional organizations. He served on a research committee of the National Eye Institute (1979–83), on a study section of the National Institutes of Health (1984–88), on the advisory board of the Eye Bank for Sight Restoration, Inc. (1985), and as chair of the Association for Research in Vision and Ophthalmology (ARVO, 1976). He also served as a trustee of ARVO from 1995 to 2000. Candia has been a member of the editorial board of four eye-related journals, including *Current Eye Research* (1981–98) and *Experimental Biology and Medicine* (2001–03).

Further Reading

"Candia, Oscar A." In *Who's Who among Hispanic Americans, 1994–95,* 3d ed., edited by Amy Unterburger, 120. Detroit: Gale Research, 1995.

"Oscar A. Candia." In *The Hispanic American Almanac,* 3d ed., edited by Sonia G. Benson. Farmington Hills, Mich.: Thomson Gale, 2003.

Cardona, Manuel
(1934–) *physicist*

Manuel Cardona is one of the world's authorities on the physical and chemical properties of germanium, silicon, and other semiconducting materials, materials whose conductivity is much less than that of conductors but greater than that of nonconductors. He has also been interested in the theory of superconductivity, the tendency of a material to continue conducting an electric current essentially forever.

Cardona was born on September 7, 1934, in Barcelona, Spain. His mother was Angela Cardona, a schoolteacher, and his father was Juan Cardona, a small businessman. Manuel showed a fascination with the physical sciences as a young child, with a special interest in the building, testing, and repairing of electrical equipment. By the time he attended high school, Cardona had already decided to pursue a career in physics. Upon graduation from high school, he entered the University of Barcelona, where he majored in physics and received his Licenciatura en Ciencias Físicas (equivalent to a bachelor's degree in physics) in 1955. He was also awarded the Spanish National Prize for Natural Sciences.

Cardona then attended the University of Madrid, where he began his studies for a doctorate in physics. While pursuing his course work, he also served as instructor in electronics at Madrid. Only a year later, however, he moved to the United States and enrolled at Harvard University, where he also began work on a doctoral degree. Two years later, he completed the requirements for his degree at Madrid and was awarded a doctorate in science, and, in 1959, he was awarded his Ph.D. in applied physics by Harvard. Cardona's doctoral studies focused on the effects of electricity, light, and magnetism on germanium and silicon and on the electrical properties of the two elements.

In 1959, Cardona returned to Europe, where he took a position as a member of the technical staff at RCA Laboratories in Zurich, Switzerland. Two years later, he took a similar post at the RCA Laboratories in Princeton, New Jersey, where he remained until 1964. He then accepted an appointment as associate professor of physics at Brown University, in Providence, Rhode Island. Two years later, he was promoted to full professor at Brown. Cardona became a naturalized citizen of the United States in 1967. In 1971, he chose to return to Europe once more, accepting a position as scientific member and director of the Max Planck Institute for Solid State Research in Stuttgart, Germany. He held that post until 2000, when he retired and became director emeritus of the institute.

Cardona is the author of more than 1,200 scientific papers, 10 monographs, and a textbook on semiconductors, *The Physics of Semiconductors* (with Peter Y. Yu), 2004. Although most of his work has dealt with the physical and chemical properties of semiconducting materials, he also worked on superconductivity during the 1960s and then, later in his career, on high-temperature superconductivity, the phenomenon in which materials lose essentially all their resistance to electrical conductivity near room temperature.

Cardona has characterized his own style of research as attempting to "extract the maximum amount of information possible from simple experiments." He has written that he "is equipped with a threefold arsenal: experimental techniques, materials, and a few theoretical methods." "Every time a new material, phenomenon, or theory appears," he has said, he "promptly tries to apply to them the rest of [the] arsenal so as to move the frontiers of Condensed Matter Physics."

Cardona has received an impressive number of honors and awards in recognition of his achievements. These awards include the N. Monturiol Medal of the Government of Catalonia (1982), the Frank Isakson Prize of the American Physical Society (1984), Spain's Grand Cross of Alfonso X el Sabio (1987) and Príncipe de Asturias Prize (1988), the Joannes Marcus Marci von Kronland Medal of the Czech Spectroscopic Society (1988), the Excellence Award for Superconductivity of the World Congress on Superconductivity (1992), the Italgas Prize for Research in Materials Science and Technology (1993), the Max Planck Research Prize (1994), the John Wheatley Prize of the American Physical Society (1997), the Sir Nevill Mott Medal and Prize of the Institute of Physics of London (2001), the Matteucci Medal of the Italian National Academy of Sciences (2004), and the Blaise Pascal Medal of the European Academy of Sciences

Manuel Cardona is the author and coauthor of more than 1,200 scientific papers on the subject of semiconductors. *(Courtesy of the Max-Planck-Institut für Festkörperforschung)*

(2004). He has also been awarded eight honorary doctorates from universities in Spain, Canada, Germany, Greece, Italy, and the Czech Republic.

Further Reading

Jones, J. Sydney. "Manuel Cardona." In *Notable Twentieth-Century Scientists,* edited by Emily J. McMurray, 307–308. Detroit: Gale Research, 1995.

"Manuel Cardona (1934–   )." In *The Hispanic American Almanac,* 3d ed., edited by Sonia G. Benson, 671. Farmington Hills, Mich.: Thomson Gale, 2003.

Olesky, Walter. *Hispanic-American Scientists,* 23–32. New York: Facts On File, 1998.

"Manuel Cardona." Prince of Asturias Foundation. Available online. URL: http://www.fundacionprincipedeasturias.org/ing/premios/galardones/galardonados/trayectorias/trayectoria509.html. Downloaded on February 23, 2005.

Cardús, David

(1922–2003) *cardiologist, biomathematician*

David Cardús was trained as a cardiologist but became interested in a wide array of medical issues dealing with the effects of gravitation on human physiology, spinal injury rehabilitation, respiratory physiology, and human aging. Some of his most influential work was in the use of computational and mathematical systems for the analysis of biological data.

Cardús was born in Barcelona, Spain, on August 6, 1922, to Jaume and Ferranda Pascual Cardús. He attended primary school in Barcelona and then, in 1932, was enrolled at the Institut-Escola, a progressive institution where children were allowed to make fundamental decisions about the courses they would study. His mother died in 1933, leaving his father as the only family he had. Cardús graduated from the Institut-Escola in 1938 and was forced to flee Spain with his father because of the spread of the Spanish civil war. The Cardúses traveled to France, where David enrolled at the University of Montpellier, from which he received both a bachelor of arts and a bachelor science in 1942. He then returned to Spain and served four years in the army. Afterward, Cardús began his medical studies at the University of Barcelona's School of Medicine, earning his M.D. in 1949. He then completed his internship at Barcelona's Hospital Clínico and his residency in respiratory diseases at the city's Sanatorio del Puig d'Olena. Over the next three years, Cardús continued his medical education in Paris and Barcelona, specializing in cardiology, and received his diploma in cardiology from Barcelona's postgraduate School of Cardiology in 1956.

In 1957, Cardús continued his studies at the University of Manchester's Royal Infirmary, in Manchester, England, before accepting an appointment as research associate at the Lovelace Foundation in Albuquerque, New Mexico. The Lovelace Foundation had originally been established to study the biological effects of nuclear radiation but later became a center for the testing of individuals for spaceflight. One of Cardús's primary responsibilities at Lovelace was the medical evaluation of candidates for the U.S. space program and selection of the first astronauts to serve in that program. After three years at Lovelace, Cardús accepted an appointment as a member of the medical staff at the Institute for Rehabilitation and Research at the Baylor College of Medicine in Houston, Texas. Cardús retained his affiliation with Baylor in one post or another until his death in Spring, Texas, on June 1, 2003.

One of Cardús's most important contributions to medical research resulted from his work for the National Aeronautics and Space Administration (NASA) on the effects of weightlessness on the anatomy and physiological functions of astronauts. Early studies had indicated that bone growth, muscle tone, fluid distribution, cardiovascular function, and other biological behaviors were likely to be affected by the loss of gravity astronauts experienced in outer space. In order to counteract this effect, Cardús invented a rotating platform with a short radius that could be installed in a space vehicle. The centrifugal (center-fleeing) effect produced by the platform produced a force on astronauts' bodies that replicated to some extent the gravitational effect experienced by humans on Earth's surface. The rotating platform was used not only in spacecraft to replicate gravity but also on Earth to study in more detail the effects of greater or lesser gravitational forces on biological functions in humans.

Cardús later adapted the rotating platform for other medical situations. For example, individuals who suffer strokes sometimes experience cardiovascular problems because they are unable to maintain upright positions. By placing such patients in the rotating platform, the effect of gravitational forces is replicated, and they may regain some of the function lost as a result of their stroke.

Cardús was also interested in the development of methods by which the rapidly developing resources of computer mathematics could be used to solve biological problems. He recognized that biological data, such as respiration rate, pulse, and temperature, could easily be expressed as discrete data points that could be entered into a computer and processed almost instantaneously. The real-time readouts of biological functions produced by this method could give physicians and researchers an opportunity to study biological functions as they were happening, providing them with a moment-by-moment summary of changes taking place in a person's body. In a now-famous demonstration of this concept, Cardús set up a system by which data obtained from a person performing exercises in Barcelona were transmitted to his office in Houston, where those data were recorded and analyzed and then retransmitted for visual display in the Barcelona laboratory.

In addition to his scientific work, Cardús maintained a strong interest in his native province of Catalonia throughout his life. Catalonia is in the northeastern corner of Spain, home to Barcelona and the Costa Brava region of the Mediterra-

nean coastline. In 1979, he founded the American Institute of Catalan Studies with the goal of educating Americans about the history, culture, art, and economy of his native province. He was largely responsible for the publication in 1995 of *The Catalan Nation and Its People* by Josep Carner-Ribalta.

Cardús was active in a number of professional associations, serving as an officer in many of them. He was president of the International Society for Gravitational Physiology, chairman of the board of the Institute for Hispanic Culture in Houston, and president of Spanish Professionals in America. He was given an honorary doctoral degree by the University of Barcelona in 1993 and was awarded the Joan d'Alòs award of the Centro Cardiovascular Sant Jordi in Barcelona in 1996.

Further Reading

"David Cardús." In *The Hispanic American Almanac,* 3d ed., edited by Sonia G. Benson, 670. Farmington Hills, Mich.: Thomson Gale, 2003.

Guerrero, Ricard. "A Man of Science." *Catalonia Today* (November 2003), 21–24. Available online. URL: http://www.aics-usa.org/CATTOD16N01.rtf. Downloaded on February 23, 2005.

Lawbaugh, Penelope. "David Cardús." In *Notable Twentieth-Century Scientists,* edited by Emily J. McMurray, 309–310. Detroit: Gale Research, 1995.

Olesky, Walter. *Hispanic-American Scientists,* 13–22. New York: Facts On File, 1998.

Carmona, Richard H.
(Richard Henry Carmona)
(1949–) *physician, surgeon general*

Richard Henry Carmona was sworn in as the 17th surgeon general of the United States on August 5, 2002, the second Latino (in addition to ANTONIA NOVELLO) to have held this post.

Carmona was born in Spanish Harlem in New York City on November 22, 1949. He came from an impoverished Puerto Rican family and

Richard H. Carmona is the 17th surgeon general of the United States. *(U.S. Department of Health and Human Services)*

was awarded an associate of arts degree. He then entered the University of California at San Francisco (UCSF), from which he received his B.S. with honors in 1976. He stayed on at UCSF for his medical training, receiving his M.D. in 1979. At graduation, Carmona was given the prestigious Gold-Headed Cane award as the graduate with the best academic record. He then completed his surgical internship and residency at UCSF and was appointed a National Institutes of Health fellow in trauma surgery, burns, and critical care at the San Francisco General Trauma Center.

Upon completing his medical education, Carmona accepted a post as director of the Trauma Care System in Tucson, Arizona, a position he held from 1985 to 2002. During the same period, he was a physician in the Pima County sheriff's department, a member of the county SWAT team, and clinical professor of surgery, public health, and family and community medicine at the University of Arizona Health Sciences Center in Tucson. In April 2002, President George W. Bush nominated Carmona for the job of surgeon general. He was confirmed unanimously by the U.S. Senate on July 23, 2002.

Further Reading

Sanchez, Brenna, "Richard Carmona." In *Contemporary Hispanic Biography,* edited by Ashyia N. Henderson, 61–63. Farmington Hills, Mich.: Thomson Gale, 2003.

U.S. Department of Health & Human Services. "Biography of Vice Admiral Richard H. Carmona, M.D., M.P.H., F.A.C.S." Available online. URL: http://www.hhs.gov/about/bios/sg.html. Downloaded on February 23, 2005.

grew up in a neighborhood in which boys and girls were seldom provided with and/or took advantage of educational opportunities by which they might better themselves. In an effort to avoid the less happy fate of many of his friends, Carmona decided to drop out of DeWitt Clinton High School in the Bronx and join the U.S. Army in 1966. Later, he studied for and passed the examinations through which he was awarded his high school equivalency degree, the army's general equivalency diploma.

Carmona volunteered for the Special Forces division of the army and served in the Vietnam War, during which he earned a Bronze Star and two Purple Hearts. At the conclusion of his service career, he returned to New York City and enrolled at Bronx Community College, where he

Casals-Ariet, Jordi
(1911–2004) *virologist*

Jordi Casals-Ariet's major contribution to science was his development of a system for classifying viruses that has become the basis of essentially all modern viral taxonomy.

Casals-Ariet was born in Viladrau (Girona), Spain, on May 15, 1911. He served in the Spanish army before attending the University of Barcelona, from which he received his bachelor's degree in 1928 and then his M.D. in 1934. In an effort to escape the disruptions of the Spanish civil war, Casals-Ariet left Spain in 1936 to accept a one-year appointment as visiting investigator at the Rockefeller Institute for Medical Research in New York City. He then spent two years at the Cornell University Medical College in New York before returning to Rockefeller as an associate in pathology. In 1952, he accepted an appointment as staff member at Rockefeller, where he worked on a group of viruses known as arborviruses. When his research unit was relocated in 1964 to Yale University, in New Haven, Connecticut, he moved with it. For the next two decades, Casals-Ariet commuted daily from his home in New York City to his laboratory at Yale. Upon his retirement from Rockefeller in 1981, Casals-Ariet joined the faculty at the Mt. Sinai School of Medicine in Manhattan. He remained employed and active at Mt. Sinai until his death on February 10, 2004. He published his last scientific paper in 1998.

Some of Casals-Ariet's earliest papers dealt with methodological issues. These papers were so carefully and clearly written that they have become, according to one of his colleagues, "classics in the field." While working on tests for the tuberculosis pathogen at Cornell Medical College, Casals-Ariet became interested in the question of viral taxonomy, the ways in which various kinds of viruses are (or are not) related to one another. He eventually established three criteria for deciding whether viruses were related. These rules have been paraphrased by one of his biographers (Charles H. Calisher) as follows:

- No virus can belong to two antigenic groups;

Jordi Casals-Ariet was one of the world's greatest virologists and discoverer of the Lassa virus in 1969. *(Yale University School of Medicine, Epidemiology and Public Health)*

- If two viruses cross-react antigenically, they are related;
- If viruses of different groups cross-react, they do not belong to different groups.

By applying these rules to the viruses that he (and others) studied, Casals-Ariet eventually constructed a well-ordered viral taxonomy that includes orders, families, subfamilies, genera, and species, paralleling taxonomies for plants and animals. Calisher suggests that Casals-Ariet's findings "may have contributed more to our current understanding of modern taxonomy [of viruses] than did those of any other individual."

In the late 1960s, Casals-Ariet became involved in one of the most dramatic viral stories in recent history. In 1969, three nurses working at a missionary camp in Nigeria became desperately ill with what appeared to be a new type of viral disease. In a short period of time, two of them died. Authorities agreed that Casals-Ariet's laboratory was probably the best research facility in the world for identifying the new virus. As a result, blood from the two dead nurses was shipped to his Yale laboratory, and the surviving nurse traveled to New York, where she recovered after a nine-week stay in Manhattan's Columbia-Presbyterian Hospital.

Meanwhile, Casals-Ariet was able to identify the virus responsible for the disease, eventually giving it the name *Lassa virus,* after the village in which the three nurses had worked. Recognizing the severe nature of the new disease, Casals-Ariet incorporated the most up-to-date techniques for ensuring the safety of his colleagues at the Yale laboratory. Unfortunately, those techniques were not good enough, and Casals-Ariet himself came down with symptoms of the disease. He became very ill and survived only because his colleagues decided to inject him with blood taken from the surviving nurse, a very risky procedure. One colleague, technician Juan Roman, was not so fortunate. He also contracted the disease and died in December 1969. At that point, Casals-Ariet terminated his work on the Lassa virus and transferred responsibility for the project to the better-equipped laboratories at the Centers for Disease Control in Atlanta, Georgia.

Further Reading

Altman, Lawrence K. "Jordi Casals-Ariet, Who Found Lassa Virus, Dies at 92." *New York Times,* February 21, 2004, p. A13.

Calisher, Charles H. "Obituary: In Memoriam: Jordi Casals-Ariet (1911–2004)." *Archives of Virology* 149, no. 6 (June 2004): 1,264–1,266.

Pu, Violet Woodward. "Virologist Casals-Ariet Dies." *Yale Daily News* (February 24, 2004). Available online. URL: http://www.yaledailynews.com/article.asp?AID=25166. Downloaded on February 18, 2005.

Castro, George

(1939–) *physical chemist, educational administrator*

George Castro was manager of the physical sciences division of the IBM San Jose Research Laboratory in San Jose, California, from 1975 to 1986. He is perhaps best known for his discovery of the mechanism by which organic materials (materials that contain the element carbon) are able to conduct an electric current when light is shined upon them. The discovery was later put to use in the development of thin plastic films used in copy machines.

Castro was born in Los Angeles, California, on March 23, 1939, of Mexican ancestry. He has written that he developed an interest in science at an early age and that he "enjoyed tearing things apart to figure out how they worked." Still, he was assigned to a college-bound course at Roosevelt High School in East Los Angeles only by accident, a lucky accident as it turned out since Castro had a chance to find out how much he really loved chemistry and physics.

He entered the University of California at Los Angeles (UCLA) in 1956, intending to major in physics. Before long, however, he found that it was chemistry, not physics, that interested him most, and he changed majors. For his first three years at UCLA, Castro was not a very motivated student, and he was satisfied with having no better than a C average. Then he had a chance to speak with a counselor from the University of California at Irvine who said that Castro would have a good chance at being admitted to graduate school if he could improve his grades. Given that his other option after graduation was military service, Castro decided to work harder and earn the grades he needed to enter graduate school. He was able to do so, posting an A average in his last year at UCLA and earning his B.S. in chemistry in 1960. He was then admitted to the University of California at Riverside for his graduate studies, where he majored in physical chemistry.

Castro completed his course work at Riverside in 1962 and took a position as research fellow with James F. Hornig at Dartmouth College, in Hanover, New Hampshire. It was at Dartmouth that Castro carried out his ground-breaking research on organic photoconductors, research that was to earn him his Ph.D. from Riverside in 1965. That same year, he began a two-year postdoctoral program at the University of Pennsylvania, in Philadelphia, which was followed by an additional one-year postdoctoral program at the California Institute of Technology in Pasadena, California.

In 1968, Castro was offered a job with the IBM Corporation in San Jose, California, as a member of the research staff. He was appointed manager of the physical sciences division in 1975, a post he held until 1986. In addition to his continued research on organic photoconductors, Castro's work at IBM focused on the laser storage of information (the process of storing data on materials using laser beams) and X-ray photomicroscopy (the microscopic examination of materials using X-rays). The latter project involved the construction of a synchrotron (atom smasher) X-ray facility in conjunction with researchers at Stanford University, in California.

When Castro retired from IBM in 1995, he was offered the post of associate dean for science outreach at San Jose State University, in California. A major part of his job was to visit schools and talk with students about opportunities in mathematics and science. He has pointed out that in these visits, "I help all kids, but in particular I focus on Latino, African-American, and Native American kids."

This emphasis reflects Castro's longtime commitment to helping underrepresented minorities improve their access to educational opportunities in science and mathematics. For example, he was president of the Society for the Advancement of Chicanos and Native Americans in Science (SACNAS) from 1991 to 1994. In recognition of his work in this area, Castro was awarded the Presidential Award for Excellence in Science, Mathematics, and Engineering Mentoring in 1999. He retired from his post at San Jose State in 2004 and now devotes his time as volunteer director of the San Jose Science Discovery Workshop. The workshop is an after-school program for children ages eight and above that makes it possible for boys and girls to learn more about science through their own discoveries and experiences.

Further Reading

"George Castro." In *The Hispanic American Almanac,* 3d ed., edited by Sonia G. Benson, 671–672. Farmington Hills, Mich.: Thomson Gale, 2003.

Jones, J. Sydney. "George Castro." In *Notable Twentieth-Century Scientists,* edited by Emily J. McMurray, 327–328. Detroit: Gale Research, 1995.

Junior Achievement of Silicon Valley and Monterey Bay, Inc. "Dr. George Castro." Available online. URL: http://www.jascc.org/hall/hfgcastro.htm. Downloaded on February 24, 2005.

Society for the Advancement of Chicanos and Native Americans in Science. "Dr. George Castro—Engineer & Associate Dean." SACNAS Biography Project. Available online. URL: http://64.171.10.183/biography/Biography.asp?mem=36&type=2. Downloaded on February 24, 2005.

Castro, Gonzalo
(1961–   ) *ecologist, wildlife administrator*

Gonzalo Castro has taught and conducted research in the field of ecology. For the past 15 years, he has served in a variety of capacities at both governmental and nongovernmental agencies that deal with environmental issues, such as the WWF (World Wildlife Fund) and the World Bank.

Castro was born in Lima, Peru, on November 21, 1961. He attended Cayetano Heredia University in Lima, from which he received his B.S. in biology in 1983 and his M.S. in biophysics in 1985. He then immigrated to the United States, where he continued his studies at the University of Pennsylvania, in Philadelphia, where he earned his Ph.D. in ecology and population biology in 1988.

Castro's teaching career began with a one-year appointment at Cayetano Heredia University, where he taught biology and ecology and directed research on bird ecology and tropical conservation. After completion of his graduate studies, he took a post as research associate at Colorado State University, in Fort Collins, from 1988 to 1990. His work there involved studies of bird migration and conservation problems in the central plains of the United States and Latin America.

In 1990, Castro left Colorado State to found Wetlands for the Americas (now Wetlands International), in Manomet, Massachusetts, an organization devoted to planning, management, and development of wetlands areas in the United States, Latin America, and other parts of the world. Castro served as chief executive officer of the organization until 1994, when he was hired as program director and acting vice president for Latin America and the Caribbean of the WWF. In this post, he was responsible for planning, budgeting, staff oversight, and program implementation and evaluation for all of WWF's activities in Latin America and the Caribbean.

In 1997, Castro was offered a position as principal biodiversity specialist with the World Bank, in Washington, D.C. In this post, he was responsible for a large portion of the bank's programs in biodiversity around the world, including the development of green markets, promoting the participation of indigenous peoples in management of their natural resources, establishment of new protected areas and trust funds for conservation of natural areas, and incorporation of biodiversity practices and principles in grants for agricultural and related

programs. In 2002, Castro added a new title to his job at the World Bank, head of the biodiversity unit at Global Environment Facility, an international nongovernmental agency that finances environmental projects around the world. In this job, he has primary responsibility for more than 500 such projects in 150 countries with a total value of more than $1.7 billion.

Castro has received recognition not only for his research work in ecology and biodiversity but also for his administrative achievements. He was given the Kathleen Anderson Award of the Manomet Bird Observatory in 1986, the Alexander Wilson Prize of the Wilson Ornithological Society in 1988, and an award from the International Association for Ecology in 1989. He was named Noyes Fellow by the Smithsonian Tropical Research Institute for 1986–87. He is the author of more than 110 scientific articles and has been an invited speaker at conferences and meetings in countries around the world, including Argentina, Bolivia, Brazil, Chile, Costa Rica, El Salvador, France, Germany, India, Jamaica, Japan, Kyrgyzstan, Malaysia, Mexico, the Netherlands, Panama, Paraguay, Peru, Slovakia, South Africa, Spain, and Uruguay.

Further Reading

"Castro, Gonzalo." In *American Men & Women of Science,* 21st ed., edited by Pamela M. Kalte and Katherine H. Nemeh, vol. 2, 105. Detroit: Thomson Gale, 2003.

New Ventures. "Foro de inversionistas de New Ventures para las empresas de la biodiversidad de la región andina y amazónica." Available online. URL: http://www.new-ventures.org/forobiodiversidad.biografias.html. Downloaded on April 6, 2005.

World Bank Group. "DM 2003 Jury." Development Marketplace. Available online. URL: http://web.worldbank.org/WBSITE/EXTERNAL/OPPORTUNITIES/GRANTS/DEVMARKETPLACE/0,,contentMDK:20135009~pagePK:180691~piPK:174492~theSitePK:205098,00.html. Downloaded on April 6, 2005.

Castro, Max
(Max José Castro)
(1951–) *sociologist, nonprofit administrator, journalist*

Max José Castro has taught sociology at the University of North Carolina at Chapel Hill and other institutions. He has been executive director of Greater Miami United, a nonprofit organization with the goal of improving racial and ethnic relations in south Florida. He also writes regular columns for three major newspapers and appears frequently on radio and television to comment on Cuban-American relations and other important current issues affecting Hispanic Americans.

Castro was born in Havana, Cuba, on April 16, 1951, the son of Bernarda Lorenzo and Máximo Castro. When he was 10 years old, he was sent to live with relatives in the United States because of rumors that Fidel Castro, who had come to power in the Cuban revolution of 1959, planned to start sending children to the Soviet Union to be educated. As he became acclimated to life in the United States, Max completed high school and entered Miami-Dade Community College, from which he received his associate's degree in 1971. He was then accepted at the University of Florida, in Gainesville, where he earned his B.A. in sociology in 1973. He chose to do his graduate studies at the University of North Carolina at Chapel Hill, where he received his M.A. in 1976 and his Ph.D. in sociology in 1985.

After completing his M.A., Castro took a variety of teaching positions at Florida International University in Miami, the University of North Carolina at Chapel Hill, and Appalachian State University in Boone, North Carolina. In 1982, he began a long career working in nonprofit organizations by accepting an appointment as a counselor with the Florida Department of Rehabilitation Services. Two years later, he went to work for Greater Miami United as a project manager and then in 1986 was appointed research director at the organization.

Greater Miami United was a nonprofit, multiethnic organization formed after the race riots of 1980 for the purpose of improving relations among Latinos, blacks, whites, and other ethnic groups. In 1988, Castro was chosen to become executive director of Greater Miami United, a post he held until 1995, when he was appointed senior research associate at the North-South Center at the University of Miami. During this period, Castro also served as director of the Vista Institute of Hispanic Studies, a private organization that conducted research on Hispanic issues and promoted the welfare of the Hispanic population. In 2003, Castro left the North-South Center to accept an appointment as visiting professor in the comparative studies program at Florida Atlantic University.

Castro is a bilingual author and speaker whose columns have appeared in newspapers across the country, including the *Miami Herald, New York Times, Newsday, San Jose* (California) *Mercury News, La Opinión* (Los Angeles), *Sun Sentinel* (south Florida), *La Prensa,* and Miami's *El Nuevo Herald.* He is the editor of *Free Markets, Open Societies, Closed Borders? Trends in International Migration and Immigration Policy in the Americas* (1999) and coeditor of *This Land Is Our Land: Immigrants and Power in Miami* (2003).

Further Reading
"Castro Max Jose." In *The Hispanic American Almanac,* 3d ed., edited by Sonia G. Benson, 145. Farmington Hills, Mich.: Thomson Gale, 2003.

College of Arts and Sciences, University of Miami. "Max J. Castro." Available online. URL: http://www.as.miami.edu/clas/faculty/castro.htm. Downloaded on March 22, 2005.

Castro, Peter
(1943–) *marine biologist*

Peter Castro is an expert in the study of the ecology, physiology, and behavior of marine organisms and the symbiosis (close relationship) among marine organisms. His special field of interest is in the study of brachyuran crabs (true crabs, in contrast to other marine organisms that look like but are not true crabs), particularly with regard to the coral reef habitats in which they live.

Castro was born in Mayagüez, Puerto Rico, on July 20, 1943. He attended the University of Puerto Rico, from which he received his B.S. in biology and chemistry in 1964. He then enrolled at the University of Hawaii, where he earned his M.S. and Ph.D. in zoology in 1966 and 1969, respectively. Throughout his life, Castro has been interested in a wide range of academic subjects and has taken more than four dozen courses on topics ranging from physical anthropology, history, and art history to philosophy and modern languages such as Russian, Catalan, and Italian. In 1992, he was awarded a B.A. in history and art history by the California State Polytechnic University in Pomona, a degree he earned over a period of 18 years.

Castro has worked as a teacher and researcher at a number of institutions, including the University of Puerto Rico (1963–65 and 1970–71); the Enewetak Marine Biological Laboratory (1967); the Moss Landing Marine Laboratories in California (1972 and 1973); the Universities of Bilbao, Madrid, Granada, and Barcelona in Spain (1978, 1981–82, and 1985–86); the University of Hawaii (1983); the University of Florence, in Italy (1986); and the Australian Museum in Sydney (1995). His primary affiliation has been with the California State Polytechnic University in Pomona, where he was appointed assistant professor in 1972. He was later promoted to associate professor (1975) and full professor (1980), a post he continues to hold.

Castro has authored and coauthored more than 40 scholarly papers. He also wrote (with Michael E. Huber) a very popular textbook on marine biology, *Marine Biology* (1991), now in its fifth edition.

Further Reading

"Castro, Peter." In *American Men and Women of Science,* 21st ed., edited by Pamela M. Kalte and Katherine H. Nemeh, vol. 2, 105. Detroit: Thomson Gale, 2003.

"Peter Castro." In *The Hispanic American Almanac,* 3d ed., edited by Sonia G. Benson, 672. Farmington Hills, Mich.: Thomson Gale, 2003.

Catalano, Carlos
(Carlos Enrique Catalano)
(1954–   ) *medicinal chemist*

Carlos Enrique Catalano was trained as a medicinal chemist, a person who studies the mechanisms by which drugs affect cells, tissues, and organs. He has developed an interest in other problems related to biochemistry, including the ways in which proteins are able to act as enzymes and the characteristics and life cycles of viruses.

Catalano was born in Hollywood, California, on October 7, 1954, into a family of Mexican heritage. After completing high school, he enrolled at California State University at San Bernardino but found that he was not yet ready to attend college. He dropped out and took a job as a buyer at Circle City Hospital in Corona, California. After two years in the job, he decided to go back to school and entered the University of California at Fullerton. It was at Fullerton that he discovered his primary academic interest, pharmacological chemistry, the study of the way drugs affect living organisms. Catalano later transferred to San Francisco State University, from which he received his B.A. in biochemistry in 1979.

Catalano has written that he was uncertain as to the next step in his life. He loved chemistry but was not sure that he could make a living with a degree in chemistry. When he learned that he could combine a very practical career in pharmacy with further studies in chemistry, he enrolled in the School of Pharmacy at the University of California at San Francisco (UCSF). He eventually earned a doctor of pharmacy (Pharm.D.) from UCSF in 1983 and then stayed on to work on his Ph.D. in medicinal chemistry, a degree he earned in 1987.

Catalano took a postdoctoral appointment at Pennsylvania State University, where he became interested in a slightly different aspect of biochemistry, the chemistry of proteins. His studies at Penn State focused on the mechanism by which an important enzyme called DNA polymerase acts on molecules to bring about chemical changes. Catalano has said that his research experience at Penn State is still "very important to my everyday life as a scientist today."

Upon completion of his postdoctoral studies, Catalano was offered an appointment as assistant professor of biochemistry in the University of Colorado Health Science Center (UCHSC)

School of Pharmacy. In 1996, he was promoted to associate professor and in 2002, to full professor. He holds a joint appointment at the UCHSC School of Medicine's department of biochemistry and molecular genetics. Catalano's current field of interest is in the study of ways by which viruses assemble, with a view toward using that information for the treatment and prevention of viral diseases.

Further Reading

Society for the Advancement of Chicanos and Native Americans in Science. "Dr. Carlos Catalano—Pharmacist/Biochemist." SACNAS Biography Project. Available online. URL: http://64.171.10.183/biography/Biography.asp?mem=37&type=2. Downloaded on February 25, 2005.

University of Colorado Health Sciences Center. "Carlos Enrique Catalano." Program in Biomolecular

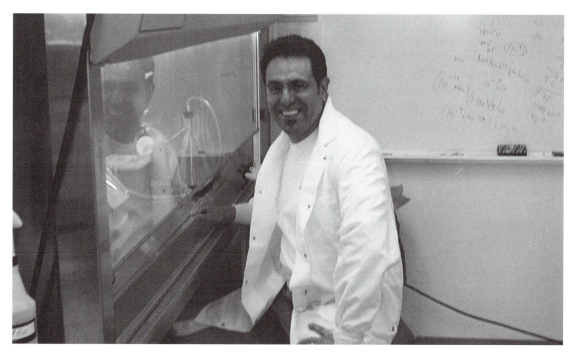

Carlos Catalano is professor of biochemistry at the University of Colorado Health Science Center's School of Pharmacy. *(Courtesy of Dr. Carlos Catalano)*

Structure: Faculty Members. Available online. URL: http://biomol.uchsc.edu/faculty/ResearchPages/catalanoResearch.html. Downloaded on February 25, 2005.

Cavazos, Lauro F.
(Lauro Fred Cavazos)
(1927–) *physiologist, health scientist, secretary of education*

Lauro Fred Cavazos was the first Hispanic American to become a cabinet officer, when he was appointed secretary of education by President Ronald Reagan in 1988. He was also the first Hispanic American to serve as president of his alma mater, Texas Tech University.

Cavazos was born on January 4, 1927, near Kingsville, Texas, on the 825,000-acre King Ranch. He was a sixth-generation Texan of Mexican heritage. His father, also named Lauro, was foreman of the division in which the ranch's famous, hardy Santa Gertrudis cattle were bred. The Cavazos family was widely credited with playing a major role in the development of the King Ranch as one of the great ranches of the American West.

After graduating from high school, Cavazos entered the U.S. Army, serving from 1945 to 1946. Upon his discharge, Cavazos enrolled at Texas Agricultural and Industrial College and then transferred to Texas Technological College (now Texas Tech University). He earned his B.A. in zoology in 1949 and his M.A. in zoological cytology in 1951. Cavazos next began a doctoral program at Iowa State University, from which he received his Ph.D. in physiology in 1954. In the same year, he took a job teaching anatomy at the Medical College of Virginia, where he remained until 1964. He then accepted an appointment as professor of anatomy at Tufts University School of Medicine, in Boston. From 1975 to 1980, Cavazos also served as dean of the medical school.

In 1980, Cavazos was offered the post of president of Texas Tech University, where he became

Lauro F. Cavazos served as secretary of education under Presidents Ronald Reagan and George H. W. Bush, the first Hispanic to hold a cabinet office in the United States. *(U.S. Department of Education)*

the first Hispanic to hold that title. He served as president at Texas Tech until 1988, when he was nominated by President Ronald Reagan to become secretary of education, the first Hispanic to hold that or any other cabinet post. He remained in office for two years, serving also under President George H. W. Bush until 1990.

After he left Washington, Cavazos returned to Tufts, where he now serves as professor of public health and family medicine and director of the graduate program in public health. He is the author or coauthor of more than 90 papers on the physiology of reproduction, the structure of cells and tissues, and medical education. He has been awarded more than 20 honorary doctorates and has been named a distinguished alumnus of Texas Tech

University and "Most Influential Hispanic" in the United States by *Hispanic Business* magazine.

Further Reading

KCBD News Channel. "Whatever Happened to Lauro Cavazos?" Available online. URL: http://www. kcbd.com/Global/story.asp?S=1101372. Downloaded on February 25, 2005.

"Lauro F. Cavazos." In *The Hispanic American Almanac,* 3d ed., edited by Sonia G. Benson, 672–673. Farmington Hills, Mich.: Thomson Gale, 2003.

Texas Archival Resources Online. "Lauro F. Cavazos: An Inventory of His Papers 1943–1991 and Undated, at the Southwest Collection/Special Collections Library." Available online. URL: http://www.lib.utexas.edu/taro/ttusw/00035/tsw–00035.html#bioghist. Downloaded on February 25, 2005.

Chang-Díaz, Franklin
(Franklin Ramón Chang-Díaz)
(1950–) *physicist, astronaut*

Franklin Ramón Chang-Díaz holds a doctorate in applied plasma physics, the study of ways in which a fourth state of matter—plasma—consisting of free electrons and positively charged ions, can be put to practical use. He became the first Hispanic American to travel in space as a crew member of the space shuttle *Columbia* in 1986.

Chang-Díaz was born in San José, Costa Rica, on April 5, 1950, to María Eugenia Díaz de Chang and Ramón A. Chang-Morales. He attended elementary school at the Colegio de La Salle in San José, where, at the age of seven, he heard about the first launch of an artificial satellite, the Soviet space probe *Sputnik I*. Fascinated by the thought of space travel, Chang-Díaz wrote the director of the U.S. National Aeronautics and Space Administration (NASA), Werner von Braun, expressing an interest in becoming an astronaut. Von Braun's suggestion that Chang-Díaz continue his studies

in the United States prompted the young man to settle with relatives in Connecticut. He eventually graduated from Hartford High School in 1969.

Chang-Díaz then enrolled at the University of Connecticut, from which he received a B.S. in mechanical engineering in 1973. He continued his studies at the Massachusetts Institute of Technology (MIT), where he was awarded a Ph.D. in applied plasma physics in 1977. He then remained at MIT to work at the Charles Stark Draper Laboratory on plasma physics and nuclear fusion, the process by which small atomic nuclei are fused (joined together) to make larger nuclei, with the release of large amounts of energy. Chang-Díaz's area of research involved the most basic problem in fusion research, developing methods for containing and controlling fusion reactions for practical applications.

In May 1980, Chang-Díaz achieved his lifelong ambition when he was selected by NASA to become an astronaut. During the next few years, he was involved in the design of the space shuttle, served on the support crew for the first Space Lab mission, was orbit capsule communicator for that flight, and was leader of the astronaut support team at the Kennedy Space Center from October 1984 to August 1985.

On January 12, 1986, Chang-Díaz had his first opportunity to fly into space as a member of space shuttle flight 61-C on the shuttle *Columbia*. During the flight, he broadcast greetings in Spanish to residents of North, Central, and South America. He was eventually to take part in six more shuttle flights, in 1989, 1992, 1994, 1996, 1998, and 2002. In all, he has spent more than 1,600 hours in space, including 19 hours and 31 minutes spent on three spacewalks. Chang-Díaz is one of only two astronauts to have flown in seven space missions.

In addition to his active service as an astronaut, Chang-Díaz has continued to conduct basic research on plasma-related problems. One of the most important of those projects is the Hybrid Plume Plasma Rocket project, designed to develop

Franklin Chang-Díaz was the first Hispanic American to travel into space, as crew member of the U.S. space shuttle. He also conducts research in the field of plasma physics. *(Courtesy National Aeronautical and Space Administration)*

and test a new, more powerful, and more efficient system of rocket propulsion than any now in use. Chang-Díaz has also continued his longtime association with MIT, where he conducts additional research on plasma physics.

Chang-Díaz has long worked to develop closer ties between the astronaut corps and the scientific community. In January 1987, he organized the Astronaut Science Colloquium Program for that purpose, an event that he later helped transform into the Astronaut Science Support Group.

Chang-Díaz has received many honors and awards, including the Liberty Medal from President Ronald Reagan in 1986, the Medal of Excellence from the Hispanic Congressional Caucus

in 1987, the Cross of the Venezuelan Air Force in 1988, the Flight Achievement Award of the American Astronautical Society in 1989, and the Wyld Propulsion Award of the American Institute of Aeronautics and Astronautics in 2001. He has been awarded honorary doctorates by four institutions, Costa Rica's Universidad Nacional, the University of Connecticut, Babson College, and the Universidad de Costa Rica.

Further Reading

Infocostarica.com. "Frankling [sic] Chang Diaz (Astronaut)." Available online. URL: http://www. infocostarica.com/people/franklin.html. Downloaded on February 15, 2005.

Meyer, Nicholas E. "Chang-Díaz, Franklin." In *Biographical Dictionary of Hispanic Americans,* 2d ed., 54–55. New York: Checkmark Books, 2001.

National Aeronautics and Space Administration. "Biographical Data: Franklin R. Chang-Díaz." Available online. URL: http://www.jsc.nasa.gov/Bios/htmlbios/chang.html. Downloaded on February 15, 2005.

Cifuentes, Inés
(1954–   ) *seismologist, science educator*

Inés Cifuentes was the first woman to earn a Ph.D. in seismology, the study of earthquakes and the way they are produced and propagated across the planet. She was director of the Carnegie Academy for Science Education of the Carnegie Institution from 1994 to 2005.

Cifuentes was born in London, England, on April 26, 1954, the daughter of a Jewish mother from New York City and a father from Quito, Ecuador, who was studying at the London School of Economics. Both of her parents were economists working for the United Nations in various countries of the Americas. For the first 12 years of her life, she lived in Ecuador, Paraguay, Chile, and Guatemala. She has said that even after all these years away, Latin America still "feels like home" to her.

Cifuentes remembers first becoming interested in science at the age of seven when her grandfather gave her a book on astronomy. From that point on, she felt certain that she wanted a career in science and that she could succeed in reaching her goals. Her parents had always valued her as being intelligent, she has written, so she never had to deal with the idea that females were somehow less capable than males in math and science.

Cifuentes's adjustment to the United States was not easy. Some of her classmates knew very little about life in Latin America and thought that she might have lived in trees in Guatemala. Still, she persevered in her studies and eventually graduated from Albert Einstein High School in Montgomery County, Maryland, in 1971. She then attended Swarthmore College, in Pennsylvania, from which she received her B.S. in physics in 1975. She next studied at Stanford University, in California, and earned an M.S. in geophysics in 1977. Upon graduation from Stanford, Cifuentes was offered a position with the U.S. Geological Survey (USGS) in Menlo Park, California, studying seismic phenomena in Guatemala and Nicaragua.

After two years with the USGS, Cifuentes enrolled at Columbia University, in New York City, with plans to continue her studies in seismology. She writes that she experienced "the classic horror story of Women in science" at Columbia, with her adviser withdrawing her funding and trying to make her leave the program. She stayed with her studies, however, eventually becoming in 1988 the first woman to have been awarded a Ph.D. in geophysics at Columbia. After completing her degree, Cifuentes spent two years in a postdoctoral program at the Institut de Physique du Globe de Paris with the support of fellowships from the National Science Foundation (NSF) and the North Atlantic Treaty Organization (NATO). Upon completion of these studies, she returned to the United States with her husband and her six-month-old son.

Back in the United States, Cifuentes had a hard time finding a job in seismology that paid more than the cost of her babysitter. Fortunately, she was soon offered a position at the Carnegie Institution in Washington, D.C., a foundation created by the philanthropist Andrew Carnegie in 1902 to "encourage investigation, research, and discovery [and] show the application of knowledge to the improvement of mankind." In the early 1990s, Maxine Singer, president of the institution, was attempting to create a new division within the organization that would study science education and provide a teacher training program. She asked Cifuentes to work on the proposal for the new program and when it was funded in 1994, to become director of the new Carnegie Academy for Science Education (CASE). Cifuentes has said that when she took the job, she knew very little about science education but rapidly became fascinated by the ways in which science can change the lives of children and the excitement involved in developing science teaching programs. Cifuentes resigned as director of CASE on January 31, 2005. She now serves as board president of CASE of Maryland, Inc.

Further Reading

Society for the Advancement of Chicanos and Native Americans in Science. "Dr. Inés Cifuentes—Seismologist." SACNAS Biography Project. Available online. URL: http://64.171.10.183/biography/Biography.asp?mem=146&type=2. Downloaded on February 28, 2005.

Cintron, Guillermo B.
(1942–) *cardiologist, medical researcher*

Guillermo B. Cintron is a researcher in cardiology, the study of the structure and function of the heart and its diseases, disorders, and treatments. His special interests are in the conditions that may lead to heart failure, heart transplantation techniques, and the use of vasodilators to treat cardiac (heart) conditions. A vasodilator is any device or substance that causes blood vessels to expand, permitting an increased flow of blood.

Cintron was born in San Juan, Puerto Rico, on March 28, 1942, the son of Rose A. Silva de Cintrón and Guillermo Cintrón-Ayuso. He attended the University of Puerto Rico, from which he received his B.S., cum laude, in 1963. He then enrolled at the Loyola University School of Medicine in Chicago, earning his M.D. in 1967. He served in Vietnam in the U.S. Navy Medical Corps from 1968 to 1970, earning the Vietnam Service Medal for his part in the war. After his discharge, Cintron completed his residency and internship in cardiology in the Washington, D.C., area before returning to Puerto Rico to take a job as director of coronary care at the Veterans Administration Hospital in San Juan from 1975 to 1983. During the same period, he was assistant professor (1975–80) and associate professor (1980–83) at the University of Puerto Rico School of Medicine in San Juan.

In 1983, Cintron returned to the United States, where he accepted a joint appointment as chief of the cardiology section at the James A. Haley VA Medical Center in Tampa, Florida, and as associate professor of cardiology at the University of South Florida, also in Tampa. He has since been promoted to full professor of cardiology. Cintron has been a fellow of the American College of Cardiology since 1975 and of the American Heart Association Council of Clinical Cardiologists since 1980. He has been a member of the Veterans Administration's Heart Transplant Board since 1992. He was also a fellow of the American College of Physicians from 1976 to 1992.

Further Reading

"Cintron, Guillermo B." In *Who's Who among Hispanic Americans, 1994–95,* 3d ed., edited by Amy Unterburger, 165. Detroit: Gale Research, 1995.

"Guillermo B. Cintrón." In *The Hispanic American Almanac,* 3d ed., edited by Sonia G. Benson, 678. Farmington Hills, Mich.: Thomson Gale, 2003.

Córdova, France Anne
(France Anne-Dominic Córdova)
(1947–   ) *astrophysicist, educational administrator*

France Anne Córdova served as chief scientist at the National Aeronautics and Space Administration (NASA) from 1993 to 1996, the youngest person and second woman to hold that post. At the conclusion of her term at NASA, Córdova accepted an appointment as professor of physics and vice chancellor for research at the University of California at Santa Barbara. In 2002, she was made chancellor of the University of California at Riverside.

Córdova was born in Paris, France, on August 5, 1947, to a Mexican father and Irish mother. At the time, her father, Frederick Córdova, was working for CARE (Cooperative for Assistance and Relief Everywhere). Baptized with the Christian name of Françoise, Córdova later shortened and Americanized her name to France.

After her father completed his assignment in Paris, Córdova's family moved back to California, where they settled in La Puente, a suburb of Los Angeles. Córdova enrolled at Bishop Amat Memorial High School in La Puente but had to devote a considerable part of every day taking care of the growing Córdova family, which eventually grew to include a dozen children. At the conclusion of her regular school day, Córdova helped out with the care of her 11 younger siblings, taking responsibility for a host of housekeeping tasks ranging from changing diapers to ironing school uniforms. Still, she found time to do well in school and in her senior year, was named one of California's Ten Outstanding Youth.

In 1965, Córdova enrolled at Stanford University, the first Hispanic from Bishop Amat to attend that prestigious California university. Although she had always been very interested in the physical sciences, Córdova decided to major in English. Her family felt that the long struggle required to earn a degree in physics was not appropriate for a woman, so they encouraged her to pursue a field in which she was also interested but that would be more suitable for her. In 1969, she graduated from Stanford with a B.A. in English.

Between her junior and senior years at Stanford, Córdova took part in an anthropological expedition to Oaxaca, Mexico. That experience aroused in her a new interest in her Hispanic heritage, and she decided to pursue a graduate degree in anthropology at Stanford. She also was inspired to write a book about her experiences in Mexico, a short novel called *The Women of Santo Domingo.* The book was chosen as one of the 10 best submissions to a contest conducted by *Mademoiselle* magazine. Córdova also submitted a cookbook of traditional Zapotecan recipes that she had found during her visit to Oaxaca. In recognition of her submissions, *Mademoiselle* made Córdova a guest editor at its New York office, where she wrote a number of articles, the best known of which was a travel article on Israel called "Shalom, We Echo Shalom." After completing her time at *Mademoiselle,* Córdova took a position with the Los Angeles Times News Service, where she wrote and edited newspaper articles.

Córdova's plans to continue her graduate studies in anthropology never came to fruition because she had a change of heart as to what she really wanted to do with the rest of her life. On July 11, 1969, astronaut Neil A. Armstrong became the first human to set foot on the Moon when the *Apollo 11* lunar module *Eagle* landed on the lunar surface. Like many other Americans, Córdova was enthralled by the accomplishments of the U.S. space program and decided that she had to return to her first love, physics. She enrolled at the California Institute of Technology (Caltech) and began a program in physics, for which she was awarded a Ph.D. in 1979.

France Anne Córdova served in a variety of administration positions at the National Aeronautics and Space Administration and is now chancellor of the University of California at Riverside. *(Courtesy of the University of California, Riverside)*

Upon graduation from Caltech, Córdova accepted a position as staff scientist in the Earth and Space Science Division of the Los Alamos National Laboratory in Los Alamos, New Mexico. In 1989, she was appointed deputy group leader of the Space Astronomy and Astrophysics Group at Los Alamos. While at Los Alamos, Córdova's research focused primarily on a study of the radiation produced by white dwarfs and pulsars. She also developed a worldwide network of both professional and amateur astronomers who collected and reported their observations about these and related astronomical phenomena.

In 1989, Córdova left Los Alamos to become professor of astronomy and astrophysics and head of the department at Pennsylvania State University. She remained at that post until 1993 when she took a leave of absence from Penn State to become chief scientist at NASA. Her primary responsibility at NASA was to coordinate the work of policymakers and scientists at the agency with the scientific community at large. She also served as the agency's principal adviser for NASA's programs in space, earth, life, and microgravity sciences. While at NASA, Córdova served as chair of the Hubble Space Telescope Time Allocation Committee and of the Working Group on the Constellation X mission and was a member of NASA's Space Science and Applications Advisory Committee and the Extreme Ultraviolet Explorer Guest Observer Working Group.

When Córdova's tenure at NASA came to an end in 1996, she accepted an appointment as professor of physics and vice chancellor for research at the University of California at Santa Barbara. One of her priorities at Santa Barbara was the development of programs through which scientists, engineers, artists, musicians, and others from a variety of fields could come together and interact. The program was one of the first in the nation that attempted to break down barriers between science and the arts. She also led a campus-wide effort to increase opportunities for students to take part in faculty research activities and to increase formal settings in which faculty and students could interact.

In 2002, Córdova was appointed chancellor of the University of California at Riverside. Many students and faculty at Riverside expressed their pleasure when Córdova's selection was announced. She was the first woman and the first Hispanic to hold the position, and as one student expressed it, the appointment of Córdova was "almost like having a double whammy. We have broken through two barriers."

The list of honors and awards given to Córdova is extensive and impressive. She was chosen as one of "America's 100 Brightest Scientists Under 40" by *Science Digest* magazine in 1984 and one of "100 Most Influential Hispanics" by *Hispanic* magazine in 1997. She was awarded NASA's Distinguished Service Medal in 1996, given an honorary doctorate by Loyola-Marymount University in 1997, named a Kilby Prize Laureate in 2000, and chosen as a National Associate of the National Academy of Sciences in 2002.

Further Reading

Bailey, Martha J. "Cordova, France Anne-Dominic." *American Women in Science, 1950 to the Present: A Biographical Dictionary,* 57–58. Santa Barbara, Calif.: ABC-CLIO, 1998.

Silverstein, Stuart. "Chancellor Tackles Image Problems; The New Head of UC Riverside Wants Respect for Her School—and the Way She Sees Herself." *Los Angeles Times,* May 27, 2003, part 2, p. 1. Available online. URL: http://nem-srvr. stsci.edu/~svwb/WRITING/2003_05_27.html. Downloaded on February 19, 2005.

Cortinas, John V., Jr.
(1964–) *meteorologist*

John V. Cortinas, Jr., is a meteorologist who works for the National Severe Storms Laboratory of the National Oceanic and Atmospheric Administration (NOAA). He is also active in educational programs designed to teach young children and young adults about weather, in general, and severe storms, in particular.

Cortinas was born in Grand Island, Nebraska, on January 28, 1964. His father was Mexican American and his mother, American. Cortinas was the oldest child in a family of four boys and one girl. He has said that he experienced only one major obstacle in achieving his educational goals: finances. Since his family could not pay his high school or college costs, Cortinas had to work at outside jobs throughout his academic life. He attended the University of Nebraska at Omaha for two years and then transferred to Metropolitan State College of Denver, in Colorado, from which he received his B.S. in meteorology in 1987. He then continued his studies at the Georgia Institute of Technology (Georgia Tech), in Atlanta, from which he earned a Ph.D. in geophysical sciences in 1992.

Upon graduation from Georgia Tech, Cortinas accepted a job as research meteorologist jointly with the National Severe Storms Laboratory (NSSL) and the University of Oklahoma's Cooperative Institute for Mesoscale Meteorological Studies (CIMMS) at Norman, Oklahoma. NSSL is an agency within NOAA whose responsibility is to carry out research on all kinds of hazardous weather, such as tornadoes, hurricanes, and severe thunderstorms.

Cortinas's own area of special interest is in the characteristics and prediction of ice storms. He has been focusing on the pattern of such storms that occur on the western shores of the Great Lakes in hopes of developing better computer models of ice storms that improve their prediction by meteorologists.

In 1997, Cortinas was appointed adjunct assistant professor in the School of Meteorology at the University of Oklahoma at Norman, and in 2001, he was made assistant director of CIMMS at the university, posts that he still holds. He has also been involved in the Earthstorm Project of the Oklahoma Climate Survey. This program endeavors to make meteorological data available to teachers at all grade levels, K–12, within Oklahoma and other states.

Cortinas has received a number of honors, including the Society of Hispanic Professional Engineers Scholarship (1985), a Hispanic Educational Scholarship (1986), and a Presidential Fellowship at Georgia Tech (1987–89). In 1999, he received NOAA's Office of Oceanic and Atmospheric Research's award for Scientific Paper of the Year.

Further Reading

Cortinas, John V., Jr., et al. "The Research Experiences for Undergraduates Program: The 1995 Program at the Oklahoma Weather Center." *Bulletin of the American Meteorological Society* 77, no. 12 (December 1996): 2,925–2,936.

Society for the Advancement of Chicanos and Native Americans in Science. "Dr. John Cortinas—Meteorologist." SACNAS Biography Project. Available online. URL: http://64.171.10.183/biography/Biography.asp?mem=38&type=2. Downloaded on February 15, 2005.

University of Oklahoma. "Dr. John Cortinas, Jr." Available online. URL: http://www.cimms.ou.edu/~cortinas/. Downloaded on February 15, 2005.

Cota-Robles, Eugene
(Eugene Henry Cota-Robles)
(1926–   ) *microbiologist, college administrator*

Eugene Henry Cota-Robles was trained as a microbiologist and taught and conducted research in this field for many years. Later in his life, however, he served in a variety of administrative positions at the University of California at Santa Cruz and with the National Science Foundation.

Cota-Robles was born in Nogales, Arizona, on July 13, 1926, to Feliciana and Amado Cota-Robles. His parents were both elementary schoolteachers in Pueblo Nuevo, Sonora, Mexico, but left their homes shortly before Eugene was born because of the disruptions caused by the Mexican Revolution. The family, which eventually included 11 children, moved to Nogales and then to Tucson, both in Arizona, where Cota-Robles spent his childhood. As with many children of Hispanic origin at the time, Cota-Robles's teachers were almost without exception Anglos. He saw only one Hispanic teacher who could serve as a role model for him. Unlike many other students, however, Cota-Robles received encouragement from many of his teachers and decided to go to college after graduating from high school.

That step was delayed, however, with the outbreak of World War II. Cota-Robles joined the U.S. Navy as a signalman in 1944 and served most of the war in the South Pacific. When he returned to the United States, he used the GI Bill to pay his way through the University of Arizona. Although he began his college education with plans to become a dentist, he soon found that he was more interested in one of the courses he had to take in his predental program, bacteriology. He switched majors and eventually received his B.S. in 1950.

His first job after graduating from Arizona was with the Gerber Baby Food company in Oakland, California, where he worked as a quality control bacteriologist. He soon tired of that job and decided to return to school. He enrolled at the University of California at Davis, from which he received his M.A. and his Ph.D. in bacteriology in 1954 and 1956, respectively. After a year's postdoctoral studies in Stockholm, Sweden, Cota-Robles returned to California, where he took a job as professor of microbiology at the University of California at Riverside. From 1969 to 1970, he also served as assistant to the chancellor of the university.

Cota-Robles's research during this period focused on the *Azotobacter agilis* bacterium, a microorganism that lives in the soil and converts atmospheric nitrogen to fixed nitrogen, nitrogen in the form of nitrates and nitrites that plants can use in their growth. Cota-Robles's research team discovered the mechanism by which enzymes in the bacterial cells brought about this important chemical change.

In 1970, Cota-Robles left California to take a teaching and research position at Pennsylvania State University (Penn State), in Philadelphia. He remained at Penn State for three years before returning to California, where he took a position as professor of microbiology at the University of California at Santa Cruz. He spent the remaining 32 years of his academic career at Santa Cruz, later serving also as academic vice-chancellor, provost of Crown College, and assistant vice president of academic affairs. Upon his retirement from Santa Cruz, Cota-Robles accepted a limited-term appointment as special assistant to the director of the National Science Foundation as director of affirmative action.

Further Reading

"Cota-Robles, Eugene Henry." In *Who's Who among Hispanic Americans, 1994–95,* 3d ed., edited by Amy Unterburger, 185. Detroit: Gale Research, 1995.

Society for Advancement of Chicanos and Native Americans in Science. "Dr. Eugene Cota-Robles." SACNAS Biography Project. Available online. URL: http://64.171.10.183/biography/Biography.asp?mem=40&type=2. Downloaded on March 2, 2005.

Cuatrecasas, Pedro
(1936–) *pharmacologist*

Pedro Cuatrecasas has participated in the development of more than 40 commercial drugs for the treatment of diseases such as the human immunodeficiency virus, diabetes, depression, respiratory distress, asthma, and hypertension. In addition, he has been involved in basic research on signal transduction, the process by which chemicals are passed through the membrane of cells, and the action of membrane receptors, chemical groups on the surfaces of cells that recognize and respond to chemicals circulating in the body.

Cuatrecasas was born in Madrid, Spain, on September 27, 1936. He immigrated to the United States to attend college at Washington University, in St. Louis, Missouri, where he earned his B.A. in 1958 and his M.D. in 1962. He completed his residency and internship at the Johns Hopkins University Hospital in Baltimore, Maryland, from 1962 to 1964 before accepting an appointment in the Clinical Endocrinology Branch of the National

Institute of Arthritis and Metabolic Diseases, in Bethesda, Maryland, for two years. He then served as a postdoctoral fellow in the Laboratory of Chemical Biology of the National Institute of Arthritis and Metabolic Diseases, in Bethesda, from 1966 to 1967 and later as a medical officer in the same laboratory from 1967 to 1970. During the same period, he was professorial lecturer in biochemistry at the George Washington University School of Medicine, in Washington, D.C.

From 1970 to 1972, Cuatrecasas held joint appointments at the Johns Hopkins University Hospital as associate professor of pharmacology and experimental therapeutics, associate professor of medicine, director of the Division of Clinical Pharmacology, and Burroughs Wellcome Professor of Clinical Pharmacology. In 1972, he was promoted to professor of pharmacology and experimental therapeutics and was named assistant physician at the Johns Hopkins hospital. In 1975, Cuatrecasas left Johns Hopkins to become director of the Burroughs Wellcome Company, in Research Triangle Park, North Carolina; vice president for research, development, and medicine at Borroughs Welcome; and head of the department of molecular biology at Wellcome Research Laboratories, in Research Triangle Park. Simultaneously, he was given joint appointments as adjunct professor in the department of medicine and the department of pharmacology and physiology at the University of North Carolina, in Durham. Cuatrecasas remained at Burroughs Wellcome until 1986, when he was named senior vice president of research and development and director at the pharmaceutical company Glaxo, Inc., also in Research Triangle Park. In 1989, he left Glaxo to become president of the Pharmaceutical Research Division of Parke-Davis, in Ann Arbor, Michigan, and vice president of the Warner-Lambert pharmaceutical company, in Morris Plains, New Jersey. As had become his custom, Cuatrecasas maintained his ties to academia by accepting a joint appointment as adjunct professor in the department of medici-

nal chemistry of the College of Pharmacy at the University of Michigan, in Ann Arbor, and at the university's medical school. Cuatrecasas's most recent move occurred in 1997, when he accepted an appointment as adjunct professor in the departments of pharmacology and internal medicine at the University of California at San Diego's School of Medicine. He also opened his own business as a consultant in the area of Rancho Sante Fe and San Diego.

Cuatrecasas has been a very prolific researcher, with more than 570 scholarly papers to his credit. He is one of the most frequently cited authors in the area of biology and biochemistry of any scientist

Pedro Cuatrecasas has spent most of his professional life conducting research on and development of new drugs. *(Courtesy of Dr. Pedro Cuatrecasas)*

in the world. He has been honored with a number of awards, including the John Jacob Abel Prize in Pharmacology (1972), the Eli Lilly Award of the American Diabetes Association (1975), the Beerman Award of the Society for Investigative Dermatology (1981), the Goodman and Gilman Award for Receptor Research of the American Society for Pharmacology and Experimental Therapeutics (1982), the Dupont Specialty Diagnostics Award of the Clinical Ligand Assay Society (1986), the Wolf Prize in Medicine of the Wolf Foundation (1987), the North Carolina Governor's Medal Award in Science (1988), the City of Medicine Award (1988), and the Distinguished Alumnus Award of Johns Hopkins University (2000). Cuatrecasas has also been awarded honorary doctoral degrees from the University of Barcelona (Spain), the Mt. Sinai School of Medicine of the City University of New York, the University of Buenos Aires (Argentina), and the University of Naples (Italy). In addition, his work has been recognized with distinguished lectureships throughout the world at locations such as the Strathclyde Institute of Biomedical Sciences, in Scotland; Washington University, in St. Louis; the University of North Carolina at Chapel Hill; the Louisiana State University Medical Center; Tulane University, in New Orleans; St. Louis University; the University of Hawaii; the West Virginia University Medical School; Texas Southwestern Medical School; the University of Kansas; the University of Arizona; the University of Toronto; and the University of Maryland.

Further Reading

"Cuatrecasas, Pedro." In *American Men & Women of Science,* 21st ed., edited by Pamela M. Kalte and Katherine H. Nemeh, vol. 2, 492. Detroit: Thomson Gale, 2003.

Freshnews.com. "Aethlon Medical Appoints Pedro Cuatrecasas, MD, to Scientific Advisory Board." Available online. URL: http://www.freshnews.com/news/tech-people-move/article_16598.html?Aethlon. Downloaded on April 7, 2005.

Cubero, Linda Garcia
(Linda Theresa Garcia)
(1958–   ) *engineer*

Linda Garcia Cubero was the first Hispanic woman to graduate not only from the U.S. Air Force Academy but indeed from any U.S. service academy. Since graduation, she has held a number of positions with large industrial corporations, including GE Aerospace, Martin Marietta, Electronic Data Systems, and Hewlett-Packard.

Born Linda Theresa Garcia in Shreveport, Louisiana, on May 14, 1958, to Sara S. and Juan G. Garcia, of Puerto Rican ancestry, she applied to the U.S. Air Force Academy, in Colorado Springs, Colorado, after graduation from high school. Legislation passed by the U.S. Congress in October 1975 had, for the first time, allowed women to attend

Linda Garcia Cubero was the first woman to graduate from the U.S. Air Force Academy and has had a successful career with various industrial corporations in the aerospace field. *(U.S. Department of Defense)*

U.S. military academies, and Garcia was one of the first women to take advantage of that opportunity. She was accepted at the U.S. Air Force Academy and received her B.S. in political science and her commission in the U.S. Air Force in 1980, after an experience that was, as she later said, "pretty rough" at times. She served seven years in the air force, reaching the rank of captain before being discharged. During her career with the air force, Cubero served for four years in the Defense Intelligence Agency at the Pentagon and three years at the Tactical Air Command at Langley Air Force Base in Virginia.

After her discharge, Cubero took a job with the GE Aerospace corporation as a systems engineer. When GE sold its aerospace division to the Martin Marietta corporation in 1992, Cubero was appointed manager of the company's Systems Engineering Program, a post she held until 1993. She then became manager of Group Development for Mergers and Acquisitions at Martin Marietta. In 1997, Cubero moved to the Case Corporation, where she was director of global supplier relations. Two years later, she took a job with EDS (Electronic Data Systems) as director of hardware and telecommunications procurement in global purchasing. In this position, she was responsible for managing more than $3.5 billion in the company's assets. In November 2004, Cubero left EDS to take her present job as a client director at Hewlett-Packard.

Cubero has served in a number of Hispanic, community, and professional organizations, including the U.S. Hispanic Chamber of Commerce, the Washington Area Diversity Council, the National Council of Hispanic Women, the Hispanic Engineer National Achievement Awards Committee, and Senator John W. Warner's Academic Review Board. She has been honored with the Woman of the Year Award by the National Conference of Puerto Rican Women in 1980, the Rockwell International Achievement Award in 1984, and the Hispanic Engineer National Achievement Awards Committee's Pioneer Award in 1991.

Further Reading

"Cubero, Linda Garcia (Linda Theresa Garcia)." In *Who's Who among Hispanic Americans, 1994–95,* 3d ed., edited by Amy Unterburger, 192. Detroit: Gale Research, 1995.

Taborn, Tyrone. "A Hispanic Century in Technology." Hispanic Engineer & Technology Information Online. Available online. URL: http://www.hispanicengineer.com/artman/publish/article_39.shtml. Downloaded on March 4, 2005.

Williams, Rudy. "First Hispanic Woman Grad Credits Academy for Her Success." American Forces Information Services, U.S. Department of Defense. Available online. URL: http://www.defenselink.mil/news/Sep2004/n09222004_2004092208.html. Downloaded on March 4, 2005.

D

Dallmeier, Francisco
(Francisco Gómez-Dallmeier)
(1953–) *wildlife biologist*

Francisco Dallmeier is one of the world's foremost wildlife biologists, with a special interest in the study of methods for protecting and maintaining the planet's biodiversity. He has made important contributions to the development of methods for studying the biodiversity of an area and for finding ways by which commercial interests and researchers can work together to protect the biodiversity of a region.

Dallmeier was born in Caracas, Venezuela, on February 15, 1953. His great-grandfather, the renowned naturalist Adolph Ernst, had emigrated from Germany to Venezuela some years earlier when the Nazi Party had confiscated the family property. His father was also a scientist who managed a cancer research institute in Caracas. With this family background, it is hardly surprising that Dallmeier himself became interested in biology at an early age. He has been quoted as saying that "At the age of three, I loved and was fascinated by nature and animals. I knew I wanted to work like my great-grandfather had with animals, and plants and to discover many of nature's secrets."

Dallmeier soon found a number of outlets through which he could express his interest in biology. He chose to become a Boy Scout because the organization provided him with a way to get out of the urban confines of Caracas and into the world of forests and nature. At the age of 14, he became a volunteer at Caracas's La Salle Museum of Natural History. His work there so impressed museum administrators that they appointed him curator of mammals four years later. Then, in 1973, at the age of 20, Dallmeier was appointed director of the museum, the youngest person in the world to hold such a post. While working at the museum, Dallmeier was also pursuing his studies at the Central University of Venezuela, from which he received his licentiate in biology, equivalent to a bachelor's degree, in 1977. In the same year, he left his position at the La Salle Museum to accept a job with INELMECA, a Venezuelan environmental engineering firm.

In 1981, Dallmeier decided that he should return to school and was awarded a Fundación Gran Mariscal Ayacucho scholarship to continue his studies. The scholarship is given by the Venezuelan government to worthy citizens to study in foreign countries. Dallmeier chose to enroll at Colorado State University, where he earned his M.S. in 1984 and his Ph.D. in wildlife ecology in 1986.

Upon completion of his studies at Colorado State, Dallmeier accepted a position with the Smithsonian Institution in Washington, D.C., where he was made program manager and assistant director of the U.S. Man and the Biosphere

Francisco Dallmeier, director of the Monitoring and Assessment of Biodiversity Program, a joint project of the Smithsonian Institution and the United Nations Educational, Scientific, and Cultural Organization, has worked with the program for 20 years. *(Smithsonian Institution SI/MAB Biodiversity Program)*

(MAB) biodiversity project. The U.S. MAB Program is a joint project of the Smithsonian and the United Nations Educational, Scientific and Cultural Organization (UNESCO), whose mission is to find ways of protecting Earth's biodiversity, the natural mix of plant and animal species found in the natural world. The greatest threat to biodiversity and the survival of plant and animal species has long been the activities of humans: the destruction of natural habitats; the poisoning of air, water, and land resources; and the direct destruction of large numbers of plants and animals. The goal of

the MAB project has been to find ways of reducing the damage caused by such activities, allowing more plant and animals species to survive and thrive in an ever more developed world.

After only two years with the Smithsonian, Dallmeier was promoted first to acting director (1988–89) and then to director of the program, whose name, by this time, had been changed to the Monitoring and Assessment of Biodiversity Program (still abbreviated as MAB) and moved to the National Zoo in Washington, D.C. Dallmeier continues to be in charge of that program today.

One of Dallmeier's most important contributions has been in the development of techniques for measuring and assessing the biological diversity of an area. It is often difficult to visit a region and decide what changes, if any, are taking place within that region, what the nature of those changes is, the rate at which change is taking place, and the extent to which human activities may be responsible for those changes. Dallmeier developed quantitative methods for dividing a region into distinct sections (a grid), each of which could be studied and analyzed in detail with respect to its biological characteristics. These characteristics are then expressed as quantitatively as possible, allowing the determination of changes in plant number, variety, size, and so on, over time. Dallmeier's system allows ecologists to discover quite precisely how an area is changing and what it and its inhabitants are likely to be like in the future.

An interesting offshoot of Dallmeier's approach to ecological monitoring was a program he initiated in 1995 called Tree Watch. In this program, teenage volunteers are assigned specific forested regions in which they are to count and measure as many types of plant and animal species as possible. This information can then be used to estimate the current biological health of the region and in the future, to determine changes in the region's biodiversity. The first Tree Watch census was taken in 1995 in a forested area of Niagara Falls National Park.

A second major contribution has been more philosophical, an approach to dealing with ecological issues promoted by Dallmeier. In many cases, development in natural areas rapidly becomes very confrontational. On the one hand, industrial and commercial interests may be pushing for the destruction of forests, savannas, and other natural areas to permit the construction of new plants, the digging of mines, the sinking of oil wells, or other projects. On the other hand, environmentalists may be taking whatever actions possible—ranging from pushing for the adoption of new laws and regulations to violent physical protests—to protect these natural areas. Dallmeier has promoted the concept that these two opposing forces, developers and environmentalists, can work together from the onset to reduce the ecological damage caused by new projects.

An example of this approach was the Shell Prospecting and Development Project, organized by Dallmeier in the mid-1990s. The project was inspired by plans of the Shell Corporation to construct a large new natural gas plant in the Lower Urubamba River Valley in Peru. According to early plans, the project would have been constructed near Peru's Manu National Park, posing a possible danger to the unique plant and animal life found in the park. Working with representatives from Shell and the Peruvian government, Dallmeier was able to work out a compromise by which the plant would have been built farther away from the park, ensuring greater safety for the natural ecosystem found there. The compromise was never acted upon, however, as Shell decided not to continue working in the area.

Dallmeier has long been interested in learning more about the role of Latinos and Latinas in American culture and promoting greater understanding of that role in general society. At the Smithsonian, he has served as acting director of the Center for Latino Initiatives, whose goal it is to integrate more freely the work and contributions of Latinos and Latinas into the Smithsonian's activities and programs.

Dallmeier has published more than 130 scholarly papers, is the author of three books on forest biodiversity in various parts of the world, and is coauthor of a children's book on biodiversity.

Further Reading

Alic, Margaret. "Francisco Dallmeier." In *Contemporary Hispanic Biography,* edited by Ashyia N. Henderson, 84–87. Farmington Hills, Mich.: Thomson Gale, 2003.

Brown, Valerie. "Francisco Dallmeier." In *Notable Twentieth-Century Scientists,* edited by Emily J. McMurray, 445–446. Detroit: Gale Research, 1995.

Kloepfer, Deanne, and Patricia Abarca. *Francisco Dallmeier.* Bloomington, Ind.: Raintree Press, 2005.

Meyer, Nicholas E. "Dallmeier, Francisco." In *Biographical Dictionary of Hispanic Americans,* 2d ed., 77–78. New York: Checkmark Books, 2001.

Olesky, Walter. *Hispanic-American Scientists,* 69–82. New York: Facts On File, 1998.

Smithsonian National Zoological Park. "Bios & Profiles: Francisco Dallmeier. Ph.D., MAB Director." Available online. URL: http://nationalzoo.si.edu/AboutUs/Staff/BiosAndProfiles/DallmeierFrancisco.cfm. Downloaded on February 18, 2005.

De La Cancela, Victor
(1952–) *psychologist*

Victor De La Cancela's research focuses on the special psychological issues and problems faced by individuals from minority communities. He is one of the psychological profession's most outspoken proponents in the field of ethnopharmacotherapy, the study of the way in which drugs are used to deal with psychological problems among individuals of various cultural backgrounds.

De La Cancela was born in New York City on December 18, 1952, to Guillermina Ortiz and Luis Fernandez De La Cancela, of Puerto Rican heritage. He attended the City College of New York, from which he received his B.A. in 1974, and the City University of New York Graduate School, which awarded him a M.Phil. in 1979 and a Ph.D. in 1981. After completing a Harvard University Medical School Department of Psychiatry (HUMSDP) two-year internship/fellowship in clinical psychology at Beth Israel Hospital, De La Cancela held numerous positions in the Boston area: assistant in psychology and instructor in psychology at Beth Israel Hospital, Boston; staff psychologist, instructor in psychology, and acting program manager at the Hispanic Family Counseling Unit of the Massachusetts Mental Health Center, in Jamaica Plains; and staff psychologist, instructor in psychology, and Hispanic Outreach team leader of the Judge Baker Guidance Center in Jamaica Plain.

After receiving his doctorate, De La Cancela moved to California, where he worked as director of the Residential Treatment Program at El Centro Community Mental Health Center, in Los Angeles (1981), and director of Outpatient Services and of the Clinical Program, Latino/Ethnic Services, at San Fernando Valley Community Mental Health Center, in Van Nuys (1981–83). He then returned to the Boston area, where he served in a number of clinical and administrative positions with HUMSDP and the Solomon Carter Fuller Mental Health Center (SCFMHC) of the Massachusetts Department of Mental Health. From 1983 to 1985, he was director of the Latino Mental Health Service, codirector of the Latino Medical Clinic, and lecturer at Cambridge Hospital, and from 1985 to 1987, he was director of Family Services at the Brookside Health Center of Brigham and Women's Hospital, in Jamaica Plain, both institutions affiliated with HUMSDP. From 1988 to 1989, De La Cancela was director of community programs at SCFMHC and from 1989 to 1990, special projects coordinator at the center.

In 1990, De La Cancela moved to New York City to become assistant vice president of Mental Hygiene Services and acting vice president for Public Affairs and Special Projects in the New York City Health and Hospitals Corporation (NYCHHC), an agency with which he was affiliated for the next five years. He later served as senior vice president and chief community health officer of NYCHHC's Community Health Division (1990–91); senior vice president of the corporation's Office of Primary Care Development (1991–92); senior assistant vice president, executive director, and chief corporate development officer of grants research and development (1992–93); and senior assistant vice president of Managed Care Education and Special Projects (1993–95). Over the following years, De La Cancela held a series of positions in New York City, including consulting psychologist at Comprehensive Habilitation Services (1995–99), clinical administrator at Gateway Counseling Center (1996–99), and member of the faculty at Beth Israel Medical Center Residency in Urban Family Practice (2000–01). He also began a relationship with the Tremont Crotona Child Development Center in the Bronx, where he served as director of organizational development (1999–2001) and then as deputy executive director, chief of staff, and mental health director (2001–03). After this, he became deputy executive director of Head Start Collaboration Services (2004–present). In addition to these jobs, De La Cancela has been president and chief executive officer of Salud Management Associates, a consulting firm specializing in addiction recovery, health education, mental health care, corporate services, and community-based primary health initiatives. He has also been a commissioned officer in the U.S. Army Medical Services Corps and has been mobilized and deployed on active duty tours to the Patterson Army Health Clinic and the Fort Dix Mills Troop Medical Clinic, both in New Jersey, and Basset Army Community Hospital, Fort Wainwright, Alaska, providing a wide variety of behavioral health services for military personnel and their families.

De La Cancela has been very active in organizations concerned with the study of psychological issues of special concern to the Latino community, including the Hispanic Coalition for Health, Inc.; the California Hispanic Psychological Association; the Massachusetts Hispanic Psychological Association; the National Hispanic Psychological Association; and the National Boricua Health Organization, an organization concerned with Puerto Rican health issues. He has been honored with an award for exemplary leadership and service from the National Hispanic Psychological Associa-

tion in 1990, a recognition of service award from the Latino caucus of the American Public Health Association in 1990, and the Nelson Mandela Award in Health from the New York Association of Black Psychologists in 1991. De La Cancela is author of more than 85 scholarly papers and coauthor of two major books, *Diversity in Psychotherapy: The Politics of Race, Ethnicity, and Gender* (1993) and *Community Health Psychology: Empowerment for Diverse Communities* (1998).

Further Reading

"De La Cancela, Victor." In *Who's Who among Hispanic Americans, 1994–95,* 3d ed., edited by Amy Unterburger, 202. Detroit: Gale Research, 1995.
"Victor De La Cancela, PhD, MPH, ABPP, FICPP." *ASAP Tablet* (2000): 5. Also available online. URL: http://www.apa.org/divisions/div55/Tablet%2010/00/page5.html. Downloaded on April 6, 2005.

de la Mora, Juan Fernández
(1952-   ) *mechanical engineer*

Juan Fernández de la Mora is a mechanical engineer whose primary research is in the field of electrosprays and ultrafine particles. Electrosprays are systems in which liquids are dispersed into very fine particles (ultrafine particles), sometimes the size of individual atoms, whose properties can then be investigated in greater detail. This field of research is one form of nanoscience, the study of the properties and behavior of particles at very small dimensions, such as those of atoms and molecules, with potential applications in the development of ionic engines for use in propelling vehicles in outer space.

De la Mora was born in Madrid, Spain, on September 20, 1952, the son of Isabel Varela and Gonzalo Fernández de la Mora. He attended the Escuela Técnica Superior de Ingenieros Aeronáuticos, in Madrid, from which he received his B.S. in 1975. He continued his studies at Yale University, in New Haven, Connecticut, where he earned his Ph.D. in physics in 1981, winning the Harding Bliss Prize for the best doctoral dissertation in engineering for the year. He then spent the following year in a postdoctoral program at the University of California at Los Angeles. From 1975 to 1986, de la Mora also worked as an aeronautical engineer for the Spanish firm Construcciones Aeronáuticos, a large corporation engaged in many aspects of aircraft design, construction, and testing.

In 1981, de la Mora was offered the position of assistant professor of mechanical engineering at Yale. He was later promoted to associate professor and full professor of mechanical engineering, a post he now holds. In addition to his work at Yale, de la Mora has served as visiting professor at the Polytechnical School of Madrid (1978–88), the Universidad Nacional de Educación a Distancia, in Madrid (1988–91), and the University of Hiroshima (1996), in Japan. He is the author or coauthor of more than 70 scientific papers dealing with electrosprays and related topics and was given the Whitby Award of the American Association for Aerosol Research in 1985.

Further Reading

"De La Mora, Juan Fernandez." In *Who's Who among Hispanic Americans, 1994–95,* 3d ed., edited by Amy Unterburger, 204. Detroit: Gale Research, 1995.

Yale University. "Juan Fernández de la Mora." Available online. URL: http://www.eng.yale.edu/faculty/vita/delamora.html. Downloaded on April 6, 2005.

Delgado, Jane L.

(1953–   ) *clinical psychologist, health care administrator*

Jane L. Delgado is president and chief executive officer of the National Coalition of Hispanic Health and Human Services Organization, the largest agency in the United States to focus exclusively on health issues faced by Latinos and Latinas. She has also served as chair of the National Health Council, an agency founded in 1920 and consisting of 115 member organizations representing many areas of health care. Delgado was the first nonwhite person to hold this position.

Delgado was born on June 17, 1953, in Havana, Cuba, the daughter of Lucila Aurora Navarro Delgado and Juan Lorenzo Delgado Borges. When Delgado was two years old, her family immigrated to the United States and settled in New York City, where her father was a publisher of Latin American magazines. When her father abandoned the family, Delgado's mother was forced to take over care of the children, often holding two jobs simultaneously to make ends meet. Having had two years of college education herself, Lucila encouraged her children to work hard in school and set their goals high in life.

Delgado entered kindergarten with something of a handicap, however, as she spoke no English. She learned the language rapidly, however, and was soon doing well in school. By the third grade, she had been placed in a special class for gifted children. In high school, she became frustrated that classes were not very challenging, and she designed a program by which she could graduate early. She did so at the age of 16 and began her college studies at the State University of New York at New Paltz in 1969. She completed her studies there in 1973 and was awarded her B.A. in psychology. She then returned to New York City, where she took a job with the Children's Television Network as talent coordinator, with responsibilities for selecting children to appear on programs. At the same time, Delgado enrolled for graduate studies at New York University (NYU). She received her M.A. in social and personality psychology from NYU in 1975.

Delgado's next goal was to earn a Ph.D. in clinical psychology. She applied to and was accepted at the State University of New York at Stony Brook in this program. In addition to taking classes at Stony Brook, she worked as a research assistant in experimental psychology and held a number of other jobs, including working as a teacher at the New York Experimental Bilingual Institute, teaching at other colleges in the area, and serving as a consultant to the Board of Cooperative Educational Services in Westbury, New York. In 1981, Delgado completed her requirements at Stony Brook and was granted her Ph.D. in clinical psychology. She had, at the same time, completed the requirements for an M.S. at the W. Averell Harriman School of Urban and Policy Sciences at Stony Brook.

While still a doctoral student at Stony Brook, Delgado began a long affiliation with the U.S. Department of Health and Human Services (HHS) when she accepted a position as social science analyst in 1979. Her primary responsibility was to manage a variety of projects dealing with minority populations, including the Hispanic Initiative, the Black Colleges Initiative, the Undocumented Workers program, and the Private Sector Initiative. She also served as a liaison officer to the department's international officer and to the White House Rural Human Services Coordinating Committee. In 1983, she became a health policy adviser at HHS, a post she held until 1985. Among her other responsibilities at HHS were oversight responsibilities for programs in alcohol and drug abuse, for mental health, and for block grants to minority programs.

In 1985, HHS secretary Margaret Heckler recommended Delgado for the position of president and chief executive officer of the National Coalition of Hispanic Mental Health and Human Services Organizations. The organization had been formed originally as the Coalition of Spanish Speaking Mental Health Organizations (COSSMHO) in 1973 in Los Angeles. A year later, it had opened its Washington, D.C., office and in 1975, changed its name, while keeping its original acronym. In 1986, the organization changed its name once more, this time to the National Coalition of Hispanic Health and Human Services Organizations but still kept its original acronym of COSSMHO. At present, COSSMHO consists of 1,300 health and human service providers as members. It conducts policy and research studies, operates national and local programs, and develops bilingual and bicultural materials.

In more than two decades on the job, Delgado has strengthened and expanded the work of COSSMHO such that she is now called, by some observers, "the nation's leading expert on Hispanic health [issues]." She has also written an important book on Latina health issues, *Salud: A Latina's Guide to Total Health* (also available as *Salud: Guía para la salud integral de la mujer latina*), which was revised in 2002. She appears regularly on Univisión, the U.S. Spanish-language television network, and on Radio Bilingüe, a bilingual radio station located in Fresno, California. She also publishes a syndicated column distributed to Spanish-language newspapers through the Los Angeles Times News Service, entitled "Ask Doctor Jane."

Further Reading

"Delgado, Jane L." In *Who's Who among Hispanic Americans, 1994–95,* 3d ed., edited by Amy Unterburger, 211. Detroit: Gale Research, 1995.

"Jane Delgado." In *Latino Women of Science,* edited by Leonard Bernstein, Alan Winkler, and Linda Zierdt-Warshaw, 6–7. Maywood, N.J.: Peoples Publishing Group, 1998.

Mele, Susan Lopez. "Jane L. Delgado." In *Notable Hispanic American Women,* edited by Diane Telgen, Jim Kamp, and Joseph M. Palmisano, 127–130. Detroit: Gale Research, 1998.

del Moral, Roger
(1943–   ) *botanist*

Roger del Moral is a botanist who specializes in the study of plant communities in forests, prairies, wetlands, and meadows, primarily in the state of Washington but also in other parts of the world. A major focus of his recent research has been the regeneration of plant life in the region surrounding Mt. St. Helens, which erupted with massive destruction of plant and animal life in 1980. He has also been conducting field research on plant communities and succession patterns in the Kamchatka Peninsula of Siberia and the region around Mt. Etna, in Sicily.

Del Moral was born on September 13, 1943, in Detroit, Michigan, the son of Amelia and Armando del Moral, of Spanish ancestry. He attended the University of California at Santa Barbara (UCSB), where he earned his B.A. in biology and botany in 1965, his M.A. in botany in 1966, and his Ph.D. in biology in 1968. He accepted an offer to join the department of biology at the University of Washington, in Seattle, immediately following his graduation from UCSB and has remained there ever since, having been promoted from assistant professor to associate professor to full professor. In 1984, he founded a consulting company, del Moral & Associates, which he continues to operate today.

In addition to his teaching and research at Washington, del Moral has served as visiting professor and researcher at a number of other institutions, including the Commonwealth Scientific and Industrial Research Organisation in Brisbane, Australia; the department of botany at the University of Melbourne, Australia; the University of East Anglia, in Norwich, United Kingdom; and the University of Catania, in Sicily. He has also conducted lecture tours in the United Kingdom (1984), Japan (1985, 1990, and 1991), Hungary (1991), and North Carolina in the United States (1995). His special interest in the regeneration of plant life in volcanic regions has taken him not only to the Mt. St. Helens region but also to volcanic areas in Hawaii, Iceland, Japan, and the Kamchatka Peninsula. Del Moral is the author or coauthor of more than 85 scholarly papers and 12 book chapters dealing with a variety of issues in the field of botany. He has served as an editor for four journals, *Tokyo Botanical Society, Vegetatio, Plant Ecology,* and *American Midland Naturalist.*

Roger del Moral is professor of biology at the University of Washington, where his special interest is in the ecology of plant communities in forests, prairies, wetlands, and meadows. *(Courtesy Roger del Moral)*

Further Reading
"del Moral, Roger." In *American Men & Women of Science,* 21st ed., edited by Pamela M. Kalte and Katherine H. Nemeh, vol. 2, 637. Detroit: Thomson Gale, 2003.

"del Moral, Roger." In *Who's Who among Hispanic Americans, 1994–95,* 3d ed., edited by Amy Unterburger, 213–214. Detroit: Gale Research, 1995.

University of Washington. "Who We Are." Available online. URL: http://faculty.washington.edu/moral/who.html. Downloaded on April 6, 2005.

Díaz, Fernando G.
(1946–) *neurosurgeon*

Fernando G. Díaz is a neurosurgeon who also holds a master's degree in administration and a law degree. He specializes in surgical procedures for the treatment of aneurysms, stroke, cervical spine reconstruction, cerebrovascular surgery, and gamma knife radiosurgery. Gamma knife radiosurgery is a procedure by which brain tumors and other abnormalities within the brain are excised by means of gamma radiation without having to actually cut into the brain.

Díaz was born in Mexico City on December 29, 1946, the son of Susana María and Fernando Díaz. He attended the Universidad Nacional Autónoma de México, from which he received his B.Sc. in 1963 and his M.D. in 1969. He did his internship at Regina General Hospital, in Regina, Saskatchewan, Canada (1969–70) and his residencies in anesthesia also at Regina General (1971), in general surgery at the University of Kansas Medical Center, in Kansas City (1971–73), and in neurosurgery at the University of Minnesota, in Minneapolis (1973–78). During the time that he was completing his medical training, he was also pursuing graduate studies, earning an M.A. in anatomy at the University of Kansas in 1973 and a Ph.D. in neurophysiology and neurosurgery at the University of Minnesota in 1979.

In 1980, Díaz accepted an appointment as neurosurgery residency coordinator at the Henry Ford Hospital in Detroit, a post he held until 1986. He then took the position of clinical associate professor at the University of Michigan School of Medicine in Ann Arbor. He held that assignment for one year before joining the Neuroscience Institute of Santa Fe, in Gainesville, Florida, as chairman. In 1990, he left Santa Fe to become professor, chair, and specialist in chief of the department of neurological surgery at Wayne State University, in Detroit. In 2000, he was promoted to full professor at Wayne State and made chief medical officer at the Detroit Medical Center, positions he continues to fill.

Díaz has also long been associated with the U.S. military, serving as a major in the U.S. Air Force Reserves (1987), flight surgeon at Eglin Air Force Base in Florida (1988–89), chief of aeromedical services at Selfridge Air Force Base in Michigan (1990–94), national neurosurgical consultant for the U.S. Air Force (1990–present), medical officer at Lackland Air Force Base in Texas during Operation Desert Storm (1991), lieutenant colonel in the U.S. Air Force (from 1992), and resident surgeon at Wilford Hall Medical Center in Texas (1994).

In addition to his assignments in the United States, Díaz has traveled widely as a consultant, researcher, and instructor in neurosurgery, visiting the Universities of Osaka and Kyoto in Japan (1982); Madrid, Spain, and Newcastle, United Kingdom (1983); and Paris, France, and Verona, Italy (1985). He is a prolific author with more than 200 scholarly papers and book chapters to his credit.

Further Reading
"Díaz, Fernando G." In *American Men & Women of Science,* 21st ed., edited by Pamela M. Kalte and Katherine H. Nemeh, vol. 2, 687. Detroit: Thomson Gale, 2003.

"Díaz, Fernando G." In *Who's Who among Hispanic Americans, 1994–95,* 3d ed., edited by Amy Unterburger, 221. Detroit: Gale Research, 1995.

Díaz, Henry F.
(Henry Frank Díaz)
(1948–) *meteorologist*

Henry Frank Díaz specializes in the study of large-scale meteorological phenomena, such as climate change and the El Niño/Southern Oscillation (ENSO) phenomenon, periodic changes in the temperature of waters off the western coast of South America that produce regular and sometimes dramatic changes in weather patterns across the United States and other parts of the Western Hemisphere.

Díaz was born in Santiago de Cuba, on July 15, 1948, the son of María Vías Díaz, of Catalan descent, and Francisco Díaz, an attorney of mixed French and Spanish ancestry. The Díaz family

Henry F. Díaz has worked at various laboratories in the National Oceanic and Atmospheric Administration since 1974, with special interest in large-scale weather phenomena, such as climate change and the El Niño/Southern Oscillation phenomenon. *(Courtesy Dr. Henry Díaz)*

moved to Havana in 1959, the year in which the Cuban Revolution led by Fidel Castro began. It was during his years in Havana that Díaz first became interested in violent storms. Cuba was often in the pathway of severe tropical storms and hurricanes that blow regularly across the Caribbean, and Díaz became fascinated by the way storms form and move across the island.

By 1961, Díaz's father, a political opponent of Castro, had decided that Havana was no longer safe for his son, and Díaz was sent to live with an uncle in New Jersey. Four years later, his parents and sister joined him in exile in Miami, where he graduated from high school in 1967. Thoroughly enthralled by weather phenomena by this time, Díaz decided to enroll at Florida State University in Tallahassee, where he majored in meteorology. He was awarded his B.S. in 1971 and began his graduate studies at the University of Miami. In 1974, Díaz received his M.S. in atmospheric science from Miami.

Díaz's first job following graduation was with the Environmental Data Center (EDC) of the National Oceanic and Atmospheric Administration (NOAA) in Washington, D.C. After one year with the EDC, he moved to the NOAA's Climate Analysis Division in Asheville, North Carolina. Over the next five years, Díaz became increasingly interested in the study of climate change, long-term variations in worldwide weather patterns, at least part of which may be a result of human activities. In 1980, he transferred to the NOAA's Climate Research Program located at Boulder, Colorado, and shortly thereafter, began a doctoral program in geography and climatology at the University of Colorado. In 1984, he was appointed acting director of the Climate Research Program and a year later was awarded his Ph.D. Díaz has continued his affiliation with the NOAA in Boulder, serving in the Climatic Research Division of its Air Resources Laboratory from 1986 to 1989, in the agency's Climate Monitoring and Diagnostics

Laboratory from 1989 to 1993, and in its Climate Diagnostics Center from 1993 to the present.

Díaz has published more than 50 scholarly papers, most of them dealing with climate change and the ENSO phenomenon. He has also edited or coedited seven books on climate variability and the ENSO effect. In addition to his work with the NOAA, Díaz has been visiting scientist at the University of Massachusetts at Amherst (1988–89), the Swiss Federal Institute of Technology in Zurich (1994), and the University of Arizona (2003). He has received three awards for Outstanding Achievement and six for Sustained Superior Performance from the NOAA.

Further Reading

DiCanio, Margaret. "Henry F. Diaz." In *Notable Twentieth-Century Scientists,* edited by Emily J. McMurray, 494. Detroit: Gale Research, 1995.

Olesky, Walter. *Hispanic-American Scientists,* 56–67. New York: Facts On File, 1998.

Diaz, Luis A.
(1942–) *dermatologist*

Luis A. Diaz is an expert in dermatology, diseases and disorders of the skin. His special interests are autoimmune disorders, in which the body reacts against its own cells, tissues, or chemicals; blistering diseases; and three human autoimmune diseases in particular, pemphigus vulgaris, pemphigus foliaceus, and bullous pemphigoid.

Diaz was born in Lima, Peru, on April 20, 1942, to Luisa C. Campodonico and Julio G. Díaz. He studied at the Universidad Nacional de Trujillo, in Peru, earning his B.S. in premedicine in 1961 and his M.D. from the School of Medicine at Trujillo in 1968. He completed his internship in the department of medicine at Ellis Hospital, in Schenectady, New York, in 1971, and his residency in dermatology at the State University of

New York Buffalo Affiliated Hospitals, in 1974. He continued his studies as a postdoctoral fellow in immunology at the Mayo Graduate School of Medicine, in Rochester, Minnesota, between 1974 and 1976.

Diaz's first academic appointment was at the University of Michigan in Ann Arbor, where he served as consulting physician in dermatology at the University Hospital and as assistant and associate professor of dermatology at the School of Medicine from 1976 to 1982. From 1979 to 1982, Diaz was also chief of dermatological services at the Veterans Administration Medical Center in Ann Arbor. He then moved to Johns Hopkins University, in Baltimore, Maryland, as associate professor and later full professor in the department of dermatology. In 1989, Diaz left Johns Hopkins to become professor and chair of the dermatology department at the Medical College of Wisconsin, in Milwaukee, a post he held until 1999. He then relocated to the University of North Carolina at Chapel Hill, where he became professor and chair of the department of dermatology, titles he continues to hold.

Diaz has been honored with the William Montagna Lecturer award of the Society for Investigative Dermatology in 1991, the Marion Sulzberger Award as Teacher of the Year by the American Academy of Dermatology in 1994, the Simón Bolívar Academic Achievement Award from the Universidad Nacional de Trujillo in 1999, and election as president of the Society for Investigative Dermatology for 2000–01.

Further Reading

"Diaz, Luis A." In *American Men & Women of Science,* 21st ed., edited by Pamela M. Kalte and Katherine H. Nemeh, vol. 2, 687. Detroit: Thomson Gale, 2003.

"Diaz, Luis A." In *Who's Who among Hispanic Americans, 1994–95,* 3d ed., edited by Amy Unterburger, 223. Detroit: Gale Research, 1995.

Diaz, Nils J.
(Nils Juan Diaz)
(1938–   ) *nuclear physicist, government official*

Nils Juan Diaz has been a nuclear physicist in both academia and industry for nearly 40 years. In 2003, he was appointed chair of the Nuclear Regulatory Commission (NRC) by President George W. Bush. The NRC is the U.S. agency responsible for licensing and regulating all nuclear power plants and other nuclear facilities in the United States.

Diaz was born in Morón, Camagüey, Cuba, on April 7, 1938, the son of Dalia Rojas and Rafael Díaz. He studied at the University of Villanova, in Havana, earning a B.S. in mechanical engineering in 1960. He left Cuba to pursue graduate studies at the University of Florida, in Gainesville, from which he received his B.S. and Ph.D. in nuclear engineering sciences in 1964 and 1969, respectively. Over the next 30 years, Diaz combined careers in academia, industry, and public service in the field of nuclear engineering. He was assistant professor of nuclear engineering sciences and reactor supervisor at the University of Florida from 1969 to 1974, associate professor and reactor supervisor at Florida from 1974 to 1979, and professor and director of nuclear facilities at Florida from 1979 to 1984. He left Florida for two years, from 1984 to 1986, to serve as associate dean for research and minorities at California State University at Long Beach before returning in 1986 as director of the university's Innovative Nuclear Space Power and Propulsion Institute.

Throughout this period, Diaz was also involved in a number of corporations concerned with the development of nuclear power. He was president and principal engineer of Florida Nuclear Associates, Inc., a high-technology research and consulting firm, and was a consultant to Exxon Nuclear Corporation, the Florida Power and Light Company, the Florida Power Corporation, and the Nuclear

Nils J. Diaz is a nuclear engineer who was appointed chair of the Nuclear Regulatory Commission by President George W. Bush in 2003. *(U.S. Nuclear Regulatory Agency)*

Safety Council of Spain. Diaz has also served in a number of governmental positions, including advisory capacities with the National Aeronautics and Space Administration, the U.S. Departments of Energy and Defense, and the Strategic Defense Initiative. He is the author of more than 70 papers in the field of nuclear engineering and is a fellow of the American Nuclear Society, the American Society of Mechanical Engineers, and the American Association for the Advancement of Science.

Diaz was first appointed for a five-year term to the NRC by President Bill Clinton in 1996. He was nominated for a second five-year term by President George W. Bush in 2001 and then nominated to become chair of the commission in 2003. In his position as chair, Diaz was principal executive officer of the NRC and its official spokesperson. He was responsible for carrying out administrative, organizational, long-range planning, budgetary, and certain personnel functions of the agency. He also had ultimate authority for all NRC activities related to any emergency that may arise at a nuclear power plant licensed by the NRC. Diaz retired from the NRC in June 2006.

Further Reading

"Diaz, Nils J." In *Who's Who among Hispanic Americans, 1994–95,* 3d ed., edited by Amy Unterburger, 224. Detroit: Gale Research, 1995.

"Diaz, Nils Juan." In *American Men & Women of Science,* 21st ed., edited by Pamela M. Kalte and Katherine H. Nemeh, vol. 2, 687. Detroit: Thomson Gale, 2003.

U.S. Nuclear Regulatory Commission. "Chairman Nils J. Diaz, Ph.D." Available online. URL: http://www.nrc.gov/who-we-are/organization/commission/diaz.html. Downloaded on April 7, 2005.

Díaz, Robert J.
(Robert James Díaz)
(1946-) *marine biologist*

Robert James Díaz's research focuses on the characteristics of marine ecosystems, especially on food production at various levels of such ecosystems. He has recently been working on benthic ecosystems, marine systems lying at the bottom of lakes, oceans, and other bodies of water, with particular attention to the interactions between organisms in those ecosystems and the sediment that makes up lake and ocean bottoms. He is also interested in the way changes that occur in these interactions alter the process by which food is processed by organisms and energy produced within the systems.

Díaz was born in Chester, Pennsylvania, on October 16, 1946, the son of Marie Esmeralda Torres and José Antonio Díaz, of Spanish ancestry. He attended La Salle College, in Philadelphia, where he earned his B.A. in biology and chemistry in 1968. He continued his studies at the University of Virginia, in Charlottesville, from which he received his M.A. in marine science in 1971 and his Ph.D. in marine biology in 1976. After completing his bachelor's degree, Díaz taught high school biology for two years and then took a job as research assistant in ecology and pollution at the Virginia Institute of Marine Science (VIMS), in Gloucester Point, Virginia. He was employed at VIMS as an ecologist (1971–72), benthic ecologist (1973–77), associate marine scientist in benthic ecology (1978–81), and senior marine scientist in estuarine and coastal ecology (1982–84).

During this period, Díaz was also a member of the faculty at the College of William and Mary, which administers VIMS, serving as instructor (1976–77), assistant professor (1978–84), associate professor (1984–90), and professor (1991–present) of marine science. In 1986, Díaz founded R. J. Díaz and Daughters, a small business specializing in environmental assessment of estuarine and marine systems ranging between intertidal, deep channel, and coastal habitats. He is the author of more than 60 papers in the field of marine biology and is coeditor (with R. O. Brinkhurst) of *Aquatic Oligochaeta: Developments in Hydrobiology* (1987). In 1996, Díaz received an honorary doctorate from Göteborg University in Sweden.

Further Reading

"Díaz, Robert James." In *American Men & Women of Science,* 21st ed., edited by Pamela M. Kalte and Katherine H. Nemeh, vol. 2, 687. Detroit: Thomson Gale, 2003.

"Díaz, Robert James." In *Who's Who among Hispanic Americans, 1994–95,* 3d ed., edited by Amy Unterburger, 225–226. Detroit: Gale Research, 1995.

Virginia Commonwealth University. "R. J. Diaz and Daughters." Available online. URL: http://www. courses.vcu.edu/ENG-esh/diaz/diaz_company. html. Downloaded on April 7, 2005.

Duran, Benjamin S.
(Benjamin Sanchez Duran)
(1939–   ) *statistician*

Benjamin Sanchez Duran specializes in the study of nonparametric statistics, a field of statistics dealing with the analysis of variables without making assumptions about the patterns in which they may be distributed, and in the application of statistics to reliability theory, risk theory, and practical problems in science and engineering.

Duran was born in Tularosa, New Mexico, on November 25, 1939, into a very poor family of Chicano ancestry. Duran and his four brothers and sisters were sent into the fields to pick cotton at an early age, and he entered elementary school with few academic ambitions. He was fortunate, however, to encounter a few key individuals who saw that he had talent, especially in the field of mathematics, and encouraged him to continue his education. In elementary school, for example, one teacher recognized Duran's talents in mathematics

Benjamin S. Duran is professor of mathematics and statistics at Texas Tech University. *(Courtesy Texas Tech University)*

and encouraged him to take more advanced classes in the subject. After graduating from high school, a friend offered to buy his books for him if Duran enrolled at a college, which he did. He attended the College of Saint Joseph and paid his own way by working as a janitor all four years he was in school. Then, in his senior year, his mathematics professor suggested that he consider going to graduate school. Duran applied to Colorado State University, where he obtained first his M.S. in 1964 and then his Ph.D. in statistics in 1966.

Duran's first teaching job was at Eastern New Mexico University, in Portales, where he taught statistics from 1966 to 1969. He then took a position at the Baylor College of Medicine from 1969 to 1971 before joining the faculty at Texas Tech University as professor of mathematics and statis-

tics, a post he continues to hold. He is the author of more than 30 scholarly papers and 20 technical reports on statistics. His text, *Statistical Methods for Engineers and Scientists* (1975), written with Robert M. Bethea and Thomas L. Boullion, is now in its third edition.

Further Reading

"Duran, Benjamin S." In *Who's Who among Hispanic Americans, 1994–95,* 3d ed., edited by Amy Unterburger, 234–235. Detroit: Gale Research, 1995.

Society for Advancement of Chicanos and Native Americans in Science. "Dr. Benjamin S. Duran—Statistician." SACNAS Biography Project. Available online. URL: http://64.171.10.183/biography/Biography.asp?mem=158&type=2. Downloaded on March 2, 2005.

E

Escalante, Jaime
(Jaime Alfonso Escalante Gutiérrez)
(1930–) *mathematics educator*

Jaime Alfonso Escalante Gutiérrez was the subject of a popular motion picture in 1988, *Stand and Deliver,* that featured his success in teaching calculus to students at Garfield High School in East Los Angeles, California, a neighborhood better known for its drug, violence, and gang problems than its academic achievements. He was also the subject of a 1988 book by Jay Matthews entitled *The Best Teacher in America.*

Escalante was born in La Paz, Bolivia, on December 31, 1930, the second child of Sara Gutiérrez and Zenobio Escalante. Escalante's parents were both schoolteachers who worked in government schools for Aymara and Quechua Indians in communities that were generally mired in abject poverty. Escalante spent most of his childhood in the town of Achacachi in the Bolivian high plains. In 1944, Escalante's mother took her five children and moved to La Paz to escape the abusive behavior of her alcoholic husband. There, Escalante was enrolled in San Calixto High School, where he rapidly demonstrated an unusual talent for physics and mathematics. By the time he graduated, however, his father had died, and there was no money for him to pursue his plans of attending college and earning an engineering degree.

Instead, he took a number of odd jobs until he reached the age of 19 and enlisted in the Bolivian army. He served for two years in the federal government's long-term fight against Marxist rebels before receiving his discharge in 1951. Escalante then enrolled in the teacher training program at San Andrés University in La Paz, Bolivia's largest university. Only halfway through his program, Escalante was offered a job teaching at the American Institute in La Paz. For the next two years, he worked there while continuing his college studies at San Andrés. His skill as a teacher was so impressive that when he was awarded his teaching certificate from San Andrés in 1955, he was offered three teaching jobs. He accepted all three and took on an ambitious schedule of teaching at his alma mater, San Calixto, in the morning; at the National Bolívar High School in the afternoon; and at La Paz Commercial High School in the evening. In 1954, Escalante married Fabiola Tapia.

For the next nine years, Escalante continued to teach physics and mathematics in a variety of institutions in La Paz. Over this period of time, however, he and his wife became convinced that prospects for his career and educational options for their children would be greater in the United States than in Bolivia. An opportunity in 1961 to study at the University of Puerto Rico for one year under President John F. Kennedy's Alliance for Progress program sealed Escalante's intention of immigrating to the United States. As a result, the Escalantes moved to Los Angeles in 1963, despite the challenges they faced. Not only was Escalante barely able to speak English, but his teaching credentials from Bolivia were not acceptable in California.

Escalante's first job in Los Angeles was as a busboy at the now-defunct Van de Kamp's restaurant, across the street from Pasadena City College (PCC). He had spent only a few days mopping floors and washing dishes before he decided to start taking courses at PCC as a first step in earning his California teaching certificate. Escalante soon found a better job working as a technician at an electronics company. He continued taking courses at PCC and, in 1969, was awarded his associate of arts from the college. He then transferred to California State University at Los Angeles, from which he received his bachelor's degree in mathematics in 1972. Two years later, he finally earned his California state teaching certificate and, at the age of 44, started looking for a teaching job.

In 1974, Escalante was offered a job teaching computer science at Garfield High School in East Los Angeles. When he reported for work, he found that the school owned no computers; he would be teaching mathematics instead. He soon found, too, that the student body, almost entirely Latino, had very few math skills and very little interest in learning the subject that he loved. He accepted the challenge of teaching math at Garfield, however, partly because he needed a job to support his family and partly because of his commitment to working with students to improve their educational experience.

Over the next 17 years, Escalante gradually increased the level of mathematics available to his students, his students' willingness to attack such courses, and their success in dealing with advanced mathematics. He reached the pinnacle of success in 1982 when all 18 students in his introductory calculus class passed the Educational Testing Service's (ETS) Advanced Placement examination in that subject. Officials at ETS were so convinced

that Escalante's students had cheated on the test that they required the class to retake the examination. To nearly everyone's surprise, all 18 students passed the test again, this time with even better scores than before.

Escalante's innovative teaching techniques have been described in detail in the film *Stand and Deliver* and the book *The Best Teacher in America*. He developed a combination of comedy, encouragement, and harsh criticism to demand that students perform at their very best, with continued success. From 1983 to 1991, he was also asked to teach calculus at East Los Angeles Community College.

Escalante's success at Garfield was not met with universal approval. Some other teachers felt that he was receiving undue attention for his work at the school, and Escalante himself was not above criticizing colleagues and administrators who he thought to be performing less well than they should. Tensions became so high in 1991 that his contract at Garfield was not renewed. At that point, however, his success was still admired widely enough that he was offered jobs at a number of other schools. He decided to take a position at Hiram Johnson High School in Sacramento, California. The school was delighted with its success in hiring Escalante and provided him with a large new teaching facility adapted for use also as an instructional space for other math teachers.

Johnson was experiencing a number of problems at the time, however. During Escalante's seven-year tenure at the school, there were three different principals and 13 vice principals. In addition, he was never able to develop the enthusiasm and success among his students that he had experienced at Garfield, and he resigned in 1998. Although he had left teaching, he was still in demand as a public speaker throughout the United States. Most recently, he was asked by California governor Arnold Schwarzenegger in 2003 to serve as consultant on educational issues to the state.

Escalante has received a number of honors from organizations both in the United States and other parts of the world. He has been awarded the Hispanic Heritage Award (1988), the Hispanic Engineer National Chairman's Award (1989), the Jefferson Award of the American Institute for Public Service (1990), the Free Spirit Award of the Freedom Forum (1998), the Andres Bello Prize of the Organization of American States (1998), and the U.S. Presidential Medal for Excellence (1998). He was inducted into the National Teachers Hall of Fame in 1999.

Further Reading

Government Technology. "Excellence: Do It Right the First Time." Available online. URL: http://www.govtech.net/magazine/visions/feb98vision/escalante.php. Downloaded on February 28, 2005.

Matthews, Jay. *Escalante: The Best Teacher in America.* New York: Henry Holt, 1988.

Meyer, Nicholas E. *Biographical Dictionary of Hispanic Americans.* 2d ed., 90–91. New York: Checkmark Books, 2001.

Santana, Alfredo. "Mr. Inspiration." Pasadena City College. Available online. URL: http://www.paccd.cc.ca.us/75th/alumni/escalante/escalante.html. Downloaded on February 28, 2005.

Stamatel, Janet P. "Jaime Escalante." In *Contemporary Hispanic Biography,* edited by Ashyia N. Henderson, 104–107. Farmington Hills, Mich.: Thomson Gale, 2003.

Escobar, Javier I.
(1943–) *psychiatrist*

Javier I. Escobar's special areas of research include psychopharmacology, the way in which drugs affect the mind and a person's behavior, and psychiatric epidemiology, the study of ways in which mental disorders occur within and spread throughout a population. He has also carried out research on the way in which mental disorders differ among various ethnic and cultural groups.

Escobar was born in Medellín, Colombia, on July 26, 1943. He attended the University of Antioquia, in Medellín, from which he obtained his M.D. in 1967. He then enrolled at the Complutense University in Madrid, Spain, where he began his specialization in the field of psychiatry. In 1969, he immigrated to the United States and began his psychiatric residency at the University of Minnesota Hospitals, in Minneapolis. During the same period, he was given a research fellowship in psychiatric genetics, the study of mental disorders caused by inherited factors, also at the University of Minnesota. In 1973, Escobar received a master's degree in psychiatry/medical genetics and was appointed assistant professor at the University of Minnesota. In 1976, he took a similar position at the University of Tennessee, in Knoxville, and in 1979, became associate professor of psychiatry at the University of California at Los Angeles (UCLA). Escobar was eventually promoted to full professor before leaving UCLA in 1985 to become vice chairman of the department of psychiatry at the University of Connecticut School of Medicine, in Farmington. He was promoted to interim chair of the department in 1992, a post he held until 1994, when he accepted an offer to become professor and chairman of the department of psychiatry at Robert Wood Johnson Medical School at the University of Medicine and Dentistry of New Jersey, in Piscataway.

Escobar is the author of more than 200 scholarly papers in the field of psychiatry and the coeditor of *Mental Health and Hispanic Americans: Clinical Perspectives* (1982). He has also served on a number of national and international committees working on psychiatric issues. He has been president of the American Society of Hispanic Psychiatry, senior adviser to the director of the National Institute of Mental Health, adviser to the World Health Organization, and member of the Food and Drug Administration's Advisory Committee on Psychiatric Drugs.

Further Reading

"Escobar, Javier I." In *American Men & Women of Science,* 21st ed., edited by Pamela M. Kalte and Katherine H. Nemeh, vol. 2, 977. Detroit: Thomson Gale, 2003.

"Javier I. Escobar." In *The Hispanic American Almanac,* 3d ed., edited by Sonia G. Benson, 695. Farmington Hills, Mich: Thomson Gale, 2003.

Estévez, L. Antonio
(1950–   ) *chemical engineer*

L. Antonio Estévez specializes in heat transfer problems, researching ways in which heat moves from one medium to another. Most recently, he has been concerned with the properties and behavior of supercritical fluids, a somewhat peculiar form of matter that exists above the so-called critical temperature and pressure for the material. Research has shown that supercritical fluids may have a number of important applications in industrial processes, especially in the separation of two or more materials from each other.

Estévez was born in Talca, Chile, on June 9, 1950, the son of Elena Victoria De Vidts Valderrama and Germán Luis Estévez. He attended the University of Santiago, in Chile, from which he received his B.S. in chemical engineering in 1975; the Central University of Venezuela, in Caracas, from which he received his M.Sc. in petroleum engineering in 1977; and the University of California at Davis, from which he received his Ph.D. in chemical engineering in 1983. Prior to his moving to the United States, Estévez was an instructor in chemical engineering at the University of Santiago (1973–75) and part-time instructor in chemical technology at the University of Chile. While working on his doctoral degree at Davis, Estévez also served as assistant professor of thermodynamics and transport phenomena at Simón Bolívar University, in Caracas (1976–84).

Upon completion of his doctoral studies, Estévez returned to Venezuela as associate professor at Simón Bolívar University before accepting an offer in 1987 to serve as visiting professor of chemical engineering at the University of Puerto Rico. When that position ended in 1990, Estévez stayed on at Puerto Rico as associate professor of chemical engineering. Since that time, he has divided his time between the University of Puerto Rico, where he was appointed full professor of chemical engineering in 1995, and Cornell University, in Ithaca, New York, where he has been summer visiting professor in 1995, 1998, 1999, and 2000 and visiting professor in 1996–97. From 2001 to 2003, Estévez was also associate dean of academic affairs and director of graduate studies at the University of Puerto Rico at Mayagüez.

In addition to his research on supercritical fluids, Estévez has been studying ways of improving water treatment, especially the removal of volatile organic chemicals that have proved to be difficult to eliminate from water during most standard methods of water purification. He is also exploring the use of supercritical carbon dioxide as a solvent in the preparation of drugs and pharmaceuticals.

Further Reading

Community of Science. "Dr. L. Antonio Estévez." Available online. URL: http://myprofile.cos.com/estevez. Downloaded on April 7, 2005.

"Estévez, L. Antonio." In *Who's Who among Hispanic Americans, 1994–95,* 3d ed., edited by Amy Unterburger, 250. Detroit: Gale Research, 1995.

F

Fernandez, Louis Anthony
(1939-) *geologist, college administrator*

Louis Anthony Fernandez was trained as a geologist, with a special interest in volcanic rocks. Later in his career, he became an educational administrator.

Fernandez was born in New York City on October 5, 1939, the son of Angelica and Luis A. Fernandez, of Puerto Rican ethnicity. He attended the City College of New York, earning his B.S. in geology in 1962. He continued his studies at the University of Tulsa, in Oklahoma, from which he received his M.S. in geology in 1964, and at Syracuse University, in New York, where he earned his Ph.D. in geology in 1969. From 1968 to 1971, Fernandez worked as a research geologist at Yale University, in New Haven, Connecticut, where he carried out analyses of lunar rocks collected during the Apollo 11 and 12 missions to the Moon.

In 1971, Fernandez joined the faculty at the University of New Orleans (UNO) as assistant professor of geology, working his way up the academic ladder to associate and full professor over the next 20 years. In addition to his teaching responsibilities at UNO, Fernandez carried out research on volcanic rocks obtained from the Sierra Madre Occidental region of Mexico. He also held a series of administrative posts at New Orleans, including chair of the department of geology (1981–85) and dean of the College of Sciences (1985–91). In 1991, Fernandez left UNO to become professor of geology and dean of the School of Natural Sciences at the University of California at San Bernardino. Three years later, in 1994, he was named provost and vice president for academic affairs at the university, a post he continues to hold.

Fernandez has long been interested in expanding the opportunities available to women and minorities in the geological sciences. He played an important role in the establishment of the American Geological Institute's Minority Participation Program and served for many years on that program's advisory committee. In recognition of his service in this field, Fernandez was honored with the Outstanding Support of Hispanic Issues in Higher Education Award by the Hispanic Caucus of the American Association for Higher Education in 2004.

Further Reading

American Geological Institute. "Biography: Louis A. Fernandez." Available online. URL: http://www.agiweb.org/career/lafbio.html. Downloaded on April 7, 2005.

"Fernandez, Louis Anthony." In *American Men & Women of Science,* 21st ed., edited by Pamela M. Kalte and Katherine H. Nemeh, vol. 2, 1,079. Detroit: Thomson Gale, 2003.

"Fernandez, Louis Anthony." In *Who's Who among Hispanic Americans, 1994–95,* 3d ed., edited by Amy Unterburger, 262. Detroit: Gale Research, 1995.

Fernandez-Baca, Jaime A.
(Jaime Alberto Fernández-Baca)
(1954–　) *nuclear physicist*

Jaime Alberto Fernandez-Baca's research is related primarily to neutron scattering experiments, studies in which beams of neutrons are directed at matter to see how they are reflected and refracted from atoms that make up that matter. The results

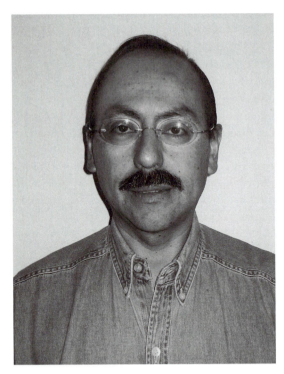

Jaime A. Fernandez-Baca is a reseacher in the Condensed Matter Sciences Division at the Oak Ridge National Laboratory (ORNL) and group leader of the U.S.-Japan Neutron Scattering Program, cosponsored by ORNL. *(Courtesy of Jaime Fernandez-Baca)*

of these experiments provide information about the structure of matter that may have many practical applications, as in the development of better ceramics, batteries, pharmaceuticals, and other products used in everyday life.

Fernandez-Baca was born in Lima, Peru, on May 23, 1954, the son of Ida Llamosas and Jorge Fernández-Baca. He attended primary and secondary Jesuit schools in Lima before enrolling at the Universidad Nacional de Ingeniería, in Lima, from which he earned his B.S. in 1977. Upon graduation, he was hired to work at the Instituto Peruano de Energia Nuclear (IPEN; Peruvian Institute for Nuclear Energy), also in Lima, on problems of radiological protection devices and techniques and nuclear reactor physics. His experience at IPEN encouraged him to apply for a fellowship in nuclear physics provided by the International Atomic Energy Agency, in Vienna, Austria. He was awarded the fellowship and studied for two years under its auspices at the University of Maryland, in College Park, while working in the field of nuclear physics at the National Bureau of Standards (now the National Institute of Standards and Technology), in Gaithersburg, Maryland. He was awarded his M.S. from Maryland in 1983 and his Ph.D. in physics in 1986.

Upon completion of his doctoral studies, Fernandez-Baca accepted a job as a member of the senior research staff in the Condensed Matter Sciences Division of the Oak Ridge National Laboratory (ORNL), in Oak Ridge, Tennessee, a post he continues to hold today. He is currently group leader of the U.S.–Japan Neutron Scattering Program cosponsored by ORNL. He is the author of more than 70 scientific papers and three book chapters on neutron scattering phenomena. In addition to his fellowship from the International Atomic Energy Agency, Fernandez-Baca was awarded the Ralph Myers Teaching Award of the College of Computer, Mathematical, and Physical Sciences at the University of Maryland in 1984.

Further Reading

"Fernandez-Baca, Jaime A." In *Who's Who among Hispanic Americans, 1994–95,* 3d ed., edited by Amy Unterburger, 267. Detroit: Gale Research, 1995.

"Fernandez-Baca, Jaime Alberto." In *American Men & Women of Science,* 21st ed., edited by Pamela M. Kalte and Katherine H. Nemeh, vol. 2, 1,079. Detroit: Thomson Gale, 2003.

Peruvian Scientists. "Jaime A. Fernandez Baca." Available online. URL: http://www.peruvianscientists. org/qesq/q-FernandezBacaJaime.htm. Downloaded on April 9, 2005.

Fernández-Pol, José A.
(José Alberto Fernández-Pol)
(1943–) *medical researcher, inventor*

José Alberto Fernández-Pol is interested in the mechanisms that control the growth of normal and cancerous cells and in the nature of oncogenes, genes that are able to transform normal cells into cancer cells. He has been issued a number of patents for discoveries he has made in these areas.

Fernández-Pol was born in Buenos Aires, Argentina, on March 17, 1943. He attended the Colegio Nacional de Vicente López, from which he received his B.A. in 1963 and the University of Buenos Aires, which awarded him an M.D. in 1969. Upon graduation, he was also awarded a Diploma de Honor by the university. Fernández-Pol completed his internship at the University of Buenos Aires's Hospital Escuela José de San Martín in 1969–70 and his residency at the Endocrine Research Laboratory of the university's Center for Nuclear Medicine from 1970 to 1971.

At the conclusion of his medical training, Fernández-Pol left Argentina to become resident physician at the State University of New York in Buffalo for one year (1971–72) and a fellow at the department of internal medicine in Canada's Institute of Medical Sciences (1972). He then took a post at the National Cancer Institute (NCI) of the National Institutes of Health as research fellow in the Nuclear Medicine Laboratory (1972–75) and as fellow in the Laboratory of Molecular Biology (1975–77). In 1977, Fernández-Pol left NCI to join the faculty of the St. Louis University School of Medicine, in Missouri, where he eventually served as assistant professor of medicine (1977–80), associate professor of medicine (1980–85), associate professor of radiology (1980–87), and professor of medicine (1980–present) and professor of radiology and nuclear medicine (1988–present). He has also served as director of the immunoassay laboratory at the Veterans Administration Medical Center in St. Louis (1977–present) and chief of the Laboratory of Molecular Oncology at St. Louis University (1987–present).

Fernández-Pol has received a number of patents on discoveries that he has made in his research, such as a newly discovered DNA sequence that codes for a protein associated with many human cancers, a new method for staining tissue samples to determine the presence of markers for tumors, and a chemical agent and method for the prevention and treatment of toxicity caused by metals, such as copper, iron, lead, nickel, tungsten, and uranium.

Further Reading

"Fernandez-Pol, Jose Alberto." In *American Men & Women of Science,* 21st ed., edited by Pamela M. Kalte and Katherine H. Nemeh, vol. 2, 1,080. Detroit: Thomson Gale, 2003.

"José Alberto Fernández-Pol." In *The Hispanic American Almanac,* 3d ed., edited by Sonia G. Benson, 697. Farmington Hills, Mich.: Thomson Gale, 2003.

Ferreyra, Guillermo S.
(1953–) *mathematician*

Guillermo S. Ferreyra's mathematical studies deal primarily with stochastic theory, the theory of ran-

Guillermo S. Ferreyra has served in the department of mathematics at Louisiana State University since 1983. *(LSU Office of University Relations)*

dom events; partial differential equations; and the theory and application of probability.

Ferreyra was born in Villa María, Argentina, on July 26, 1953, the son of Wilma A. Castellini and Segundo R. Ferreyra. He studied mathematics at the Universidad Nacional de Córdoba, in Córdoba, Argentina, earning his *licenciatura* (equivalent to a bachelor's degree) in 1977. He then chose to continue his education in the United States, enrolling for graduate studies at Rutgers University, in New Brunswick, New Jersey. He received his Ph.D. in mathematics from Rutgers in 1983.

Ferreyra has spent all of his academic career at Louisiana State University (LSU), in Baton Rouge, earning promotions from assistant professor (1983–89) to associate professor (1989–96) to

full professor (1996–present). From 1986 to 1987, Ferreyra also served as assistant research professor of mathematics at Brown University, in Providence, Rhode Island. He was chosen to serve as chair of the department of mathematics at LSU from 2000 to 2003, when he resigned that post to become dean of the university's College of Arts and Sciences.

Ferrerya is author of more than 30 journal papers and reports for mathematical proceedings. He is also coeditor of two books, *Evolution Equations* (with G. Goldstein and F. Neubrander, Marcel Dekker, 1994) and *Differential Geometry and Control* (with R. Gardner, H. Hermes, and H. Sussmann, 1999). Ferrerya has also served on a number of university committees, including the Committee on Graduate Studies in Mathematics at LSU, the Academic Standards and Honors Committee of LSU, the Planning Review Panel for the department of finance, the Campus Advisory Board of the Academic Center for Student-Athletes, the LSU Retention Committee, and the Core Information Technology Meta-committee of the Center for Computation and Technology at LSU. He has been secretary-treasurer for the Society for Industrial and Applied Mathematics Activity Group on Control and Systems Theory and has served as organizer and co-organizer of more than a dozen professional meetings on stochastics, control theory, and related mathematical problems. In 1990, he was plenary speaker at the Fifth Inter-University Seminar of Mathematical Research, held at the University of Puerto Rico at Arecibo.

Further Reading

"Ferreyra, Guillermo S." In *Who's Who among Hispanic Americans, 1994–95,* 3d ed., edited by Amy Unterburger, 270. Detroit: Gale Research, 1995.

Louisiana State University. "Guillermo Ferreyra, Professor." Available online. URL: http://www.math.lsu.edu/~ferreyra/. Downloaded on April 9, 2005.

Figueroa, Orlando
(1955–) *mechanical engineer, space program administrator*

Orlando Figueroa is director of the Mars Exploration Program of the National Aeronautics and Space Administration (NASA). The office is responsible for administering all existing space probes designed for the study of the planet Mars. He has worked on a variety of space projects for NASA over the past 25 years.

Figueroa was born in San Juan, Puerto Rico, on September 9, 1955. He grew up in the neighborhood of Villa Palmeras, on the city's outskirts, where he became interested in space sciences at an early age. He remembers watching once or twice a week a half-hour program produced by NASA called *NASA Report* on his family's black-and-white television set and deciding that a career with NASA was what he wanted for his life. "I didn't care [what my job was]," he has said, "as long as I worked for NASA."

He began to put that plan into action when he enrolled at the University of Puerto Rico at Mayagüez, where he majored in mechanical engineering. After earning his B.S. in 1978, he immediately submitted his application at every NASA facility that he could think of. He was offered a job at the Goddard Space Flight Center (GSFC) in Greenbelt, Maryland. Over the next 19 years, he worked on a number of projects at GSFC, including the Heat Capacity Mapping Mission (a satellite that measured heat radiated from Earth's surface), the Cosmic Background Explorer (a satellite designed to measure infrared and microwave radiation in the universe), the Diffuse InfraRed Background Experiment (a satellite designed to measure cosmic infrared radiation), and the Cryogenic Optical Assembly (a low-temperature measuring device). He served as project manager for the Superfluid Helium on Orbit Transfer project (an experiment on the properties of helium carried out on space shuttle flight STS–57) and the Small Explorers (SMEX) program, which supports frequent flight opportunities for small, inexpensive space experiments.

In May 2001, Figueroa was appointed director of NASA's Mars Exploration Program, at the time the largest single program in the agency with an annual budget of about $500 million. The program is responsible for all Mars projects currently in operation, including the *Mars Global Surveyor* spacecraft, launched in 1996; the *Odyssey* probe, launched in 2001; the two Mars Exploration Rovers, *Spirit* and *Opportunity,* launched in 2003; the *Mars Reconnaissance Orbiter,* launched on August 12, 2005; and the *Mars Smart Lander,* scheduled for launch in 2009.

During his tenure at NASA, Figueroa has continued to take graduate courses at the University of Maryland at College Park. His work with the agency has earned him a number of honors, including a NASA Outstanding Leadership Medal for his work on the SMEX project and the Maryland Science Commission's Community Stars Award for his work in developing innovative educational programs involving NASA, industry, and Maryland schools.

Further Reading
HENAAC, Inc. "Pioneer Award Winner, 2002." Available online. URL: http://www.henaac.org/about/02figueroa.htm. Downloaded on March 1, 2005.

Rifkin, Janey. "NASA's Exploration to Mars Is Directed by Latino." *Hispanic Times* (Spring 2003). Available online. URL: http://www.findarticles.com/p/articles/mi_m0FWK/is_1_26/ai_102909919. Accessed on August 6, 2006.

Finlay, Carlos Juan
(1833–1915) *physician, medical researcher*

Carlos Juan Finlay spent more than 20 years of his life in a search of the causative agent for the dreaded disease yellow fever. His hypothesis that the disease was spread by the female mosquito, first announced in 1881, was widely disparaged by his colleagues, although the suggestion was finally verified more than 10 years later by American physician Walter Reed.

Finlay was born in the city of Puerto Príncipe (now Camagüey), Cuba, on December 3, 1833. His father, Edward, was a physician of Scottish heritage, and his mother, Isabel de Barres, was a native of France. During the first decade of his life, Finlay divided his time between the family home in Havana and the countryside around the village of Guanimar, where his father owned a coffee plantation. During this period, his education consisted of tutoring sessions by his father's sister. In 1844, Finlay's family sent him to France to pursue his education at Le Havre. After two years of study, he developed cholera and returned to Cuba to recover from the disease. One lasting effect of the condition was a stammer that, although much improved, remained with Finlay for the rest of his life.

In 1848, Finlay's family decided that he was well enough to return to Europe, although revolutionary movements taking place across the continent made it unwise for him to return to Le Havre or any other place in western Europe. As a result, he traveled to London to continue his schooling. He remained only a short time, however, before moving on to another school in Mentz, Germany. Upon completing his secondary education, he decided to begin his medical training in Rouen, France, where his father had earned his medical degree. Once again, disease interrupted Finlay's plans. He came down with typhoid fever in 1851 and was forced once more to return to Cuba. After he had recovered, he found that Cuban medical schools would not accept the earlier training he had had in Europe, so Finlay applied to the Jefferson Medical College in Philadelphia. He completed his studies and received his M.D. from Jefferson on March 10, 1855.

Over the next few years, Finlay displayed a wanderlust that, according to one of his biographers, "prevails in the Finlay family." He traveled first to Lima, Peru, where he set up a medical practice with his father. After a short time in Peru, Finlay returned to Cuba, where he again set up a medical practice, only to leave after a few months to visit Paris, where he continued his medical studies in various hospital clinics. He finally returned to Cuba, where he once more established a medical practice in the city of Matanzas, two hours east of Havana.

Finlay's interest in contagious diseases probably resulted from a number of factors. His own problems with cholera and typhoid fever were likely of primary importance. Such diseases were common, in fact, across the island of Cuba (and in many other tropical areas) so that almost anyone interested in infectious diseases would have given some thought to their etiology (how they are caused) and how they are spread. Finally, one of Finlay's instructors at Jefferson Medical College was John Kearsley Mitchell, an early proponent of the germ theory of disease.

In any case, by 1881, Finlay had become convinced that the causative agent in yellow fever was a mosquito, probably a member of the species *Aëdes aegypti*. Finlay based his hypothesis on a series of experiments in which the presence of the female member of the species could be demonstrated in every case of yellow fever that he observed. He lacked, however, positive proof that showed how the disease was transferred from the mosquito to a human. Indeed, that proof would not be produced for more than a decade, when experiments carried out by Walter Reed showed beyond a doubt that the virus that causes yellow fever is carried in a mosquito's saliva and is transmitted to humans as the result of a mosquito bite.

In 1881, however, Finlay was virtually alone in accepting the mosquito–yellow fever connection. His speech to the International Sanitary Conference in Washington, D.C., of that year fell essentially on deaf ears. In spite of the rejection of

Carlos Juan Finlay is best known for his research on the transmission of yellow fever. *(Courtesy of Historical Collections & Services, Claude Moore Health Sciences Library, University of Virginia)*

Further Reading

Guiteras, Juan. "Who Was Dr. Carlos J. Finlay?" Finlay-online.com, Finlay Medical Society. Available online. URL: http://www.finlay-online.com/welcome/whowasdrfinlay.htm. Downloaded on March 1, 2005.

Leonard, Jonathan. "Carlos Finlay's Life and the Death of Yellow Jack." *Bulletin of the Pan American Health Organization* 23 (Winter 1989): 438–452.

Phillip S. Hench Walter Reed Yellow Fever Collection. "Carlos Juan Finlay (1833–1915)." University of Virginia Health Sciences Library. Available online. URL: http://etext.lib.virginia.edu/healthsci/reed/finlay.html. Downloaded on March 1, 2005.

Fischbarg, Jorge
(1935–   ) *ophthalmologist*

Jorge Fischbarg is an authority on the physical and chemical mechanisms by which water and electrolytes are transported across the epithelial membranes that make up the outer portions of the eye. An explanation of these mechanisms is of importance to understanding the way eyes function and for the treatment of a variety of eye diseases and disorders.

Fischbarg was born in Buenos Aires, Argentina, on August 14, 1935. He attended the Colegio Nacional de Buenos Aires, from which he received his bachelor's degree in 1953, and the University of Buenos Aires, from which he received his M.D. in 1962. He then immigrated to the United States, where he attended the University of Chicago. He was awarded his Ph.D. in physiology from Chicago in 1971. Fischbarg has held three postdoctoral appointments, one at the University of Buenos Aires, in the department of biophysics; one at the University of Louisville, in Kentucky, in the Division of Ophthalmic Research; and one at the University of Chicago, on the Committee on Mathematical Biology and in the department of physiology.

In 1970, Fischbarg was appointed assistant professor of ophthalmology at Columbia University's

his ideas by his colleagues, Finlay continued his research on yellow fever and other infectious diseases for the next 20 years. In recognition of his contributions to medicine, the Cuban government appointed him the nation's chief health officer and president of the Superior Board of Health in 1902.

Unfortunately, even Reed's final report on the etiology of yellow fever failed to mention Finlay's work in the field. It was not, in fact, until 1954 that the International Congress of Medical History formally and officially acknowledged Finlay's contribution to the solution of the yellow fever problem. By that time, Finlay had been dead for 39 years, having passed away in Havana on August 20, 1915.

College of Physicians and Surgeons (CPS) in New York City. He was later promoted to associate professor of clinical ophthalmology and head of the Laboratory of Membrane Biology in 1978 and then to professor of physiology and cellular biophysics at CPS. In 2002, he was named to the Laszlo Z. Bito Chair of Physiology and Cellular Biophysics at CPS. In addition to his work at Columbia, Fischbarg has served as visiting scientist in the Département de Biologie at the Centre d'Énergie Nucléaire, in Saclay, France (1974 and 1978), and at the Physiological Laboratory of the University of Cambridge, in the United Kingdom (1976–77), and as visiting professor in the department of biological sciences at the University of La Plata, Argentina (1992).

Fischbarg has written more than 120 scholarly papers and is the author, coauthor, or editor of nearly two dozen books and book chapters. He was given the 1986 Alcon Recognition Award by the Alcon Research Institute of Fort Worth, Texas, for outstanding service to the field of ophthalmology and was named Fellow Commoner at the Churchill College in Cambridge, England, for 1976–77.

Further Reading

"Fischbarg, Jorge." In *American Men & Women of Science,* 21st ed., edited by Pamela M. Kalte and Katherine H. Nemeh, vol. 2, 1,117. Detroit: Thomson Gale, 2003.

"Jorge Fischbarg." In *The Hispanic American Almanac,* 3d ed., edited by Sonia G. Benson, 701–702. Farmington Hills, Mich.: Thomson Gale, 2003.

Foyo, George
(George William Foyo)
(1946–) *engineer, telecommunications and business executive*

George William Foyo earned his bachelor's and master's degrees in engineering, and then moved into managerial positions in various telecommunications businesses. In 2004, he became chief executive officer of the Greater Miami Chamber of Commerce.

Foyo was born in Havana, Cuba, on August 21, 1946. He immigrated to the United States with his family at the age of 16 and attended high school in Naperville, Illinois. After graduation, he attended the University of Illinois at Chicago (UIC), from which he earned his B.S. in mechanical engineering in 1968. He then enrolled at Purdue University, where he was awarded his M.S. in industrial engineering in 1972.

After completing his studies at UIC, Foyo took a job with the giant telecommunications company AT&T, which he held while studying at Purdue. For the next 18 years, he managed a variety of engineering projects within the company. Then, in 1984, he was appointed managing director and chief executive officer (CEO) of AT&T Microelectrónica de España, a joint venture between AT&T and Telefónica of Spain. In this post, Foyo had an important role in AT&T's efforts to expand its international operations. Five years later, he was appointed managing director and CEO of AT&T Microelectronics Europe, with responsibilities for marketing and sales in six European nations.

In 1990, Foyo returned to the United States, where he was made vice president for sales in AT&T's Mid-Atlantic region and, later, in its Southeast region. He was then promoted to president of the company's Caribbean and Latin American division, where he was responsible for the acquisition of several smaller telecommunications companies, as well as managing agreements between AT&T and telephone companies in 42 Latin American countries. In 2000, Foyo severed his long-term ties with AT&T to take a position as president of DIRECTV Latin America, a division of Galaxy Latin America, an operation with facilities in 28 Latin American countries. He was largely responsible for making DIRECTV the leading provider of pay-TV operations in that part of the world.

In 2002, Foyo left DIRECTV to become chairman and CEO of LJ International, a consulting firm that provides training and advice to companies looking for ways to improve and expand their businesses in Latin America. After two years with LJ International, he resigned to become president and CEO of the Greater Miami Chamber of Commerce.

Foyo was named Executive of the Year by the Madrid Chamber of Commerce in 1988, AT&T Hero for 1988, Hispanic Engineer of the Year by the Hispanic Engineer National Achievement Award program in 1993, and Outstanding Alumni of the UIC College of Engineering in 2004. He has served on the board of directors of the European Institute of Technology (1987–89), the American Chamber of Commerce of Spain (1987–89), Fundesco of Spain (1986–89), and the U.S. Cuban American National Council (1991–present). He is a member of American Society of Mechanical Engineers, the Hispanic Association of AT&T Employees, and the Hispanic Association on Corporate Responsibility.

Further Reading

DIRECTV. "Hughes Electronics Names George Foyo President of Galaxy Latin America, LLC." Available online. URL: http://www. directvla.com/newcc/news/archives/news. asp?December%207,%201999.htm. Posted on December 7, 1999.

"Foyo, George William." In *Who's Who among Hispanic Americans, 1994–95,* 3d ed., edited by Amy Unterburger, 283. Detroit: Gale Research, 1995.

UIC–College of Engineering. "George Foyo." Available online. URL: http://www.uic.edu/depts/enga/ alumni/georgefoyo.htm. Downloaded on March 5, 2005.

G

Garcia, Carlos Ernesto
(1936–2003) *mechanical engineer*

Carlos Ernesto Garcia worked as an engineer for the federal government at a variety of locations from 1967 until his death in 2003. His special area of expertise was in the hydromechanical properties of missile systems (the disturbances in a fluid caused by passage of a missile through the fluid) and shock wave phenomena. He was also an authority in the characteristics of underground nuclear explosions.

Garcia was born in Las Vegas, New Mexico, on May 14, 1936, into a family of Mexican ancestry. He attended New Mexico State University in Las Cruces, where he earned his B.S. in 1958, his M.S. in 1962, and his D.Sc. in 1966, all in the field of engineering. Upon graduation from New Mexico State, he took a job with the LTV (Ling-Temco-Vought) Corporation at the White Sands Test Facility, in southwestern New Mexico, where the National Aeronautics and Space Administration (NASA) conducted tests of spacecraft materials, components, and rocket propulsion systems used in its space programs. In 1970, he was hired by the Atomic Energy Commission (whose responsibilities have since been divided between the Nuclear Regulatory Commission and the U.S. Department of Energy [DOE]) to work as a program analyst in the development of the Space Nuclear Auxiliary Power program, a system for using nuclear power as a source of energy in satellites and space probes.

In 1973, Garcia was reassigned to work in weapons production and in 1981, was appointed branch chief of the Nuclear Materials Management program of the DOE. He also served as director of the DOE's Environmental Safety and Health Division (1984–86) and as director of its Energy Technologies Division (1986–89). In 1989, Garcia became a program manager at the Los Alamos National Laboratory in Los Alamos, New Mexico. He was killed on September 29, 2003, when a 1947 Beechcraft Bonanza airplane that he was flying alone crashed near Belen, New Mexico. At the time, he was working at Los Alamos as a project leader in the Environmental Applications Division of the laboratory.

Further Reading

"Carlos Ernesto Garcia." In *The Hispanic American Almanac,* 3d ed., edited by Sonia G. Benson, 705. Farmington Hills, Mich.: Thomson Gale, 2003.

"Garcia, Carlos E(rnesto)." In *American Men & Women of Science,* 21st ed., edited by Pamela M. Kalte and Katherine H. Nemeh, vol. 3, 30. Detroit: Thomson Gale, 2003.

"Garcia, Carlos Ernesto." In *Who's Who among Hispanic Americans, 1994–95,* 3d ed., edited by Amy Unterburger, 301. Detroit: Gale Research, 1995.

Garcia, Catalina Esperanza
(1947–) *anesthesiologist*

Catalina Esperanza Garcia was the first Latina to earn a medical degree from Southwest Medical School in Dallas, Texas. In addition to her medical practice, she has been active in organizations designed to encourage other Latinas to achieve their goals, both professionally and personally.

Garcia was born in El Paso, Texas, on October 18, 1947, the daughter of Catalina Galindo and Arturo Ramos Garcia, of Mexican heritage. She attended the University of Texas at El Paso, from which she received her B.S. in 1964. She continued her education at the University of Texas Southwestern Medical Center at Dallas, from which she earned her M.D. in 1969. She then interned at the Baylor University Medical Center in Dallas in general medicine and completed her residency in anesthesiology at the Parkland Hospital, also in Dallas. In 1972, she became a partner at the Dallas Anesthesiology Group, where her practice is still located.

In addition to her medical career, Garcia has been active in promoting both the personal and professional development of Latinas. She was one of the founders of the Mexican American Business and Professional Women, an organization formed between 1972 and 1974 in Austin, Dallas, and San Antonio. The organization was the first group in Texas formed by and for Mexican women for the purpose of promoting their career development, civic involvement, and cultural awareness. In 1985, Garcia was involved in the creation of the Dallas Women's Foundation, an organization created to raise money for the purpose of supporting community programs that help women and girls realize their full potential. She was also a founding member of the Hispanic Women's Network of Texas in 1987 and of the Hispanic Jewish Dialogue of Dallas in 1989.

Garcia has served in a number of capacities in the medical profession, including serving as vice chair of the American Medical Women's Association and alternate delegate to the Texas Medical Association House of Delegates. She has also been active in a number of Hispanic and community organizations, including the Mayor's Hispanic Task Force (of which she was chair in 1987–88), the National Council of La Raza (of which she was a board member for 11 years, beginning in 1987), and the National Network of Hispanic Women (of which she was a board member in 1989). In 1994, Garcia was appointed by Secretary of Health and Human Services Donna E. Shalala to the department's Practicing Physicians Advisory Council, one of only four such appointees from a group of 130 physicians nominated for the post.

Among the honors that Garcia has received are the Dallas Independent School System's Volunteer of the Year Award in 1985, President and Mrs. Carlos Salinas of Mexico's Encuentros Mujeres award in 1990, a Gold Nugget Award from the University of Texas at El Paso in 1994, and an Excellence in Community Service award from the Dallas Historical Society in 2003.

Further Reading

"Garcia, Catalina Esperanza (Hope)." In *Who's Who among Hispanic Americans, 1994–95,* 3d ed., edited by Amy Unterburger, 301. Detroit: Gale Research, 1995.

Poythress, Stephanie. "Catalina Esperanza Garcia." In *Notable Hispanic American Women,* edited by Diane Telgen, Jim Kamp, and Joseph M. Palmisano, 166. Detroit: Gale Research, 1998.

García, Celso-Ramón
(1921–2004) *medical researcher*

Celso-Ramón García was a leading researcher in the field of women's reproductive health issues. He was leader of a team that conducted the first large-scale tests in Puerto Rico of the oral contraceptive pill (the Pill) developed by American researchers Gregory C. Pincus and John Rock that has transformed human reproductive practices throughout the world.

García was born on October 31, 1921, in New York City to Celso García y Ondina and Olivia Menéndez del Valle García, immigrants to the United States from Spain. He studied at Queens College in New York, earning his B.S. in 1942, and at the Downstate Medical Center of the State University of New York, in Brooklyn, from which he received his M.D. in 1945. He then joined the U.S. Army Medical Corps, where he served at hospitals in Fairbanks, Alaska, and Phoenixville, Pennsylvania. Upon his discharge in 1948, he completed his residency in pathology at the Cumberland Hospital in Brooklyn (1948–49) and in obstetrics and gynecology, also at Cumberland (1950–53).

In 1953, García took a position as assistant professor of obstetrics and gynecology at the University of Puerto Rico's School of Medicine at San Juan. It was during this period that García conducted extensive tests of the Pill on women in Puerto Rico, work for which he was later nominated for the Nobel Prize. Late in his life, he expressed the view that the discovery of the Pill was probably worthy of a Nobel Prize but that the Nobel committee had been reluctant to offend the Catholic Church by awarding the prize for this accomplishment.

Two years later, in 1955, García left Puerto Rico to accept an appointment at the Free Hospital for Women in Brookline, Massachusetts, a post he held for the next 10 years. During that period, he also served as senior scientist and director of the training program in reproductive physiology at the Worcester Foundation for Experimental Biology, in Worcester, Massachusetts (1960–62), as assistant surgeon and chief of the Infertility Clinic at the Massachusetts General Hospital in Boston, and as clinical associate professor of obstetrics and gynecology at the Harvard Medical School, also in Boston (1962–65).

García joined the faculty of the University of Pennsylvania School of Medicine, in Philadelphia, in 1965, where he remained until his retirement in 1992. During this time, he held a number of titles, including director of reproductive surgery (1987–92) and William Shippen, Jr., Professor of Human Reproduction. In addition to his perhaps better-known work on the Pill, García conducted research on the treatment of tubal disease and methods of artificial fertilization. He was awarded the Carl G. Hartman Award of the American Society for the Study of Sterility in 1961; the University of Michigan Sesquicentennial Award in 1967; the Wyeth/Ayerst Public Recognition Award in 1993; the CHOICE Award for major accomplishments in contraception, reproductive endocrinology, and infertility in 1993; and the Scientific Leadership Award of the Global Alliance for Women's Health in 2000. García died on February 1, 2004, in New York City.

Further Reading

"Celso Ramón García." In *The Hispanic American Almanac,* 3d ed., edited by Sonia G. Benson, 705–706. Farmington Hills, Mich.: Thomson Gale, 2003.

Downey, Sally. "Celso-Ramon Garcia, 82, Pill Pioneer." *Philadelphia Inquirer,* February 5, 2004, p. B9. Available online. URL: http://www.philly.com/mld/inquirer/news/obituaries/7877351.htm. Posted on February 5, 2004.

Strauss, Jerome F., III, and Luigi Mastroianni, Jr. "In Memoriam: Celso-Ramon Garcia, M.D. (1922–2004), Reproductive Medicine Visionary." *Journal of Experimental & Clinical Assisted Reproduction* 2 (January 2005): 2–5.

García, Héctor P.
(Héctor Pérez García)
(1914–1996) *physician, activist*

Héctor Pérez García was a physician who worked primarily as a family practitioner but is best known for his political activities. He was founder and president of the American GI Forum, an organization of Latino veterans of the U.S. military; founder and first president of the Political Association of Spanish-Speaking Organizations; and national coordinator of the Viva Kennedy clubs, which worked for the election of John F. Kennedy as president of the United States.

García was born on January 17, 1914, in Llera, in the state of Tamaulipas, Mexico. His parents were José and Faustina Pérez García, both teachers. In 1917, the García family emigrated from Mexico because of the disruptions caused by the Mexican Revolution, settling eventually in Mercedes, Texas. Unable to continue as a teacher because his credentials were not valid in the United States, García's father became a partner in a dry goods store in Mercedes.

In 1929, at the age of 15, García joined the Citizens Military Training Corps (CMTC), a branch of the U.S. Army similar to the modern-day National Guard, in which young men attended military drills for a month out of each year. Three years later, he graduated from a segregated, Mexican-only high school and was commissioned as a second lieutenant in the U.S. Army. He also enrolled at Edinburg Junior College, 30 miles from his home in Mercedes, commuting each day to attend classes. After completing his studies at Edinburg, García entered the University of Texas at Austin, where he majored in zoology. He was granted his B.A. from Texas in 1936. He then continued his studies at the University of Texas at Galveston, earning his M.D. in 1940.

García completed his residency shortly after the onset of World War II. He volunteered for active service and was given command of a company, first, of infantry and, later, of combat engineers. Late in 1942, he was transferred to the U.S. Medical Corps, serving in the European theater of operations from 1942 to 1945. During his service, he was promoted to captain and then to major, also earning the Bronze Star with six Battle Stars for his services.

After discharge from the army, García returned to Texas, where he opened a private medical practice in Corpus Christi. He also took his first step into the political arena, joining the League of United Latin American Citizens (LULAC). Almost immediately, in 1947, he was elected president of the local chapter of LULAC. In the same year, García was hospitalized with acute nephritis, a potentially life-threatening disease. While he was recuperating, he heard of the superintendent of schools describing with pride the system's program of segregating Mexican-American students from their white counterparts. García was so angry that he decided to commit his energies to overcoming the unfair treatment of his fellow citizens. A year later, he called a meeting at a local school to organize Mexican-American veterans, a meeting that resulted in the formation of the American GI Forum. The mission of the forum was to ensure the civil and educational rights of all Hispanic Americans.

Over the next three decades, García became increasingly active in state and national politics and was sought out more and more frequently by political leaders as a spokesperson for the Hispanic-American community. For example, in 1962 he was asked by President Kennedy to represent the United States in negotiations with the Federation of West Indies Islands to create a defense treaty between the two nations. The appointment represented the first time that a Mexican American had been asked to represent a U.S. president. Two years later, García was appointed by President Lyndon B. Johnson as special ambassador for the inauguration of Dr. Raúl Leoni as president of Venezuela. In 1967, Johnson appointed García alternate ambassador to the United Nations, providing García with the opportunity to present the first speech to the international assembly by an American representative in a language (Spanish) other than English. And, in one of Johnson's last official acts as president, he appointed García a member of the U.S. Commission on Civil

Rights, the first Hispanic American to hold that office.

Throughout his life, García's work was recognized by a number of honors and awards. These awards included a Bronze Plaque "Democracy Forward" by the Texas Council of Negro Organizations (1955), the Presidential Medal of Freedom (1984), the Mexican Honor Al Merito Medalla Cura José María Morelos y Pavón (1986), the Hispanic Heritage Award of the National Hispanic Leadership Conference (1989), the Matt Garcia Public Service Award of the Mexican-American Legal Defense and Educational Fund (1989), a Distinguished Alumnus Award from the University of Texas Ex-Students Association (1989), a National Hispanic Hero Award from the Midwest/Northeast Voter Registration Project (1989), the MAPA Award for outstanding service to Hispanics throughout the United States from the Mexican-American Physician's Association (1990), a Distinguished Lifetime Service Award from the National Association of Hispanic Journalists (1990), the Equestrian Order of Pope Gregory the Great from Pope John Paul II (1990), and the Maclovio Barraza Award of the National Council of La Raza (1990). In 1988, the U.S. Postal Service renamed the main post office in Corpus Christi in honor of García, and in 1999, the U.S. Department of the Treasury chose to memorialize García with his picture on the $75 I Bond series.

On March 8, 1996, after 50 years of medical service in the same location, García closed his offices in Corpus Christi. Four months later, on July 26, García died.

Further Reading

KEDT-TV. "Justice for My People: Dr. Hector P. Garcia—Biography." Available online. URL: http://www.justiceformypeople.org/drhector.html. Downloaded on March 2, 2005.

"Héctor Pérez García." In *The Hispanic American Almanac,* 3d ed., edited by Sonia G. Benson, 706–707. Farmington Hills, Mich.: Thomson Gale, 2003.

Saavedra, Rebecca. "Hector P. Garcia: A Texas Legend." University of Texas Medical Branch. Available online. URL: http://www.utmb.edu/drgarcia/. Downloaded on March 2, 2005.

Garcia, Jose Dolores, Jr.
(1936–) *theoretical physicist*

Jose Dolores Garcia, Jr., is a theoretical physicist whose special interest is in atomic structure as understood by quantum theory, a collection of ideas that describe the behavior of matter at the very smallest levels. He is also involved in the development of programs for the improvement of science education, in general, and for science programs for minorities, in particular.

Garcia was born in Santa Fe, New Mexico, on January 3, 1936, to a family of Mexican ethnicity. As a young child, he moved to the small village of Alcalde in northern New Mexico, which had been founded by Spanish-speaking people hundreds of years earlier. He has written that although the town was very small, it had a culture "very rich in tradition and folklore." Garcia was fortunate enough to be able to attend a boarding school in Santa Fe, Saint Michaels, about 30 miles from his home. He was fortunate not only because of the school's strong academic traditions, especially in the area of science and mathematics, but also because the school provided him an opportunity to earn a scholarship that allowed him to attend New Mexico State University, where he enrolled in 1953. He earned his B.S. in physics from New Mexico State in 1957 and, in the same year, was named a Fulbright Scholar. He chose to use his Fulbright Scholarship to spend a year at the University of Göttingen in Germany, home of some of the greatest theoretical physicists in the world.

When Garcia returned to the United States, he applied to the University of California at Berkeley, from which he received his M.S. in physics in 1959. He joined the U.S. Air Force, where he reached the rank of captain before being discharged in 1963. At that point, Garcia began his doctoral studies at the University of Wisconsin at Madison, completing his program and earning his Ph.D. in 1966. He was then offered a job in the department of physics at the University of Arizona, where he has remained ever since. He was named full professor in 1975.

Garcia's research is concerned with the electronic and nuclear structure of atoms, using the equations developed through quantum theory to obtain better understandings of the way atoms are constructed and the way they interact with each other. As an example, a paper he coauthored while still a doctoral student dealt with the electronic structure of the first 20 elements and the line spectra (type of light) they emit, using certain basic equations from quantum theory. The paper was named a "citation classic" in 1980 because it was mentioned so often (more than 100 times) by other physicists in their own reports.

Garcia is also very much interested in improving the type of science education programs available to students, especially to those who come from underrepresented minorities, such as Hispanics and blacks. For example, he and other members of his department annually sponsor a physics "phun night" in which they perform demonstrations for high school students, their parents, and the general public.

Further Reading

"Garcia, José D., Jr." In *Who's Who among Hispanic Americans, 1994–95,* 3d ed., edited by Amy Unterburger, 310. Detroit: Gale Research, 1995.

"José D. Garcia." In *The Hispanic American Almanac,* 3d ed., edited by Sonia G. Benson, 707. Farmington Hills, Mich.: Thomson Gale, 2003.

Society for Advancement of Chicanos and Native Americans in Science. "Dr. J. D. Garcia—Physicist." SACNAS Biography Project. Available online. URL: http://64.171.10.183/biography/Biography.asp?mem=46&type=2. Downloaded on March 6, 2005.

García, Julio H.
(Julio Hernán García)
(1933–1998) *neuropathologist*

Julio Hernán García was an internationally known and highly esteemed researcher of microscopic changes that occur in the brain as the result of stroke, shock, or other types of injury. He was especially skilled at studying such changes with the electron microscope, a magnifying device with resolution powers much greater than that of the ordinary light microscope. He was also interested in the effects of methanol (wood alcohol) poisoning on the brain.

García was born in Armenia, Colombia, on December 22, 1933. He received his bachelor's degree from the College of St. Bartholomew, in Bogotá, in 1951, and his M.D. from the National University of Colombia, also in Bogotá, in 1958. He completed his internship in pathology at the Hospital San Juan de Dios, in Bogotá, between 1958 and 1959 before immigrating to the United States, where he did two residencies, one in the department of pathology at Long Island Jewish Hospital of New York in 1959–60 and one in the department of pathology and neuropathology at Kings County Hospital, in Brooklyn, from 1960 to 1964. After completing this training, García held a series of academic appointments that included assistant professor of pathology at the Medical College of Virginia, in Richmond, from 1964 to 1967; associate professor of pathology and neuropathology at the University of Tennessee, in Memphis, from 1967 to 1970; associate professor of pathology and neuropathology at Baylor College of Medicine, in Waco, Texas, from 1970 to 1971; professor of pathology and head of the Neuropathology Division at the University of Maryland's School of Medicine, in Baltimore (UMB), from 1971 to 1979; professor of pathology and neurology at the Schools of Medicine and Dentistry of the University of Alabama at Birmingham (UAB), from 1979 to 1990; and director of the department of neuropathology at the Henry Ford Hospital, in Detroit, from 1991 until his death in 1998. Ironically, García died unexpectedly in Birmingham, Alabama, on November 8, 1998, as the result of a ruptured cerebral aneurysm (a weakness in the wall of an artery), a type of injury that he had long studied in his own laboratory.

Concurrent with his academic appointments, García held a number of clinical positions, such as physician in the Office of the Chief Medical Examiner of Virginia, in Richmond (1964–66); consultant to the Eastern State Hospital, in Williamsburg, Virginia (1964–66); and consultant at the Baptist Memorial Hospital, in Memphis (1967–70). He was honored with a Teacher of the Year Award by the sophomore medical class at UMB in 1986 and a Best Basic Science Coursemaster Award at UAB in 1987. He was elected a fellow of the Council on Cerebrovascular Disease of the American Heart Association and an honorary member of the Spanish Neurological Society.

Further Reading

Cervós-Navarro, J. "In Memory of Dr. Julio García." *Brain Pathology* 9 (Spring 1999): 419.

"Garcia, Julio H." In *American Men & Women of Science,* 21st ed., edited by Pamela M. Kalte and Katherine H. Nemeh, vol. 3, 30. Detroit: Thomson Gale, 2003.

Martí-Vilalta, José-Luis, and Carlos S. Kase. "Julio Hernán García." *Stroke* (January 1999): 183–184.

Garcia, Marcelo H.
(Marcelo Horacio Garcia)
(1959–   ) *hydraulic engineer*

Marcelo Horacio Garcia has sometimes been called "the river doctor" because of his interest in studying the problems of rivers, such as erosion and deposition, and in developing solutions to those problems. His specific areas of research include environmental hydrodynamics, the characteristics of water flow with relation to the land over which it travels; transport of sediments; the flow of water in open channels; and river and seabed mechanics.

Garcia was born in Córdoba, Argentina, on April 22, 1959. He attended the Universidad Nacional del Litoral (UNL), in Santa Fe, Argentina, where he received his Ing. Dipl. (equivalent to a bachelor's degree) in water resources in 1982. After graduation, Garcia worked as an assistant engineer at the Paraná Medio Project in Argentina (involving the construction of a dam on the Paraná River) from 1982 to 1983 and as a research docent at UNL from 1982 to 1987. He continued his graduate studies in the United States, earning his M.S. and Ph.D., both in civil engineering, at the University of Minnesota, in Minneapolis, in 1985 and 1989, respectively. Following receipt of his doctorate, Garcia was a research fellow at the St. Anthony Falls Hydraulic Laboratory of the University of Minnesota, in Minneapolis.

In 1990, Garcia accepted an offer to become assistant professor in the department of civil and environmental engineering at the University of Illinois at Urbana-Champaign (UIUC), where he was later promoted to associate professor (1997) and full professor (2000). He is now Chester and Helen Siess Professor of Civil Engineering at UIUC. Garcia has also been on the staff of the Ven Te Chow Hydrosystems Laboratory at UIUC, where he was made director in 1997. In addition to his work at UIUC, Garcia has served as visiting professor and consultant at a number of academic institutions and industrial corporations, including the Northern States Power Company, the Hokkaido (Japan) River Research Foundation, the Universidad Nacional del Litoral (Argentina), the University of Genoa (Italy), the California Institute of Technology, the École Polytechnique Fédérale de Lausanne (Switzerland), the Universidad de Castilla–La Mancha (Spain), and the Universidad Nacional de Córdoba (Argentina). Among the awards he has received are the National Science Foundation Research Initiation Award (1992), the

MUCIA (Midwest Universities Consortium for International Activities) International Program Development Award (1995), the Karl Emil Hilgard Hydraulic Prize of the American Society of Civil Engineers (1996 and 1999), the Walter L. Huber Research Prize of the American Society of Civil Engineers (1998), and the Arthur Thomas Ippen Award of the International Association of Hydraulic Engineering and Research (2001).

Further Reading

"Garcia, Marcelo Horacio." In *American Men & Women of Science,* 21st ed., edited by Pamela M. Kalte and Katherine H. Nemeh, vol. 3, 30. Detroit: Thomson Gale, 2003.

Prow, Tina W. "The River Doctor." *Engineering Outlook* 14 (2001). Available online. URL: http://www.engr.uiuc.edu/communications/outlook/Text,%2041–2/garcia.htm. Downloaded on April 30, 2005.

"Marcelo H. Garcia." University of Illinois at Urbana-Champaign, Department of Civil and Environmental Engineering. Available online. URL: http://www.cee.uiuc.edu/Faculty/mhgarcia.htm. Downloaded on April 30, 2005.

García, Oscar N.
(Oscar Nicolas García)
(1936–) *electrical engineer, inventor*

Oscar Nicolas García's research has spanned a wide range of topics in electrical engineering and computer sciences, including human-computer interaction; bioinformatics, the science of analyzing and managing biological information using computing techniques; artificial intelligence; speech-driven facial animation; computer architecture; testing of digital circuits; and arithmetic coding theory.

García was born in Havana, Cuba, on September 10, 1936, to Leonor Hernández and Oscar Vicente García. He attended North Carolina State University, in Raleigh, earning his B.S. and M.S. in electrical engineering in 1961 and 1964, respectively, and the University of Maryland, in College Park, from which he received his Ph.D. in electrical engineering in 1969. While still a graduate student, García was assistant professor of electrical engineering at Old Dominion University, in Norfolk, Virginia (1963–66), and research assistant and instructor in the department of electrical engineering at the University of Maryland (1966–69).

After completing his doctoral studies, García returned to Old Dominion as associate professor for one year before accepting an appointment as associate professor of electrical engineering at the University of South Florida, in Tampa (1970–75). He was later promoted to professor, a post he held from 1975 to 1985, also serving during that period as assistant chair of the department of electrical engineering, in charge of B.S., M.S., and Ph.D. programs in the computer science option in the engineering science degree (1974–79). In 1979, García was appointed chair of the newly formed department of computer science and engineering at South Florida, a position he held until 1985.

In 1985, García left South Florida to become professor in the department of electrical engineering and computer science at the George Washington University (GWU) School of Engineering and Applied Science, in Washington, D.C. He remained at GWU until 1995, except for a three-year period during which he was program director for Interactive Systems in the Information, Robotics, and Intelligent Systems Division at the National Science Foundation (1992–94). In 1995, García was named NCR Endowed Distinguished Professor and chair of the department of computer science and engineering of the College of Engineering and Computer Science at Wright State University, in Dayton, Ohio. He served in that post until 2003, when he was named founding dean of the newly established College of Engineering at the University of North Texas, in Denton, a post he continues to hold.

In addition to his academic appointments, García has been a consultant to many governmental, industrial, academic, and other agencies and organizations, including Goddard Space Flight Center, National Aeronautics and Space Administration (1969; Interplanetary Monitoring Platform IV satellite computer); Sperry Microwave Systems (1975; computer-aided test generation); Honeywell Aerospace Division (1976–77; microprocessor development systems); Corporate Computer Sciences Center, Honeywell, Inc. (1979–80; design systems for testability, multiprocessing for simulation, and discrete harmonic analysis); General Telephone and Electronics Data Services (1985; curriculum development and employee educational assessment); Institute for Defense Analysis (1986–92; procurement of highly reliable software and statistical aspects of software engineering); Graduate School of North Carolina State University (1990; review of its graduate program in computer science); International Access Corporation (1991–92; artificial intelligence programs); State Council of Higher Education for Virginia (1999–2000; computer science doctoral program evaluations); and Puerto Rico Board of Higher Education (2000; evaluation of a doctoral program in computer engineering and computational science).

García has received an impressive number of honors and awards in connection with his work. They include the Centennial Medal of the Florida West Coast Section of the Institute of Electrical and Electronics Engineers (IEEE; 1984); the Distinguished Service Award of the IEEE Computer Society, "for many years of outstanding leadership representing the Computer Society" (1985); the Richard E. Merwin Distinguished Service Award of the IEEE Computer Society (1988); the Meritorious Service Award of the IEEE Computer Society (1990); the Centennial Certificate of the American Society for Engineering Education (1993); the Richard M. Emberson Award of the IEEE Board of Directors (1994); and the IEEE Third Millennium Medal (2000). He has also been asked to give special lectures at conferences and meetings throughout the United States and countries around the world, including Brazil, China, Costa Rica, Greece, Hong Kong, India, Japan, Mexico, Puerto Rico, and Spain. He is coauthor (with Yi-Tzuu Chien) of *Knowledge-Based Systems: Fundamentals and Tools* (1992).

Further Reading

The Computer Society. "Oscar N. Garcia." Available online. URL: http://www.computer.org/csinfo/boards/OSCAR%20N.htm. Downloaded on April 9, 2005.

"García, Oscar Nicolas." In *American Men & Women of Science,* 21st ed., edited by Pamela M. Kalte and Katherine H. Nemeh, vol. 3, 31, Detroit: Thomson Gale, 2003.

"Garcia, Oscar Nicolas." In *Who's Who among Hispanic Americans, 1994–95,* 3d ed., edited by Amy Unterburger, 315. Detroit: Gale Research, 1995.

University of North Texas News Service. "Oscar N. Garcia Named Founding Dean of New College of Engineering." Available online. URL: http://web2.unt.edu/news/story.cfm?story=8520. Posted on February 7, 2003.

Garcia-Luna-Aceves, J. J.
(José Joaquin Garcia-Luna-Aceves)
(1955–   ) *electrical engineer, inventor*

José Joaquin Garcia-Luna-Aceves is an electrical engineer whose current research interests include the analysis and design of algorithms and protocols for computer communication, focusing in particular on wireless networks and systems for working on the Internet.

Garcia-Luna-Aceves was born in Mexico City on October 20, 1955. He attended the Universidad Iberoamericana, in Mexico City, thinking, he later wrote, that he was interested in becoming an artist. Instead, he ended up majoring in engineering. He received his B.S. in electrical engineering in 1977 and then spent a year as a lecturer at Iberoamericana while he tried to improve his English-language skills. In 1978, he entered the University of Hawaii at Manoa, from which he received his M.S. and Ph.D. in electrical engineering in 1980 and 1983, respectively. He claims that he chose Hawaii for his graduate studies in order to "get a tan" and spend his time surfing but instead had to settle for a degree in electrical engineering.

After completing his doctoral studies in Hawaii, Garcia-Luna-Aceves took a job as a center director at SRI International, in Menlo Park, California, an independent nonprofit that conducts research and development for government agencies, commercial businesses, foundations, and other organizations. In 1993, Garcia-Luna-Aceves left SRI to become associate professor of electrical engineering at the University of California at Santa Cruz (UCSC). He was later appointed to the Baskin Chair of Computer Engineering at UCSC, a post he still holds. In addition to his chair at UCSC, Garcia-Luna-Aceves was visiting professor at Sun Labs in Menlo Park in 1999, and principal of protocol design for the telecommunications company Nokia from 1999 to 2003. He is also a principal scientist at the Palo Alto Research Center, in Palo Alto, California.

Garcia-Luna-Aceves is the author of more than 270 scholarly papers and coeditor of the book *Multimedia Communications: Protocols and Applications* (with Wolfgang Effelsberg and Franklin F. Kuo, 1997). He received SRI International's Exceptional Achievement Award in 1985 for his work on multimedia communications and again in 1989 for his work on adaptive routing algorithms. He has been very active on a number of professional committees and working groups, such as the Institute of Electrical and Electronic Engineers (IEEE) Internet Technology Award Committee, the IEEE Richard W. Hamming Medal Committee, and the National Research Council Panel on Digitization and Communications Science of the Army Research Laboratory Technical Assessment Board. He was also a founding member of IEEE's special interest group on multimedia.

Further Reading

UCSC Engineering. "J. J. Garcia-Luna-Aceves." Baskin SOE Faculty. Available online. URL: http://www.soe.ucsc.edu/people/faculty/jj/html. Downloaded on September 10, 2006.

University of California, Santa Cruz. "UCSC to Lead Ambitious Multidisciplinary Research Project on Wireless Communication Networks." Available online. URL: http://www.ucsc.edu/news_events/press_releases/text.asp?pid=663. Downloaded on November 15, 2005.

Garzoli, Silvia L.
(1941–) *oceanographer*

Silvia L. Garzoli's primary field of interest is in ocean dynamics and the ways in which Earth's oceans affect climate. Most of her work is done at sea, having directed more than a dozen scientific cruises since 1983, primarily to the Atlantic Ocean. She employs the use of fixed, moored instruments with which to collect data about ocean circulation patterns, which she then uses in the development of mathematical models to describe ocean dynamics and the interaction between oceans and the atmosphere. In addition to her studies in the tropical Atlantic, Garzoli has been maintaining research projects in other parts of the world, including the Benguela Current system south of South Africa, the North Brazil Current north of Brazil, and the Indonesian throughflow currents at the strait of Makassar, between the Java and Celebes Seas.

Garzoli was born in Buenos Aires, Argentina, on November 16, 1941. She attended the University of Buenos Aires, from which she received her Licenciatura en Ciencias Físicas, a six-year program equivalent to a master's degree in physical science. She continued her studies at La Plata University,

Silvia L. Garzoli specializes in the study of ocean currents and the relationship between the oceans and climate change. *(Courtesy Dr. Silvia Garzoli)*

oceanography at the Laboratoire d'Océanographie Physique, in Paris, where she remained until June 1980. A month later, Garzoli began a long association with the Lamont-Doherty Earth Observatory of Columbia University, in New York City, when she began a one-year assignment as visiting research scientist. She was later named associate research scientist (1981–85), senior research scientist (1985–88), and continued as an adjunct senior research scientist (1998–present) at Lamont-Doherty.

Garzoli started her affiliation with the National Oceanic and Atmospheric Administration (NOAA) in 1996, when she took a leave of absence from Lamont-Doherty to work at the agency as senior research oceanographer. In October 1997, she was appointed director of the Physical Oceanography Division of NOAA's Atlantic Oceanographic and Meteorological Laboratory, in Miami, Florida, a post she continues to hold. From 1992 to 1994, Garzoli was also on leave of absence from Lamont-Doherty to serve as program director of the Physical Oceanography Division of the National Science Foundation, in Washington, D.C. In addition to her work with Lamont-Doherty and NOAA, Garzoli is adjunct professor at the Rosenstil School of Marine Science of the University of Miami.

Garzoli is the author of more than 85 scholarly articles, book chapters, reports, and other publications. She has been elected a member of the Inter-American Institute for Global Change Research Scientific Advisory Committee, a fellow and member of the Council of Fellows of the Cooperative Institute for Climate and Ocean Research, a Steinbach Scholar of the Woods Hole Oceanographic Institute, and a fellow of the Cooperative Institute of Marine and Atmospheric Science. She has also been a visiting scientist at the Cooperative Institute for Marine and Atmospheric Studies at the University of Miami (1989) and invited TOKTEN (Transfer of Knowledge Through Expatriates Nationals) professor at the University of Mar del Plata, Argentina (1987).

in La Plata, Argentina, earning her Ph.D. in physics in 1968 in a joint program with the University of Maryland at College Park. Garzoli's first work assignment was with the Argentine Institute of Radioastronomy, in Villa Elisa, where she was an associate research scientist, a post she held until 1972. She then joined the physics department of the Faculty of Sciences at the University of Buenos Aires, first as instructor and later as associate professor and member of the Physical Oceanography Group of researchers.

In October 1974, Garzoli moved to the Naval Technology Research Center, in Buenos Aires, as associate research scientist and member of the Scientific Research Career of the Argentine National Research Council for three months, before taking a position as associate research scientist in physical

Further Reading

"Garzoli, Silvia L." In *American Men & Women of Science*, 21st ed., edited by Pamela M. Kalte and Katherine H. Nemeh, vol. 3, 52. Detroit: Thomson Gale, 2003.

"Garzoli, Silvia L." *Oceanography* 18 (March 2005): 121.

Gigli, Irma
(1931–) *dermatologist, medical researcher*

Irma Gigli was trained as a dermatologist but has expanded her expertise to include research on the immune system in general. She has been particularly interested in the structure and function of proteins that make up the complement system, a group of about 20 proteins that are responsible for the destruction of foreign cells that invade the body.

Gigli was born in Córdoba, Argentina, on December 22, 1931. She earned a teacher's degree from the Escuela Normal Superior in Córdoba in 1948 and her B.A. from the Colegio Nacional Manuel Belgrano in Buenos Aires in 1950. She studied for her medical degree at the Universidad Nacional de Córdoba, which she received in 1957. During her last three years of medical school, she also served at the Universidad Nacional as a teaching fellow in biochemistry.

After receiving her M.D. in Argentina, Gigli immigrated to the United States, where she completed her internship in internal medicine at the Cook County Hospital in Chicago in 1957–58 and her residency in dermatology at the same hospital from 1958 to 1960. She then spent a year as a research fellow at New York University (NYU), in Manhattan, before taking a job as visiting investigator in immunology at the Howard Hughes Medical Institute in Miami, Florida, from 1961 to 1964. After a two-year term as research investigator at the University of Frankfurt in Germany, she returned to the United States and was appointed research associate at the Harvard University Medical School, in Boston. She remained at Harvard for most of the next decade, serving as assistant and associate professor at the medical school, chief dermatologist at the Peter Bent Brigham Hospital (which is associated with Harvard), and senior associate dermatologist at the medical school.

In 1976, Gigli left Harvard to spend a year as visiting scientist in biochemistry at the University of Oxford, in England, before taking a position as professor of dermatology and experimental medicine at NYU. In 1983, Gigli was appointed professor of medicine and chief of the Division of Dermatology at the University of California at San Diego, posts she held until 1995. She next moved to the University of Texas Health Science Center at Houston (UTHCS-H), where she was named professor of medicine and dermatology and vice chair of medical sciences at the center. She was later made Walter and Mary Mischer Professor in Molecular Medicine, director of the Center for Immunology and Autoimmune Diseases, and deputy director of the Brown Foundation Institute of Molecular Medicine.

Gigli is the author of more than 160 scholarly papers and book chapters dealing with problems of dermatology and the immune system. In 2002, she was elected a fellow of the American Academy of Arts and Sciences, and in 2003, she received the Distinguished Professional Woman of the Year Award from UTHSC-H. In 2004, Gigli was appointed to the U.S. Civilian Research and Development Foundation, a nonprofit organization authorized by the U.S. Congress for the purpose of promoting international scientific and technical collaboration between the United States and other nations of the world.

Further Reading

"Gigli, Irma." In *American Men & Women of Science*, 21st ed., edited by Pamela M. Kalte and Katherine H. Nemeh, vol. 3, 125. Detroit: Thomson Gale, 2003.

"Irma Gigli." In *Latino Women of Science,* edited by Leonard Bernstein, Alan Winkler, and Linda Zierdt-Warshaw, 10–11. Maywood, N.J.: Peoples Publishing Group, 1998.

Gilbert, Fabiola Cabeza de Baca
(Fabiola Cabeza de Baca)
(1894–1991) *home economist*

Fabiola Cabeza de Baca Gilbert was trained as a teacher but became interested in home economics soon after she began teaching. She studied the nutritional patterns of traditional Mexican cooking and integrated those patterns with the best information then available on the preparation of attractive and nutritious meals. Her best-known books deal with cooking recipes from and for Mexican, Indian, Spanish, and Anglo cultures, such as *Historic Cookery,* as well as later fiction and nonfiction works that reflect the traditions and character of the Hispanic culture in which she grew up and spent most of her life.

Born Fabiola Cabeza de Baca on May 16, 1894, in La Liendra, near Las Vegas, New Mexico, she was raised by her father, Graciano Cabeza de Baca, and her paternal grandmother, Estefanita Delgado Cabeza de Baca, after her mother died when she was four. The Cabeza de Baca family were members of the *patrón* class, with large landholdings and a substantial degree of wealth. Cabeza de Baca attended New Mexico Normal University (now New Mexico Highlands University), in Las Vegas, where she received her teaching degree in 1921. One of the classes she was assigned to teach was domestic science, equivalent to modern home economics, a subject in which she had relatively little experience but in which she soon became very interested. She eventually decided to return to school and pursue formal studies in home economics. In 1929, she graduated from New Mexico State University, in Las Cruces, with her bachelor's degree in home economics and took a job with the New Mexico State Extension Service.

As part of her work with the Extension Service, Cabeza de Baca visited homes and communities throughout northern New Mexico, bringing information about proper methods of cooking and food preservation, as well as educating people as to ways in which they could market their homemade products. She was more than a teacher, however, as she carefully observed cooking and household methods of the people she visited, attempting to integrate the best practices handed down from generation to generation with the newest research on sound nutritional practices.

In 1939, Cabeza de Baca married Carlos Gilbert, an insurance agent, a marriage that lasted only a short time. In the same year, she published the book for which she is perhaps best known, *Historic Cookery;* it eventually sold more than 100,000 copies and was reissued in 1970 and again in 1997. In 1941, she published an important article reflecting her views about the integration of modern and traditional cooking, "New Mexican Diets," in the *Journal of Home Economics.* In that article, she suggested ways in which her colleagues in the home economics profession could pay more careful attention to the traditions and practices of their clients as they attempted to educate them about good nutritional practices.

In her next book, *The Good Life: New Mexico Traditions and Food,* Gilbert began to combine her expertise in nutritional practices with a growing interest in fiction writing. The book tells of the cultural traditions of a typical Hispanic community in northern New Mexico with information about cooking practices and the use of herbal materials for medical purposes. The book was released in 1949 and revised in 1982. In 1953, she produced a third book, *We Fed Them Cactus* (reprinted in 1954, 1989, and 1994), a historical account of the settlement of the southwestern United States by Spanish explorers. Gilbert formally retired from the Extension Service in 1959, but she continued to lecture and write. She died in Albuquerque on October 14, 1991.

Further Reading

Davis, Kate K. "Cabeza de Baca, Fabiola." In *American Women Writers, 1900–1945: A Bio-Bibliographical Critical Sourcebook,* edited by Laurie Champion, 159–160. Portsmouth, N.H.: Greenwood, 2000.

Poythress, Stephanie. "Fabiola Cabeza de Baca Gilbert." In *Notable Hispanic American Women,* edited by Diane Telgen, Jim Kamp, and Joseph M. Palmisano, 178–179. Detroit: Gale Research, 1998.

Gómez, Cynthia A.
(Cynthia Ann Gómez)
(1958–   ) *psychologist*

Cynthia Ann Gómez is a nationally and internationally known expert in the field of human immunodeficiency virus (HIV) diseases. Her special interests involve the development and implementation of HIV/AIDS prevention programs among women, gay men, injection drug users, Latinos, children, and sero-discordant couples, couples in which one person is HIV positive and the other is HIV negative.

Gómez was born in Long Beach, California, on September 9, 1958, the daughter of Lilly Gonsalez and Augustine U. Gómez, of Mexican descent. She was educated at Boston University, from which she received her B.A. in psychology in 1979; at Harvard University, in Cambridge, Massachusetts, where she earned her Ed.M. in consulting psychology in 1982; and Boston University, from which she received her Ph.D. in clinical psychology in 1990. Her earliest professional and research position was as a community outreach worker at the Upham's Corner Health Center, in Dorchester, Massachusetts (1979–81), after which she became a psychology intern at the Cambridge Guidance Center, in Cambridge, Massachusetts (1981–82), and a bilingual psychotherapist at the AtlantiCare Medical Center, in Lynn, Massachusetts (1982–84). Over the next few years, she held a variety of jobs in the Boston area, including psychology intern at the Brookline Community Mental Health Center, in Brookline (1984–85); mobile crisis team therapist with the AtlantiCare Medical Center, in Lynn (1984–86); staff psychologist at the Southern Jamaica Plain Health Center, in Jamaica Plain (1986–87); clinical psychology fellow at the Harvard Medical School Mental Health Center, in Cambridge (1987–89); and director of the Children's Mental Health Service of the Southern Jamaica Plain Health Center (1987–91).

In 1991, Gómez left the Boston area to accept a position as specialist at the Center for AIDS Prevention Studies in the department of epidemiology and biostatistics of the University of California at San Francisco (UCSF). In 1997, she was appointed assistant professor at the Center for AIDS Prevention Studies in the department of general internal medicine of UCSF, a position she continues to hold.

Gómez is the author or coauthor of more than 20 scholarly papers dealing with HIV and AIDS issues and has made presentations at more than 25 conferences and meetings in the United States, Canada, Japan, and Switzerland. She has served on a number of committees and other groups that deal with HIV and AIDS issues, including the Advisory Committee on Women of the Substance Abuse and Mental Health Service Administration, the Presidential Advisory Council on HIV and AIDS, the Scientific Advisory Panel of the Alan Guttmacher Institute, the Advisory Committee on the Prevention of HIV and STDs of the Centers for Disease Control and Prevention, and the Board of Directors of Planned Parenthood Federation of America.

Further Reading

Center for AIDS Prevention Studies. "Cynthia A. Gómez, Co-Director, CAPS." Available online. URL: http://www.caps.ucsf.edu/people/gomezbio.html. Downloaded on April 9, 2005.

"Gomez, Cynthia Ann." In *Who's Who among Hispanic Americans, 1994–95,* 3d ed., edited by Amy Unterburger, 334–335. Detroit: Gale Research, 1995.

Gomez, Frank A.
(1964–) *chemist*

Frank A. Gomez specializes in the study of main group elements, those elements in groups 1, 2, and 13–18 of the periodic table, as well as the use of capillary electrophoresis to study biological molecules and reactions. Capillary electrophoresis involves the use of thin-diameter glass tubes and electrical charges to separate molecules of different sizes and composition from each other.

Gomez was born on April 14, 1964, in Montebello, California, to parents of Mexican extraction. He studied at California State University at Los Angeles (CSULA), where he originally planned to major in physics. Largely through the influence of a dynamic professor, Dr. Thomas Onak, Gomez changed his major to chemistry, a field in which he received his B.S. in 1986. He continued his studies at the University of California at Los Angeles, where he earned his Ph.D. in chemistry in 1991. He then spent three years at Harvard University, in Cambridge, Massachusetts, as a postdoctoral student from 1991 to 1994, working under a Damon Runyon–Walter Winchell Cancer Research Fund scholarship. It was at Harvard, Gomez later wrote, that he began to see the ways in which chemistry could be connected to other fields of science, such as biology, connections that have become fundamental to his research.

Upon completing his postdoctoral studies at Harvard, Gomez accepted a position as assistant professor of chemistry at CSULA, where he was later promoted to associate professor in 1997 and to full professor in 2002. In 2003, he was also appointed visiting research associate at the California Institute of Technology (Caltech), in Pasadena, and director of the CSULA–Caltech Partnership for Research and Education in Materials Collaborative.

Gomez is the author of more than 45 articles, and, with his students and colleagues, he has presented more than 65 papers at professional meetings and conferences. He has been active in a number of professional and community organizations, having served as a member of the Committee on Education, the Task Force on Teacher Professional Development, and the Minority Affairs Committee of the American Chemical Society; the East Los Angeles Community Union Scholarship Committee of the City of Commerce, California; the Montebello (California) Unified School District Board of Education; and the

Frank A. Gomez is professor of chemistry at California State University at Los Angeles. *(Courtesy Dr. Frank Gomez)*

Eastmont (California) Community Center Board of Directors. Gomez's work has been recognized with a Hispanic Engineer National Achievement Award Conference Most Aspiring Scientist award (1993), a California Educator of the Year award from the California Junior Chamber of Commerce (1998), and a Society for Advancement of Chicanos and Native Americans in Science Undergraduate Institution Mentor Award (2003).

Further Reading

California State University at Los Angeles, Department of Chemistry. "About Dr. Gomez." Available online. URL: http://www.calstatela.edu/dept/chem/gomez/h-about.htm. Downloaded on April 18, 2005.

Society for Advancement of Chicanos and Native Americans in Science. "Dr. Frank A. Gomez—Chemist." SACNAS Biography Project. Available online. URL: http://64.171.10.183/biography/Biography.asp?mem=48&type=2. Downloaded on April 18, 2005.

Gomez-Cambronero, Julian
(1959–   ) *cell biologist*

Julian Gomez-Cambronero's research interests are related to essential biochemical changes that take place in healthy and abnormal cells. In one line of study, he has investigated the way in which chemical signals are transmitted between cells and across cell membranes in neutrophils, the most common type of white blood cells involved in the immune response system. He has also focused on the way in which proteins interact with one another and the ways in which molecules can be structured to inhibit the action of enzymes.

Gomez-Cambronero was born in Manzanares, Spain, on September 29, 1959. He attended the Complutense University, in Madrid, earning his B.S. in 1982, his M.S. in 1983, and his Ph.D. in biochemistry and immunology in 1986. He immi-grated to the United States to complete his postdoctoral training in cell biology at the University of Connecticut Health Center, in Farmington. After completing his postdoctoral studies in 1991, Gomez-Cambronero accepted an appointment as instructor in physiology at Connecticut's School of Medicine, also in Farmington, where he was later promoted to assistant professor. In 1995, he transferred to Wright State University, in Dayton, Ohio, where he became assistant professor in the department of physiology and biophysics. He was promoted to associate professor in 2000 and to full professor in 2004, a post he currently holds.

Gomez-Cambronero has published more than 60 papers in peer-reviewed journals, made more than 60 presentations at conferences and professional meetings, and is the author of five book chapters. He has also written a number of science fiction stories and articles in Spanish about science for the general reader. His honors include the New Investigator Research Award from the Donaghue Medical Research Foundation in 1992, the Frontiers in Physiology National Research Award from the American Physiological Society in 1996, and a STARS Scholar Distinguished Service Award from Ohio University, in Athens, in 1998. In 2005, Gomez-Cambronero was given the Sembrador Award from his hometown of Manzanares, Spain. The award is normally given to artists, musicians, poets, or historians but was conferred on Gomez-Cambronero to recognize his research on blood leukocytes (neutrophils).

Further Reading

"Gomez-Cambronero, Julian." In *American Men & Women of Science,* 21st ed., edited by Pamela M. Kalte and Katherine H. Nemeh, vol. 3, 217. Detroit: Thomson Gale, 2003.

Wright State University School of Medicine. "Wright State Researcher at the Forefront of New Field." Office of Public Relations. Available online. URL: http://www.med.wright.edu/whatsnew/

newsreleases/archive/2004/gomezcambronero. html. Posted on March 22, 2004.

Gómez-Pompa, Arturo
(1934–   ) *botanist*

Arturo Gómez-Pompa is one of the world's foremost authorities on the ecology of tropical rain forests. He is one of the first individuals to have drawn attention to the threat posed by the destruction of these valuable resources and to have pointed out some of the untapped resources available from rain forests, resources such as undiscovered chemicals that may be used as drugs. He has founded a number of institutions for the purpose of improving scientists' understanding of the nature of tropical rain forests and the ways in which they can be conserved and put to the best use.

Gómez-Pompa was born in Mexico City on October 21, 1934. He attended the Instituto México and Centro Universitario México, in Mexico City, from which he received his B.S. in 1951, and the National Autonomous University of Mexico (UNAM), from which he received his professional degree in biology in 1956 and his doctor of science in biology in 1966. Soon after receiving his bachelor's degree, Gómez-Pompa was appointed technical director of the Commission for the Study of Dioscorea Ecology of the Mexican National Institute of Forestry Research, a post he held from 1959 to 1965. His task on the commission was to survey tropical plants that might prove to have medicinal value and, hence, that could be developed by drug companies that were cosponsors of the commission's work. For one year during this period (1962–63), Gómez-Pompa also served as professor of botany at the National School of Agriculture and Graduate College in Chapingo, in the state of México.

In 1965, Gómez-Pompa was appointed professor in the department of botany at the UNAM, a post he held until 1980. During that period of time, he also served as executive director of the National Program of Ecology of Mexico's National Council of Science and Technology. In 1975, he founded the first of a number of institutions for the study of forest ecology, the National Research Institute of Biotic Resources in Xalapa, Veracruz, of which he served as director general until 1984. From 1984 to 1985, he worked as consultant director in the Division of Ecological Sciences at the United Nations Educational, Scientific and Cultural Organization and then in 1985, as Charles Bullard Research Fellow at Harvard University, in Cambridge, Massachussets.

In 1986, Gómez-Pompa was appointed professor of botany at the University of California at Riverside, marking the beginning of a long relationship with the university that has lasted to the present day. In 1998, he was named distinguished professor of botany at Riverside, and in 1999, he was made university professor. During his association with Riverside, Gómez-Pompa has continued to pursue his research on tropical forests in Mexico and other parts of Latin America. He has also served in a number of consulting positions. From 1991 to 1993, for example, he was adviser to the president of Mexico on tropical ecology issues. Among the other organizations that he has founded are the Programa de Acción Forestal Tropical, of which he was also chairman from 1993 to 1999; ProNatura, México, where he served as a member of the board of governors from 1993 to 2000; and the United States–Mexico Foundation for Science, of which he was acting executive director after its founding in 1992.

Among the awards presented to Gómez-Pompa are the Al Mérito Botánico Medal of the Botanical Society of Mexico (1978); the Alfonso L. Herrera Medal of the Mexican government for contributions to ecology and conservation in Mexico (1984); the Golden Arch medal of the Netherlands government for contributions to the conservation of natural resources (1984); the Luis Elizondo Prize in Science and Technology of the

Monterrey Technological Institute for Higher Education, Monterrey, Mexico (1993); the Tyler Prize for Environmental Achievement (1994); and the Chevron Prize in Conservation (1997). He has been elected to membership of the General Health Council of the Mexican Republic; the Third World Academy of Sciences; the Smithsonian Council of the Smithsonian Institution; the Advisory Committee to the House Committee on Science, Space, and Technology of the U.S. House of Representatives; and the Academy of Sciences of Latin America. He has had three plants named in his honor, *Rhamnus pompana, Opsiandra gomez pompae,* and *Marasmiellus gomez pompae.* He is the author or coauthor of more than 200 scholarly papers and the editor, coeditor, or author of four books.

Further Reading

"Arturo Gómez-Pompa." In *Contemporary Hispanic Biography,* edited by Ashyia N. Henderson, 121–123. Farmington Hills, Mich.: Thomson Gale, 2003.

University of Southern California. "1994 Tyler Laureate: Arturo Gomez-Pompa," Tyler Prize for Environmental Achievement. Available online. URL: http://www.usc.edu/admin/provost/tylerprize/tyler94.html. Downloaded on March 23, 2005.

Elma González is professor of organismic biology, ecology, and evolution at the University of California at Los Angeles. *(Photo by Herman Kabe)*

González, Elma
(1942–) *cell biologist*

Elma González is a biologist who studies the biochemical molecules that make up cells, especially the units known as organelles. Her latest research focuses on molecular changes that occur during the process of calcification in a group of algae known as the coccolithophorids. The coccolithophorids are the only known organisms with the ability to make calcium carbonate shells inside the cells of which they are made and then move those shells outside their cells to make an external cell cover, known as a coccosphere.

González was born on June 6, 1942, in Ciudad Guerrero, in the state of Tamaulipas, Mexico, within walking distance of the Mexican-U.S. border. She was the daughter of Efigenia and Nestor González, who were both field-workers who expected their children to leave school after eighth grade and join the family as pickers in the fields. Indeed, that was how González spent her summers, traveling from Texas to Nebraska to Illinois to Wisconsin to pick cotton, cucumbers, tomatoes, cherries, and other crops, causing her and her siblings to start school late each fall.

But González had plans for her life different from those of her parents' goals. She wanted to finish high school, go to college, and have a career. She took the first step in that plan by enrolling in Texas Woman's University (TWU), in Denton, after graduating from high school. She started out by majoring in medical technology, with the assumption that with that kind of practical training she would always be able to support herself. She soon found, however, that she could do more with her life and decided to pursue a career in biology. She eventually received her B.S. in biology and chemistry at TWU and took a job in the rheumatology unit at Southwest Medical School, in Dallas. Her experiences there convinced González that she wanted to continue her studies in biology, and she enrolled at Rutgers University, in New Brunswick, New Jersey, where she was granted her Ph.D. in cell biology in 1972.

For her postdoctoral studies, González spent two years at the University of California at Santa Cruz before accepting an offer to become assistant professor of cell biology at the University of California at Los Angeles (UCLA), where she has remained ever since. She was promoted to associate professor in 1981 and to full professor in 1993. She is now professor of organismic biology, ecology, and evolution at UCLA.

González has also been involved for more than 25 years in programs at UCLA that help minority students pursue careers in scientific research. She is director of the university's Minority Access to Research Careers (MARC) program, funded by the National Institutes of Health to support undergraduates as they complete their education and research projects in science. In 2005, González was chosen to receive UCLA's first Distinguished Teaching Award for "superb mentorship to undergraduate students engaged in research and/or creative scholarly projects."

Further Reading

"Gonzalez, Elma." In *American Men & Women of Science,* 21st ed., edited by Pamela M. Kalte and Katherine H. Nemeh, vol. 3, 219. Detroit: Thomson Gale, 2003.

Society for Advancement of Chicanos and Native Americans in Science. "Dr. Elma González—Cell Biologist." SACNAS Biography Project. Available online. URL: http://64.171.10.183/biography/Biography.asp?mem=51&type=2. Downloaded on April 22, 2005.

University of California at Los Angeles, Center for Academic and Research Excellence. "Faculty Profile: Dr. Elma Gonzalez." Available online. URL: www.care.ucla.edu/assets/images/Page_6.PDF. Downloaded on April 22, 2005.

Gonzalez, Paula
(Sister Paula Gonzalez)
(1932–) *biologist, environmentalist, futurist*

Sister Paula Gonzalez was trained as a biologist but has become a well-known environmentalist and student of the future of human society. She has given presentations on topics such as learning from the Earth, ecospirituality, renewable energy, and ecojustice.

Paula Gonzalez was born on October 25, 1932, in Albuquerque, New Mexico, to Emilia Sanchez and Hilario C. Gonzalez, of Mexican ancestry. She was born in a hospital operated by the Sisters of Charity, a religious organization founded in 1809 by Elizabeth Bayley Seton, also known as Mother Seton. Gonzalez was educated in schools operated by the organization and in 1948 received a scholarship to study at Mt. St. Joseph College, in Cincinnati, Ohio. She earned her B.A. in biology in 1952 and then returned to Albuquerque to teach biology at the Regina School of Nursing. She had planned to become a nun in the Sisters of Charity herself but decided to delay taking vows in order to help support her parents in their old age. She finally took her vows in 1954 and spent five years teaching biology at Seton High School in Cincinnati before continuing her studies at the Catholic University of America, in Washington, D.C. There, she earned her M.S. in 1962 and her Ph.D. in cell physiology in 1964. Upon completion of her graduate studies, Gonzalez was assigned to teach at her alma mater, the College of Mt. St. Joseph, where she worked her way up the ranks from assistant professor to associate professor to full professor. She also served as chair of the department of biology at Mt. St. Joseph from 1968 to 1973.

With the rise of the environmental movement in the early 1970s, Gonzalez began to consider the ways in which she could incorporate the goals of this movement with her own biology teaching. She eventually reached the conclusion that she wanted to spend more time out of the classroom, working on environmental projects and speaking about environmental issues. Thus, in 1975, her responsibilities at Mt. St. Joseph were reduced to half time, allowing her to pursue these other interests. One of her first activities was the construction of an energy-efficient building, which she called La Casa del Sol (House of the Sun), out of an old chicken coop. She and another nun moved into the building to demonstrate that a living space could be constructed making use of sound environmental principles. She later directed the construction of a second energy-efficient building called EarthConnection in west Cincinnati that is still open to visitors. Today, Gonzalez is affiliated with the Future Awareness Center, in Cincinnati, and calls herself a futurist-environmentalist-educator.

Further Reading

"Gonzalez, Paula." In *American Men & Women of Science,* 21st ed., edited by Pamela M. Kalte and Katherine H. Nemeh, vol. 3, 220. Detroit: Thomson Gale, 2003.

"Gonzalez, Sister Paula." In *Who's Who among Hispanic Americans, 1994–95,* 3d ed., edited by Amy Unterburger, 359. Detroit: Gale Research, 1995.

"Paula Gonzalez, SC, Ph.D.," Linking Contemplation with Social Justice, Faith with Action, Hill Connections. Available online. URL: http://www.hillconnections.org/ri/gonzalez0ap.htm. Downloaded on April 22, 2005.

Gonzalez, Rafael C.

(1942–) *digital image processing engineer, inventor*

Rafael C. Gonzalez is an internationally famous authority on digital image processing, pattern recognition, machine learning, and related technologies in which computers are used to scan, recognize, and interpret visual data. Among the devices he has invented are a machine for reading the license plates of moving vehicles, laser discs that can hold up to a trillion bytes of data, and a digital system for processing and collecting data used by the U.S. Navy.

Gonzalez was born in Havana, Cuba, on August 26, 1942, the son of Mercedes and Emérito R. González. He received his B.S.E.E. (bachelor of science in electrical engineering) from the University of Miami, in Coral Gables, Florida, in 1965 and his master's and Ph.D. in electrical engineering from the University of Florida, in Gainesville, in 1967 and 1970, respectively. Upon receipt of his doctorate, Gonzalez accepted a position with the University of Tennessee at Knoxville (UTK), where he remained throughout his academic career serving as assistant professor (1970), associate professor (1973), full professor (1978), IBM professor (1981), Distinguished Service Professor (1984), and, finally, professor emeritus in the department of electrical and computer engineering. During his tenure at Tennessee, Gonzalez served as chair of the department from 1994 through 1997 and founded the Image and Pattern Analysis Laboratory and the Robotics and Computer Laboratory at UTK. In 1982, he also founded a private company, Perceptics Corporation, that focuses on the development of image processing, laser disc storage technologies, and methods for using computer devices for visual interpretations.

Gonzalez is author or coauthor of more than 100 articles in peer-reviewed journals and five textbooks: *Pattern Recognition Principles* (with Julius T. Tou, 1974); *Digital Image Processing* (1977), now in its third edition (with Richard E. Woods); *Syntactic Pattern Recognition: An Introduction,* (1978); *Robotics: Control, Sensing, Vision, and Intelligence* (with K. S. Fu and C. S. G. Lee, 1987); and *Digital Image Processing Using MATLAB* (with Woods and Steven L. Eddins, 2003). Among the honors that Gonzalez has received are the UTK College of Engineering Faculty Achievement Award (1977), the UTK Chancellor's Research Scholar Award (1978), the Magnavox Engineering Professor Award (1980), the M. E. Brooks Distinguished Professor Award (1980), a Distinguished Alumnus Award from the University of Miami (1985), the Phi Kappa Phi Scholar Award (1986), the IEEE (Institute of Electrical and Electronic Engineers) Outstanding Engineer Award for Commercial Development in Tennessee (1987), the Albert Rose National Award for Excellence in Commercial Image Processing (1988), the B. Otto Wheeley Award for Excellence in Technology Transfer (1989), the Coopers and Lybrand Entrepreneur of the Year Award (1989), UTK's Nathan W. Dougherty Award for Excellence in Engineering (1992), the IEEE Region 3 Outstanding Engineer Award (1992), and the Automated Imaging Association National Award for Technology Development (1993).

Further Reading

"Gonzalez, Rafael C." In *American Men & Women of Science,* 21st ed., edited by Pamela M. Kalte and Katherine H. Nemeh, vol. 3, 220. Detroit: Thomson Gale, 2003.

University of Tennessee, Electrical and Computer Engineering. "Biographical Sketch." Available online. URL: http://www.ece.utk.edu/~gonzalez/rcgbio/. Downloaded on April 30, 2005.

Rafael C. Gonzalez is an internationally recognized authority on digital image processing, pattern recognition, machine learning, and related computer technologies. *(Courtesy of Rafael Gonzalez)*

Gonzalez-Lima, Francisco
(1955–   ) *behavioral neuroscientist*

Francisco Gonzalez-Lima earned his Ph.D. in neurological anatomy at the University of Puerto Rico's School of Medicine and has focused his research studies on problems in neuroanatomy (the structure of nerve cells), neurobiology (the function of nerve cells), physiological psychology (the physiological basis of human behavior), learning and memory, and neural mechanisms of behavior (changes in nerve cell structure and function that correspond to various types of behaviors).

Gonzalez-Lima was born in Havana, Cuba, on December 7, 1955, the son of Jacinta and Francisco González-Lima. Gonzalez-Lima attended Tulane University, in New Orleans, Louisiana, from which he received his B.S. in biology in 1976 and his B.A. in psychology in 1977. One of Gonzalez-Lima's advisers at Tulane, Dr. Joan C. King, encouraged him to concentrate his studies on the brain, which

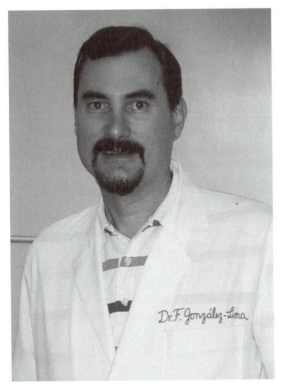

Francisco Gonzalez-Lima specializes in the study of changes in nerve cells that accompany learning, memory, and other mental functions. *(Photo by Susanna Douglas)*

he served as associate professor of neuroanatomy (1983–85), acting chair of the department (1985), associate director of neurosciences (1981–84), and director of neurosciences (1984–85).

In 1985, Gonzalez-Lima was recruited to join the faculty at the newly established College of Medicine at Texas A&M University, in College Station, as assistant professor in the department of anatomy and neurobiology. In 1990, Gonzalez-Lima joined the University of Texas at Austin's new Institute for Neuroscience as associate professor in the university's department of psychology. In 1997, he was promoted to full professor and made head of the Behavioral Neuroscience Division of the Institute for Neuroscience, positions he continues to hold. He is now George I. Sanchez Centennial Professor at Texas.

Gonzalez-Lima, his colleagues at Texas, and his students have been responsible for some crucial breakthroughs in the study of the structure and function of the nervous system. He produced some of the earliest research on metabolic changes that take place in the brain as the result of learning, conditioning, and sensitization and published the first book on images of neural modifications that occur in the brain as the result of such changes (*Advances in Metabolic Mapping Techniques for Brain Imaging of Behavioral and Learning Functions,* with T. Finkenstädt and H. Scheich, 1992). In recent years, he has focused on biochemical changes involved in the production of energy in the brain, especially in connection with the onset of Alzheimer's disease. He has also been at the forefront of the development and implementation of mathematical techniques for an improved understanding of neural anatomy.

Gonzalez-Lima has received a number of honors in recognition of his work, including a Merit Certificate "Escuela Superior Dr. Pila" from the Ponce School of Medicine (1981); teaching awards of the Medical Class of 1984 at the Ponce School of Medicine (1981) and the "Programa de Entrenamiento Científico Estudiantes Sobresalientes,"

strongly motivated the direction of his future career in science. During his final summer at Tulane, he worked in the university's neuroendocrinology laboratory, studying the effects of the endocrine system on the nervous system and vice versa.

In 1977, Gonzalez-Lima was accepted in the doctoral program at the University of Puerto Rico's School of Medicine, where he earned his Ph.D. in neurological anatomy in 1980. His doctoral studies dealt with changes that occur in single nerve cells when the brain is stimulated electrically. Upon receipt of his doctoral degree, Gonzalez-Lima was offered the position of assistant professor of anatomy at the newly formed Ponce School of Medicine, in Ponce, Puerto Rico. Over the next five years, also from Ponce (1982); a research fellowship of the Alexander von Humboldt Foundation, Germany (1982–83); Certificates of Recognition for Scientific Contributions from the Department of Public Instruction of Puerto Rico (1983 and 1985); visiting research professor travel awards sponsored by the German Science Foundation, the German Institute of Zoology, and the Technical University of Darmstadt, Germany (1984 and 1985); a visiting senior scientist award from the Medical Research Council Unit on Neural Mechanisms of Behaviour, Department of Anatomy, University College London, United Kingdom (1985); Best Lecture Award from the College of Medicine, Texas A&M University (1988–89); Lecture Award of Medical Class of 1993 of the College of Medicine, Texas A&M University; the first Neuroscience Award Lecture of the Texas A&M Chapter of the Society for Neuroscience (1990); and Outstanding Professor of the Year Award for 1991–92 of the National Chicano Health Organization (1992).

Further Reading

"Gonzalez-Lima, Francisco." In *American Men & Women of Science,* 21st ed., edited by Pamela M. Kalte and Katherine H. Nemeh, vol. 3, 230. Detroit: Thomson Gale, 2003.

"Gonzalez-Lima, Francisco." In *Who's Who among Hispanic Americans, 1994–95,* 3d ed., edited by Amy Unterburger, 365. Detroit: Gale Research, 1995.

The University of Texas at Austin, Department of Psychology. "Francisco Gonzalez-Lima, Ph.D." Available online. URL: http://www.psy.utexas.edu/psy/FACULTY/Gonzalez-Lima/Gonzalez-Lima.html. Downloaded on April 11, 2005.

Guerrero, Jorge

(1942–) *veterinary parasitologist*

Jorge Guerrero's research deals with the cultivation and study of parasites that prey on animals and the development of new chemical compounds that can

be used against such parasites. He has developed models for parasite-host relationships and diagnostic systems for studying parasitic infections that can be used in such studies.

Guerrero was born in Andahuaylas, Peru, on October 20, 1942. He studied at the Universidad Nacional Mayor de San Marcos (UNMSM), in Lima, Peru, where he earned his B.V.M. (bachelor's degree in veterinary medicine) in 1964 and his D.V.M. (doctorate in veterinary medicine) in 1965. Guerrero has said that he became interested in the subject of parasitology when he took a course in it during veterinary school and decided to make it his life's work. The first summer after completing the course, he traveled with a research team to the Andes Mountains to study sheep parasites, an assignment for which he was paid, he said, "a new pair of rubber boots." After graduation, Guerrero worked for two years as assistant professor of veterinary parasitology at UNMSM before winning a Fulbright Scholarship that allowed him to attend the University of Illinois at Urbana-Champaign (UIUC) for further study. He eventually earned his M.S. and Ph.D. at UIUC in 1969 and 1971, respectively.

Guerrero spent another year as research associate at UIUC before taking the post of professor of medical parasitology at the Escola Paulista de Medicina, in São Paulo, Brazil, where he remained from 1973 to 1976. He then accepted a job with the pharmaceutical firm of Johnson & Johnson in São Paulo, as manager of veterinary research. That assignment began a 30-year career with the pharmaceutical industry in which he concentrated on the development of antiparasitic chemical compounds for use against a host of diseases affecting animals. In 1976, he left Brazil to become director of preclinical research at Pitman Moore, Inc., a subsidiary of Johnson & Johnson, in Washington Crossing, New Jersey, where he remained until 1984. He then moved to the Merck Company, in Rahway, New Jersey, where he was associate director and, later, director of technical services. In 1993, Guerrero was offered the position of managing director of MSD AgVet Spain and Portugal, in Madrid, where he worked until 1996. He then returned to the United States where he took the post of senior director of technical services (1996–97) and then executive director of veterinary professional services at Merck AgVet, in Iselin, New Jersey (1997–2001). He is now head of veterinary services for the North American operations of Merial Pharmaceuticals. Since 1984, Guerrero has also served as adjunct professor of veterinary parasitology in the department of pathobiology of the School of Veterinary Medicine at the University of Pennsylvania, in Philadelphia.

Guerrero was honored with the Chairman's Award of the Merck Company in 1993 and has been elected a foreign member of the Royal Spanish Academy of Veterinary Sciences and an associate member of the Peruvian Academy of Veterinary Sciences.

Further Reading

"Guerrero, Jorge." In *American Men & Women of Science,* 21st ed., edited by Pamela M. Kalte and Katherine H. Nemeh, vol. 3, 367. Detroit: Thomson Gale, 2003.

University of Illinois at Urbana-Champaign. "Jorge Guerrero: The 'Life Cycle' of a Parasitologist . . ." *Life Sciences Alumni Newsletter* (Winter 2000–01). Available online. URL: http://www.life.uiuc.edu/alumni/guerrero.htm. Downloaded on on April 30, 2005.

Ana Sol Gutiérrez was trained as a chemist and a specialist in information technology and became active in politics in 1990, when she was elected to the Montgomery County (Maryland) Board of Education. *(Courtesy of Maryland State Delegate Ana Sol Gutiérrez)*

Gutiérrez, Ana Sol

(1942–   ) *aerospace engineer, politician, government official*

Ana Sol Gutiérrez was trained as a chemist and a specialist in information technology and worked for more than 30 years in the latter field. In midlife, she became interested in politics and was elected to the Montgomery County (Maryland) Board of Education in 1990 and to the Maryland House of Delegates in 2002.

Gutiérrez was born in Santa Ana, El Salvador, on January 11, 1942, to Ana de Sol and Jorge Sol Castellanos. She attended the University of Geneva, in Switzerland, from which she received her diploma in arts and letters in 1962 and Pennsylvania State University, from which she earned her B.S. in chemistry in 1964. She continued her studies at American University, in Washington, D.C., receiving her M.S. in technology of information in 1975. She also completed postgraduate studies in applied engineering at George Washington University.

From 1975 to 1981, Gutiérrez worked as a management consultant in South America, while also teaching computer science and engineering courses at the Universidad Simón Bolívar in Venezuela (1975–78) and the Universidad San Andrés in La Paz, Bolivia. In 1981, Gutiérrez returned to the United States and became district technical support manager at Wang Laboratories' Federal Systems Division. A year later, she left Wang to join Computer Sciences Corporation (CSC) as manager of the company's technical department, a post she held until 1985. She then accepted an offer to become senior associate in the Information Technology Center of Booz, Allen & Hamilton, Inc., a management and technology consulting firm. After two years with Booz, Allen & Hamilton, Gutiérrez was appointed senior systems engineer in the Technology Programs Division of Loral Aerosys, formerly Ford Aerospace, where she worked until 1992. She then returned to CSC as a senior consulting engineer.

In 1994, President Bill Clinton asked Gutiérrez to serve as deputy administrator of the U.S. Department of Transportation's Research and Special Programs Administration. When she left that position in 1996, she founded her own consulting firm, SOL Quality Systems, Inc., in Chevy Chase, Maryland. In 1999, Gutiérrez again returned to CSC as director and principal information technology consultant with its Strategic Information Technology Consulting group.

In 1990, Gutiérrez was elected to the Montgomery County Board of Education, the first Latina to have earned that post. She served on the board for four terms before deciding to run for the Maryland House of Delegates. She was elected to the house in 2002, the first Latina and the first El Salvadoran to have reached that high office in the state.

Gutiérrez has been active in a number of professional, community, and Hispanic organizations, including the Society of Hispanic Professional Engineers (SHPE), the Association for Computing Machinery (ACM), the National Management Association (NMA), and the National School Boards Association (NSBA). She has twice been selected as one of the 100 Most Influential Hispanics in the United States by *Hispanic Business Magazine* (1991 and 1996) and has received the Hispanic Achievement Award in Science from Apple Computers and SHPE (1993), the Outstanding Women in Nontraditional Careers award from *VISTA* magazine (1991), and the Outstanding Public Service and Leadership Award of the Maryland State Teachers Association (1999).

Further Reading

Apodaca, Sylvia P. "Ana Sol Gutiérrez." In *Notable Hispanic American Women,* edited by Diane Telgen, Jim Kamp, and Joseph M. Palmisano, 191. Detroit: Gale Research, 1998.

"Gutiérrez, Ana Sol." In *Who's Who among Hispanic Americans, 1994–95,* 3d ed., edited by Amy Unterburger, 379. Detroit: Gale Research, 1995.

House of Delegates, Maryland. "Ana Sol Gutiérrez." Available online. URL: http://mlis.state.md.us/Other/Roster/House.pdf. Downloaded on March 6, 2005.

Gutierrez, Orlando A.

(1928–   ) *aerospace engineer*

Orlando A. Gutierrez was trained as a mechanical engineer but spent most of his working life in the field of aerospace engineering. He was affiliated with the National Aeronautics and Space Administration (NASA) for 31 years. Gutierrez has also long been active in organizations designed to promote the role of Latinas and Latinos in the sciences, having served as treasurer and president of the Society of Hispanic Professional Engineers (SHPE).

Gutierrez was born in Havana, Cuba, on July 23, 1928, the son of Flora María Izaguirre and Antonio María Gutiérrez, the manager of a local newspaper. He attended a prestigious private school, Academia Baldor, from which he graduated in 1945. His parents then allowed him to leave Cuba to attend college in the United States, hoping for him to become a medical doctor. Instead, he enrolled at Rensselaer Polytechnic Institute, in Troy, New York, where he earned his B.S. in mechanical engineering in 1949. After graduation, Gutierrez accepted a job with the IBM World Trade Corporation as a mechanical engineer, working on projects in both the United States and Cuba. Two years later, he took a position as design and test engineer with the American Locomotive Company in Schenectady, New York, where he remained until 1961.

In that year, Gutierrez moved to NASA at its Lewis Research Center, in Cleveland, Ohio, as a researcher on heat transfer problems. Over time, his interests shifted more to aeronautical and space problems, eventually settling on jet acoustics (sound problems related to the use of jet engines). He authored more than 25 papers in peer-reviewed journals dealing with space power generation and jet noise suppression systems. Gutierrez remained at Lewis for two decades before moving from research to human resources, taking a job as manager of NASA's Hispanic Employment Program in Washington, D.C. In 1990, he moved to the agency's Minority University Program, where he served as manager until his retirement in 1992.

Gutierrez has garnered a number of honors for his scientific research and efforts on behalf of minority scientists, including SHPE's highest award, the Jaime Oaxaca Award; NASA's Equal Opportunity and Exceptional Services medals; the Medalla de Oro of the Society of Mexican American Engineers; and the Honor a Quien Honor Merece award of the U.S. Office of Personnel Management.

Further Reading

Bruno, Leonard C. "Orlando A. Guttierez." In *Notable Twentieth-Century Scientists,* edited by Emily J. McMurray, 831–832. Detroit: Gale Research, 1995.

Gutierrez, Orlando A. "Society of Hispanic Professional Engineers." In *Diversity in Engineering: Managing the Workforce of the Future,* 59–60. Washington, D.C.: National Academy Press, 2002.

Gutierrez, Peter L.
(Peter Luis Gutierrez)
(1939–   ) *biochemist, molecular biologist*

Peter Luis Gutierrez was trained as a physicist but has spent much of his life dealing with chemical and biological problems, such as the action of oxygen on essential chemicals that make up the body, the mechanisms by which chemotherapeutic agents (chemicals used to treat disease) work, and the new science of proteomics, the study of the structure and function of proteins.

Gutierrez was born in Montería, Colombia, on June 9, 1939, the son of Fanny and Pedro A. Gutiérrez. He immigrated to the United States for his college education, earning a B.S. in physics at Wheaton College, in Wheaton, Illinois, in 1962; his M.S. in physics from California State University in Los Angeles in 1971; and his Ph.D. in molecular physics at Southern Illinois University, in Carbondale, in 1973. After receiving his doctorate, Gutierrez spent one year as an instructor at Tulane University, in New Orleans, Louisiana, before taking a job as staff biophysicist at the National Biomedical ESR (electron spin resonance) Center at the Medical College of Wisconsin, in Milwaukee, a post he held until 1979. He was then appointed senior investigator at the National Cancer Institute–National Institutes of Health Baltimore Cancer Research Center, in Baltimore, Maryland. In 1982, he resigned from that position to become assistant professor at the University of Maryland Greenebaum Cancer Center (UMGCC), in Baltimore. Gutierrez has remained at Greenebaum ever since. He is currently professor of biochemistry and director of the UMGCC Proteomics Research Facility.

For more than 25 years, Gutierrez has been studying the behavior of free radicals in biological systems. Free radicals are atoms or molecules with at least one unpaired electron. They are highly reactive substances and are thought to be involved in a number of essential biological processes, such as the development of cancer and other disorders and the process of aging. Gutierrez's research has been focused on the chemical changes for which free radicals may be responsible in certain medical disorders, particularly the development of breast cancer, and the effects they may have on chemotherapeutic agents used to treat cancer.

Further Reading

"Gutierrez, Peter Luis." In *American Men & Women of Science,* 21st ed., edited by Pamela M. Kalte and Katherine H. Nemeh, vol. 3, 388. Detroit: Thomson Gale, 2003.

"Gutierrez, Peter Luis." In *Who's Who among Hispanic Americans, 1994–95,* 3d ed., edited by Amy Unterburger, 383. Detroit: Gale Research, 1995.

Gutiérrez, Sidney
(Sid Gutiérrez, Sidney McNeill Gutiérrez)
(1951–   ) *astronaut, engineer*

Sidney McNeill Gutiérrez is a graduate of the U.S. Air Force Academy and joined the U.S. astronaut corps in 1984. He flew on two spaceflight missions: STS-40, a Spacelab Life Sciences mission, and STS-59, a Space Radar Laboratory mission, of which he was commander. After leaving the astronaut corps in 1994, Gutiérrez joined the Sandia National Laboratories, in Albuquerque, New Mexico.

Gutiérrez was born in Albuquerque on June 27, 1951, to Sarah E. and Robert A. Gutiérrez, of Mexican ancestry. He attended Valley High School, in Albuquerque, where he graduated in 1969. He was then accepted at the U.S. Air Force Academy, in Colorado Springs, Colorado, where he earned his B.S. in aeronautical engineering in 1973. After completing his undergraduate pilot training

at Laughlin Air Force Base, in Del Rio, Texas, he stayed on as an instructor pilot in the T–38 aircraft from 1975 to 1977. In 1978, he was assigned to the 7th Tactical Fighter Squadron, at Holloman Air Force Base, in Albuquerque, where he flew F-16 aircraft. Three years later, Gutiérrez enrolled in the U.S. Air Force Test Pilot School, at Edwards Air Force Base in California, qualifying him to become a test pilot for the air force. Gutiérrez has also been certified a master parachutist by the air force, with more than 550 jumps to his credit.

Gutiérrez was selected by the National Aeronautics and Space Administration (NASA) as an astronaut in 1984 and went on active duty for NASA in June 1985. In addition to his two spaceflights, he has served in a number of support capacities, including commander of the Shuttle Avionics Integration Laboratory (SAIL), a program designed to test shuttle flight software; astronaut officer for shuttle software development, verification, and future requirements definition; and member of the support staff for shuttle flights STS-28, 30, 32, 33, and 34 and spacecraft communicator for flights STS-42, 45, 46, 49, and 52.

Gutiérrez left NASA and the astronaut corps in 1994 with the rank of colonel in the U.S. Air Force to become manager of the Strategic Initiatives Department at Sandia. He was later appointed manager of the Airborne Sensors and Integration Department in the laboratory's Exploratory Systems Development Center. In 2001, a new charter school in Roswell, New Mexico, was named for him, the Sidney Gutiérrez Middle School.

Further Reading

"Gutiérrez, Sidney (Sidney McNeill Gutiérrez)." In *Biographical Dictionary of Hispanic Americans,* 2d ed., edited by Nicholas E. Meyer, 124. New York: Checkmark Books, 2001.

Lyndon B. Johnson Space Center. "Astronaut Biography: Sidney M. Gutierrez." Available online. URL: http://www.jsc.nasa.gov/Bios/htmlbios/gutierrez-sm.html. Downloaded on April 18, 2005.

H

Hernández, Enrique
(1951–) *physician, medical researcher*

Enrique Hernández is a specialist in gynecological oncology, the study of cancer in the genital and reproductive systems of females. He is coauthor of one of the basic books in that field of research, *Manual of Gynecological Oncology.*

Hernández was born in Vega Baja, on the northern coast of Puerto Rico, on October 25, 1951, to Ana López and Nathaniel Hernández. He attended the University of Puerto Rico, from which he received his B.S. in biology magna cum laude in 1973 and his M.D. in 1977 from the university's School of Medicine. He did his internship and residency in obstetrics and gynecology at the Johns Hopkins Hospital, in Baltimore, Maryland, from 1977 to 1981. He was named assistant resident at the hospital in 1978 and chief resident in 1980.

Upon completion of his medical training, Hernández was offered a postdoctoral fellowship at the Johns Hopkins Oncology Center. He was made an instructor at the university's School of Medicine in 1981 and an assistant professor a year later. In 1983, Hernández was given a commission as major in the U.S. Army Medical Corps and assigned as chief of the gynecologic oncology services at Tripler Army Medical Center in Honolulu, Hawaii. After his discharge from the army in 1987, Hernández took a position as associate professor at the Medical College of Pennsylvania (MCP) in Philadelphia. He was promoted to full professor in 1989 and, in 1997, made professor of pathology. During his tenure at MCP, Hernández held a number of other appointments, including president of the medical staff at MCP (1992–93), director of the Division of Gynecologic Oncology at MCP (1987–98), senior vice chair of the department of gynecology and obstetrics (1995), and chief of the ob-gyn (obstetrics and gynecology) service at the Allegheny University Hospital for Women and at MCP.

In 1998, Hernández was offered the post of director of gynecologic oncology and director of the residency program in ob-gyn at the Temple University School of Medicine in Philadelphia. He has remained at Temple since that time, serving as professor of obstetrics, gynecology, and reproductive sciences and professor of pathology and laboratory medicine. In 2002, he was named Abraham Roth Professor and Chairman of Obstetrics, Gynecology, and Reproductive Sciences.

Hernández has coauthored two fundamental books in gynecologic oncology, *Manual of Gynecologic Oncology* (with Neil B. Rosenshein, 1989) and *Clinical Gynecologic Pathology* (with Barbara F. Atkinson, 1995). He has also published more than 100 scholarly papers and has given numerous lectures throughout the United States and in other parts of the world.

Among his many honors are the Frank G. Books award of Beta Beta Beta, the National Biological Honor Society (1973), the Council on Resident Education in Obstetrics and Gynecology award for teaching at the Medical College of Pennsylvania (1994), the Association of Professors of Obstetrics and Gynecology award for excellence in teaching (1998), and the Volunteer Achievement Award of the American Cancer Society Southwest Pennsylvania Division (2000). Hernández has also held a number of positions in professional organizations, such as president of the Obstetrical Society of Philadelphia, president of the Metropolitan Philadelphia Chapter of the American College of Surgeons, and president of the Society of Ibero–Latin American Medical Professionals.

Further Reading

"Enrique Hernández." In *The Hispanic American Almanac,* 3d ed., edited by Sonia G. Benson, 718. Farmington Hills, Mich.: Thomson Gale, 2003.
"Hernández, Enrique." In *Who's Who among Hispanic Americans, 1994–95,* 3d ed., edited by Amy Unterburger, 391. Detroit: Gale Research, 1995.

Hernández, John W.
(John Whitlock Hernández)
(1929–   ) *environmental engineer*

John Whitlock Hernández has been interested in a variety of environmental issues, many of which relate to water resources. His research has focused on problems such as the treatment of wastewaters, the management of wastewaters and endangered species, the desalination of water for drinking water purposes, and the development and use of water laws in the United States, in general, and of New Mexico, in particular.

Hernández was born in Albuquerque, New Mexico, on August 8, 1929. (Some sources list his birth date as August 17, 1929.) His family has a long and honorable tradition in the area dating to the days before New Mexico became a state. His grandfather, Benigno Cárdenas Hernández, was a member of the U.S. House of Representatives from 1915 to 1917 and from 1919 to 1921. His uncle, Ben Hernández, served as chief justice of the state court of appeals and U.S. ambassador to Paraguay from 1965 to 1968.

Hernández did his undergraduate studies at the University of New Mexico (UNM), in Albuquerque, where he earned his B.S. in civil engineering in 1951. He then enlisted in the U.S. Navy and served on active duty from 1951 to 1954. After being discharged, he continued to serve in the Navy Reserve until 1981, when he retired with

John W. Hernández served for the better part of four decades in the department of civil engineering at New Mexico State University. *(Courtesy Dr. John Hernández)*

the rank of captain in the Navy Civil Engineering Corps.

In 1954, Hernández returned to his studies, receiving his M.S. in sanitary engineering in 1959 from Purdue University, in Lafayette, Indiana. For his doctoral studies, he enrolled at Harvard University, in Cambridge, Massachusetts, earning his Ph.D. in water resources management in 1965. During the period between 1954 and 1963, Hernández also worked as assistant engineer for dam design with the New Mexico State Game and Fish Department, as an engineer for waterworks design with the state Engineers Office, and as associate engineer in the state Health Department.

In 1965, Hernández became associate professor in the civil engineering department at New Mexico State University (NMSU), where he was promoted to full professor in 1968. He remained at NMSU until his retirement in 1999, serving as dean of the School of Engineering from 1975 through 1980. One of his proudest accomplishments during this period was increasing the number of Hispanics, Native Americans, and women enrolled in engineering. He also was cofounder of the New Mexico Environmental Institute in 1970, an agency whose purpose is to improve understanding of New Mexico's natural resources and to make data on water, land, and biodiversity in the state available to scientists, land managers, and policymakers.

In 1981, Hernández took a leave of absence from NMSU to take the post of deputy administrator of the U.S. Environmental Protection Agency (EPA). During the last two months of his term at the EPA (March–May 1983), Hernández served as acting administrator of the agency. He then worked briefly at the U.S. Department of Energy before returning to NMSU in January 1984.

In addition to his academic and government appointments, Hernández has been a consultant to a number of state, national, and foreign governments. He was assistant to the state engineer of New Mexico from 1991 to 1999; consultant for Engineering-Sciences, Inc., in Bangkok, Thailand, Kuwait, and Beijing, China; and visiting professor in Malaysia and at the University of Auckland, New Zealand. He has been given the Governor's Award for Public Service (1980), the NMSU College of Engineering's Donald C. Roush award for teaching excellence (1990), the Outstanding Alumni Award from the civil engineering department of UNM (1992), and the UNM Zia Award (1998). In 1980, he was named the New Mexico Society of Professional Engineers' Engineer of the Year, and in October 2005, he was made an honorary member of the American Society of Civil Engineers.

Further Reading

College of Engineering, New Mexico State University. "Donor Profile of John Whitlock Hernandez." Supporters and Friends. Available online. URL: http://engr.nmsu.edu/supporters_friends/hernandez.htm. Downloaded on May 1, 2005.

"Hernandez, John W(hitlock)." In *American Men & Women of Science,* 21st ed., edited by Pamela M. Kalte and Katherine H. Nemeh, vol. 3, 655. Detroit: Thomson Gale, 2003.

"Hernández, John Whitlock." In *Who's Who among Hispanic Americans, 1994–95,* 2d ed., edited by Amy Unterburger, 327–328. Detroit: Gale Research, 1992.

Hernández, José
(1935–   ) *sociologist*

José Hernández is author of a groundbreaking book, *People, Power and Policy: A New View on Population,* which argues for a new approach to the development of Latin American nations, namely, better educational and economic opportunities for the citizens of those nations, rather than the imposition of birth control and foreign investment. He has long been an authority on the Puerto Rican community in the United States and the changes produced by migration from their home island to the mainland.

Hernández was born in Jersey City, New Jersey, on August 22, 1935. His parents were Blanca Alvarez Hernández, formerly a teacher in Utuado, Puerto Rico, and José Hernández, formerly a dentist in San Juan, who had come to the United States in the so-called Big Migration in the 1950s and early 1960s and settled in Jersey City. Hernández attended Xavier High School and Fordham University, in New York City, earning his B.A. and M.A. in 1958 and 1960, respectively. He then took a job as a seventh-grade teacher in Río Piedras, Puerto Rico, before deciding to go on to graduate studies at the University of Minnesota. He was awarded his Ph.D. in sociology by Minnesota in 1966.

For the next five years, Hernández lived in Brazil, where he worked as a community development adviser and visiting professor. His experiences during this period provided both the data and the ideas that later led to his book on community development in developing nations, *People, Power and Policy* (1974). When he returned to the United States in 1970, he accepted an appointment as associate professor in the department of sociology at the University of Arizona. He left Arizona in 1975 to accept a Fulbright Scholarship that allowed him to work with the government of Portugal in the decolonization of the country's African nations. He then returned to the United States, where he worked as an advocate for Native American students with the Western Interstate Higher Education Commission. His work there brought an invitation from the U.S. Commission on Civil Rights to work on a project for the development of social indicators of equality for women and minorities.

In 1976, Hernández moved to the University of Wisconsin at Milwaukee, where he served as professor of sociology until 1983. He then served for one year as research director at the Latino Institute in Chicago, where he produced a monograph on housing and employment patterns among Latinos in the city. During his tenure at Milwaukee, Hernández also served as chair of the Spanish Origin Advisory Committee to the U.S. Census Bureau. In 1984, Hernández was offered a position in the department of black and Puerto Rican studies at Hunter College in New York City, a post he held until his retirement in 2003. At Hunter, Hernández also served as coordinator of Puerto Rican studies until 1996.

In addition to *People, Power, and Policy,* Hernández has written a textbook, *Conquered Peoples in America,* now in its sixth edition, and the lead chapter in the four-volume encyclopedia *Handbook of Hispanic Cultures in the United States* (1994).

Further Reading

"Hernández, José." In *Who's Who among Hispanic Americans, 1994–95,* 3d ed., edited by Amy Unterburger, 394. Detroit: Gale Research, 1995.

"José Hernández." In *The Hispanic American Almanac,* 3d ed., edited by Sonia G. Benson, 719. Farmington Hills, Mich.: Thomson Gale, 2003.

J

José, Jorge V.
(1949–) *physicist*

Jorge V. José's research covers a diverse array of topics in theoretical physics, ranging from studies of the nature and theory of chaos, a system of extreme disorder, and the properties of condensed matter, with special emphasis on the phenomena of superfluidity (a state completely lacking in viscosity) and superconductivity (the flow of an electric current without resistance), to the fundamental properties of certain important biological systems, such as molecular motors (combinations of protein molecules that convert chemical energy into kinetic motion in cells).

José was born in Mexico City on September 13, 1949, the son of Adriana and Guillermo José. He attended the Universidad Nacional Autónoma de México (UNAM), receiving his B.S. in physics in 1971, his M.S. in physics in 1973, and his Ph.D. in physics in 1976. While studying for his doctorate, José was a research associate at the UNAM (1972–74) and at Brown University, in Providence, Rhode Island (1974–76). After receiving his Ph.D., he stayed on at Brown for one year as assistant research professor in physics. From 1977 to 1979, José studied at the James-Franck Institute at the University of Chicago as a James Franck Fellow. He was then guest scholar at the Yukawa Institute of Kyoto University, in Japan.

After completing his studies in Kyoto, José took the position of assistant research professor at Rutgers University, in New Brunswick, New Jersey (1979–80), before serving as professor titular B at the Instituto de Física at the UNAM in 1981. During the next year, he was a consultant in the Department of Corporate Research and Engineering at the Exxon Corporation. In 1984, José began a long affiliation with Northeastern University (NU), in Boston, when he accepted an appointment as assistant professor of physics. He was promoted to associate professor (1984) and later to full professor (1988) at NU before being named Matthews University Distinguished Professor in 1996. In 1995, José was also named director of the newly established Center for Interdisciplinary Research on Complex Systems (CIRCS). CIRCS is staffed by researchers from a variety of fields, including biology, chemistry, mathematics, mechanical engineering, and physics, with common interests in complex problems, such as nanotribology (the physics of friction at the nanoscale), glasses, superconductivity, molecular biophysics, protein motors, cardiac fibrillation, and neuroscientific modeling. José served as interim chair of NU's physics department from 2002 to 2004 and was named chair of the department in 2004. In the same year, José left Northeastern to become vice president for research at the State University of New York at Buffalo, in Buffalo, New York. In this position, he is responsible for management of all sponsored programs and research at Buffalo.

José is the author of more than 130 scholarly papers in physics and has given more than 200 invited talks in more than 20 countries. He has been honored with the Chercheur Étranger d'Haut Niveau et de Renommée Internationale of the French government (2002) and the Manuel Sandoval-Vallarta Award of the Metropolitan University of Mexico (2004). He has served as visiting professor and visiting scientist at a number of international institutions, including the Metropolitan University of Mexico; Schlumberger/Doll Research Center, in Ridgefield, Connecticut; Université de Neûchatel, Switzerland; Von Laue-Langevin Institut, in Grenoble, France; Centre d'Études Nucléaires de Scalay, France; Centro Atómico Bariloche, Argentina; Van der Waals Institute, University of Amsterdam, the Netherlands; and the Salk Institute for Biological Studies, La Jolla, California.

Further Reading

Center for Interdisciplinary Research on Complex Systems at Northeastern University. "Jorge V. José." Available online. URL: http://www.circs.neu.edu/members/jose.htm. Downloaded on April 12, 2005.

"Jose, Jorge V." In *American Men & Women of Science,* 21st ed., edited by Pamela M. Kalte and Katherine H. Nemeh, vol. 4, 155. Detroit: Thomson Gale, 2003.

"José, Jorge V." In *Who's Who among Hispanic Americans, 1994–95,* 3d ed., edited by Amy Unterburger, 424. Detroit: Gale Research, 1995.

Kalnay, Eugenia
(1942–) *meteorologist*

Eugenia Kalnay was formerly director of the Environmental Modeling Center (EMC) of the National Centers for Environmental Prediction, an agency of the National Weather Service. She is a specialist in numerical weather prediction, which involves the development of computer models of atmospheric dynamics. The quality of national weather forecasts improved markedly during her tenure at EMC, such that three-day forecasts are now, on average, at least as good as those for one-day forecasts available only 20 years ago.

Kalnay was born in Buenos Aires, Argentina, on October 1, 1942, the daughter of Susana Zwicky and Jorge Rodrigo Rivas. Her father died when Kalnay was 14 years old, and her mother became a strong influence in her life. Indeed, Kalnay's mother not only worked to make sure that Kalnay could have a college education but also directed her into the field of meteorology, rather than physics (which Kalnay favored), because there were more scholarships available in the field. Kalnay attended the University of Buenos Aires, from which she received her licentiate in science in 1965. Then, with the assistance of her principal professor at Buenos Aires, Rolando García, she was offered an opportunity to continue her studies at the Massachusetts Institute of Technology (MIT), in Cambridge, where she earned her Ph.D.

in meteorology in 1971, the first woman to receive that degree from MIT.

Upon completion of her doctoral studies at MIT, Kalnay returned to South America, where she was assistant professor of meteorology at the University of Montevideo, in Uruguay, from 1971 to 1973. Afterward, she went back to MIT as research associate and assistant (later associate) professor of meteorology. Kalnay left MIT in 1978 to become senior research associate at the National Aeronautics and Space Administration's (NASA) Goddard Space Flight Center, in Greenbelt, Maryland. In 1983, she was made branch chief of Goddard's Global Modeling and Simulation Branch, which is internationally recognized for the atmospheric and climate models that it has developed. During her tenure at Goddard, Kalnay developed an atmospheric and climate model known as the Fourth Order Global Model, which, for more than 15 years, was the basic model used for incorporating weather data and making weather forecasts.

In 1987, Kalnay left Goddard to join the National Oceanic and Atmospheric Administration as director of its Environmental Modeling Center (EMC), a division of the National Weather Service, located in Camp Springs, Maryland. All of the atmospheric and climate models used in weather forecasting by the National Weather Service and private organizations are developed by EMC, and it was improvements in these models that eventually led to greater accuracy in daily

Eugenia Kalnay is an expert in the field of numerical meteorology and computer modeling of meteorological phenomena. *(Courtesy Dr. Eugenia Kalnay)*

Bulletin of the American Meteorological Society in March 1996, the paper summarizes data from a large variety of sources, using many different measuring techniques, to provide a broad overview of the planet's climatic patterns. It eventually became the most cited research paper in the geosciences in the decades following its publication.

Kalnay left EMC in 1998 to take one of the most prestigious appointments in meteorology in the world, the Robert E. Lowry Chair of Meteorology at the University of Oklahoma, in Norman. After a year at Oklahoma, she was appointed professor and chair of the department of meteorology at the University of Maryland at College Park. In 2001, she was named distinguished university professor at Maryland, a post she continues to hold.

Among the honors Kalnay has received are the NASA Medal for Exceptional Scientific Achievement (1981), the Department of Commerce Silver Medal for outstanding leadership (1990), the Jule Charney Award of the American Meteorological Society (1995), and the Department of Commerce Gold Medal for the Reanalysis Project (1997). She has been elected a fellow of the American Meteorological Society, the National Academy of Engineering, the Academia Europaea, the Argentine National Academy of Physical Sciences, and the American Geophysical Union.

Further Reading

"Kalnay, Eugenia." In *American Men & Women of Science,* 21st ed., edited by Pamela M. Kalte and Katherine H. Nemeh, vol. 4, 189. Detroit: Thomson Gale, 2003.

"Kalnay, Eugenia." In *Who's Who among Hispanic Americans, 1994–95,* 3d ed., edited by Amy Unterburger, 427. Detroit: Gale Research, 1995.

University of Maryland. "Eugenia Kalnay." Available online. URL: http://www.atmos.umd.edu/~ekalnay/. Downloaded on April 12, 2005.

weather forecasts made available for the government, industry, and the general public. One of Kalnay's most notable achievements during her time at EMC was the publication of a scientific paper of which she was senior author, "The NCEP/NCAR 40-Year Reanalysis Project," (commonly known as the "reanalysis paper"). Published in the

L

Llamas, Vicente J.
(Vicente José Llamas)
(1944–) *physicist, science educator*

Vicente José Llamas is a solid-state physicist with special interest in problems of air pollution. He is also active in programs for the improvement of science education curricula and teaching methods, especially for young people from underrepresented minorities, such as Hispanics and blacks.

Llamas was born on February 15, 1944, in Boyles Height, a predominantly Hispanic neighborhood in Los Angeles. Although his Mexican-born parents had little formal education themselves, they strongly encouraged their three children to stay in school as long as possible and get the best education they could. Llamas was interested in mathematics and science early in his life, attracted especially by electrical appliances. At one point, he built his own stereo receiver with the help of his father.

After graduating from high school, Llamas entered Loyola Marymount University in Los Angeles intending to concentrate on some aspect of electricity. As he later wrote, at the time, he wanted to be an electrician and did not realize that majoring in electrical engineering was different from studying to become an electrician. He eventually discovered the difference and completed his studies for a B.S. in physics in 1966. He then received a scholarship to continue his studies in physics at the University of Missouri at Rolla.

The move from Los Angeles to Rolla proved to be quite traumatic. Whereas he was part of the majority population (Chicano) in Boyles Height, he was very much in the minority in Rolla, one of only two Latinos in his classes. He found that the people of Rolla knew very little about Latinos and decided that he could improve that situation by becoming active in a variety of community affairs.

Llamas eventually earned his M.S. in physics at Rolla in 1968 and his Ph.D. in physics two years later. While completing his doctoral studies, he worked as a science teacher at Cuba Middle School, outside Rolla, and as an instructor in the department of physics at the university. After completing his doctorate, Llamas applied to 268 colleges and universities, looking for a teaching position. He was finally offered a job as assistant professor at New Mexico Highlands University in Las Vegas, New Mexico. He was later promoted to associate professor in 1973 and to full professor in 1984. He retired in 1994 with the rank of emeritus professor of physics. Over a period of 24 years, Llamas spent only one year away from New Mexico Highlands when, in 1984, he was visiting professor of physics at the United World College of the Southwest. From 1978 to 1980, he also taught physics at the local West Las Vegas High School.

As is obvious from his history, Llamas has always had an interest in teaching science at all levels, from elementary school to university. Beginning in the mid-1980s, he became increasingly active in a variety of programs to promote the development of improved science education programs for precollege students. For example, he served as associate director and then director of the Science Education Resource Center at New Mexico Highlands from 1987 to 1990 and as assistant director and then director of the NSF (National Science Foundation) Young Scholars Program at the university from 1989 to 1991. In 1989, he founded the New Mexico Alliance for Science Education,

of which he served as chair from 1989 to 1991. He then became copresident of the New Mexico Partnership for Mathematics and Science Education, a post he continues to hold. Among other committees and groups on which he has served are the Governor's Writing Team on Systemic Change in Science and Math Education (1990–91); Los Alamos Summer Science Student Program (1991); New Mexico Council for the Advancement of Mathematics and Science Education, Alternatives in Science, Technology, and Mathematics Educa-

Vicente J. Llamas is a solid-state physicist with special interest in science education programs for young people from underrepresented minorities, such as Hispanics and blacks. *(Photo by Soile Cordova)*

tion (1992–present); the NSF Minority Institutes for Excellence Blue Ribbon Committee Member (1994–99); National Advisory Board of the National Urban League (1995–97); and National Association of State Science and Math Coalitions (1995–present).

Further Reading

"Llamas, Vicente José." In *Who's Who among Hispanic Americans, 1994–95,* 3d ed., edited by Amy Unterburger, 444. Detroit: Gale Research, 1995.

Society for Advancement of Chicanos and Native Americans in Science. "Dr. Vicente Llamas—Physicist." SACNAS Biography Project. Available online. URL: http://64.171.10.183/biography/Biography.asp?mem=156&type=2. Downloaded on March 8, 2005.

"Vicente José Llamas." In *The Hispanic American Almanac,* 3d ed., edited by Sonia G. Benson, 729–730. Farmington Hills, Mich.: Thomson Gale, 2003.

López, Ann
(Ann Aurelia López)
(1945–) *environmental scientist*

Ann Aurelia López was trained as an environmental biologist and has taught at San Jose City College for four decades. In 2002, she earned her Ph.D. in environmental science, the first Latina in the United States to have attained this degree.

López was born on May 17, 1945, in San Bernadino, California, to Billie Ann Whitaker and David Amado López. Her father was a Mexican American who "came from the wrong side of the tracks," while her mother was an Anglo-American from a wealthy southern family that had once owned slaves. She has written that she sometimes feels that her survival in life and later success are something of a miracle because of her biracial background.

López experienced many of the frustrations common to Latina and Latino teenagers in her high school years. Although she earned good grades, her counselor encouraged her to attend beauty school and forget about college. She ignored that advice, enrolled at the University of California at Riverside, and received her B.A. in biology in 1967. She then continued her studies at the University of California at Santa Barbara, receiving her M.A. in biology in 1969. Upon her graduation, she was offered a position in the department of biology at San Jose City College, which she accepted. Her entire academic career has been spent at San Jose, where she is now the senior member of the department.

López had never given any thought to continuing her education until 1994. Then, she became interested in the problems confronted by poor Mexican farmworkers in the United States. She decided to enroll in a new doctoral program in environmental studies offered by the University of California at Santa Cruz. She chose to study the traditional knowledge that farmworkers bring with them to their new jobs in the United States, with the goal of developing an educational curriculum for the children of those workers. López completed her research in 2002 and, at the age of 57, received her Ph.D. Although she continues to teach at San Jose State, she also hopes to carry on with her research on migrant farmworkers with the goal of helping to create healthier and safer working conditions for them.

The organizations to which López belongs reflect her interests and concerns. She is a member of the Latina Educators Association, the Ecological Society of America, Greenpeace, the Sierra Club, the Nature Conservancy, the Hunger Project, and Educators for Social Responsibility. She was named San Jose City College Student Body Humanitarian of the Year in 1989.

Further Reading

"Lopez, Ann Aurelia." In *Who's Who among Hispanic Americans, 1994–95,* 3d ed., edited by Amy Unterburger, 447–448. Detroit: Gale Research, 1995.

Society for Advancement of Chicanos and Native Americans in Science. "Dr. Ann López—Environmental Scientist." SACNAS Biography Project. Available online. URL: http://64.171.10.183/biography/Biography.asp?mem=157&type=2. Downloaded on March 7, 2005.

López, Jorge A.
(Jorge Alberto López)
(1955–) *physicist*

Jorge Alberto López's research deals with a variety of topics in physics, including the study of nuclear structure and nuclear reactions, heavy ion reactions (reactions between atoms of heavy elements that have lost one or more electrons), the nature of materials, and the construction of a radio telescope designed to study the concentration of neutral hydrogen gas in the Milky Way.

López was born in Monterrey, Mexico, on January 23, 1955, the son of Trinidad Gallardo and Fortino López. He attended the University of Texas at El Paso (UTEP), where he earned his B.S. in physics in 1977 and his M.S. in physics in 1979. López continued his studies at Texas A&M University, in College Station, where he was awarded his Ph.D. in physics in 1983. While still a student, López worked as a graduate teaching assistant at UTEP (1977–79) and at Texas A&M (1979–81) and as a graduate research assistant at Texas A&M's Cyclotron Institute. Upon completion of his doctoral studies, López spent two years in a postdoctoral program at the Niels Bohr Institute of the University of Copenhagen, in Denmark (1985–87), and two more years at the Nuclear Science Division of the Lawrence Berkeley National Laboratory, in Berkeley, California (1987–89).

In 1989, López was offered the position of assistant professor of physics at California State Polytechnic University, in San Luis Obispo. He served in that post until 1990, when he took a similar assignment at UTEP. He has since been promoted to associate professor (1994) and full professor (2000) and in 2001, was named Shumaker Professor of Physics at UTEP. López has also served as chair of the physics department since 2001, and from 1999 to 2001, he was assistant dean of the College of Science at UTEP.

López is the author of more than 65 articles, one book chapter, and two articles included in books. He is coauthor of the book *Lecture Notes on Phase Transitions in Nuclear Matter* (with C. O. Dorso, 2000) and the coeditor of *Heavy Ion Physics* (with E. Chavez, M. Moshinsky, and M. E. Borunda, 2002) and *Proceedings of the IV Latin American Symposium on Nuclear Physics* (with E. Chavez, M. Moshinsky, and M. E. Borunda, 2001). He has given more than 100 presentations at 40 national and international meetings, 11 regional meetings, and 46 seminars. He has also been the organizer of seven national, regional, and local conferences and served as chair for 15 sessions at national, regional, and local conferences.

Further Reading

"Lopez, Jorge Alberto." In *American Men & Women of Science,* 21st ed., edited by Pamela M. Kalte and Katherine H. Nemeh, vol. 4, 907. Detroit: Thomson Gale, 2003.

"Lopez, Jorge Alberto." In *Who's Who among Hispanic Americans, 1994–95,* 3d ed., edited by Amy Unterburger, 452. Detroit: Gale Research, 1995.

University of Texas at El Paso. Physics Department. "Jorge A. López, Chair and Shumaker Professor." Available online. URL: http://academics.utep.edu/Default.aspx?tabid=18741. Downloaded on April 13, 2005.

Lopez, Ramon E.
(1959–) *space physicist*

Ramon E. Lopez is a widely recognized authority on storms that occur in the magnetosphere, the region of space that is influenced by Earth's magnetic field. He is also interested in problems of science education at the college and precollege level, especially trends in physics education in the United States.

Lopez was born in Aberdeen, Maryland, on September 7, 1959. His parents were both from Puerto Rico, his father then serving as a surgeon in the U.S. Army, and his mother working as an elementary schoolteacher. He was strongly influenced as a young man, as were so many other young Americans, by the U.S. space program of the 1960s and 1970s and decided that he wanted to be a physicist. After his father retired from the army, the family moved to Freeport, Illinois, where he attended Pearl City High School. He never officially graduated from high school but rather "outgrew" the educational opportunities available to him there and entered the University of Illinois at Urbana-Champaign in 1976. Although he did poorly at first, he persevered and graduated with his B.S. in physics in 1980. For his graduate studies, Lopez chose Rice University, in Houston, Texas, eventually receiving his M.S. and Ph.D., both in space physics, in 1984 and 1986, respectively.

Upon completion of his studies at Rice, Lopez took a job as a researcher at Applied Research Corporation, in Landover, Maryland, operating under contract to the Johns Hopkins University Applied Physics Laboratory, located in Baltimore. He left that position in 1992 to become research associate in the department of astronomy at the University of Maryland at College Park (UMCP). Lopez remained affiliated with UMCP until 1999, also serving as assistant director for research at the university's East-West Space Science Center. Between 1994 and 1999, Lopez was also director for outreach and education programs of the American Physical Society, in College Park.

In 1999, Lopez left Maryland to take the post of C. Sharp Cook Distinguished Professor of Physics and chair of the department of physics at the University of Texas at El Paso (UTEP). He remained at UTEP until 2004, when he accepted an appointment as professor in the department of physics and space sciences at the Florida Institute of Technology, in Melbourne.

In addition to his research and teaching, Lopez has long been active in efforts to improve science education at the precollege level. In 2003, he was elected vice chair of the American Physical Society Forum on Education and in 2005, advanced to chair of the organization. He has also been co-organizer of the Introductory Calculus-Based Physics Course Conference, a meeting sponsored by the American Association of Physics Teachers to discuss the development of a physics course in which the use of calculus is a basic component. In addition, he was coprincipal investigator on a program for the development of a series of workshops on science education reform for space scientists and codirector of the Electric Space project, a program that produced a traveling museum exhibition about the space environment.

Lopez has authored more than 80 papers for refereed journals and another 90 papers for nonrefereed publications. His book *Storms from the Sun* (with Michael J. Carlowicz, 2002) has become very popular among both scientists and the general public. He has been honored with NASA (National Aeronautics and Space Administration) Group Achievement Awards (1990 and 1998), an Outstanding Service to Education award by the Montgomery County (Maryland) Public Schools (1992), the Scientist in Education Achievement Award of the Space Science Institute (1999), and the Nicholson Medal for Humanitarian Service to Science of the American Physical Society (2002). He was elected a fellow of the American Physical Society in 1999.

Further Reading

Florida Institute of Technology. "Homepage for Ramon E. Lopez." Available online. URL: http://my.fit. edu/~relopez/home.html. Downloaded on April 20, 2005.

Society for Advancement of Chicanos and Native Americans in Science. "Dr. Ramon E. Lopez—Physicist." SACNAS Biography Project. Available online. URL: http://64.171.10.183/biography/Biography.asp?mem=58&type=2. Downloaded on April 20, 2005.

Lugo, Ariel E.
(1943-   ) *ecologist*

Ariel E. Lugo is currently director of the International Institute of Tropical Forestry, a division of the U.S. Department of Agriculture's Forest Service, based in Río Piedras, Puerto Rico. He is a

Ariel E. Lugo is an authority on tropical forests and the response of tropical flora to changes brought about by human activities. *(Courtesy Ariel E. Lugo, director, FS International Institute of Tropical Forestry)*

widely recognized authority on a variety of ecological topics, including the ecology of tropical forest landscapes; dry, moist, wet, and rain forest mangroves; the flow of carbon and other nutrients through ecosystems; the responses of ecosystems to disturbance from humans and other sources; strategies for management and conservation of ecosystems; and tree plantations.

Lugo was born in Mayagüez, Puerto Rico, on April 28, 1943. He attended public schools in Mayagüez and graduated from the city's Hostos High School in 1959. He enrolled at the University of Puerto Rico, from which he received his B.S. in biology in 1963 and his M.S. in biology in 1965. For his doctoral studies, Lugo attended the University of North Carolina at Chapel Hill, receiving his Ph.D. in ecology in 1969.

Lugo's career has combined traditional teaching assignments at academic institutions with consultancies for many different organizations and administrative appointments with agencies concerned with ecological issues. His teaching jobs have included general zoology laboratory assistant (1962) and cell physiological laboratory assistant (1963) at the University of Puerto Rico; general botany laboratory assistant at the University of North Carolina at Chapel Hill (1967); assistant professor (1969–76) and associate professor (1976–79) in the department of botany at the University of Florida, in Gainesville; ad honorem lecturer and professor at the University of Puerto Rico (1974–76 and 1980–present); ad honorem associate professor at the department of public health, School of Medicine, University of Puerto Rico (1985–86); and graduate faculty member of the department of environmental, population, and organismic biology at the University of Colorado, in Boulder (1990–91). In 1992, Lugo was appointed acting director of the International Institute of Tropical Forestry in Río Piedras. In 1994, he was made director of the institute, a post he continues to hold.

Lugo's consulting experience has included assignments with a range of international, national, and state organizations, such as the U.S. Environmental Protection Agency (1974); U.S. Justice Department (1974 and 1978); United Nations Educational, Scientific and Cultural Organization, with service in Thailand (1975–76), Colombia (1978), and Malaysia (1983); Southwest Florida Regional Planning Council (1976 and 1977); County of Lee, Florida (1977); National Audubon Society, in the Bahamas (1977); National Wildlife Federation (1978); World Bank, in Mexico (1978); Organization of American States, in Venezuela (1979 and 1980); Florida Defenders of the Environment (1980–81); Islands Resources Foundation of the U.S. Virgin Islands (1980–present); Rhode Island University coastal zone program for tropical countries (1985–88); Yale Tropical Resources Institute (1985–90); Department of Forestry, School of Forest Resources and Conservation, University of Florida (1989); Center for Microbial Ecology, Michigan State University, in East Lansing (1993–98); Conservation Trust of Belize, at the Rio Bravo Reserve (1996); Organization for Tropical Studies Research Advisory Committee (1998–present); and the National Science Foundation Committee of Visitors, Division of Environmental Biology (1999).

Lugo's research has brought him to virtually every type of subtropical ecosystem, including palm wetlands in subtropical wet and subtropical rain forests in Puerto Rico; a sandhill forest, a freshwater prairie and associated lakes, and a forest in Gainesville, Florida; the Oklawaha River and floodplain wetlands in Florida; the Río Dulce region in Guatemala; a subtropical dry forest in Puerto Rico; mangrove forests of Florida; a tropical wet forest on the Osa Peninsula in Costa Rica; granite outcrops in southeastern United States; and a subtropical wet forest at El Verde in Puerto Rico.

Lugo has published more than 400 research papers and has been recognized with a Distinguished Service Award from the U.S. Department of Agriculture (1988), a Distinguished Scientist Award from the Forest Service (1990), a Distinguished Scientist Award from InterAmerican University in San Juan (1992), a Premio Amigos de la Planificación award from the Association of Planners of Puerto Rico (2003), a Meritorious Executive Rank Award from President George W. Bush (2004), a Distinguished Scientific Career Award, and an honorary doctorate from the University of Puerto Rico at Cayey (2004).

Further Reading

International Center for Tropical Ecology. "Ariel Lugo Delivers 1999 Jane and Whitney Harris Lecture." Newsletter 6, no. 2 (May 1999). Available online. URL: http://www.umsl.edu/-biology/icte/newsletter/may99.html. Downloaded on April 13, 2005.

"Lugo, Ariel E." In *American Men & Women of Science,* 21st ed., edited by Pamela M. Kalte and Katherine H. Nemeh, vol. 4, 947. Detroit: Thomson Gale, 2003.

Macagno, Eduardo R.
(Eduardo Roberto Macagno)

(1943–) *physicist, biologist, college administrator*

Eduardo Roberto Macagno earned his bachelor's and doctoral degrees in physics but became more interested in the field of biology over time and eventually spent more than 30 years as a teacher and researcher in that field. He has also filled some important administrative posts at the university level, most recently having been named founding dean of the division of biological sciences at the University of California at San Diego.

Macagno was born on June 13, 1943, in San Juan, Argentina. He immigrated with his family to the United States in 1956. Macagno attended the University of Iowa, at Iowa City, earning his B.A. in physics in 1963. For his graduate studies, he enrolled at Columbia University, in New York City, an institution with which he was to be affiliated in one capacity or another for the next 40 years. He received both his M.A. and his Ph.D. in physics at Columbia, in 1968 and 1973, respectively. During his postdoctoral studies at Columbia, Macagno became increasingly interested in biological questions and focused his research on both physics and neurobiology, the study of the biology of the nervous system, especially the brain.

Macagno's earliest teaching and research assignments were also at Columbia, where he was research associate in the department of physics from 1968 to 1970, research associate in the biological sciences from 1970 to 1973, assistant professor of biological sciences from 1973 to 1980, and associate professor of biological sciences from 1980 to 1985. In 1985, he was named professor of biological sciences at Columbia, a post he held until 2001. During his tenure at Columbia, Macagno was also codirector of the Neural Systems and Behavior Course at the Marine Biological Laboratory from 1980 to 1984 and instructor of the course from 1985 to 1994, chair of the department of biological sciences from 1991 to 1993, dean of the Graduate School of Arts and Sciences from 1993 to 2001, and associate vice president of Arts and Sciences for Research and Graduate Education from 1993 to 2001.

In 2001, Macagno retired from Columbia, earning the title of professor emeritus, and took on a new challenge at the University of California at San Diego (UCSD). He was named Richard C. Atkinson Professor and Founding Dean of the school's newly established Division of Biological Sciences. Macagno's task at UCSD has been to expand the scope and influence of the university's program in the biological sciences, with special emphasis on ties between the university and San Diego's biotechnology

Eduardo R. Macagno was trained as a physicist, spent much of his academic career on topics from the biological sciences, and was founding dean of the Division of Biological Sciences at the University of California at San Diego. *(University of California, San Diego)*

community and developing new ways in which practical applications can be found for break-throughs now occurring in the biological sciences. One of his first steps has been the creation of an Academy of Neuroscience for Architecture, whose purpose it is to find ways of making use of knowledge about the human brain to develop better living and working environments for structures such as classrooms, libraries, offices, and hospitals.

Further Reading

McDonald, Kim. "Dean of Biological Sciences at UCSD Named One of '50 Most Important Hispanics In Technology' for 2004." UCSD News. Available online. URL: http://ucsdnews.ucsd.edu/newsrel/science/mchispanicengineer.asp. Posted on April 19, 2004.

———. "Founding Dean Named for UCSD's Division of Biology." UCSD News. Available online. URL: http://ucsdnews.ucsd.edu/newsrel/awards/mcmacagno.htm. Posted on November 21, 2000.

Macari, Emir Jose
(1957–   ) *civil engineer*

Emir Jose Macari's research deals with the mechanics of granular materials, that is, changes that occur in materials made of small particles, particularly when stress is applied to those materials. An important application of his work has been in the study of certain types of soil that may tend to liquefy when stress is placed on them, as may occur during an earthquake. A recent study has focused on earthquake hazards that may exist in western Puerto Rico as a result of this condition.

Macari was born in Mexico City on July 22, 1957. His parents had met at Louisiana State University (LSU), in Baton Rouge, when both were students there. His father had come from Mexico originally and was studying chemical engineering at LSU, and his mother was Cuban American, studying nutrition at LSU. Macari was born in Mexico City after his parents had moved there, and he grew up in both Mexico and the United States, eventually graduating from high school in Mexico City. He returned to the United States for college, earning his B.S. in civil engineering, with a specialization in geomechanics, at Virginia Tech (Virginia Polytechnic Institute and State University), in Blacksburg. Macari went to the University of Colorado at Boulder for his graduate studies, receiving his M.S. and Ph.D., both in civil engineering with specializations in geomechanics, in 1982 and 1989, respectively.

During his years at Colorado, Macari held a number of jobs in industry, as a geotechnical engineer with McClelland Engineers, in Houston, Texas, in 1983; as a geotechnical staff engineer with Seafloor Engineers, of Houston, in 1984;

and as chief engineer with Kiso-Jiban Consultants, LTD, of Singapore, in 1985. After receiving his doctorate, Macari was research fellow for the National Aeronautics and Space Administration's Marshall Space Flight Center, in Huntsville, Alabama, before taking a job as assistant professor of civil engineering at the University of Puerto Rico, in San Juan. He was later made associate professor and director of the Civil Infrastructure Research Center at the university. In 1993, Macari was also made adjunct professor in the department of civil engineering at the University of Puerto Rico in Mayagüez, a title he continues to hold.

In 1993, Macari moved to Georgia Institute of Technology (Georgia Tech), in Atlanta, as associate professor of civil and environmental engineering. Two years later, he was also given an appointment in the School of Public Policy at Georgia Tech, posts he held until 1999 when he was named Bingham C. Stewart Distinguished Professor and chair of the department of civil and environmental engineering at LSU. He left LSU in 2004 to become dean of the College of Science, Mathematics, and Technology at the University of Texas at Brownsville, a position he continues to hold.

Macari is the author of more than 50 peer-reviewed articles and has been awarded more than $3 million in research grants. He has been honored with an Illustrious Visitor Certificate from the department of chemistry and chemical engineering of the National University of the South, in Bahía Blanca, Argentina, as well as Distinguished Visitor Certificates from the Mexican cities of Boca del Río and Veracruz. He was awarded the Best Journal Paper of the Georgia Tech School of Engineering in 1998 and was named Aldo Leopold Leadership Fellow in 2001 and a member of the Mexican National Academy of Engineering in 2004.

Further Reading

Aldo Leopold Leadership Program. "Emir Jose J. Macari Ph.D." Fellows Directory. Available online. URL: http://www.leopoldleadership.org/content/fellows/search-detail.jsp?id=70. Downloaded on April 18, 2005.

Society for Advancement of Chicanos and Native Americans in Science. "Dr. Emir Jose Macari—Civil Engineer." SACNAS Biography Project. Available online. URL: http://64.171.10.183/biography/Biography.asp?mem=59&type=2. Downloaded on April 18, 2005.

University of Texas at Brownsville and Texas Southmost College. "UTB/TSC Selects Macari to Lead College of Science, Math and Technology." Office of News and Information. Available online. URL: http://blue.utb.edu/newsandinfo/news/archive/2004_07_26%20new%20dean.htm. Downloaded on April 18, 2005.

Maidique, Modesto A.
(Modesto Alex Maidique)
(1940–) *electrical engineer, inventor, college administrator*

Modesto Alex Maidique was trained as an electrical engineer and has worked in both the academic and corporate worlds in a variety of positions. He is currently president of Florida International University, which claims to be "the fastest growing research university in the United States," a status attributable to a considerable degree to the initiatives Maidique has implemented during his tenure there. He has been awarded three patents for semiconductor devices.

Maidique was born on March 20, 1940, in Havana, Cuba. His mother, Hilda Rodríguez Sarabia, was a home economics teacher who had earned her education degree in Havana and completed postgraduate work in education at Columbia University, in New York City. His father was Modesto Maidique, a former congressman and senator in Cuba with a doctorate in education from the University of Havana. Maidique attended elementary schools in Havana, New York City, and Corpus

Christi, Texas, and graduated first in his class from Ruston Academy in Havana, claimed to be Cuba's most prestigious prep school. He attended the Massachusetts Institute of Technology (MIT), in Cambridge, earning his B.S., M.S., M.E.E., and Ph.D. in electrical engineering, with a specialization in solid-state physics, in 1962, 1964, 1966, and 1970, respectively. He later completed the Program for Management Development at Harvard University, also in Cambridge, receiving his P.M.D. there in 1975.

Maidique's first academic appointments were at MIT, where he was teaching assistant (1967) and instructor (1967–69) in the department of electrical engineering. While still working on his doctorate, however, he also became involved in the corporate world, founding with three other engineers a company called Nova Devices, Inc., in Wilmington, Massachusetts. He served as vice president and general manager of the company until 1976, when he left to join the faculty at the business administration department of the Harvard Business School as assistant professor. In 1981, he left Harvard to become associate professor in the engineering management department at Stanford University, in Stanford, California. Three years later, Maidique was appointed professor of management at the University of Miami (UM), in Coral Gables. At UM, he was also cofounder and director of the Innovation and Entrepreneurship Institute—an organization that conducts research on small businesses, entrepreneurship, and technological innovation and fosters entrepreneurship and economic development in the state of Florida—and executive director of the UM Venture Council/MIT Enterprise Forum—an advisory and support program to showcase entrepreneurial companies and offer them expert counsel and advice. In 1986, Maidique was chosen to become the fourth president of Florida International University, in Miami.

Maidique has continued to remain active in the business world. He was president and chief executive officer of Collaborative Research, Inc.,

a company that develops methods and materials used in genetic research (1981–83), and general partner in American Technology Fund and Hombrecht & Quest Venture Partners, venture capital funds that invest in high-technology companies (1984–present).

In recognition of his academic and business accomplishments, Maidique has been awarded a Best Paper Award by the Institute of Electrical and Electronics Engineering Circuits Conference (1972); the Lincoln-Marti Citizenship Award of the U.S. Department of Health, Education, and Welfare (1973); the Industrial Engineering Management Departmental Teaching Award of Stanford University (1983); and the PICMET (Portland International Center for Management of Engineering and Technology) '01 Award (2001). He is the author of 10 research papers in peer-reviewed journals and the author or coauthor of or contributor to 11 books in the field of electrical engineering and business management.

Further Reading

Florida International University. "Modesto Maidique." College of Business Administration. Available online. URL: http://cba.fiu.edu/web/eg/mgmt/maidique.htm. Downloaded on January 3, 2005.

Lion Strategy Advisors. "Dr. Modesto Maidique." Advisor Network. Available online. URL: http://www.lionstrategy.com/wcms/index.php?id=7,14,0,0,1,0. Downloaded on April 20, 2005.

"Maidique, Modesto A." In *Who's Who among Hispanic Americans, 1994–95,* 3d ed., edited by Amy Unterburger, 475. Detroit: Gale Research, 1995.

Mares, Michael A.
(Michael Allen Mares)
(1945–   ) *mammologist*

Michael Allen Mares is widely regarded as the world's primary authority on the natural history of desert rodents. For 20 years, he was director of the

Sam Noble Oklahoma Museum of Natural History and professor in the department of zoology at the University of Oklahoma, in Norman.

Mares was born in Albuquerque, New Mexico, on March 11, 1945, the son of Rebecca Gabriela Devine and Ernesto Gustavo Mares, of Mexican heritage. After graduation from high school, he enrolled at the University of New Mexico in Albuquerque, with plans to follow a premedical program. During his sophomore year, however, he changed his mind and decided to major in zoology instead. One of the factors affecting this decision was his experiences on field trips conducted as part of his college courses. He found that he was fascinated by the opportunity of getting out into the field and learning about plants and animals in their natural habitats.

After receiving his B.S. in biology from New Mexico in 1967, Mares completed his M.S. in zoology at Fort Hays Kansas State University in 1969. He then earned his Ph.D., also in zoology, at the University of Texas in Austin in 1973. During the last two years of his doctoral studies at Texas, Mares also served as adjunct professor of zoology at the Universidad Nacional de Córdoba, Argentina, in 1971, and at the Universidad Nacional de Tucumán, also in Argentina, in 1972. He returned to Tucumán in 1974 for one year as visiting professor of ecology.

Mares's first job after receiving his Ph.D. was at the University of Pittsburgh, in Pennsylvania, where he served first as assistant professor and later as associate professor in the department of biological sciences from 1973 to 1981. In 1981, he accepted an appointment as associate professor of zoology at the University of Oklahoma, in Norman, and associate curator of mammals at the university's Stovall Museum (later renamed the Sam Noble Oklahoma Museum of Natural History). Mares spent the rest of his academic career at Oklahoma, where he later became professor of zoology and director of the museum. He retired in 2003 and was named distinguished research professor in the department of

zoology and distinguished research curator at the Sam Noble museum.

Mares's field studies have focused on desert mammals and the mechanisms they have evolved for surviving in relatively inhospitable environments. His doctoral research dealt with the ways in which different types of desert rodents develop similar methods of adapting to desert conditions over long periods of time. He also became interested in the ecology of tropical mammals and traveled to Brazil and Argentina to conduct his field studies. In recognition of his work, Mares has had three animals named after him: *Maresomys boliviensis,* a Bolivian rodent; *Tonatia saurophila maresi,* a neotropical bat; and *Lukoschus maresi,* a parasitic mite that lives on neotropical rodents.

Mares was also very successful as a museum administrator. He realized early in his career that museums had to change the way they presented

Michael A. Mares is one of the world's authorities on desert rodents and was director of the Sam Noble Oklahoma Museum of Natural History for more than 20 years. *(Sam Noble Oklahoma Museum of Natural History)*

information to the general public, making exhibits more interactive and more interesting to visitors. In the 1990s, he oversaw a massive development program at the university's natural history museum that involved a fund-raising project of more than $50 million. The design and mission of the new museum turned out to be very successful, dramatically increasing the number of people visiting the museum each year.

Mares is the author or editor of 10 books, including *The Mammals of Oklahoma* (1989), *Latin American Mammalogy: History, Biodiversity and Conservation* (1991), *Encyclopedia of Deserts* (1999) and *A Desert Calling: Life in a Forbidding Landscape* (2002). He has received honors and awards from a number of organizations, such as the University of Oklahoma Associates' Distinguished Lectureship Award (1984), the Don W. Tinkle Research Excellence Award of the Southwestern Association of Naturalists (1989), the Outstanding Academic Book for 1999 of *Choice Magazine* (for *Encyclopedia of Deserts*), the C. Hart Merriam Award of the American Society of Mammalogists (2000), and the first Otis Sullivant Award for Perceptivity (2002). In 2002, he was inducted into the Oklahoma Higher Education Hall of Fame and was elected a fellow of the American Association for the Advancement of Science.

Mares has also held a number of special appointments in the United States and other nations, including serving as a representative to the United Nations Committee on the Progress of Science and Technology for Development in Latin America and the Caribbean (1989); cochair of the International Programs Committee for SYSTEMATICS 2000, a national plan to revitalize teaching and research in systematics; consultant to the Interim Working Group on Biodiversity, Ecology, and Ecosystems for the treaty on global climate change (1992); member of the U.S. Department of the Interior's Advisory Board for the Center for Biological Diversity; member of the Advisory Board of the Claes Olrog Institute of Conservation Biology in Tucumán, Argentina; and member of the Smithsonian Institution Council.

Further Reading

Mares, Michael A. *A Desert Calling: Life in a Forbidding Landscape.* Cambridge, Mass.: Harvard University Press, 2002.

"Michael Allen Mares." In *The Hispanic American Almanac,* 3d ed., edited by Sonia G. Benson, 736. Farmington Hills, Mich.: Thomson Gale, 2003.

"Mares, Michael Allen." In *Who's Who among Hispanic Americans, 1994–95,* 3d ed., edited by Amy Unterburger, 481. Detroit: Gale Research, 1995.

Sanchez, Brenna. "Michael A. Mares." In *Contemporary Hispanic Biography,* edited by Ashyia N. Henderson, 132–134. Farmington Hills, Mich.: Thomson Gale, 2003.

Marquez, Victor E.
(Victor Esteban Marquez)
(1943–) *medicinal chemist, inventor*

Victor Esteban Marquez is acting chief of the Laboratory of Medicinal Chemistry at the National Cancer Institute (NCI) of the National Institutes of Health (NIH), in Bethesda, Maryland. His research specialty is nucleosides and nucleotides, the components of nucleic acids such as DNA (deoxyribonucleic acid) and RNA (ribonucleic acid). The goal of this research is to find out how these compounds are implicated in the development of cancerous cells and how that information can be used to prevent and/or treat cancer.

Marquez was born in Caracas, Venezuela, on August 7, 1943. He was educated at the Central University of Venezuela, in Caracas, where he earned his B.S. in pharmacy in 1966. He continued his graduate studies in the United States at the University of Michigan, in Ann Arbor, from which

Victor E. Marquez is acting chief of the Laboratory of Medicinal Chemistry at the National Cancer Institute of the National Institutes of Health, in Bethesda, Maryland, where he studies the role of nucleic acids in the growth of cancerous cells. *(Courtesy Victor Marquez)*

he received his M.S. and Ph.D., both in medicinal chemistry, in 1968 and 1970, respectively. He spent a year in a postdoctoral fellowship at the NCI of the NIH in 1970–71 before returning to Venezuela to serve as research director in chemistry at Labs Cosmos, in Caracas. In 1977, he returned to NCI as visiting scientist, a post he held until being named to the permanent position of senior scientist in 1987. He has remained with NCI since that time.

Marquez is the author of more than 250 publications and holder of more than 20 patents on chemical compounds and chemical procedures that he has developed in his research. Among the patented compounds are substances that have shown the ability to inhibit allergic reactions, to reduce or inhibit the activity of the human immunodeficiency virus, and to inhibit the growth of cancer cells.

Further Reading

Center for Cancer Research, National Cancer Institute. "Scientists: Victor E. Marquez, Ph.D." Available online. URL: http://ccr.cancer.gov/staff/staff.

asp?profileid=5808. Downloaded on May 2, 2005.

"Marquez, Victor Esteban." In *American Men & Women of Science,* 21st ed., edited by Pamela M. Kalte and Katherine H. Nemeh, vol. 5, 222. Detroit: Thomson Gale, 2003.

Márquez-Magaña, Leticia
(1963–   ) *molecular biologist*

Leticia Márquez-Magaña studies the molecular mechanisms that cause a particular gene to be turned on or off, thereby beginning or stopping the transcription of a genetic message that will lead to the production of necessary proteins in the cell.

Márquez-Magaña was born in Sacramento, California, on August 15, 1963. Her parents are from two small towns in the state of Zacatecas, Mexico—Jalpa and Tepechitlán. She first became interested in science when she was still quite young, fascinated, as she later wrote, by media portrayals of "distinguished men with wild white hair, running around the laboratory in white coats." She decided she wanted to be part of that scene, although the all-girls Catholic school that she attended offered only the bare minimum of science courses. In fact, it was not until she began taking science classes at Stanford University, in Stanford, California, that she was able to take advantage of the best of science instruction and to begin to realize her own potential as a scientist. In spite of her weak preparation in the sciences, Márquez-Magaña persevered at Stanford and earned her B.S. and M.S. in biological sciences in 1986. She then went on to the University of California at Berkeley, where she earned her Ph.D. in biochemistry in 1991. From 1991 to 1994, Márquez-Magaña worked as a postdoctoral fellow in molecular pharmacology at Stanford University.

Upon completion of her postdoctoral studies, Márquez-Magaña was hired by San Francisco State University, where she has worked her way up the ranks to the position of full professor. Her accomplishments have been acknowledged by a number of organizations. She received a Presidential Award for Promising Teachers and Scholars in 1996, was featured in a 1999 issue of *Latina* magazine and a television program, "Profiles of Excellence," was honored in a television "Salute to Prominent Bay Area Latinos," and was awarded a National Mentor Award by the American Association for the Advancement of Science in 2001.

Leticia Márquez-Magaña is a molecular biologist at San Francisco State University researching the biochemical factors involved in the transcription of genetic messages in the synthesis of proteins. *(Photo by Christine Jegan)*

Further Reading

"Marquez-Magaña, Leticia Maria." In *Who's Who in America—2005,* edited by Karen Chassie, 2,981. New Providence, N.J.: Marquis Who's Who, 2004.

San Francisco State University. "Dr. Leticia Márquez-Magaña." Márquez-Magaña Lab. Available online. URL: http://userwww.sfsu.edu/~magana/about/LM-M.htm. Downloaded on April 20, 2005.

Society for Advancement of Chicanos and Native Americans in Science. "Dr. Leticia Márquez-Magaña—Molecular Biologist." SACNAS Biography Project. Available online. URL: http://64.171.10.183/biography/Biography.asp?mem=63&type=2. Downloaded on April 20, 2005.

Martínez, Cleopatria
(1948–) *mathematician*

Cleopatria Martínez has taught mathematics in the Maricopa County (Arizona) community colleges since 1985. Prior to that time, she taught high school in Denver, Colorado, and was professor of mathematics at Auraria Community College in Denver.

Martínez was born on April 21, 1948, in Las Vegas, New Mexico. Her family was of Mexican-American heritage dating back to the days before New Mexico was part of the United States. Martínez grew up in U.S. government housing projects in Denver with her mother, Mary Jane Martínez, a younger brother, and a younger sister. Although her mother usually had jobs outside the home, her family survived on welfare, often living far below the poverty level. Martínez's mother, with only a third-grade education, was unable to help Martínez with her schoolwork. Still, Martínez did well at Smedley Elementary School, Horace Mann Junior High School, and North High School in Denver and was able to enter the University of Denver in 1967. This latter accomplishment was significant because, as Martínez later wrote, her teachers and counselors constantly reminded her of her minimal chance of graduating from high school and going on to college. She discovered that she was likely to have greater success with mathematics, which seemed to have rules that applied to everyone, compared to English and history, where she was never sure what one had to do to succeed.

Martínez was awarded her B.S. in mathematics from Denver in 1971 and then went on to the University of Colorado at Boulder, from which she received her M.S. in mathematics in 1976. She then continued her studies at Colorado and was granted her Ph.D. in mathematics in 1985. Given her difficult financial background, it was necessary for her to work while she pursued her graduate degrees. She taught mathematics in the Denver public schools from 1970 to 1974 and was professor of mathematics at the Denver Auraria Community College from 1974 to 1984. When she finally completed her doctoral studies, she accepted an appointment at Scottsdale Community College, one of the 10 institutions that make up the Maricopa County community college system. She is now professor of mathematics and chair of the department of mathematics at Phoenix College, also a Maricopa County community college.

Further Reading

"Martínez, Cleopatria." In *Who's Who among Hispanic Americans, 1994–95,* 3d ed., edited by Amy Unterburger, 490. Detroit: Gale Research, 1995.

Society for Advancement of Chicanos and Native Americans in Science. "Dr. Cleopatria Martínez—Mathematician." SACNAS Biography Project. Available online. URL: http://64.171.10.183/biography/Biography.asp?mem=65&type=2. Downloaded on March 9, 2005.

Martinez, Joe L., Jr.
(1944–) *neuroscientist*

Joe L. Martinez, Jr., earned his bachelor's and master's degrees in psychology and then concentrated on the field of physiological psychology for his doctoral work. In his research, he has focused on the neural basis of many psychological phenomena, such as the neurobiology of learning, memory, and sleep, as well as the study of Chicano psychology.

Martinez was born in Albuquerque, New Mexico, on August 1, 1944, of Mexican ancestry. He attended the University of San Diego, in California, where he earned his B.A. in psychology in 1966. He went to New Mexico Highlands University, in Las Vegas, for his graduate studies, receiving an M.S. in psychology in 1968. He then enrolled at the University of Delaware, in Newark, for his doctoral studies, earning his Ph.D. in physiological psychology in 1971. Physiological psychology is a science that deals with the biological basis of learning, memory, emotions, and other psychological phenomena.

Following receipt of his doctorate, Martinez completed four postdoctoral programs, the first in the field of neurobiology at the Worcester Foundation for Experimental Biology, in Shrewsbury, Massachusetts (1970–72); the second, also in the field of neurobiology, in the Frontiers in Teaching and Research Program at the Marine Biological Laboratory at Woods Hole, Massachusetts (1974); the third in psychobiology at the University of California at Irvine (1975–77); and the fourth at Organon's CNS Pharmacology Laboratories, in Oss, the Netherlands (1979). He later completed a fifth postdoctoral program as a Ford Foundation Senior Fellow in behavioral neurobiology at the Salk Institute in La Jolla, California (1982–83).

Concurrently with his postdoctoral appointments, Martinez held a series of teaching and research appointments, the first at California State College at San Bernardino, where he was assistant professor (1972–76) and associate professor (1976–77) of psychology. These appointments overlapped with similar posts at the University of California at Irvine, where Martinez was visiting

assistant professor in the Program in Comparative Cultures (1975–76), visiting associate professor in the department of psychobiology and the Program in Comparative Cultures (1976–77), and associate research psychobiologist and lecturer in the department of psychobiology (1977–82).

In 1982, Martinez was appointed professor in the department of biology at the University of California at Berkeley, a post he held until 1995. During his tenure at Berkeley, he was also professor in the Graduate Group in Endocrinology (1985–95), professor in the Graduate Group in Neurobiology (1986–95), head of the Biopsychology Group (1987–90), and faculty assistant to the vice chancellor for affirmative action (1990–92). In 1995, Martinez left Berkeley to take the Ewing Halsell Distinguished Chair in Biology at the University of Texas at San Antonio (UTSA), a position he continues to hold. He has also been director of the Division of Life Sciences at UTSA (1995–2001), associate vice provost for research (2001–present), codirector of the University of Texas Health Science Center at San Antonio (UTHSCSA, 2003–present), and director of the Cajal Neuroscience Institute (2003–present). Martinez has held a number of other positions at UTHSCSA, including member of the graduate faculty in the department of pharmacology (1998–present), member of the Aging Research and Education Center (1997–present), member of the Nathan Shock Aging Center (1997–present), member of the faculty team for Fundamentals of Neuroscience (2002–03), and member of the Executive Research Committee (2003–05).

Martinez is the author of more than 160 scholarly papers and editor or coeditor of five books: *Chicano Psychology* (1977), *Neurobiology of Sleep and Memory* (with R. R. Drucker-Colin, J. L. McGaugh, and R. A. Jensen, 1977), *Endogenous Peptides and Learning and Memory Processes* (with R. A. Jensen, R. B. Messing, H. Rigter, and J. L. McGaugh, 1981), *Learning and Memory: A Biological View* (with R. Kesner, 1986), and *Neurobiology: Learning and Memory* (with R. Kesner, 1998).

Martinez is a popular speaker, having been invited to address more than 70 colloquia throughout the United States, Canada, the Caribbean, Germany, Mexico, the Netherlands, and Switzerland. He has been honored with the University of California's Raza Recognition Award (1986); the McNair Trustee Award of the University of California, Berkeley (1994); the American Association for the Advancement of Science Mentor Award for Lifetime Achievement (1994); the Million Dollar Scholar Award of the University of Texas at San Antonio (1998); the National Hispanic Science Network on Drug Abuse Outstanding Mentorship Award (2001); the Association of Neuroscience Departments and Programs 2003 Education Award; and the National Hispanic Network on Drug Abuse 2004 National Award of Excellence in Research by a Senior Investigator.

Further Reading

Association of Neuroscience Departments and Programs. "2003 Award for Education in Neuroscience." Available online. URL: http://www.andp.org/activities/awards/education/2003a.htm. Downloaded on April 13, 2005.

"Martinez, Joe L., Jr." In *American Men & Women of Science,* 21st ed., edited by Pamela M. Kalte and Katherine H. Nemeh, vol. 5, 247. Detroit: Thomson Gale, 2003.

University of Texas at San Antonio, Department of Biology. "Joe L. Martinez, Jr." Specialized Neuroscience Research Programs. Available online. URL: http://bio.utsa.edu/SNRP/bio_martinez.html. Downloaded on April 13, 2005.

Martínez, Richard I.
(Richard Isaac Martínez)
(1944–   ) *physical chemist, inventor*

Richard Isaac Martínez's research deals with methods for the study of complex organic reactions, especially those involving ozone and other chemical compounds that occur in the atmosphere. Since 1992, he has worked at the National Institute of General Medical Sciences, where he has been scientific review administrator in the Office of Scientific Review.

Martínez was born in Havana, Cuba, on August 16, 1944, the son of Susan and Joseph Louis Martínez. He earned his B.S. in chemistry at McGill University, in Montreal, Canada, in 1964, and his Ph.D. in physical chemistry at the University of California at Los Angeles (UCLA) in 1976. Prior to completing his doctoral degree, Martínez worked as a lab assistant at Dupont of Canada, Ltd. (1962); as a teaching research assistant at San Diego State University (1965–67); as a chemist at the Shell Chemical Company (1967–70), in Torrance, California; and as a research chemist at UCLA (1971–76).

Martínez took a position as research chemist at the National Institute of Standards and Technology (NIST) in the U.S. Department of Commerce, in Gaithersburg, Maryland, in 1976. Martínez's research at NIST focused on the use of mass spectrometry (MS), an instrumental technique for the identification of chemical compounds based on differences in their molecular weights. This research was used to study the products of the reaction between compounds of sulfur and ozone, between unsaturated hydrocarbons and ozone, and among a variety of nitrogen-containing compounds found in the atmosphere and ozone. For this work, Martínez received the Bronze Medal Award for Outstanding Scientific Achievement of the U.S. Department of Commerce. He also received the I-R 100 Award of *R&D Magazine* for a patent he received on a method for removing sulfur from flue gases produced in industrial operations, a process known as the Martinez-Herron desulfurization process.

Further Reading

"Martinez, Richard Issac." In *American Men & Women of Science,* 21st ed., edited by Pamela M. Kalte and

Katherine H. Nemeh, vol. 5, 246. Detroit: Thomson Gale, 2003.

"Martinez, Richard Issac." In *Who's Who among Hispanic Americans, 1994–95,* 3d ed., edited by Amy Unterburger, 739. Detroit: Gale Research, 1995.

Medina, Miguel A., Jr.
(Miguel Angel Medina, Jr.)
(1946–   ) *civil and hydraulic engineer*

Miguel Angel Medina, Jr.'s research deals with a range of water-related problems, including the flow of surface and subsurface water, the transport and interaction of dissolved substances in water, mathematical models for water quality, wetlands and groundwater models, and the development of water models that can be used for the purposes of risk assessment and decision making in water quality situations.

Medina was born in Havana, Cuba, on December 9, 1946. He attended Ruston Academy, in Havana, until he was 14 years old. He did his undergraduate studies at the University of Alabama, at Tuscaloosa, where he earned his B.S.C.E. (bachelor of science in civil engineering) and M.S.C.E. (master of science in civil engineering) in 1968 and 1972, respectively. His doctoral studies were completed at the University of Florida, in Gainesville, where he was awarded his Ph.D. in water resources and environmental engineering sciences in 1976. Prior to completing his graduate studies, Medina worked as a consultant at the University of Florida Industrial and Experimental Station; assistant post engineer for design and construction at the Third U.S. Army headquarters at Fort McPherson, in Atlanta, Georgia; researcher on water pollution at the University of Alabama; and researcher on urban stormwater at the University of Florida.

In 1976, Medina was appointed assistant professor in the department of civil and environmental engineering at Duke University, in Durham, North Carolina. He was later appointed to associate professor (1981) and full professor (1998) at Duke. In 1984, Medina was also Visiting Fulbright Scholar at Monash University, in Melbourne, Australia. He is currently director of the International Honors Program of the School of Engineering and codirector of the School of Engineering's joint master's degree program with Duke's Fuqua School of Business. Medina has taught postgraduate courses on urban hydrology for the United Nations Educational, Scientific and Cultural Organization in Costa Rica, the Dominican Republic, El Salvador, Guatemala, Honduras, and Panama. He has also worked with hydrologists and water professionals in the United States and Argentina to develop better links between the two nation's water programs. Medina has been awarded the U.S. Environmental Protection Agency's William Simpson Keller Prize, the Earl I. Brown II Outstanding Civil Engineering Faculty Award of the Duke University chapter of Chi Epsilon, the School of Engineering Distinguished Faculty Teaching Award, and the Award Plaque of the E.I. Du Pont de Nemours Company for "outstanding contributions and dedication toward furthering the science of environmental modeling."

Further Reading

Edmund T. Pratt, Jr., School of Engineering, International Honors Program. "Miguel Medina, Professor of Civil and Environmental Engineering, Pratt School of Engineering." Available online. URL: http://ceeweb.egr.duke.edu/~medina/Medina/index.html. Downloaded on May 2, 2005.

"Medina, Miguel A., Jr." In *Who's Who among Hispanic Americans,* 2d ed., edited by Amy Unterburger, 428. Detroit: Gale Research, 1992.

"Medina, Miguel Angel, Jr." In *American Men & Women of Science,* 21st ed., edited by Pamela M. Kalte and Katherine H. Nemeh, vol. 5, 313. Detroit: Thomson Gale, 2003.

Mesa-Lago, Carmelo
(1934–   ) *economist*

Carmelo Mesa-Lago is a highly respected economist who specializes in Latin American issues. He has written or edited more than 60 books and 200 scholarly articles and served as consultant to governmental and nongovernmental agencies in the United States, Latin America, and other parts of the world.

Mesa-Lago was born on August 11, 1934, in Havana, Cuba, the son of Ana María Lago and Rogelio Mesa. He attended the University of Havana's School of Law, from which he received his LL.M. in civil law in 1956. He then attended the School of Law at the University of Madrid, in Spain, where he earned his LL.D. degree in labor and social security in 1958. After completing his doctoral degree in Madrid, Mesa-Lago accepted a joint appointment as professor of labor and social security at the University of La Salle and the University of Villanueva, both in Havana. In 1959, he also became head of the law department and member of the board of directors at the Cuban Bank of Social Insurance in Havana. In 1961, he left Havana to become assistant professor of social security and labor law at the University of Madrid, a post he held for one year. He then immigrated to the United States, where he served as research associate in the department of economics at the University of Miami, Florida.

Mesa-Lago next began a long association with the University of Pittsburgh, Pennsylvania, by joining the university's Center for Latin American Studies as assistant director and its department of economics as assistant professor. He was later promoted to associate director of the center and associate professor in 1970; director of the center in 1974, a post he held until 1986; and professor of economics in 1976, a title he held until 1980. Mesa-Lago served as research professor at the University Center for International Studies at the University of Pittsburgh from 1980 to 1999, when he

retired from the university with the title of Distinguished Service Professor Emeritus on Economics and Latin American Studies.

During his academic career, Mesa-Lago also held appointments at more than a dozen universities and institutes in a half dozen countries around the world, including as visiting professor at Oxford University, in England, in 1977–78; research associate at the Instituto Torcuato Di Tella in Buenos Aires, Argentina, in 1986; visiting researcher at the Instituto Universitario Ortega y Gasset in Madrid, in 1991, 1998, and 2003; Fulbright Distinguished Lectureship in Social Sciences at the Centro Latinoamericano de Economía Humana in Montevideo, Uruguay, in 1995; and Alexander von Humboldt Researcher at the Max-Planck-Institut für ausländisches und internationales Sozialrecht in Munich, Germany, in 1991–92 and 2002.

Mesa-Lago has served as a consultant on social security and pension reform in more than two dozen countries in Latin America, Asia, and western Europe. He has also consulted on these issues for a number of governmental and nongovernmental agencies, such as the U.S. Agency for International Development, the Organization of American States, the Inter-American Foundation, the U.S. State Department, the U.S. Department of Labor, the Interamerican Development Bank, the World Bank, and a number of United Nations agencies.

Among Mesa-Lago's long list of honors and awards are his selection by the *Miami Herald* as one of the 20 most prominent Cuban Americans in 1983, the Middle Atlantic Council of Latin American Studies' Arthur Whitaker Prize for best book on Latin America in 1983 (*The Economy of Socialist Cuba: A Two Decade Appraisal*), the Bicentennial Medallion of the University of Pittsburgh (1987), the University of Pittsburgh President's Distinguished Senior Research Award (1991), the Alexander von Humboldt Collaborative Research Award on Economies in Transition (1997), the Homage of Organización Iberoamericana de Seguridad Social in 2004, and the Homage of the Institute of

Cuban Studies for life work on the Cuban economy in 2004.

Further Reading

"Carmelo Mesa-Lago." In *The Hispanic American Almanac,* 3d ed., edited by Sonia G. Benson, 743. Farmington Hills, Mich.: Thomson Gale, 2003.

"Mesa-Lago, Carmelo." In *Who's Who among Hispanic Americans, 1994–95,* 3d ed., edited by Amy Unterburger, 529. Detroit: Gale Research, 1995.

Towns, Elizabeth, and Gustavo Guerrero. "Homenaje a Carmelo Mesa-Lago." *Encuentro de la Cultura Cubana,* nos. 34/35 (Autumn/Winter 2004).

Mexía, Ynés
(Ynés Enriquetta Julietta Mexíia, Ynés Mexía de Reygades)
(1870–1938) *naturalist*

Ynés Enriquetta Julietta Mexía was a naturalist and collector of botanical specimens who started her profession late in life but still managed to accumulate more than 150,000 samples of plant material that have proved to be invaluable in later botanical studies.

Mexía was born in the Georgetown section of Washington, D.C., on May 24, 1870. Her father, Enrique Mexía, was a member of the Mexican consulate to the United States, and her mother, a housewife who cared for six children from a previous marriage, as well as Ynés. Mexía came from a distinguished Mexican family that included General José Antonio Mexía, who had served in the Mexican senate and had been involved in the political uprisings in Mexico in the early 1830s. When Mexía was still a young child, her parents divorced, and she moved with her mother and siblings to Limestone County, Texas, where the family owned a large ranch on the site of what was to become the modern-day city of Mexia, Texas.

In 1886, the Mexía family left Texas to return to the East Coast, settling first in Philadelphia and then in the province of Ontario, Canada. During this time, Mexía was educated at local Quaker schools until she was old enough to enter St. Joseph's Academy, in Emmitsburg, Maryland, where she remained until 1887. She then went to Mexico City, where she lived with her father for the next 10 years.

In 1897, Mexía married Herman Lane, a Spanish-German merchant, who died only seven years later. In 1907, she remarried, this time to Augustín A. de Reygades. That marriage lasted only a year, and, after her divorce, Mexía moved to San Francisco, California, where she lived largely in isolation for more than a decade.

In 1921, she decided to make a new beginning with her life and enrolled at the University of California at Berkeley. The turning point in this experience occurred when she took a course in botany and discovered that she was fascinated by plants. After three years at Berkeley, she set out on her own to begin collecting plant specimens. She traveled through the Mexican states of Chihuahua, Guerrero, Hidalgo, Jalisco, Nayarit, Oaxaca, Puebla, and Sinaloa and through much of the western United States, including Alaska, Arizona, California, Nevada, and Utah, as well as making two trips to South America. Of the 150,000 specimens she eventually collected, about 500 were previously unknown, and two were species that had never been observed.

Mexía became a widely popular lecturer on botany, and her collections are now preserved in a number of locations, including the California Academy of Sciences, in San Francisco; Catholic University, in Washington, D.C.; the Field Museum of Natural History, in Chicago; Gray Herbarium of Harvard University, in Cambridge, Massachusetts; the Philadelphia Academy of Natural Sciences; the University of California at Berkeley; and various botanical gardens and museums in Copenhagen (Denmark), Geneva and Zurich (Switzerland), London, Paris, and Stockholm (Sweden). Mexía died on July 12,

1938, after becoming sick on a collecting trip to Oaxaca.

Further Reading

García, María-Cristina. "Mexía de Reygades, Ynés." Handbook of Texas Online. Available online. URL: http://www.tsha.utexas.edu/handbook/online/articles/view/MM/fme54.html. Downloaded on November 15, 2005.

"Ynes Mexia." In *Latino Women of Science,* edited by Leonard Bernstein, Alan Winkler, and Linda Zierdt-Warshaw, 34–35. Maywood, N.J.: Peoples Publishing Group, 1998.

Molina, Mario
(Mario Jose Molina)
(1943–) *atmospheric chemist*

Mario Jose Molina shared the 1995 Nobel Prize in chemistry for his role in discovering the fate of chlorofluorocarbons (CFCs) in the atmosphere and the damage caused by the products of their dissolution on the Earth's ozone layer. CFCs are a class of compounds with a host of industrial uses that are very stable in the lower atmosphere (troposphere) but that break down into potentially dangerous products in the upper atmosphere (stratosphere). The ozone layer is a thin band of ozone, a form of oxygen, located about 9–25 miles (15–40 kilometers) above the Earth's surface.

Molina was born in Mexico City on March 19, 1943, to Roberto Molina Pasquel and Leonar Henríquez de Molina. His father was an attorney who taught part time at the Universidad Nacional Autónoma de México (UNAM) and was later ambassador from Mexico to Australia, Ethiopia, and the Philippines. Molina became interested in science at an early age, at one point converting an unused bathroom in the family home into a chemical laboratory. He was fortunate enough to have an aunt who was a chemist and who encouraged and fostered his interest in the subject.

At the age of 11, Molina was sent to Europe to continue his studies, as was often the case among wealthy Mexican families. During his time overseas, he vacillated between a career in music and continuing his studies in chemistry. He eventually chose the latter and in 1960 returned to Mexico and enrolled as a chemical engineering major at UNAM. At the time, he was deficient in many of the subjects he would have liked to study, such as mathematics and physics, so he could not enroll in the chemistry curriculum. The chemical engineering curriculum was the closest Molina could come to majoring in chemistry.

Molina was awarded his bachelor's degree in chemical engineering in 1965 and chose to continue his graduate studies at the University of Freiberg, in Germany. After receiving the equivalent of an M.S. from Freiberg in 1967, Molina realized that he was still deficient in some of the fundamental courses in chemistry, physics, and mathematics, which had not been available at UNAM, and decided to pursue additional graduate studies in the United States. He first returned to Mexico for a year, where he served as assistant professor of chemistry at UNAM, before enrolling as a doctoral student at the University of California at Berkeley. At Berkeley, he found the well-rounded mix of courses for which he had been looking, in addition to many opportunities to explore the forefront of chemical research. In 1972, he was awarded his Ph.D. for a study of energy changes in molecules that take place during chemical and photochemical (light-induced) changes.

After a year of postdoctoral research at Berkeley, Molina began a second postdoctoral program at the University of California at Davis under the direction of F. Sherwood Rowland (with whom Molina was eventually to share the 1995 Nobel Prize). Among the possible research problems that Rowland suggested to Molina was a study of the fate of CFCs in the upper atmosphere. CFCs had first been discovered in the late 1920s by the

American mechanical engineer–turned–chemist Thomas Midgley, Jr. They had rapidly become widely popular for a variety of commercial applications, including refrigeration, air-conditioning, aerosols, and blowing agents. Production of CFCs in the United States mushroomed from about 2.2 million pounds (1 million kilograms) in 1935 to just over 1.5 billion pounds (700 million kilograms) in 1985.

In the early 1970s, there was relatively little concern about the possible environmental impacts of CFCs. The compounds were so stable that they were known to remain unchanged in the troposphere for hundreds or thousands of years. Still, some chemists realized that they would ultimately migrate into the stratosphere, where they would be exposed, some 10 miles above the Earth's surface, to a greater concentration of solar radiation. And that solar radiation would probably be energetic enough to cause CFC molecules to break apart. What, then, would the products of that reaction be, and how, if at all, would those products affect the natural components of the atmosphere, such as oxygen and nitrogen?

Within a short time, Molina and Rowland had found the answer to that question. They demonstrated that solar energy causes CFC molecules to decompose into a variety of chemical products, one of which is atomic chlorine (a single atom of chlorine). Atomic chlorine is a very active chemical species with the ability to react with ozone molecules in the atmosphere, causing them to break apart into ordinary molecules of oxygen.

This discovery was therefore environmentally significant for two reasons. First, ozone in the upper atmosphere has the ability to absorb certain types of radiation from sunlight, which, if they reach Earth's surface, can cause serious damage to plant and animal life. Reductions in the concentration of ozone in the upper atmosphere, then, may pose a serious threat to all life on Earth. Second, when a chlorine atom attacks and

Mario Molina was corecipient of the 1995 Nobel Prize in chemistry for his research on chemical factors involved in destruction of the Earth's ozone layer by members of the chlorofluorocarbon family of organic compounds. *(© The Nobel Foundation)*

destroys a molecule of ozone, it is not itself used up. Instead, it lives on to attack another ozone molecule, and another, and another. Indeed, a single chlorine atom may cause the decomposition of a thousand or more ozone molecules before being carried away by some other chemical process.

Rowland and Molina published their first scientific paper on CFCs on June 28, 1974, a paper that was to form the basis for the Nobel Prize they received more than 20 years later. The two researchers continued their studies of CFCs and ozone, expanding and refining their understanding of the chemical changes that take place in the stratosphere and their environmental effect on the Earth. They also began to communicate their findings to the nonscientific community, eager to make the world aware of the potential risks that had been developing because of the extensive use of CFCs. Their efforts were fundamentally important to the adoption in 1987 of the Montreal Protocol on Substances That Deplete the Ozone Layer, an international agreement that has led to a virtual halt in the production of CFCs worldwide and a gradual improvement in the "health" of the ozone layer.

Meanwhile, Molina continued his research and teaching at Davis, earning a promotion to associate professor in 1979. Three years later, he accepted a job with the Molecular Physics and Chemistry Section of the Jet Propulsion Laboratory (JPL) in Pasadena, California, a position in which he could devote all of his time to research. He remained at JPL until 1989 when he moved to the Massachusetts Institute of Technology (MIT), in Cambridge, where he was given a joint appointment as professor in the department of chemistry and in the department of earth, atmosphere, and planetary sciences. He has remained at MIT ever since, now serving as institute professor in the two departments.

In addition to the Nobel Prize, Molina has received the Tyler Environmental Prize (1983), the Esselen Award of the American Chemical Society (1987), the Newcomb-Cleveland Prize of the American Association for the Advancement of Science (1988), a NASA (National Aeronautics and Space Administration) Medal for Exceptional Scientific Achievement (1989), the Max Planck Research Award (1994), the Walker Prize of the Boston Museum of Science (1996), the Willard Gibbs Medal of the American Chemical Society (1998), the American Chemical Society Award for Creative Advances in Environmental Science and Technology (1998), and the Sasakawa Environment Prize presented by the United Nations Environment Programme (1999).

Further Reading

Leerburger, Benedict A. "Mario Molina." In *Notable Twentieth-Century Scientists,* edited by Emily J. McMurray, 1,402–1,403. Detroit: Gale Research, 1995.

Massachusetts Institute of Technology. "Mario J. Molina." Available online. URL: http://www-eaps.mit.edu/molina/. Downloaded on March 22, 2005.

Nobelprize.org. "Mario J. Molina—Autobiography." Available online. URL: http://nobelprize.org/chemistry/laureates/1995/molina-autobio.html. Downloaded on March 22, 2005.

"Molina, Mario Jose." In *American Men & Women of Science,* 21st ed., edited by Pamela M. Kalte and Katherine H. Nemeh, vol. 5, 457. Detroit: Thomson Gale, 2003.

Mora, Miguel A.
(1950–) *ecotoxicologist*

Miguel A. Mora is a specialist in ecotoxicology, the study of toxins (poisons) that occur in the environment and the effects these toxins have on wildlife. His research also includes studies of avian (bird) ecology, the ways in which birds interact with their physical and biological environment. Mora has worked for the federal government for most of his professional career, first with the U.S. Fish and Wildlife Service, and later with the U.S. Geological Survey.

Mora was born on September 28, 1950, in Totolán, Michoacán, Mexico. He attended high school in Mexico City and then enrolled at the Instituto Politécnico Nacional in Mexico City, from which he earned his B.S. in biochemical engineering in 1977. After completing his bachelor's degree, Mora worked as a laboratory supervisor for two years in the Division of Wildlife of the Secretariat of Agriculture and Water Resources. He then moved to the United States and earned his M.S. in ecology at the University of California at Davis.

While studying for his doctorate at Davis over the next six years, Mora also worked as research associate in the department of veterinary pharmacology and toxicology and as research assistant in the diagnostics laboratory system at the University of California's School of Veterinary Medicine. He was awarded his Ph.D. in ecology at Davis in 1990.

Upon completion of his doctoral studies, Mora accepted an appointment as research associate at the Department of Fisheries and Wildlife and Pesticide Research Center at Michigan State University, in East Lansing. In 1993, he left that position to become research wildlife biologist with the U.S. Fish and Wildlife Service, National Biological Survey, National Biological Service, and U.S. Geological Survey (USGS) in College Station, Texas, a post he held until 2000. In that year, he was promoted to field station leader and research wildlife biologist with the USGS at College Station, a post he continues to hold. In addition to his research assignments, Mora has served as adjunct faculty member at Texas A&M University (1995–present) and Texas Tech University (1999–present).

Mora is author or coauthor of more than 50 scholarly and popular articles and technical reports, primarily on the presence of toxins in the environment and their effects on animals living in an area. He has also been active in organizations and activities that promote the participation of Latinas and Latinos in the sciences. For example, he has served on the board of directors of the Society for the Advancement of Chicanos and Native Americans in Science (SACNAS) and as SACNAS representative to the American Association for the Advancement of Science. In 2004, he was elected an honorary member of the Science Advisory Board of the Instituto Tecnológico de Jiquilpan in Jiquilpan, Michoacán.

Further Reading

GulfBase.org. "Dr. Miguel A. Mora." Available online. URL: http://www.gulfbase.org/person/view. php?uid=mmora. Downloaded on April 8, 2005.

School of Natural Resources and Environment, University of Michigan. "Profiles of Minority Environmental Professionals: Miguel A. Mora." Available online. URL: http://www.umich.edu/&meldi/4_ profiles_minprof.html#MAM1950. Downloaded on August 16, 2005.

Society for Advancement of Chicanos and Native Americans in Science. "Dr. Miguel Mora—Wildlife Toxicologist." SACNAS Biography Project. Available online. URL: http://64.171.10.183/beta/ pdf/moraMS.pdf. Downloaded on April 8, 2005.

Morales, Manuel F.
(Manuel Francisco Morales)
(1919–   ) *biophysicist*

Manuel Francisco Morales's most significant research in recent years has dealt with molecular motors, molecules in living organisms with the ability to convert chemical energy into kinetic energy, or physical motion. Examples of such molecular motors to which Morales has directed his attention are the molecules myosin and actin that occur in muscles and that use chemical energy to cause muscular contraction. In recent years, Morales has also become a spokesperson for increasing the scientific emphasis in dental education, making the teaching of dentistry based more in biological principles than in its traditional "mechanistic" emphasis, as has already happened to a large extent in medical education.

Morales was born in San Pedro Sula, Honduras, on July 23, 1919, the son of Saturna Bogran and Manuel Medina Morales. He was educated at home until he was old enough to attend high school, for which he moved to the United States. Morales received his undergraduate education at the University of California at Berkeley, earning his A.B. in physiology and chemistry in 1939. He continued his studies at Harvard University, in Cambridge, Massachusetts, receiving his A.M. in mathematics and physics in 1941. He then returned to Berkeley for his doctoral studies, completing his Ph.D. in biophysics in 1943. At that point, Morales joined the U.S. Navy, serving until August 1945 with the rank of lieutenant, senior grade.

After his discharge, Morales took a job as instructor in mathematical biophysics and physiology at the University of Chicago, where he remained until 1948. He then became a civilian scientist at the U.S. Naval Medical Research Institute (USNMRI), in Bethesda, Maryland, where he served as head of the Physical Biochemistry Division from 1949 to 1958. In 1958, he left USNMRI to become chair of the biochemistry department at Dartmouth Medical School, in Hanover, New Hampshire, a post he held for two years before moving to the University of California at San Francisco, where he was professor of biochemistry and biophysics until his retirement in 1989. At that point, he accepted an appointment as adjunct professor at the Arthur A. Dugoni School of Dentistry

of the University of the Pacific, in San Francisco, a post he continues to hold.

Morales has long served on a number of professional and governmental committees and for nearly three decades was one of 14 career investigators of the American Heart Association. He worked as scholar in residence at the National Institutes of Health from 1990 to 1994, was elected president of the Biophysical Society in 1968 and to membership in the National Academy in 1975, and was awarded Japan's Order of the Rising Sun in 1989.

Further Reading

"Morales, Manuel Francisco." In *Who's Who among Hispanic Americans,* 2d ed., edited by Amy Unterburger, 456. Detroit: Gale Research, 1992.

"Morales, Manuel Frank." In *American Men & Women of Science,* 21st ed., edited by Pamela M. Kalte and Katherine H. Nemeh, vol. 5, 486. Detroit: Thomson Gale, 2003.

N

Niebla, Elvia
(Elvia Elisa Niebla)
(1945–) *soil scientist, scientific administrator*

Elvia Elisa Niebla has spent most of her adult life in government service, first with the Western Archaeological Center (WAC), then with the U.S. Environmental Protection Agency (EPA), and most recently with the U.S. Forest Service, a division of the U.S. Department of Agriculture (USDA). At the Forest Service, she has worked primarily with the Global Change Research Program, designed to improve the nation's understanding, assessment, prediction, and response to global change.

Niebla was born in Nogales, Arizona, on March 12, 1945, the youngest of four children in a family of Mexican heritage. Although her favorite subjects in school were science and mathematics, she was discouraged by her teachers and counselors from considering a career in these fields. At the time, Hispanic girls were encouraged to think in terms of a secretarial career or, if they decided to attend college, of becoming a Spanish teacher. With her parents' support, however, Niebla decided to pursue her interest in science and mathematics. When she graduated from Nogales High School in 1963, she had studied a full range of science and math courses, including biology, chemistry, physics, and calculus.

After graduation from high school, Niebla enrolled at Fullerton Junior College, from which she received her associate's degree in 1965. She then moved on to the University of Arizona, where she received her B.S. in chemistry and zoology in 1967. A year later, she was awarded her M.Ed. from Arizona. Niebla's first job was as a teacher of science and mathematics in special education classes in California. After three years of teaching, she decided to return to school for her graduate studies. She attended the University of Arizona, where she earned her Ph.D. in chemistry in 1979.

In the same year, Niebla took a job at the U.S. National Park Service's WAC as a physical scientist. Her primary assignment at WAC was to carry out experiments on the kinds of materials used in building adobe structures in seven southwestern states and to learn more about the ecosystems in historic areas. She also worked to make federal employment opportunities more accessible to people living in rural areas of the Southwest.

In 1984, Niebla took a job with the EPA in Washington, D.C., as a soil scientist. She was assigned the task of developing regulations for the use of sludge on agricultural lands. Sludge is the material formed when garbage decays. It may be valuable as a fertilizer on farmlands, although it sometimes contains substances that are toxic to plants and animals that live on the land. In recognition of her work on this project, the EPA awarded Niebla its Bronze Medal for Commendable Service in 1989.

Niebla left the EPA in 1989 to take a position with the USDA Forest Service as national coordinator of the Global Change Research Program. Her job was to oversee the allocation of funds for research on the ways in which changes in global climatic conditions are likely to affect plants and animals and, therefore, the nation's agricultural industry. Since beginning to work for the Forest Service in 1989, she has continued to work in one part or another of their climate change program.

Further Reading

"Niebla, Elvia Elisa." In *Who's Who among Hispanic Americans, 1994–95*, 3d ed., edited by Amy Unterburger, 569. Detroit: Gale Research, 1995.

Society for Advancement of Chicanos and Native Americans in Science. "Dr. Elvia Niebla—Soil Scientist." SACNAS Biography Project. Available online. URL: http://64.171.10.183/biography/Biography.asp?mem=69&type=2. Downloaded on March 10, 2005.

Noriega, Carlos
(1959–) *computer scientist, astronaut*

Carlos Noriega has bachelor's and master's degrees in computer science and a master's degree in space systems operations. He was selected to train as an astronaut by the National Aeronautics and Space Administration (NASA) in 1994 and has spent more than 22 hours in space, traveling 3.6 million miles in 144 orbits of the Earth.

Noriega was born on October 8, 1959, in Lima, Peru, to Nora and Rodolfo Noriega. He grew up in California, where he graduated from Wilcox High School, in Santa Clara, in 1977. He then attended the University of Southern California (USC), from which he received his B.S. in computer science in 1981. While in college, Noriega was a member of the Navy ROTC and was commissioned a lieuten-

ant in the U.S. Marine Corps upon graduation from USC. He was assigned to the Marine Corps Air Station Kaneohe Bay, in Hawaii, where he learned to fly CH-46 Sea Knight helicopters. After two tours of duty in the South Pacific and Indian Oceans, Noriega was transferred to the Marine Corps Air Station Tustin, in California, where he served as aviation safety officer and instructor pilot. In 1988, he was selected to attend the Naval Postgraduate School, in Monterey, California, where he eventually earned two master's degrees in 1990, one in computer science and another in space systems operations. Noriega was then transferred to the U.S. Space Command, in Colorado Springs, Colorado, where he was space surveillance center commander.

Carlos Noriega, a computer scientist and astronaut, served on two shuttle missions to the space station *Mir* and the *International Space Station*. *(National Aeronautics and Space Administration)*

In December 1994, NASA selected Noriega as one of its new astronauts, and he began training for the program four months later. His first flight assignment was on space shuttle mission STS-84 on the shuttle *Atlantis.* The flight delivered supplies and a replacement astronaut to the space station *Mir,* a mission that lasted from May 17 to 24, 1997. Noriega's second mission was on flight STS-97 aboard the shuttle *Endeavour,* the fifth shuttle mission involved in the assembly of the *International Space Station.* Noriega performed three space walks during the mission and spent a total of 10 days, 19 hours, and 57 minutes on a 4.47 million-mile trip between November 30 and December 11, 2000.

Noriega retired from the U.S. Marine Corps in 2002 with the rank of lieutenant colonel but remains active with the astronaut program at NASA. He was chosen as backup commander of mission STS-121 but had to be replaced because of a temporary medical condition. While awaiting future flight assignment, he is working as manager of the Exploration Systems Engineering Office at the Johnson Space Center, in Houston, Texas.

Further Reading

Innerview. "Building a House in Heaven." *Networker@ USC* (September/October 1998). Available online. URL: http://www.usc.edu/isd/pubarchives/ networker/98–99/v9n1-Sept_Oct_98/innerview-noriega.html. Downloaded on April 19, 2005.

Latino Leaders. "Carlos Noriega, Lieutenant Colonel, USMC, RET." Available online. URL: http://www. latinoleaders.com/articulos.php?id_sec=1&id_ art=89&num_page= 274. Posted on October 1, 2004.

National Aeronautics and Space Administration. "Biographical Data." Available online. URL: http:// www.jsc.nasa.gov/Bios/htmlbios/noriega.html. Posted in January 2005.

SpaceRef.com. "First-Ever Spanish-Language Interactive Online Chat with NASA Astronaut Carlos Noriega from the Space Shuttle *Endeavour.*" Available online. URL: http://www.spaceref.com/ news/viewpr.html?pid=3235. Posted on December 6, 2000.

Novello, Antonia
(Antonia Coello)
(1944–) *physician, health administrator, surgeon general*

Antonia Novello was trained and worked as a pediatrician, but she has spent most of her adult life in public health service. Among other positions, she was surgeon general of the United States from 1990 to 1993 and has been commissioner of the New York State Department of Health since 1999.

Born Antonia Coello on August 23, 1944, in Fajardo, Puerto Rico, she was raised primarily by her mother, a middle school mathematics and science teacher and principal, as her father died when she was eight years old. Novello's childhood was made more difficult by a congenital disorder of the large intestine with which she was diagnosed at birth. Although surgical treatment was available for the condition, Novello did not have the necessary surgery until she was 18 years old because of an oversight by her doctors. That experience had a lasting impact on her, and she later said that it convinced her that "when I grow up, no other person is going to wait 18 years for surgery."

A gifted, motivated student who benefited from her mother's tutoring, Novello graduated from high school at the age of 15 and entered the University of Puerto Rico at Rió Piedras (UPR-RP). Her academic career was interrupted, however, by a recurrence of her health problems. Additional surgeries were, at first, unsuccessful, but an operation at the world-famous Mayo Clinic in 1964 eventually solved the problem. Novello returned to Puerto Rico and completed her B.S. at the University of Puerto Rico at San Juan (UPR-

Antonia Novello was surgeon general of the United States from 1990 to 1993 and has been commissioner of the New York State Department of Health since 1999. *(U.S. Department of Health and Human Services)*

SJ). She then began her medical studies at UPR-SJ and was awarded her M.D. in 1970.

In the same year, she met and married Joseph Novello, a surgeon in the U.S. Navy. The couple moved to Ann Arbor, Michigan, where she was to complete her internship in pediatrics. During her internship at the University of Michigan, Novello's favorite aunt died from kidney failure, and she herself experienced a series of kidney problems. These events inspired in Novello a special interest in nephritic (kidney) issues, and she decided to specialize in pediatric nephrology (the study of kidney disorders in children). She left the Uni-

versity of Michigan in 1973 at the completion of her internship to begin a three-year fellowship in pediatric nephrology at Georgetown University in Washington, D.C.

Having finished her fellowship at Georgetown in 1976, Novello set up a private practice in pediatrics in Springfield, Virginia. After only two years, however, she abandoned the practice. Although she had much to offer her patients and their parents, Novello realized that the emotional price she paid in dealing with sick children was too great. She decided instead to join the military services as a doctor.

Novello's efforts to enlist in the U.S. Navy were thwarted when a recruiting officer pointed out the disadvantages of having female physicians in the navy. She had more success with the U.S. Public Health Service, an agency that accepted her application in 1978.

Over the next decade, Novello held a number of positions in the federal government's public health system. Her first appointment was as a project officer in the National Institutes of Health's (NIH) Institute of Arthritis, Metabolism, and Digestive Disease. Her assignment there was to work on the institute's artificial kidney and chronic uremia program. In 1979, she was appointed a staff physician at NIH and then, a year later, executive secretary of the NIH Division of Research Grants. She remained in that post until 1986, when she became deputy director of the NIH's National Institute of Child Health and Human Development.

During these years, Novello also continued her own education, earning a master's degree in public health from Johns Hopkins University in Baltimore in 1982. From 1982 to 1983, she worked as a congressional fellow with the Senate Committee on Labor and Human Resources. Two of the committee's important projects during this period were the drafting of legislation dealing with organ transplants and the development of warning messages for cigarette packaging. Novello next completed a program for senior managers in governmental service at Harvard University's John F. Kennedy School of Government in 1987. She was also appointed clinical professor of pediatrics at Georgetown that same year.

In 1989, President George H. W. Bush asked Novello to become surgeon general of the United States. She was officially nominated on October 17 of that year, easily confirmed by the U.S. Senate, and sworn into office on March 9, 1990. She was the first woman and the first person of Hispanic extraction to hold this high office. An important factor in Bush's choice was Novello's strong and public opposition to abortion, a position that reflected Bush's own views on the controversial issue.

During her three years in office, Novello focused her attention on special health issues faced by women, children, and minorities; domestic violence; AIDS and HIV-related problems; alcohol and tobacco use; and accident injury prevention. She took special aim at advertising companies that seemed to suggest that cigarette smoking and alcohol use were associated with good looks and health. In March 1992, she took issue with the R. J. Reynolds Tobacco Company's campaign using the cartoon character Joe Camel as an appealing temptation to start smoking aimed at young children. Novello was also very interested in special health problems of Latinos and Latinas, such as smoking and diabetes, initiating an educational program that was later to become the National Hispanic/Latino Health Initiative.

At the conclusion of her term as surgeon general in 1993, Novello was invited to become special representative to the United Nations Children's Fund. Her assignment was to expand the fund's efforts to address the health and nutritional needs of women, children, and adolescents around the world. She held that post until 1996, when she became visiting professor of health policy and management at Johns Hopkins School of Health and Hygiene. Her task there was to advise the university on health service programs for poor communities. In 1999, New York governor George Pataki nominated her to be commissioner of health for the state of New York, a post she continues to hold and one in which she is responsible for one of the largest public health agencies in the country.

Further Reading

Las Mujeres. "Antonia Novello." Available online. URL: http://www.lasmujeres.com/antonianovello/background.shtml. Downloaded on February 14, 2005.

Meier, Matt S., with Conchita Franco Serri and Richard A. Garcia. *Notable Latino Americans.* Westport, Conn.: Greenwood Press, 1997.

National Library of Medicine. "Dr. Antonia Novello." Celebrating America's Women Physicians. Available online. URL: http://www.nlm.nih.gov/changingthefaceofmedicine/physicians/biography_239.html. Downloaded on February 14, 2005.

Stamatel, Janet P. "Antonia Novello." In *Contemporary Hispanic Biography,* edited by Ashyia N. Henderson, 142–145. Farmington Hills, Mich.: Thomson Gale, 2003.

Ocampo, Adriana C.
(Adriana Christian Ocampo, Adriana C.
Ocampo-Uria)
(1955–   ) *planetary geologist*

Adriana Christian Ocampo has worked on a variety of space projects for the Jet Propulsion Laboratory (JPL) of the National Aeronautics and Space Administration (NASA) and the European Space Agency (ESA). She has also carried out groundbreaking research on the Chicxulub Crater on the Yucatán Peninsula in Mexico, a crater thought to have been caused by the collision of a large asteroid with the Earth's surface about 65 million years ago.

Ocampo was born in Barranquilla, Colombia, on January 5, 1955. Her parents were Victor Alberto Ocampo, an electrical engineer, and Teresa Uria de Ocampo, a teacher at a Montessori school. When Ocampo was only a few months old, the family moved to Buenos Aires, Argentina, where she grew up and attended elementary and high school. Ocampo has said that she was always "more interested in a chemistry set than in dolls," and her playtime involved the construction of spaceships out of kitchen utensils and astronauts out of dolls.

In middle school, Ocampo seemed destined for a traditional woman's career when counselors suggested she study business or accounting. That changed, however, when her parents decided to move the family to the United States to improve their children's educational opportunities. In 1970, the family settled in Pasadena, California, where Ocampo entered high school.

The choice of Pasadena as a new home for the family was fortuitous for Ocampo. Pasadena is home to NASA's JPL, the nation's primary center for interplanetary spacecraft and robotic space exploration and experimentation. While still a junior in high school, Ocampo was offered a summer job at JPL. She accepted and continued to work part time on a variety of assignments at the laboratory for the next 10 years. One such assignment involved an analysis of the electrical characteristics of earthquakes.

After high school, Ocampo enrolled at Pasadena City College, where she majored in aerospace engineering. She later transferred to the University of California at Los Angeles (UCLA) and began to study for a bachelor's degree in geology, with a specialization in planetary science. That program provides training in the geology of all the planets, rather than concentrating exclusively on the Earth alone, as is the case with most geology programs. Ocampo was awarded her B.S. from UCLA in 1983.

After graduating from UCLA, Ocampo became a full-time employee at JPL. One of the high points of her early career at JPL was her work on images obtained by the Viking spacecrafts of Phobos, one of the moons of Mars. As a member

Adriana C. Ocampo is a planetary geologist who has worked with the National Aeronautics and Space Administration and the European Space Agency. *(National Aeronautics and Space Administration)*

of the JPL Multi-Mission Image Processing Laboratory, her job was to interpret the string of zeroes and ones obtained from the spacecraft and turn them into actual images of the moon's surface. This work was published in 1984, and it remains the only atlas of Phobos available. It proved to be invaluable in the planning of the 1988 Russian *Phobos I* spacecraft sent to study Mars (although contact with the spacecraft was lost about two months after launch).

Over the next decade, Ocampo worked on a number of space projects for NASA. For example, she was in charge of designing the thermal emission spectrometer (TES) for the *Mars Observer* launched in August 1993. The TES was designed to collect information on minerals found on the planet's surface, properties of the dust and clouds in its atmosphere, and its surface temperature. Unfortunately, the spacecraft was lost just three days prior to reaching the planet, and almost no useful data were collected on the mission.

Ocampo's next assignment at NASA was with the agency's Project Galileo mission to Jupiter. Launched in 1989, *Galileo* was designed to study the physical characteristics and chemical composition of Jupiter and some of its satellites. Ocampo's responsibility in the project was the design of the spacecraft's Near Infrared Mapping Spectrometer. This instrument was designed to collect and analyze radiation in the near infrared region of the electromagnetic spectrum (radiation with wavelengths ranging from about 700 to 1,500 nanometers), information that would tell scientists more about the atmosphere and clouds of Jupiter, its satellites, and the surface characteristics of the satellites.

In addition to her studies of astronomical bodies, Ocampo somewhat unexpectedly became involved in a fundamental problem in terrestrial geology. In 1989, Ocampo, Kevin O. Pope (her husband at the time), and Charles Duller were studying water resources in the Yucatán Peninsula using images obtained from NASA satellites. The team noticed a semicircular series of cenotes (sinkholes) along the Yucatán coast in the images. The cenotes appeared to surround a craterlike region first discovered almost a decade earlier by petroleum geologists working in the area. Researchers had hypothesized that the fossil crater had been created about 65 million years earlier when an asteroid had collided with the Earth's surface. The force of that collision, scientists believed, had produced so much smoke and dust that the amount of sunlight reaching the Earth had been dramatically reduced for more than a year. That loss of sunlight had, the theory continued, caused the widespread death of plant life across the planet, resulting, in turn, in the extinction of as much as half of Earth's animal species, including the dinosaurs.

After her initial discoveries, Ocampo continued to work on studies of the impact crater. She and her colleagues later discovered two large regions in which material thrown out by the asteroid, called ejecta, had accumulated. These regions were of interest not only because of the information they provided about the collision but also because of their similarity to features on Mars. Ocampo observed, "The discovery of these new ejecta sites is very exciting. It is like seeing a bit of Mars on Earth."

While working full time on planetary and terrestrial problems for NASA, Ocampo also found time to continue her academic studies at California State University at Northridge. In 1997, she was awarded her M.S. in geology. Ocampo has as yet not earned a Ph.D., which should be an inspiration to all students. It shows that one can reach the very highest levels in one's chosen field even without the "academic stamp of approval" offered by a Ph.D.

In 2002, Ocampo severed her longtime association with NASA by accepting a position with the ESA. She went to work on the agency's Mars Express mission, launched on June 3, 2003. In 2007, the spacecraft was in orbit around the Red Planet, taking pictures of its surface and collecting other information about its physical and chemical characteristics.

In addition to her own research, Ocampo has long been active in a variety of educational programs. In 1987, she offered a course in planetary geology, sponsored by the Planetary Society, in Mexico City. The course was so successful that it was later repeated in Costa Rica and Colombia in 1992, in Nigeria in 1993, in Egypt in 1994, in Argentina in 2002, and in China in 2003.

Ocampo has also been committed to improving the general public's understanding of space research throughout the Western Hemisphere. In 1990, she was largely responsible for organizing the first Space Conference for the Americas: Prospects in Cooperation, held in San José, Costa Rica. At home, she has also been active in Hispanic organizations, serving as vice president, secretary, and member of the Space and International Affairs Committees of the Society of Hispanic Professional Engineers. In 1992, she was awarded the Woman of the Year in Science award by the Comisión Femenil, an organization in Los Angeles that promotes the advancement of Hispanic women.

Further Reading

National Aeronautics and Space Administration. "Adriana C. Ocampo." Women of NASA. Available online. URL: http://quest.arc.nasa.gov/people/bios/women/ao.html. Downloaded on February 15, 2005.

Alic, Margaret. "Adriana C. Ocampo." In *Contemporary Hispanic Biography,* edited by Ashyia N. Henderson, 154–157. Farmington Hills, Mich.: Thomson Gale, 2003.

Meyer, Nicholas E. *Biographical Dictionary of Hispanic Americans,* 2d ed., 209–211. New York: Checkmark Books, 2001.

Olesky, Walter. *Hispanic-American Scientists,* 83–93. New York: Facts On File, 1998.

Ochoa, Ellen

(1958-) *electrical engineer, astronaut, inventor*

Ellen Ochoa became the first Latina to travel into space when she served as mission specialist on the space shuttle *Discovery* on April 4–17, 1993. She has also made important discoveries and inventions in the field of optical information processing, in which photons of light, rather than electrons, are used to store and transmit data.

Ochoa was born on May 10, 1958, in Los Angeles to Rosanne Deardoff Ochoa and Joseph Ochoa, of Mexican descent. She was raised in La Mesa, California, just south of San Diego, where she attended Grossman High School. Her parents divorced when Ochoa was still a teenager, and her mother was faced with the challenge of raising her five children as a single mother. She not only met this challenge but also managed to take a number of college courses to advance her own education. In 1981, Ochoa's mother finally earned her bachelor's degree from San Diego State University (SDSU).

In 1975, Ochoa graduated from high school and was offered a scholarship to Stanford University, Stanford, California. She decided to decline that offer and, instead, enrolled at San Diego State University, where she could be closer to her family. Based on her interest and considerable talent in playing the flute, Ochoa decided to major in music. She remained in the San Diego State music program for only a relatively brief period of time, however, mainly because her academic interests ranged over so many fields. She switched her major first to journalism, then to business, then to computer science, and finally to physics. With the last change, she finally discovered the subject for which she had the greatest passion, and, in 1980, she was awarded her B.S. in that subject. She was valedictorian of her class, as she had been in her high school graduating class.

Upon graduation from San Diego State, Ochoa enrolled for graduate studies at Stanford. She completed the requirements for her M.S. in 1981 and her Ph.D. in 1985, both in electrical engineering. Her studies at Stanford were supported by a Stanford Engineering Fellowship from 1980 to 1981 and an IBM Predoctoral Fellowship from 1982 to 1984. While at Stanford, Ochoa continued to pursue a variety of interests. For example, she played flute with the Stanford Symphony Orchestra, win-ning a student soloist award from the orchestra in 1983.

After completing her doctoral studies, Ochoa accepted a job at Sandia National Laboratories in Livermore, California. There, she worked as a research engineer in the laboratory's Imaging Technology Branch. Her assignment was to work on the development of optical systems for the processing of data obtained from space projects. In 1988, Ochoa was appointed chief of the Intelligent Systems Technology Branch at the National Aeronautical and Space Administration's (NASA) Ames Research Center in Mountain View, California. There, she supervised a group of 35 scientists and engineers working on computational systems for aerospace missions. During her time at Sandia and Ames, Ochoa contributed to the development

Ellen Ochoa was the first Latina to travel in space as a member of the U.S. astronaut corps aboard the space shuttle *Discovery* on the 1992 mission STS-56. *(National Aeronautics and Space Administration)*

of three new optical-based technologies for collecting and analyzing data and for removing "noise" (unwanted background data) from optical images.

Ochoa's interest in becoming an astronaut dated to her years at Stanford, at a time when the space shuttle flights were just getting under way. She realized that she had many of the qualifications expected of an astronaut and, in 1985, applied to become a candidate for the NASA spaceflight team. She was selected in January 1990, one of five women and 18 men chosen to enter the astronaut program that year. A year later, Ochoa left her job at Ames and began her training as an astronaut.

During her first three years in the astronaut program, Ochoa was assigned to a number of support roles, including flight software verification; crew representative for robotics development, testing, and training; and lead spacecraft communicator at Mission Central in Houston, Texas. She also served as acting deputy chief of the Astronaut Office at the Johnson Space Center in Houston.

In 1992, Ochoa was selected as a member of the five-person crew of space shuttle flight STS-56 on the shuttle *Discovery.* The flight's primary mission was to conduct atmospheric and solar studies in order to obtain a better understanding of the effects of solar activity on Earth's climate and environment. One of Ochoa's primary responsibilities was operation of the shuttle's Remote Manipulator System (RMS), a mechanical arm used to capture the Spartan satellite, which had been in orbit collecting data on the solar corona, the outermost part of the Sun's atmosphere.

Ochoa later flew on three other spaceflights, the STS-66 mission on *Atlantis,* the STS-96 mission on *Discovery,* and the STS-110 mission, again on *Atlantis.* On the first of these flights, Ochoa was payload commander and again used the RMS arm to capture a satellite, this time the CRISTAS-SPAS atmospheric research satellite, which had been mapping ozone concentrations in Earth's atmosphere. The primary goal of STS-96 was the first docking of a shuttle with the *International Space Station* (*ISS*), on which occasion four tons of food, supplies, and other materials were transferred to the station. STS-110 also rendezvoused with the *ISS,* at which time supplies and crew members were delivered to the station.

In addition to her work as an astronaut, Ochoa has been active as a spokesperson for NASA, especially for school groups. She has given more than 150 talks describing her experiences and the opportunities in science and engineering available to young students. Among the honors she has received are two Space Act Tech Brief Awards (1992), Space Flight Medals (1993, 1994, 1999, and 2002), the Outstanding Leadership Medal (1995), NASA's Exceptional Service Medal (1997), the Hispanic Engineer Albert Baez Award for Outstanding Technical Contribution to Humanity (1995), the Hispanic Heritage Leadership Award (1995), the Women in Aerospace Outstanding Achievement Award (1997), and San Diego State University Alumna of the Year (1998).

Further Reading

Brennan, Carol. "Ellen Ochoa." In *Contemporary Hispanic Biography,* edited by Ashyia N. Henderson, 149–151. Farmington Hills, Mich.: Thomson Gale, 2003.

Fedunkiw, Marianne. "Ellen Ochoa." In *Notable Twentieth-Century Scientists,* edited by Emily J. McMurray, 1,496–1,497. Detroit: Gale Research, 1995.

National Aeronautics and Space Administration. "Biographical Data: Ellen Ochoa." Available online. URL: http://www.jsc.nasa.gov/Bios/htmlbios/ochoa.html. Downloaded on November 15, 2005.

Olesky, Walter. *Hispanic-American Scientists,* 107–115. New York: Facts On File, 1998.

Ochoa, Severo

(1905–1993) *physiologist, biochemist*

Severo Ochoa was corecipient of the 1959 Nobel Prize in physiology or medicine (with his former graduate student Arthur Kornberg) for his discovery of the chemical mechanisms involved in the synthesis of RNA (ribonucleic acid) and DNA (deoxyribonucleic acid), the two families of chemical compounds that carry and transmit the genetic code in organisms. Ochoa also made important discoveries in a number of other areas, including the character and functions of enzymes involved in some biological processes and of vitamin B_1.

Ochoa was born in Luarca, in the province of Asturias, in northern Spain, on September 24, 1905. His parents were Carmen de Albornoz and Severo Ochoa, an attorney and businessman. While still a young child, Ochoa moved with his family to the south of Spain, where he was educated at and graduated in 1921 from, according to some sources, the Instituto de Bachillerato or, according to others, the Colegio de Málaga.

Ochoa developed an interest in the sciences early in his high school career, inspired especially by his chemistry teacher and the works of the great Spanish neurologist Santiago Ramón y Cajal. He decided to pursue a career in biochemical research, the study of chemical compounds involved in living processes, and enrolled at the University of Madrid. Since there were no research facilities in biochemistry at Madrid (or anywhere else in Europe) at the time, Ochoa majored in medicine, receiving his M.D. in 1929.

Although the University of Madrid had no research facilities, Ochoa was able to do some original experiments at a private laboratory owned by one of his instructors. These experiments dealt with a method for the isolation of an important nitrogen-containing compound from urine, creatine. He published the results of his research in English in the *Journal of Biological Chemistry* in 1929, the first of his many scientific papers. In 1931, Ochoa married Carmen María Cobián.

Over the next 13 years, Ochoa moved from laboratory to laboratory—an even dozen in all—in Europe and the United States. One reason for this seemingly endless travel was his interest in working at the forefront of biochemical research. Another

Severo Ochoa shared the 1959 Nobel Prize in physiology or medicine for his research on the synthesis of RNA and DNA. (© *The Nobel Foundation*)

reason was the turbulence occasioned by the disruptions and wars that spread across the European continent and Great Britain during the 1930s, first by the Spanish civil war that raged from 1936 to 1939, then by the persecution of Jews after the rise of the Nazi Party in Germany, and finally by the onset of World War II itself. As a consequence of these disturbances and his own drive to make new contacts, Ochoa moved from Madrid in 1929 to the Kaiser Wilhelm Institut für Medizinische Forschung at Heidelberg, in Germany, back to Madrid in 1931, where he held the title of lecturer in physiology, and then on to the National Institute for Medical Research in London in 1932. In 1934, Ochoa returned to Madrid as lecturer in physiology and biochemistry, before moving to the University of Heidelberg in 1936, the Plymouth Marine Biological Laboratory in England in 1937, and to Oxford University in 1938, where he conducted his studies on vitamin B_1.

With the outbreak of World War II in Europe, Ochoa immigrated to the United States, where he took a post as instructor and research associate in pharmacology at the Washington University School of Medicine, in St. Louis, Missouri. He remained at Washington only one year before moving to the New York University (NYU) School of Medicine, where he finally found a permanent home. Over the next three decades, Ochoa served as research associate in medicine (1942–45), assistant professor of biochemistry (1945), professor of pharmacology (1946–54), professor of biochemistry (1954–74), and chair of the department of biochemistry (1954–74). He became an American citizen in 1956.

It was at NYU that Ochoa carried out the research for which he was awarded the Nobel Prize. During the 1930s, the German biochemist Hans Krebs had hypothesized a sequence of chemical reactions by which glucose is metabolized in cells to produce carbon dioxide, water, and energy, a process the understanding of which Arnold Kornberg has called "the Holy Grail of biochemistry." Ochoa, assisted by Kornberg, was able to determine the character and role of a number of enzymes involved in the so-called Krebs cycle and, purely by chance along the way, discovered an enzyme essential to the synthesis of RNA. The discovery of that enzyme, named polynucleotide phosphorylase, eventually proved to be fundamental to understanding the mechanism by which the individual units of RNA and DNA (nucleotides) are assembled into the long chain polymers that make up these molecules. It also proved to be an essential tool in unraveling the genetic code, the combination of chemical units found in DNA that determines an organism's genetic constitution.

Ochoa's award of the Nobel Prize in 1959 provided him with an opportunity to return to Spain, where he would have been welcomed with open arms for the place he had earned in science, but his opposition to the dictator Francisco Franco then in power made that an unlikely option for him. He chose to remain at NYU. When the date of his formal retirement at NYU arrived in 1974, Ochoa chose to continue working at his old laboratory, and simultaneously, he accepted an appointment as researcher at the Roche Institute of Molecular Biology, in Nutley, New Jersey.

In 1985, Ochoa and his wife returned to Spain, where she died within a year of pneumonia. Ochoa himself died six years later of pneumonia, on November 1, 1993, in Madrid. Throughout his long career, Ochoa garnered many honors and awards in addition to his Nobel Prize. He was awarded the Carl Neuberg Medal of the American Society of European Chemists in 1951, the Medal of the French Société de Chimie Biologique in 1959, and the Medal of New York University, also in 1959. He received honorary doctoral degrees from a number of institutions, including Washington University of St. Louis, Wesleyan University, and the Universities of Glasgow (Scotland), Oxford, Salamanca (Spain), and Brazil.

Further Reading

Kornberg, Arthur. "Reflections: Remembering Our Teacher." *Journal of Biological Chemistry* 276 (January 5, 2001): 3–11.

———. "Severo Ochoa." *Nature* 366 (December 2, 1993): 408.

———. "Severo Ochoa." *Proceedings of the American Philosophical Society* 141 (December 1997): 479–491.

Meier, Matt S., with Conchita Franco Serri and Richard A. Garcia. "Severo Ochoa." In *Notable Latino Americans,* 280–282. Westport, Conn.: Greenwood Press, 1997.

Nobelprize.org. "Severo Ochoa—Biography." Available online. URL: http://nobelprize.org/cgi-bin/print?from=/medicine/laureates/1959/ochoa-bio.html. Downloaded on March 16, 2005.

Ondetti, Miguel A.
(Miguel Angel Ondetti)
(1930-2004) *pharmaceutical chemist, inventor*

Miguel Angel Ondetti is best known for his discovery of a class of drugs known as ACE (angiotensin-converting enzyme) inhibitors, compounds used in the treatment of hypertension (high blood pressure). One of the most familiar of those drugs is a compound with the trade name of Capoten, first approved for use in the United States in 1981.

Ondetti was born in Buenos Aires, Argentina, on May 14, 1930, the son of Sara Cerutti and Emilio Ondetti. He received his education at the University of Buenos Aires, which granted his licentiate in chemistry in 1955 and his D.Sc. in chemistry, with a specialization in organic chemistry, in 1957. Upon receipt of his doctoral degree, Ondetti took a position with the Squibb Corporation as senior research chemist at its Institute for Medical Research (IMR) in Buenos Aires. Ondetti was eventually to spend more than three decades with Squibb, moving to the United States and taking the post of senior research chemist at Squibb's IMR in New Brunswick, New Jersey (1960–66). He later became research group leader for peptide synthesis at IMR (1966–73), section head for peptides, steroids, and antibiotic research (1973–76), director of the department of biological chemistry at IMR (1976–79), associate director for chemical and microbiological research (1980–81), vice president for basic research (1981–83), senior vice president for cardiovascular drug discovery (1984–89), and senior vice president for cardiovascular and metabolic diseases (1990). In 1991, Ondetti left Squibb to begin a private consulting firm, a line of work he continued until his death on August 23, 2004, in Princeton, New Jersey.

Ondetti was holder or coholder of 122 patents for methods of isolating and/or synthesizing a variety of pharmaceutically active chemical compounds, primarily those consisting of amino acids and peptides. Amino acids are organic (carbon-containing) compounds that also contain the element nitrogen, while peptides are compounds consisting of two or more amino acids joined to each other. In recognition of his achievements, Ondetti was awarded the 1999 Albert Lasker Award for Clinical Medical Research, an award sometimes said to be the equivalent of a Nobel Prize, as well as the Alfred Burger Award in Medicinal Chemistry of the American Chemical Society (1981); the Thomas Alva Edison Patent Award of the Research and Development Council of New Jersey (1983); the Ciba Award for Hypertension Research of the Council on High Blood Pressure Research of the American Heart Association (1983); the Chairman's Edward Robinson Squibb Award, awarded by the board of directors of E. R. Squibb & Sons (1986); the Pharmaceutical Manufacturers Association and National Health Council Award for contributions to medical science (1988); the Inventor of the Year Award, presented by the New Jersey Inventors Congress (1988); the Perkin Medal, given for outstanding work in applied chemistry by the American Section of the Society of Chemical Industry (1991); the Warren Alpert Foundation Prize, presented by Harvard Medical School (1991); the American Chemical Society Award for Creative Invention (1992); and the first Herman Bloch Award, for scientific excellence in industry, administered by the University of Chicago (1992).

Further Reading
Town Topics. "Obituaries." Available online. URL: http://www.towntopics.com/sep0104/obits.html. Posted on September 1, 2004.

"Ondetti, Miguel Angel." In *Who's Who in America—2005,* edited by Karen Chassie, 3,504. New Providence, N.J.: Marquis Who's Who, 2004.

"Ondetti, Miguel Angel." In *American Men & Women of Science,* 21st ed., edited by Pamela M. Kalte and Katherine H. Nemeh, vol. 5, 770. Detroit: Thomson Gale, 2003.

Ortega, Sonia

(1953–   ) *marine biologist, science administrator*

Sonia Ortega was trained as a marine biologist but has spent much of her professional career as a scientific administrator at the National Science Foundation (NSF), where she has been manager and director of many programs.

Ortega was born in Carazo, Nicaragua, on May 19, 1953. Her father died when she was 11 years old, and she grew up with her mother and three sisters in Honduras, where she attended both elementary and high school. Life was difficult for her mother, who had no formal education and had to work two jobs to provide for her children's needs. Still, her mother believed strongly that her children should get an education so that their lives would be different from and better than her own. Ortega learned that lesson well, loved school, and was eventually able to attend the University of Costa Rica, in San José, where she earned her B.S. in biology in 1975. She continued her studies at Duke University, in Durham, North Carolina, from which she received her M.A. in zoology in 1978, and the University of South Carolina, in Columbia, which awarded her a Ph.D. in biology in 1986. Prior to completing her doctoral studies, Ortega was a teaching instructor at the University of Costa Rica for one year (1975), program director in the department of research and technology at the Central Bank of Nicaragua, in Managua (1979), teaching assistant at the University of South Carolina (1981), visiting professor at the National University of Costa Rica (1983), and research assistant at the University of South Carolina (1984).

After receiving her Ph.D., Ortega worked from 1987 to 1989 as research associate at Duke University's Marine Laboratory, in Beaufort, North Carolina. She then began her long affiliation with the NSF by accepting an appointment as program manager of the Minority Research Initiation Program, a post she held for one year. Ortega then held a series of appointments with the Faculty Awards for Women Scientists and Engineers Program (1990–95); the Presidential Faculty Fellows Awards Program (1992–96); the Postdoctoral Fellowships in Science, Mathematics, Engineering, and Technology Education program (1996–2001); the Graduate Teaching Fellowships in K–12 Education program (1999–2001 and 2004–present); and as NSF representative to the U.S. Antarctic Program at Palmer Station (1997). From 2001 to 2004, she was on leave from the NSF so that she could serve as program director of the Education and International Activities, Long Term Ecological Research (LTER) Network Office at the University of New Mexico, in Albuquerque. At the end of that assignment she returned to her position at the NSF.

Ortega has written a number of articles and made a number of presentations dealing with marine biology, funding of scientific activities, and the role of women and minorities in science. She has been honored with an Outstanding Young Woman of America award by the foundation of the same name (1987), Outstanding Performance Awards of the NSF (1991 and 1995), an Achievement Award from the Washington Area Hispanic Employment Program (1993), a Special Act/Service Award for organizing the Hispanic Cause of NSF (1994), and a Certificate of Recognition for six years of service in the Diversity Committee of Sigma Xi (2001).

Further Reading

Reslmaier, Christine. "Ortega, Sonia, Ph.D." Just Garcia Hill: A Virtual Community for Minorities in Science. Available online. URL: www.justgarciahill.org/jghdocs/webbiographydtl.asp. Downloaded on October 28, 2004.

Society for Advancement of Chicanos and Native Americans in Science. "Dr. Sonia Ortega—Program Director and Marine Biologist." SACNAS Biography Project. Available online. URL: http://64.171.10.183/biography/Biography.asp?mem=73&type=2. Downloaded on April 23, 2005.

Ortiz, Vilma
(1954–   ) *sociologist*

Vilma Ortiz is an authority on Latino/Latina sociology; racial, ethnic, and minority relationships; immigration characteristics and problems; and sex and gender issues. She was codirector of one of the largest and most complete long-term studies of Hispanic populations ever conducted in the United States.

Ortiz was born on April 15, 1954, in New York City, to Haydee and José Ortiz, of Puerto Rican background. She attended the City College of New York, from which she received her B.A. in sociology in 1976, and New York University, where she earned her M.A. and Ph.D. in sociology in 1979 and 1981, respectively. She then completed postdoctoral fellowships at Fordham University in New York City from 1981 to 1982, the University of Michigan in Ann Arbor from 1982 to 1983, and the University of Wisconsin in Madison from 1983 to 1985. At the completion of her postdoctoral studies, she accepted a position as a research scientist with the Educational Testing Service in Princeton, New Jersey, from 1985 to 1987, and then with Manpower Demonstration Research Corporation in New York City as a senior research associate from 1987 to 1988. In 1988, Ortiz returned to academia by accepting a position as assistant professor of sociology at the University of California at Los Angeles (UCLA). She has remained at UCLA ever since, becoming first associate professor in 1990 and then full professor of sociology in 2000.

In 1993, the original data of one of the most famous studies of Hispanic culture in the United States, "The Mexican-American People: The Nation's Second Largest Minority," were accidentally discovered at the UCLA library. These data were, according to Ortiz's colleague at UCLA Edward Telles, a "gold mine" of information. Ortiz and Telles decided to initiate a follow-up study of the participants in the original 1970

Vilma Ortiz is a sociologist who specializes in the study of racial, ethnic, and minority relationships; immigration characteristics and problems; and sex and gender issues. *(Photo by Reed Hutchinson, UCLA Photographic Services for UCLA Today)*

study to find out how the Hispanic population had changed and developed over the following two decades. The results of that study, known as the Mexican American Study Project, were first announced in the early 2000s, with some of the most complete and richest information ever produced on the Latino/Latina culture in this country.

Ortiz is coeditor (with Mary Romero and Pierrette Hondagneu-Sotelo) of a widely used reference book in Latino sociology, *Challenging Fronteras: Structuring Latina and Latino Lives in the U.S.* (1997).

Further Reading

"Ortiz, Vilma." In *Who's Who among Hispanic Americans, 1994–95,* 3d ed., edited by Amy Unterburger, 594. Detroit: Gale Research, 1995.

"Vilma Ortiz." In *The Hispanic American Almanac,* 3d ed., edited by Sonia G. Benson, 763. Farmington Hills, Mich.: Thomson Gale, 2003.

Ortiz de Montellano, Paul R.
(Paul Richard Ortiz de Montellano)
(1942–   ) *chemist*

Paul Richard Ortiz de Montellano's research is focused on problems of protein structure, mechanisms by which proteins carry out their function, the design of proteins that act as inhibitors in biochemical reactions, and the development of drugs for the treatment of AIDS (acquired immunodeficiency syndrome) and AIDS-related conditions and of drug-resistant tuberculosis.

Ortiz de Montellano was born in Mexico City on September 6, 1942. He earned his B.S. in chemistry at the Massachusetts Institute of Technology, in Cambridge, in 1964, and his M.A. and Ph.D. in chemistry at Harvard University, also in Cambridge, in 1966 and 1968, respectively. He then spent a year as a North Atlantic Treaty Organization postdoctoral fellow at the Eidgenössische Technische Hochschule, in Zurich, Switzerland, from 1968 to 1969. Upon his return to the United States, Ortiz de Montellano took a job as group leader at Syntex Research, in Palo Alto, California. After two years at Syntex, he accepted an appointment as assistant professor of chemistry in the department of pharmaceutical chemistry and pharmacology at the University of California at San Francisco (UCSF). He has remained at UCSF ever since, earning promotions to associate professor in 1976 and full professor in 1980. Over the last three decades, he has also been *professeur associé* at the Institut de Chimie of the Université Louis Pasteur, in Strasbourg, France

(1978–79); visiting professor in the department of biochemistry at University College, in London (1985–86); Rhone-Poulenc Professor at the Université René Descartes, in Paris (1993–94); and honorary research fellow in the department of biochemistry at University College, London (2000–01).

Ortiz de Montellano has more than 320 publications to his credit, including a book of which he is editor, *Cytochrome P-450: Structure, Mechanism and Biochemistry* (1986), now in its second edition. Among the many honors he has received are selection as a fellow of the American Association

Paul R. Ortiz de Montellano is a chemist who specializes in the study and function of proteins and in the design of drugs for the treatment of HIV and AIDS-related health problems. *(Courtesy Dr. Paul Ortiz de Montellano)*

for the Advancement of Science, the John Moffat Lectureship at the University of British Columbia (1989), the B. B. Brodie Award in Drug Metabolism of the American Society of Pharmacology and Experimental Therapeutics (1994), and several Long Foundation Awards for Excellence in Teaching at UCSF (1989, 1996, 1997, 1999, and 2000). Ortiz de Montellano was also King/Chavez/Parks Visiting Professor at the University of Michigan in Ann Arbor in 1991, Distinguished University Lecturer at the University of Utah in Salt Lake City in 1991, and Wellcome Visiting Professor in Basic Medical Sciences at Washington State University in Pullman in 1994.

Further Reading

"Ortiz de Montellano, Paul Richard." In *American Men & Women of Science,* 21st ed., edited by Pamela M. Kalte and Katherine H. Nemeh, vol. 5, 788. Detroit: Thomson Gale, 2003.

UCSF Cancer Center. "Paul R. Ortiz de Montellano, PhD." Available online. URL: http://cc.ucsf.edu/people/ortiz-de-montellano_paul.html. Downloaded on April 14, 2005.

P

Padilla, Amado M.
(Amado Manuel Padilla)
(1942–) *psychologist*

Amado Manuel Padilla's special area of interest is in the development of young people from minority backgrounds, especially those in which support for educational achievement tends to be weak. He is interested in learning how such individuals manage to do well in their education and later development, even lacking the encouragement and/or support of parents and family members.

Padilla was born in Albuquerque, New Mexico, on October 14, 1942, to Esperanza Lopez and Manuel S. Padilla, of Mexican heritage. He earned his B.S. from New Mexico Highlands University in Las Vegas in 1964, his M.S. from Oklahoma State University in Stillwater in 1966, and his Ph.D. in experimental psychology from the University of New Mexico in Albuquerque in 1969. His first teaching position was at the State University of New York at Potsdam, where he was assistant professor from 1969 to 1971. He then moved to the University of California at Santa Barbara, where he was assistant professor from 1971 to 1974 and to the University of California at Los Angeles, where he was associate professor from 1974 to 1978 and then full professor from 1978 to 1988. In 1988, he was offered the position of professor of education at Stanford University, in Stanford, California, a post he continues to hold.

In addition to his primary responsibilities in the Stanford School of Education, Padilla serves as director of the California Foreign Language Project and director of the Bay Area Foreign Language Project. In these posts, he pursues one of his most important research interests, the way in which children learn a second language in school-based foreign language. He attempts to discover the way curriculum, teaching strategies, and parent involvement affect a student's ability to learn a second language in a school setting. The research focuses not only on English and Spanish learning but also on the way less commonly taught languages, such as Chinese and Korean, are acquired by students.

Padilla is author, editor, coauthor, or coeditor of a number of publications, including *Crossing Cultures in Therapy: Pluralistic Counseling for the Hispanic* (with Elaine S. Levine, 1980), *Invitation to Psychology* (with John P. Houston, Constance Hammen, and Helen Bee, 1989), *Hispanic Psychology: Critical Issues in Theory and Research* (1994), *Hispanic Mental Health Research: A Reference Guide* (with Frank Newton and Esteban L. Olmedo, 1981), *Chicano Ethnicity* (with Susan E. Keefe, 1987), and *Foreign Language Education: Issues and Strategies* and *Bilingual Education: Issues and Strategies* (both with Halford H. Fairchild and Concepcion M. Valadez, 1990).

Among the honors that Padilla has received are a Distinguished Scholar Award from the American Education Research Association (1987), the Paul Pimsleur Award for Research in Foreign Language Education of the American Council of Teachers of Foreign Languages (1989), a Distinguished Contribution through Research Award from Division 45 of the American Psychological Association (1990), a Lifetime Achievement Award also from Division 45 of the American Psychological Association (1996), and the 6th Annual Latino Behavioral Health Institute Award for Leadership, Innovation, and Dedication to the Advancement of Latino Behavioral Health Research (2000).

Further Reading

"Amado Manuel Padilla." In *The Hispanic American Almanac,* 3d ed., edited by Sonia G. Benson, 765. Farmington Hills, Mich.: Thomson Gale, 2003.

"Padilla, Amado Manuel." In *Who's Who among Hispanic Americans, 1994–95,* 3d ed., edited by Amy Unterburger, 600. Detroit: Gale Research, 1995.

Peralta, Richard C.
(Richard Carl Peralta)
(1949–) *agricultural engineer*

Richard Carl Peralta is an authority in irrigation engineering, with a special interest in problems of groundwater modeling, movement of contaminants through the subsurface layer of the ground and systems for the control of such movement, the relationship of water movement in streams and aquifers, and planning for large-scale, long-term use of water supplies.

Peralta was born in Enid, Oklahoma, on November 8, 1949, to Christina M. and John F. Peralta, of Chilean ancestry. He attended the Uni-

Richard C. Peralta is currently director of the Water Dynamics Laboratory at Utah State University, a research facility of the Utah State University Research Foundation. (*© Utah State University*)

versity of South Carolina, in Columbia, earning his B.S. in chemistry with a minor in biology in 1971. His graduate studies were delayed while he served in the U.S. Air Force, where he eventually reached the rank of major. After being discharged from the military in 1975, Peralta spent one year as an Environmental Protection Agency (EPA) trainee in agricultural and irrigation engineering at Utah State University, in Logan. Concurrently with this training, he pursued his graduate studies at Utah State and qualified for his M.S. in agricultural and irrigation engineering in 1976. He then attended Oklahoma State University, in Stillwater, earning his Ph.D. in agricultural (water resources) engineering in 1979.

In 1980, Peralta accepted an offer to become assistant professor of agricultural engineering at the University of Arkansas, in Fayetteville, where he eventually rose to the level of associate professor. While he was at Arkansas, Peralta directed more then 20 projects designed to ensure long-term access to groundwater supplies in a number of regions. He also worked on computer models to analyze and project the availability of water from aquifers and other sources. In 1988, Peralta left Arkansas to accept a position as associate professor of water systems engineering in the department of biological and irrigation engineering at Utah State University. He has since been promoted to full professor, a position he continues to hold. In 2003, he was named director of the Water Dynamics Laboratory at Utah State, a research facility of the Utah State University Research Foundation.

A major thrust of Peralta's work at Utah State has been the supervision of more than 40 projects for the development of groundwater optimization models (models for deciding the best way of using groundwater) and water quality management. Much of his work has involved the coordination of efforts by a variety of federal, state, and local agencies in dealing with water quality education, training, and activities.

Peralta is in demand as a consultant and adviser on water engineering problems throughout the United States and other nations of the world. He has traveled to China, Costa Rica, Egypt, Guatemala, India, Peru, and Senegal to work with local and national agencies on such issues. He is the author of more than 45 peer-reviewed papers in scientific journals and 125 reports dealing with water issues. Peralta has been honored with the Outstanding Researcher Award by the Department of Biological and Irrigation Engineering (1997) and by the College of Engineering (1998) at Utah State and the Halliburton Education Foundation Outstanding Researcher Award by the Department of Agricultural Engineering (1984, 1985, and 1987). He was also chosen one of the United States Jaycees' Outstanding Young Men of America in 1981, 1984, 1985, and 1990.

Further Reading

"Peralta, Richard Carl." In *American Men & Women of Science,* 21st ed., edited by Pamela M. Kalte and Katherine H. Nemeh, vol. 5, 939. Detroit: Thomson Gale, 2003.

"Peralta, Richard Carl." In *Who's Who among Hispanic Americans, 1994–95,* 3d ed., edited by Amy Unterburger, 615. Detroit: Gale Research, 1995.

Perez, Edith A.

(1956–   ) *medical researcher*

Edith A. Perez is professor of medicine at the Mayo Clinic College of Medicine in Rochester, Minnesota, and director of the Cancer Clinical Study Unit at the Mayo Clinic in Jacksonville, Florida. Her current research interests involve the study of new chemotherapeutical agents (chemicals used to treat disease) and biological therapies for the treatment of breast cancer.

Perez was born in Humacao, Puerto Rico, on April 30, 1956, to Edith Maldonado and Rubén Pérez. She received her B.S. in biology from the University of Puerto Rico at Río Piedras in 1975 and her M.D. from the University of Puerto Rico School of Medicine in 1979. She did her residency in internal medicine at the Loma Linda University Medical Center in Loma Linda, California, from 1979 to 1982. Perez then worked for two years as a general internist in the Division of National Health Service Corps in Los Angeles before accepting a fellowship in hematology and oncology at the Martinez Veterans Administration (VA) Medical

Center of the School of Medicine, University of California at Davis (UCD).

In 1987, Perez was appointed assistant professor of medicine in the department of internal medicine at the UCD School of Medicine. Two years later, she was made director of clinical oncology studies at the Martinez VA Medical Center, and in 1990, director of the Oncology Tumor Cell Laboratory. In 1992, Perez was appointed director of the Medical Breast Cancer Clinic at the UCD School of Medicine, and in 1993, she became acting chief of the Section of Hematology Oncology at the VA clinic.

In 1995, Perez left the UCD School of Medicine and the VA clinic to join the staff at the Mayo Clinic College of Medicine in Rochester, Minnesota. There she became professor of medicine, specializing in hematology and oncology. She was also named director of clinical investigations and director of the Breast Cancer Program in the Division of Hematology and Oncology for the Jacksonville, Florida, campus of the Mayo Clinic.

Perez currently serves as chair of the Breast Committee of the North Central Cancer Treatment Group. She is also a member of several committees of the American Society of Clinical Oncology and program director of the National Cancer Institute's Special Populations Working Group. She is the author of more than 60 scholarly papers in journals such as *Chest, Cancer, The Oncologist,* and the *Journal of Clinical Oncology.*

Further Reading

Daily News Health. "Edith A. Perez, MD." Available online. URL: http://nydailynews.healthology.com/nydailynews/1775.htm. Downloaded on March 11, 2005.

Health Talk. "Edith A. Perez, M.D." Available online. URL: http://www.healthtalk.com/bios/breastcancer/perez_edith.cfm. Downloaded on March 11, 2005.

"Perez, Edith A." In *Who's Who among Hispanic Americans, 1994–95,* 3d ed., edited by Amy Unterburger, 619. Detroit: Gale Research, 1995.

Pérez, Francisco L.
(Francisco Luis Pérez)
(1950–) *ecologist*

Francisco Luis Pérez specializes in the study of plant ecology, with particular attention to the relationships among plants, soils, microclimates, and geomorphic processes (changes in the Earth such as those produced by running water, glacial action, and volcanic activity). Most of his research has been conducted in high mountain ecosystems in the Sierra Nevada range of California, the Andes Mountains, and upper elevations of the Hawaiian Islands.

Pérez was born in Jumilla, Murcía, Spain, on July 16, 1950, the son of Josefina Sánchez Muñoz and Francisco Pérez Conca. He studied at the Universidad Central de Venezuela, in Caracas, from which he received his B.Arch. (bachelor of architecture) in 1973. He continued his studies at the University of California at Berkeley, where he earned his M.L.A. (master of landscape architecture) in 1976. He then returned to Venezuela, where he worked with the environmental planning company of Stoddart & Tabora, in Caracas, from 1976 to 1978, and the Venezuelan Ministry of the Environment, in 1978. Concurrently with these jobs, he served as assistant professor at the Universidad Central de Venezuela from 1976 to 1978.

In 1979, Pérez returned to Berkeley, where he became a teaching research assistant from 1979 to 1985 while working on his doctoral degree. At the completion of his doctoral studies, he took the post of visiting assistant professor of geography at the University of Georgia, in Athens, for one year. He then accepted an offer to join the faculty at the University of Texas at Austin as assistant professor in the department of geography and the environment. He has since been promoted to associate and then full professor, a position he continues to hold. His current areas of interest include alpine geomorphology, mountain geoecology, vegetation dynamics, ecological biogeography, and soil evolution.

Further Reading

"Pérez, Francisco Luis." In *American Men & Women of Science,* 21st ed., edited by Pamela M. Kalte and Katherine H. Nemeh, vol. 5, 941. Detroit: Thomson Gale, 2003.

"Pérez, Francisco Luis." In *Who's Who among Hispanic Americans, 1994–95,* 3d ed., edited by Amy Unterburger, 620. Detroit: Gale Research, 1995.

Quesada, Antonio R.
(1948–   ) *mathematician, mathematics educator*

In addition to his research in a number of areas of abstract mathematics, Antonio R. Quesada has long been interested in the philosophy and practice of mathematics education in the United States, has written extensively on the subject, and has been an invited speaker at a number of professional meetings about developments in mathematics education.

Quesada was born in Melilla, Spain, on January 29, 1948, the son of Milagros Rettschlag and Antonio Quesada. After completing high school, he became a teacher at the elementary and secondary level in Granada, Spain, while attending classes at the University of Granada, from which he obtained his Licenciatura en Matemáticas in 1971. He then took a position as instructor of mathematics at the Catholic University of Puerto Rico, in Ponce, where he was later promoted to assistant professor in 1974. He took a sabbatical leave from his post at the Catholic University in 1975 to begin a doctoral program in mathematics at the University of Florida, at Gainesville, completing the requirements for his Ph.D. in 1978. He then returned to his job at Catholic University, where he advanced from assistant professor (1978–80) to associate professor and chair of the mathematics department (1980–84).

In 1984, Quesada accepted an offer to become associate professor in the department of mathematical sciences at the University of Akron, in Akron, Ohio. From 1991 to 1993, he served as mathematics division coordinator in the department of mathematics, and in 1995, he was promoted to full professor of mathematics.

In his mathematical writings, Quesada has focused on a group of algebraic functions known as ring theory and on an algorithm known as the sieve of Eratosthenes, a very old method of determining all of the prime numbers up to a given number *n*. He has also been very interested in trends in high school mathematics and has written and spoken about topics such as teaching algebra with handheld computers, mathematical discoveries made by secondary math students, and the use of technology in mathematics classrooms. Quesada's work has been recognized by the George B. Thomas Scholarship, which is given "in recognition of contributions made to the advancement of mathematics education" (1992), and has received an award for outstanding achievements from the Board of Trustees Recognition Program of the University of Akron (1993–94), the Outstanding Achievement in Professional and Community Services award from the Buchtel College of Arts and Sciences of the University of Akron (2000), and the Teaching Award given by the Buchtel College of Arts and Sciences (1999–2000).

Further Reading

"Quesada, Antonio R." In *Who's Who among Hispanic Americans, 1994–95,* 3d ed., edited by Amy Unterburger, 643. Detroit: Gale Research, 1995.

University of Akron, Theoretical and Applied Mathematics. "Antonio R. Quesada." Welcome to My Homepage. Available online. URL: http://www.cs.uakron.edu/~quesada/. Downloaded on April 16, 2005.

R

Rael, Eppie D.
(Eppie David Rael)
(1943–) *microbiologist, inventor*

Eppie David Rael's research interests include immunology and immunotoxins (a plant or animal toxin that is attached to a monoclonal antibody, used to destroy a specific target cell), the biochemistry of snake venoms, the process of blood coagulation, human leukocyte antigens, and the general field of molecular biology.

Rael was born on January 17, 1943, in the Indian village of Cochiti, New Mexico, the youngest of 17 children. He has traced his ancestry to Alonzo Rael de Aguilar, who came to America in 1690 during the second wave of immigration by Spaniards into northern New Spain (later Mexico) and what was to become the state of New Mexico. Rael grew up speaking Spanish and the Indian language of Keresan and only learned to speak English when he started attending school. He graduated from Our Lady of Sorrows High School, in Bernalillo, New Mexico, in 1960, and then enrolled at the University of Albuquerque, expecting to major in government. After his first class in botany, however, Rael changed his mind and decided to major in biology. He was awarded his B.S. in 1965 and then continued his studies at New Mexico Highlands University (NMHU), in Las Vegas, New Mexico. After a year at NMHU, Rael joined the

U.S. Army, where he served as a clinical laboratory technician before returning to the university. He received his M.S. in biology from NMHU in 1970 and then moved to the University of Arizona, in Tucson, where he earned his Ph.D. in microbiology with a specialization in immunology and a minor in biochemistry in 1975.

Upon completion of his doctoral studies, Rael was hired as assistant professor at the University of Texas at El Paso (UTEP), beginning an association that was to last more than 30 years. He was eventually promoted to associate professor in 1983 and to full professor in 1990, a post he continues to hold. In addition to his teaching and research assignments, Rael has been involved with programs that promote the participation of minorities in the biological sciences. From 1983 to 1990 and again from 1998 to 1999, he was director of UTEP's Minority Biomedical Research Support (MBRS) Program, and since 1999, he has been director of the university's MBRS/SCORE (Support of Continuous Research Excellence) Program. Since 1999, he has also been chair of the department of biological sciences at UTEP and director of the Border Biomedical Research Center at UTEP.

Rael has written more than 40 scholarly articles and more than 400 abstracts of reports and research. He has received a patent for a monoclonal antibody for the Mojave toxin and served as a consultant to a number of academic institutions and industrial organizations, including Allergy, Immunology, and Rheumatology Health Associates, of El Paso; the International Science and Technology Center, Ulitsa Luganskaya, Moscow, Russia; the Howard Hughes Medical Institute, in Washington, D.C.; the Hispanic Association of Colleges and Universities; and the U.S.-Mexico Border Health Commission Project on Early Warning Infectious Disease Surveillance.

Further Reading

"Rael, Eppie David." In *American Men & Women of Science,* 21st ed., edited by Pamela M. Kalte and Katherine H. Nemeh, vol. 6, 24. Detroit: Thomson Gale, 2003.

Society for Advancement of Chicanos and Native Americans in Science. "Dr. Eppie David Rael—Molecular Biologist." SACNAS Biography Project. Available online. URL: http://64.171.10.183/biography/Biography.asp?mem=76&type=2. Downloaded on April 20, 2005.

University of Texas at El Paso. "Eppie Rael." Available online. URL: http://academics.utep.edu/Default.aspx?tabid=7730. Downloaded on April 20, 2005.

Eppie D. Rael is an immunologist with special interests in the study of immunotoxins and snake venom. He has long been active in science education programs for minority students. *(Courtesy of Eppie Rael)*

Ramírez, Mario E.
(Mario Efraín Ramírez)
(1926–   ) *physician, health administrator*

Mario Efraín Ramírez has been a practicing physician for more than a half century, during which time he also served on a number of medical and educational boards. In 1991, the Texas House of Representatives adopted a special resolution recognizing Ramírez's "many outstanding contributions . . . made to the betterment of this state and nation as a physician, educator, and public servant."

Ramírez was born on April 3, 1926, in Roma, Texas, to Carmen H. and Efren M. Ramírez, of Mexican ancestry. He attended elementary school in Roma and graduated from Rio Grande City High School in 1942. He then enrolled at the University of Texas at Austin, from which he earned his B.A. in 1945. He completed his medical studies at the University of Tennessee College of Medicine, in Memphis, receiving an M.D. in 1948. Upon completion of his residency at the Shreveport (Louisiana) Charity Hospital, Ramírez returned to his hometown of Roma, where he opened a private practice. Except for his service in the U.S. Army from 1955 to 1957, Ramírez maintained his Roma medical office until 1975, when he moved his office to Rio Grande City, Texas. He has continued to operate his Rio Grande City office for more than three decades and remained active in local and national medical groups.

Ramírez has long been highly regarded as a physician. Dr. John P. Howe III, president of the Health Science Center at the University of Texas, has called him "a physician's physician." However, he has also been interested in public service and has been appointed and elected to a number of important boards and commissions. In 1969, he was appointed judge and county health officer in Starr County, Texas, in which both Roma and Rio Grande City are located. He was then elected to the bench in 1970 and again in 1974. Ramírez has also long been associated with the state of Texas's program in medical education, having been appointed assistant professor in the Family Practice Program at the University of Texas Medical School at Houston and at the University of Texas Medical School at San Antonio in 1973.

Among the many positions of responsibility that Ramírez has held are member of the board of directors of Blue Cross and Blue Shield of Texas, the South Texas Development Council, the Council for South Texas Economic Progress, the Governor's Committee on Mental Retardation and Committee on Tuberculosis, the State of Texas Medical Care Advisory Committee of the Department of Public Welfare, the Greater South Texas Cultural Basin Commission, and the Texas Higher Education Coordinating Board. On the national scene, Ramírez served on the Ad Hoc Committee on Health Professions and the National Health Advisory Council and as regent of the Uniformed Services University of the Health Sciences. In 1988, he was appointed to the Board of Regents of the University of Texas System, an office he held until 1995.

Ramírez was awarded the *Good Housekeeping* magazine Family Doctor of the Year award

Mario E. Ramírez is a highly respected and honored physician who has served on a number of medical and educational commissions and boards. *(University of Texas at Austin)*

in 1978, the first Hispanic to have received that honor. He was also given the Dr. Benjamin Rush Award for Citizenship and Community Service of the American Medical Association in 1985 and the Mirabeau B. Lamar Medal from the Association of Texas Colleges and Universities in 1997.

Further Reading

Gutierrez, Roberto. "Resolution." Texas House of Representatives. Available online. URL: http://www.

capitol.state.tx.us/tlo/74R/billtext/HR00280I.
HTM. Downloaded on March 11, 2005.
"Mario E. Ramírez." In *The Hispanic American Alma-
nac,* 3d ed., edited by Sonia G. Benson, 774. Farm-
ington Hills, Mich.: Thomson Gale, 2003.
"Ramirez, Mario Efrain." In *Who's Who among Hispanic
Americans, 1994–95,* 3d ed., edited by Amy Unter-
burger, 654. Detroit: Gale Research, 1995.
University of Texas System. "Mario E. Ramírez, M.D."
Board of Regents. Available online. URL: www.
utsystem.edu/bor/regents/regentbios/Ramirez.pdf.
Downloaded on March 11, 2005.

Renteria, Hermelinda

(1960–) *construction engineer*

Hermelinda Renteria has filled a number of
responsible positions with Pacific Gas and Electric
(PG&E), of California, where she has worked since
1984. Among her assignments, she has been field
engineer at the Diablo Canyon Power Plant, in San
Luis Obispo, California, and contracts and technical services supervisor at PG&E's San Francisco
Bay Power Plant.

Renteria was born in Los Llamas, Zacatecas,
Mexico, on June 8, 1960, to María del Refugio
Chávez and Santiago Rentería. Her parents were
farmworkers who moved to Chico, California,
when Renteria was still a child to make a better life
for themselves and their four children. Between
1963 and 1966, the Renteria family moved around
the state, like many of their compatriots, trying to
find enough work to make a decent living. They
finally settled in Watsonville, California, where
Renteria, her sister, and her two brothers attended
local schools.

After graduating from high school, Renteria
decided to move back to Mexico to learn more
about her culture and heritage. She enrolled at the
Universidad Autónoma de Guadalajara, one of only
three women in a class of 123 students. Eventually,
all three of the women graduated but only half of
the men did. During her years at Guadalajara,
Renteria became something of a political activist, reacting especially to her teachers' and elders'
traditional expectations for women. In reaction to
the popular Miss Universe contest, for example,
she proposed that a "King Ugly" contest be held
on campus.

After receiving her B.S. in civil engineering
in 1983, Renteria returned to Watsonville to work
at her parents' business. A year later, she moved
to Ventura, California, where she took a series of
jobs that included engineering aide in the city
of Ventura Engineering Department, draftsperson at the Ventura County Road Maintenance
Department, draftsperson at Gerald Graebe &
Associates, and farm manager at Linda's Farms.
Finally, she was offered a job in civil engineering, the field for which she had been trained,
with PG&E. At first, she was given assignments
appropriate to those of a civil engineer but also
was treated by her colleagues, in many cases, as a
glorified secretary. When she complained to her
superiors about this treatment, she was finally
given a significant assignment, supervising a mil-
lion-dollar construction project for the company.
From there, she went on to the Diablo Canyon
and San Francisco Bay projects and a successful
career at PG&E.

Renteria has long been active in professional
organizations in engineering, for women, and for
Hispanics. She has been an active member of the
American Society of Civil Engineers, the Society
of Women Engineers, the League of Latin American Citizens, and the Society of Hispanic Professional Engineers (SHPE), of which she has been
San Francisco chapter president for four terms
and national secretary from 1988 to 1991. She
has been awarded the Women on the Move Certificate of Honor of the Anti-Defamation League
of B'nai B'rith; a Certificate of Merit by the
Young Women's Christian Association; a certificate of appreciation from Skyline College of San
Bruno, California; a Performance Recognition

Award from PG&E; and an award for outstanding leadership and dedication to her field from SHPE.

Further Reading

Bernstein, Leonard, Alan Winkler, and Linda Zierdt-Warshaw. "Hermelinda Renteria." *Latino Women of Science,* 50–51. Maywood, N.J.: Peoples Publishing Group, 1998.

"Hermelinda Renteria." In *Notable Hispanic American Women,* edited by Diane Telgen, Jim Kamp, and Joseph M. Palmisano, 337. Detroit: Gale Research, 1998.

"Renteria, Hermelinda." In *Who's Who among Hispanic Americans, 1994–95,* 3d ed., edited by Amy Unterburger, 664. Detroit: Gale Research, 1995.

Reyes, José N., Jr.
(1955–) *nuclear physicist*

José N. Reyes, Jr., is a nuclear engineer with a special interest in thermal hydraulics (the application of heat transfer principles to nuclear power plants), advanced light water reactor safety, reactor system design, and risk assessment of nuclear systems. He is currently working on safety studies of the new Westinghouse AP1000 nuclear reactor, which some experts believe to be one of the most promising new nuclear reactor designs to have been developed in decades.

Reyes was born in New York City on November 21, 1955, the son of Melba and José Napoleón Reyes, of Dominican ancestry. He attended the University of Florida, in Gainesville, earning his B.S. in nuclear engineering in 1978. He attended the University of Maryland at College Park for his graduate studies, receiving his M.S. in nuclear engineering in 1984 and his Ph.D., also in nuclear engineering, in 1986. While studying at Maryland, Reyes worked for the U.S. Nuclear Regulatory Commission (NRC), the federal agency responsible for licensing and safety of all nuclear power reactors in the United States. At NRC, he was a nuclear engineering intern from 1977 to 1979, a member of the technical staff in 1980, and a research engineer from 1980 to 1987.

After receiving his doctoral degree, Reyes took a job as assistant professor at Oregon State University, in Corvallis, where he has remained ever since. He now holds the Henry W. and Janice J. Schutte Chair in Nuclear Engineering and Radiation Health Physics and serves as director of the university's Advanced Thermal Hydraulics Research Laboratory. From 1988 to 1989, Reyes was also consultant to the Westinghouse Corporation at its Hanford, Washington, nuclear facility.

Reyes's research on the AP1000 reactor is of considerable interest to the nuclear industry. The plant is designed with significantly fewer working parts than most existing nuclear reactors, resulting in a reduced risk of accident or malfunction. If the plant turns out to be as safe as its proponents expect, a question Reyes is testing in his experimental facility, prospects for the expansion of nuclear power reactors throughout the world should be significantly increased.

Reyes has been honored for his work in nuclear reactor safety with a Special Achievement Award for Outstanding Contributions to the NRC (1986), the Austin-Paul Engineering Faculty Award at Oregon State (1990), and the College of Engineering Research Award for 1997.

Further Reading

Oregon State University. "José N. Reyes, Jr." Nuclear Energy and Radiation Health Physics. Available online. URL: http://ne.oregonstate.edu/people/faculty/reyes.html. Downloaded on April 15, 2005.

"Reyes, José N., Jr." In *Who's Who among Hispanic Americans, 1994–95,* 3d ed., edited by Amy Unterburger, 668. Detroit: Gale Research, 1995.

Ricardo-Campbell, Rita
(Rita Ricardo)
(1920–) *economist*

Rita Ricardo-Campbell has made a number of breakthroughs in the field of business, including being the first woman to teach economics at Harvard University, to serve on the President's Economic Policy Advisory Board, and to win an appointment as senior fellow at the Hoover Institution at Stanford University.

Ricardo was born in Boston, Massachusetts, on March 16, 1920, the daughter of Elizabeth Jones and David A. Ricardo. She is of Spanish background and descended from the eminent economist David Ricardo (1772–1823). She attended Simmons College, an all-women's institution in Boston, earning her B.S. in library sciences in 1941. She then enrolled at Harvard University, in Cambridge, Massachussets, and majored in economics, receiving her M.A. in that subject in 1945 and her Ph.D. in 1946. In 1946, she also married fellow economist Wesley Glenn Campbell and changed her name to Ricardo-Campbell.

Ricardo-Campbell was fortunate to have been at Harvard during the early 1940s when the relative scarcity of men on campus because of World War II made it easier for her to get a job at the university. While still a graduate student, she served first as a research assistant from 1942 to 1946 and as a teaching fellow and tutor from 1944 to 1946, before being appointed as instructor in the department of economics in 1946. In 1948, Ricardo-Campbell left Harvard to take a job as assistant professor of economics at Tufts University in Boston. After three years, she took a position with the Wage Stabilization Board in 1951. Two years later, she joined the staff of the U.S. House of Representative's Ways and Means Committee as an economics adviser. She then left government in 1956 to work for four years as a consulting economist.

In 1960, Ricardo-Campbell left the East Coast to spend a year as visiting professor of economics at San Jose State University in San Jose, California. At the conclusion of that assignment, she took a position as archivist and research fellow at the Hoover Institution at Stanford University, in Stanford, California. She was then promoted to senior fellow at Hoover in 1968, a title she continues to hold.

In addition to her early jobs in Washington, Ricardo-Campbell has served on a number of governmental committees and commissions. She was a member of the President's Economic Policy Advisory Board from 1981 to 1989, the President's National Council on the Humanities from 1982 to 1988, and the President's Committee on the National Medal of Science in 1988. From 1967 to 1975, she was commissioner for the state of California on the Western Interstate Commission for Higher Education. In addition, Ricardo-Campbell has held important positions in the business community, serving on the board of directors of the Gillette Company, the Watkins-Johnson Company, and the Samaritan Medical Center. She is the author of a number of important books, including *Social Security: Promise and Reality* (1977), *The Economics and Politics of Health* (1982), and *Resisting Hostile Takeovers: The Case of Gillette* (1997).

Further Reading

Hoover Institution. "Rita Ricardo-Campbell." Available online. URL: http://www-hoover.stanford.edu/bios/rrc.html. Downloaded on March 11, 2005.

"Ricardo-Campbell, Rita." In *Who's Who among Hispanic Americans, 1994–95,* 3d ed., edited by Amy Unterburger, 672. Detroit: Gale Research, 1995.

Vachon, Michelle. "Rita Ricardo-Campbell." In *Notable Hispanic American Women,* edited by Diane Telgen, Jim Kamp, and Joseph M. Palmisano, 339–340. Detroit: Gale Research, 1998.

Rios, Miguel, Jr.
(1941–   ) *physicist*

Miguel Rios, Jr., worked for 10 years at Sandia National Laboratories on a diverse array of projects, including photovoltaics (the use of light to produce electricity), nuclear reactor safety, and nuclear weapons safety and security. In 1985, he founded his own company, Orion International Technologies, Inc., which provides engineering and technical support services to the Department of Energy National Laboratories, the Federal Aviation Administration, other federal agencies, and contractors working on federal projects. Orion also contracts with the U.S. Department of Defense for projects related to the development, testing, and evaluation of new defense systems.

Rios was born in El Paso, Texas, on July 18, 1941, to Felicitas Cumplido and Miguel Rios. He grew up in a family with strong cultural ties to Mexico and that valued education. As he later reported, he learned mathematics from his grandfather before he learned to speak English. Rios became interested in science at an early age, largely because of the launch of the first artificial satellite, *Sputnik I,* by the Soviet Union in 1957. That event made it clear to him, he later said, "that people in science were going to be respected in our society," and he wanted to be one of those people.

Rios attended the University of Southern California, in Los Angeles, where he earned his B.S. in physics in 1965. He then continued his studies at California State University at Los Angeles (CSULA), from which he was awarded his M.S. in physics in 1967. He completed his doctoral studies in experimental nuclear physics at the University of Maryland at College Park in 1971. His first teaching position was at California State Polytechnic University, in Pomona, where he served as assistant professor from 1971 to 1974. Concurrent with this appointment, Rios pursued further studies in the field of nuclear astrophysics as a visiting research assistant at the Kellogg Laboratory at the California Institute of Technology, in Pasadena, from 1972 to 1974.

Rios moved to Sandia National Laboratories in 1975 as a member of the technical staff, a post he held until 1984. He then decided to establish his own company, Orion International, based in Albuquerque, New Mexico, which he now leads as chief executive officer. In 2000, Rios created a subsidiary to Orion, Orion Information Technologies, created to offer electronic business (e-business) solutions and support services to companies operating in the commercial, state, and municipal market sectors. Rios added another important title to his résumé in 2001 when he was elected chairman of the board of the National Center for Genome Resources (NCGR), in Santa Fe, New Mexico. NCGR is an independent nonprofit research institution that develops software and computer programs for use in biological research. It was founded in 1994 (when Rios first joined its board of directors) for the purpose of working with the Los Alamos National Laboratory in developing the Genome Sequence Data Base, the first database of human genome sequences available to the general public.

Rios was voted Outstanding Physics Teacher of the Year and Distinguished Alumnus at CSULA in 1981 and chosen Hispanic Engineer Entrepreneur of the Year by *Hispanic Business* magazine in 1992. He was also named National Minority Entrepreneur of the Year for 1999 by the Office of Minority Business Development Agency of the U.S. Department of Commerce. Both Rios and his wife, Maria Estela de Rios, managing director at Orion, have been given the Award of Entrepreneurship from the Ministry of Foreign Relations of the government of Mexico.

Further Reading
Alvarez, Maria Elena. "Discussing Life after Physics at Maryland." *Photon* (February 2002) 1. Avail-

able online. URL: www.physics.umd.edu/news/
photon/Archives/Issue18_Alum.pdf. Downloaded
on April 15, 2005.

Orion International Technologies. "Corporate Background." Available online. URL: http://www.
orionint.com/AboutORION/corpbkground.cfm.
Downloaded on April 15, 2005.

"Rios, Miguel, Jr." In *Who's Who among Hispanic Americans, 1994–95,* 3d ed., edited by Amy Unterburger,
674. Detroit: Gale Research, 1995.

Rivero, Juan A.
(1923–   ) *zoologist*

Juan A. Rivero is one of the world's authorities on
the taxonomy of South American amphibians, having discovered and named more than 100 species
of amphibians and reptiles. He is also interested
in a number of other biological topics, including
organic evolution, distribution of plant and animal life, and endemism, the condition in which a
particular plant or animal species is restricted to a
specific geographical area.

Rivero was born in San Juan, Puerto Rico,
on May 3, 1923. He received his B.S. in biology
at the Agricultural University of Puerto Rico, in
Mayagüez, in 1945. He then worked as an assistant
plant physiologist at the Institute of Tropical Agriculture in Mayagüez for one year before taking the
post of instructor in the biology department at the
University of Puerto Rico at Mayagüez (UPRM).
He retained that title until 1953, while continuing his studies at Harvard University, in Cambridge, Massachusetts, where he earned his M.S.
in 1951 and his Ph.D. in biology in 1953. Rivero
then returned to UPRM, where he has remained
ever since. He was made assistant professor of biology (1953–54), then associate professor (1954–
58), and finally full professor (1958–present) at
UPRM.

During the period between 1954 and 1963,
Rivero devoted his efforts to the creation of two
major biological facilities in Mayagüez, the Zoological Garden and the Institute of Marine Biology. The Zoological Garden, since named the
Dr. Juan A. Rivero Zoo in his honor, is a particularly attractive facility in which animals are
displayed in open spaces similar to their own
natural habitats. In addition to his teaching and
research activities, Rivero has been director of
the UPRM biology department (1959–60); dean
of the School of Arts and Sciences at UPRM
(1962–66); research associate at Harvard University studying the origin, evolution, and ecology of Andean fauna (1966–68); visiting scientist
at the Instituto Venezolano de Investigaciones
Científicas, in Caracas, working on the origin,
evolution, and ecology of the Andean fauna; and
consultant to Puerto Rico University, in San
Juan.

Rivero has written more than 150 articles of
scholarly and general interest and is the author
of 11 books and monographs, including *Sali-
entia of Venezuela* (1961), *Los anfibios y reptiles
de Puerto Rico* (The amphibians and reptiles of
Puerto Rico, 1978), and *El dolor de la espalda
baja: De paciente a paciente* (Lower back pain:
Patient to patient, 2000). Rivero was a Guggenheim Fellow in 1970 and was awarded first prize
by the Instituto de Literatura Puertorriqueña for
his book *Los anfibios y reptiles de Puerto Rico* in
1979. Since 1986, he has been involved in the
production of *Ciencia al Día,* a television program about the latest in science, sponsored by
the Puerto Rican Department of Instruction. In
1987, he was named Distinguished Professor at
the University of Puerto Rico, the highest academic honor conferred by the university on its
professors.

Further Reading
"Rivero, Juan A." In *American Men & Women of Science,*
21st ed., edited by Pamela M. Kalte and Katherine
H. Nemeh, vol. 6, 214. Detroit: Thomson Gale,
2003.

"Rivero, Juan A." In *Who's Who among Hispanic Americans, 1994–95,* 3d ed., edited by Amy Unterburger, 685. Detroit: Gale Research, 1995.

Robles, Bárbara J.
(1957–   ) *economist*

Bárbara J. Robles is an expert in taxation, management of public finances, and microeconomics, the study of individual components of an economy, such as families and individual businesses. She was formerly an economist for the Joint Committee on Taxation of the U.S. Congress.

Robles was born in Dilley, Texas, on November 29, 1957, the daughter of Edna Lozano Sanchez and Patricio Garcia Sanchez, of Mexican descent. She attended the University of Texas at Austin, from which she received her B.A. in Spanish and French comparative literature in 1978. She then transferred to the University of Maryland at College Park, where she majored in economics, earning her Ph.D. in 1990. Her areas of specialization at Maryland were econometrics, the application of statistical and mathematical methods to the study of economic problems, and monetary theory and policy.

After receiving her doctorate, Robles took a job as assistant professor of economics at the University of Colorado at Boulder, where she taught and did research until 1995. She then accepted a position as economist and revenue estimator for Congress's Joint Committee on Taxation from 1995 to 1997. In 1998, Robles became assistant professor of economics in the Lyndon B. Johnson School of Public Affairs at the University of Texas at Austin, a position she continues to fill. In spring 2003, she took a leave of absence from Texas to serve as visiting faculty fellow at the Institute for Latino Studies at the University of Notre Dame in South Bend, Indiana.

Robles has made a number of conference and seminar presentations on a variety of economic issues, with special emphasis on those affecting Latinos and their communities. Some examples include "Is Your Credit Union 'Hispanic Ready'?" (Credit Union National Association), "Wealth Building in Latino Communities" (Congressional Hispanic Caucus Institute), "Wealth Inequality Indicators for Latinos in the U.S." (Ford Foundation Conference on Asset Building in Communities of Color), and "Latino Purchasing Power" (Latino Economic Summit, Organization of American States). She has also served as consultant to a number of governmental and nongovernmental bodies, including the Annie E. Casey Foundation, the Asian-Pacific Economic Commission, the University of Colorado, and the University of Maryland.

In addition to writing papers for journals such as *Applied Economics, Review of Economics and Statistics,* and *Aztlán: International Journal of Chicano Studies Research,* Robles is working on four books, *Rich Latino/Poor Latino: Wealth Inequality, Cultural Capital, and Asset Building Policies; The Growth of Microenterprise in the Borderlands: Latino Entrepreneurs, Family Well Being, and Community Asset Building* (with Perla Cavazos); *Revisiting the Melting Pot: The Politics and Policies of Multiculturalism in the US* (edited with Xavier Torrens and Federico Subervi); and *The Color of Wealth: How Government Policies Widened the Racial Wealth Divide* (with Meizhu Lui, Betsy Leondar-Wright, Rose M. Brewer, and Rebecca Adamson).

Further Reading
Federal Reserve Bank of Chicago. "Financial Access for Immigrants: Learning from Diverse Perspectives—Presenter Biographies." Available online. URL: http://www.chicagofed.org/news_and_conferences/conferences_and_events/financial_access_for_immigrants_learning_from_diverse_perspectives_presenter_biographies.cfm. Downloaded on March 11, 2005.

"Robles, Bárbara." In *Who's Who among Hispanic Americans, 1994–95,* 3d ed., edited by Amy Unterburger, 686. Detroit: Gale Research, 1995.

Rodón-Naveira, Miriam

(1963–) *marine ecologist, science administrator*

Miriam Rodón-Naveira has an undergraduate degree in psychology and a doctorate in biology, with a specialization in aquatic microbial ecology. She has been a teacher, a researcher, and an administrator of science programs in a variety of capacities for the National Aeronautics and Space Administration (NASA).

Rodón-Naveira was born in San Juan, Puerto Rico, on April 2, 1963, into a family that she has described as "highly educated and goal oriented." Her mother is the Honorable Miriam Naveira Merly, the first woman to become chief justice of the Supreme Court of Puerto Rico. Rodón-Naveira graduated from the Academia Perpétuo Socorro High School, in San Juan, and attended Georgetown University, in Washington, D.C., from which she received her B.S. in psychology in 1985. She continued her graduate studies at Georgetown, changing her major to biology and earth science, with a specialization in microecology of aquatic systems.

After graduation from Georgetown, Rodón-Naveira took a job with the Environmental Pro-

Miriam Rodón-Naveira has been a researcher and administrator at the U.S. Environmental Protection Agency and the National Aeronautics and Space Administration since 1990. *(National Aeronautics and Space Administration)*

tection Agency (EPA) as biologist and technical assistant to the associate director of the Office of Research and Development in the EPA's Environmental Monitoring and Assessment Program (EMAP, 1990–91), in Washington, D.C. She was promoted to scientific and international coordinator in the same office the following year and then became environmental research scientist in the EPA's Quality Assurance Technical Support Division at Research Triangle Park, North Carolina. Over the next decade, she also served as principal investigator for the EPA in a part-time research project at the College of Veterinary Medicine of North Carolina State University, in Raleigh (1995); chief of the Exposure Assessment Branch of the EPA's Air Exposure Research Division, in Research Triangle Park (1995–97); chief of the National Exposure Research Laboratory's (NERL) Landscape Characterization Branch, in Research Triangle Park (1997–98 and 1999–2000); and acting deputy director of the Environmental Sciences Division of NERL, in Las Vegas, Nevada (1998–99). During this period, she was the first woman minority branch chief to serve at NERL and the first Latina to be named deputy director with NERL.

In 2000, Rodón-Naveira left the EPA to join NASA as Earth science remote sensing physical scientist in its Aerospace Projects Directorate at the Dryden Flight Research Center (DFRC), in Edwards, California. In 2001, through a special agreement with NASA, she was named distinguished visiting professor at the Bayamón campus of the Inter-American University, in Puerto Rico, a post she continues to hold. In February 2003, Rodón-Naveira was named chief science adviser and higher education director in the Office of Academic Investments at DFRC, her current position with NASA. Her assignment in this job is the management of DFRC's higher-education academic programs. She has also been involved in the ongoing development of the Unmanned Aerial Vehicle by NASA.

Rodón-Naveira has received a Congressional Certificate of Recognition (1999), the Outstanding Leadership in Management Award of the Southern Nevada Federal Executive Association (1999), the Silver Medal Award of the EPA (2001), and the EPA's Suzanne Olive EEO (Equal Employment Opportunity) and Diversity Award (2000).

Further Reading
National Aeronautics and Space Administration. "Miriam Rodón-Naveira, Ph.D." Latina Women of NASA. Available online. URL: http://oeop.larc.nasa.gov/hep/lwon/LWONbios/dfrc-MRodonNaveira.html. Downloaded on April 19, 2005.

Rodríguez, Clara E.
(Clara Elsie Rodríguez)
(1944–) *sociologist*

Clara Elsie Rodríguez's fields of special interest include race and ethnicity, media, Latino studies, labor markets, and migration. She has written more than 50 articles and nine books on Latinos in the United States.

Rodríguez was born in New York City on March 29, 1944, the daughter of Clarita Pérez and Angel Manuel Rodríguez, of Puerto Rican descent. She attended the City College of New York, from which she received her B.A. in sociology in 1965; Cornell University, where she earned her M.A. in Latin American studies in 1969; and Washington University, in St. Louis, Missouri, which granted her a Ph.D. in sociology and urban and regional studies in 1973. Rodríguez's first teaching appointment was as adjunct professor of sociology at Pace University in New York City in 1973. She was then appointed assistant professor and chair of the Puerto Rican studies department at Fordham University, in New York City. In 1976, she became dean of the School of General Studies at

Fordham and project director of the Pre-Health Professions program, posts she held until 1981. In that year, Rodríguez was promoted to associate professor at Fordham. She has been affiliated with Fordham ever since, having been made full professor in 1991.

During the past two decades, however, she has also served at a number of other universities and institutions. During the 1987–88 academic year, she was visiting scholar in the department of urban studies and planning at the Massachusetts Institute of Technology, in Cambridge, Massachusetts. She was also visiting fellow at Yale University, in New Haven, Connecticut, in 1992; visiting scholar at the Russell Sage Foundation in New York City during 1993–94; senior fellow at the archives center of the National Museum of American History of the Smithsonian Institution in Washington, D.C., in spring 1999; and visiting professor at Columbia University, in New York City, in 1998.

Rodríguez has been very active as a consultant to both governmental and nongovernmental agencies such as the American Association for the Advancement of Science, the U.S. Bureau of the Census, the Children's Television Workshop, the Center for Latino Family Policy, the Educational Testing Service, the Ford Foundation, the Gallup Organization, the Hispanic Research Center at Fordham, the Institute for Puerto Rican Policy of the Puerto Rican Legal Defense Fund, the Interuniversity Program for Contemporary Latino Research, the Mayor's Advisory Committee on Appointments, the National Council of La Raza, the National Institute of Education, the National Puerto Rican Coalition, the New-York Historical Society, the Prescriptive Cosmetic Company, the Screen Actors Guild, the Social Science Research Council, the Commission on Civil Rights of the State of New York, the U.S. Commission on Civil Rights, the U.S. Department of Health and Human Services, and the U.S. Department of Labor.

The titles of Rodríguez's books provide a suggestion of the range of her research interests. They include *The Ethnic Queue in the U.S.: The Case of Puerto Ricans* (1974), *Puerto Ricans: Born in the U.S.A.* (1991), *Changing Race: Latinos, the Census, and the History of Ethnicity in the United States* (2000), and *Heroes, Lovers, and Others: The Story of Latinos in Hollywood* (2004). She has also published a number of chapters in anthologies dealing with Latinos and other racial and ethnic issues. These include "Puerto Ricans in Historical and Social Science Research," in *Handbook of Research on Multicultural Education* (1995); "Issues of Race and Class among Puerto Rican Women," in *Confrontations et Métissages* (1996); "Racial Themes in the Literature on Puerto Ricans," in *Latinos in New York: Communities in Transition* (1996); and "Latino Performing Arts," in *Encyclopedia of American Studies* (2001).

Among the many honors that Rodríguez has received are the Star Award of the New York Women's Agenda (1992), the National Society of Hispanic MBAs Leadership in Educational Excellence Award (1995), the Premio Ciencias Sociales (Distinguished Prize in Social Sciences) of the Instituto de Puerto Rico of New York (1997), the Alumni Association Plaque of Fordham University's College at Lincoln Center (1991), the Award for Distinguished Contribution to Research of the American Sociological Association (2001), and the Fordham University Award for Distinguished Teaching in the Social Sciences (2003).

Further Reading

"Clara Rodríguez." In *The Hispanic American Almanac,* 3d ed., edited by Sonia G. Benson, 781–782. Farmington Hills, Mich.: Thomson Gale, 2003.

"Rodríguez, Clara Elsie." In *Who's Who among Hispanic Americans, 1994–95,* 3d ed., edited by Amy Unterburger, 693. Detroit: Gale Research, 1995.

Rodríguez, Eloy
(1947–   ) *biochemist*

Eloy Rodríguez is probably best known as the founder of the science of zoopharmacognosy, the study of plants that animals use for their own self-medication. Research in this field holds the potential for discovering many new drugs that can be used for human health needs also.

Rodríguez was born in Edinburg, Texas, on January 7, 1947, the son of Hilaria Calvillo and Everardo Rodríguez. He grew up in a very poor but tightly knit Chicano community in which he had 67 cousins within a five-block radius of his home. Even though the county was then the poorest in the nation, on the basis of per capita income, 64 of his 67 cousins managed to earn college degrees, and 11 received a Ph.D.

The schools Rodríguez attended in Edinburg were similar to many other schools in the Southwest at that time. They consisted primarily of Chicano boys and girls being taught by non-Chicanos who had low expectations of their students. Rodríguez's teachers and counselors suggested that he attend vocational school rather than college. But, as he later wrote, he felt that he was capable of more than "fixing cars," so he enrolled at the University of Texas at Austin (UTA), planning to become an accountant. He soon learned that accounting was not what he most enjoyed, however, and switched his major to zoology, with a minor in organic chemistry. In 1969, he was awarded his B.A. in biology, and in 1975, he received his Ph.D. in phytochemistry (the study of chemicals obtained from plants) and plant biology from UTA.

Rodríguez received his first academic appointment in 1976, when he joined the University of California at Irvine's College of Medicine with a joint appointment in the School of Biological Sciences' toxicology program and department of community and environmental medicine. He remained at Irvine, eventually reaching the level of full professor, until 1995, when he was offered the James

Eloy Rodríguez is widely recognized as the founder of the science of zoopharmacognosy, the study of plants that animals use for their own self-medication. *(Cornell University Photography)*

Perkins Chair of Environmental Studies at Cornell University, in Ithaca, New York. Rodríguez continues to hold that post today.

Rodríguez first became interested in the field that is now known as zoopharmacognosy in the mid-1980s when a researcher from Harvard University, Richard Wrangham, sent him plant material that Wrangham had seen chimpanzees use in an apparent attempt to treat the illnesses with which they were afflicted. Rodríguez extracted from the plants a reddish oil containing a chemical known as thiarubrin-A, which acts as an antibiotic and attacks parasites that are found in the gut. The chimps that Wrangham had studied had apparently evolved the ability to select plant materials from their environment with which to treat their own medical problems. Researchers later found that thiarubrin-A is effective against other diseases, too, including the retroviruses responsible for human immunodeficiency virus infection and AIDS (acquired immunedeficiency syndrome). Rodríguez realized the enormous potential of studying plants that animals other than humans used for self-medication and named this field of research *zoopharmacognosy*. He now conducts much of his own research in the field, in places such as the Amazon forest, trying to find plants that may yield drugs that can eventually be used for the treatment of human diseases also.

In addition to his research work, Rodríguez has long been interested in programs for the improvement of educational opportunities for underrepresented minorities. At Irvine, for example, he served on the California Alliance for Minority Participation Program, as director of the National Chicano Council on Higher Education, and as national vice president of the Society for Advancement of Chicanos and Native Americans in Science. He has been honored with the first annual Hispanic Educator Award from the League of United Latin American Citizens (1984), the Professional Research Accomplishment Recognition Award of the *Los Angeles Times* (1989), and the Martín de la Cruz Silver Medal for Outstanding Research on Medicinal Plants of the Mexican Academy of Traditional Medicine (1992). In 1991, he was named Outstanding College Professor by *Hispanic Engineer* magazine.

Further Reading

"Eloy Rodríguez." In *The Hispanic American Almanac*, 3d ed., edited by Sonia G. Benson, 782. Farmington Hills, Mich.: Thomson Gale, 2003.

North Carolina Society of Hispanic Professionals. "Keynote Speakers." Available online. URL: http://www.thencshp.org/HispanicSummit2003/Speakers.htm. Downloaded on March 12, 2005.

Rodríguez, Eloy. "I'd Never Really Thought about Being a Scientist . . . ," *IDRA Newsletter* (June–July 1996), 8ff. Available online. URL: http://www.idra.org/Newslttr/1996/Jun/Eloy.htm#I_d_Never_Really_Thought. Downloaded on March 12, 2005.

"Rodríguez, Eloy." In *Who's Who among Hispanic Americans, 1994–95,* 3d ed., edited by Amy Unterburger, 695. Detroit: Gale Research, 1995.

Society for Advancement of Chicanos and Native Americans in Science. "Dr. Eloy Rodríguez—Natural Products Chemist." SACNAS Biography Project. Available online. URL: http://64.171.10.183/biography/Biography.asp?mem=77&type=2. Downloaded on March 12, 2005.

Rodriguez, Juan G.
(Juan Guadalupe Rodriguez)
(1920–   ) *entomologist*

Juan Guadalupe Rodriguez is a highly respected authority on the nutritional ecology of insects and mites, the study of the relationships between nutrients required by insects and mites and their health patterns. He also served for many years as a volunteer at the Kentucky Academy of Sciences, where he has held every office in the association, including serving as president from 1982 to 1983.

Rodriguez was born in Espanola, New Mexico, on December 23, 1920, the son of Lugardita S. and Manuel D. Rodriguez, of Mexican ancestry. He attended New Mexico State University, in Las Cruces, from which he received his B.S. He then continued his studies at Ohio State University, in Columbus, where he earned his M.S. in 1946 and his Ph.D. in entomology in 1949. Upon receiving his doctorate, Rodriguez took a job as assistant at the University of Kentucky's Experimental Station, in Lexington. He then served as assistant entomologist and associate entomologist at the university from 1949 to 1959 before receiving an appointment as associate professor in the department of entomology. Two years later, in 1961, he was promoted to full professor, a post he held until his retirement in 1987. He now holds the title of emeritus professor of entomology at Kentucky.

Rodriguez has long been active in the Kentucky Academy of Sciences, serving as a volunteer in every office within the association. For many years, he was executive secretary, a position he filled without pay. For his many contributions to the academy, he was given an Outstanding Academy Service award in January 2003.

Rodriguez is the author of more than 150 scientific papers on the nutritional ecology of insects and mites, as well as the editor or coeditor of five books, including *Insect and Mite Nutrition: Significance and Implications in Ecology and Pest Management* (1972), *Recent Advances in Acarology* (1979), and *Nutritional Ecology of Insects, Mites, Spiders, and Related Invertebrates* (1987). He has been elected a fellow of the Entomological Society of America, the American Association for the Advancement of Science, and the Royal Entomological Society of London.

Further Reading

"Rodriguez, Juan G." In *Who's Who among Hispanic Americans, 1994–95,* 3d ed., edited by Amy Unterburger, 784. Detroit: Gale Research, 1995.

"Rodriguez, Juan Guadalupe." In *American Men & Women of Science,* 21st ed., edited by Pamela M. Kalte and Katherine H. Nemeh, vol. 6, 261. Detroit: Thomson Gale, 2003.

Rodriguez-Iturbe, Ignacio
(1942–) *civil engineer*

The interaction among climate, soil, and vegetation is the primary focus of Ignacio Rodriguez-Iturbe's research. He has been awarded the Robert E. Horton Medal of the American Geophysical Union for "outstanding contributions to the geophysical aspects of hydrology" and the Stockholm Water Prize, widely recognized as the "Nobel Prize in hydrology."

Rodrdiguez-Iturbe was born in Caracas, Venezuela, on March 8, 1942. He earned his undergraduate degree at the Universidad del Zulia, in Maracaibo, Venezuela, in 1963. After immigrating to the United States, Rodriguez-Iturbe received his M.S. from the California Institute of Technology, in Pasadena, in 1965, and his Ph.D. from Colorado State University, in Fort Collins, in 1967, both in engineering. He then returned to Venezuela, where he became associate professor in the civil engineering department at the Universidad del Zulia (1967–69) and associate researcher at the Instituto Venezolano de Investigaciones Científicas in Caracas (1969–1971). In 1971, he left Venezuela to take the post of associate professor in the civil engineering department at the Massachusetts Institute of Technology (MIT), in Cambridge. Two years later, he was made associate head of the water resources division of the civil engineering department at MIT.

In 1975, Rodriguez-Iturbe was named professor of engineering at the Universidad Simón Bolívar in Caracas, a post he held for 20 years. While at Simón Bolívar, he was also head of the graduate program in hydrology and water resources (1975–77), dean of research (1975–79), dean of graduate studies (1980–81), and professor at the Instituto Internacional de Estudios Avanzados, in Caracas (1987–93). Rodriguez-Iturbe maintained his relationship with MIT during this period, holding a part-time assignment as visiting professor and senior lecturer in the civil engineering department from 1987 to 1993. He was also endowed professor of civil and environmental engineering at the Iowa Institute of Hydraulic Research, at the University of Iowa, in Iowa City, from 1989 to 1991 and R. P. Gregory Professor and head of the civil engineering department at Texas A&M University, in College Station, from 1993 to 1999.

In 1999, Rodriguez-Iturbe moved to his present assignment at the department of civil and environmental engineering and the Princeton Environmental Institute at Princeton University, in Princeton, New Jersey, where he has been director of the Center for Energy and Environmental Studies (1999–2002) and is professor (1999–present) and Theodora Shelton Pitney Professor of Environmental Sciences (2001–present). In addition to the Horton and Stockholm prizes, Rodriguez-Iturbe has received, among others, the Huber Research Prize of the American Society for Civil Engineers (1975); the James B. Macelwane Award of the American Geophysical Union (1977); the Medal "Orden 27 de June" for Merits in Education granted by the government of Venezuela (1977); the Francisco J. Torrealba Prize awarded by the Universidad Simón Bolívar (1985); Order "Andrés Bello," 1st Class by the government of Venezuela (1988); the Medal Dr. Antonio Borjas, Distinguished Alumnus Award by the Universidad del Zulia (1991); the Academic Medal of the University of Florence, Italy, (1991); an honorary doctor's degree by the University of Genoa, Italy (1992); the Academic Medal of the University of Padua, Italy (1992); the Colorado State University Honor Alumnus Award (1994); the Premio México de Ciencia y Tecnología of the Republic of Mexico (1994); the National Engineering Research Prize by the government of Venezuela (1998); the Order Francisco Miranda, 1st Class by the government of Venezuela (1998); the Ven Te Chow Award for lifetime achievements in the field of hydrology awarded by the Environmental Water Resources Institute/American Society of Civil Engineers (2001); the Hydrology Days Award of Colorado State University (2002); and an honorary doctor's degree from the Universidad del Zulia (2003).

Further Reading

American Geophysical Union. "Rodriguez-Iturbe Receives Horton Medal." Available online. URL: http://www.agu.org/inside/awards/rodriguez. html. Downloaded on May 2, 2005.

Downey, Mike. "Ignacio Rodriguez-Iturbe Named Distinguished Professor." Aggie Daily, Office of University Relations. Available online. URL: http://www.tamu.edu/univrel/aggiedaily/news/ stories/archive/072397–5.html. Downloaded on May 2, 2005.

Schultz, Steve. "Princeton Scientist Wins 'Nobel Prize of Water,'" *Equad* (Spring 2002). Available online. URL: http://www.princeton.edu/~seasweb/eqnews/ spring02/feature7.shtml. Downloaded on May 2, 2005.

Rodríguez-Johnson, Elizabeth
(Elizabeth Rodríguez)
(1953–) *mathematician, research analyst*

Elizabeth Rodríguez-Johnson has worked for the U.S. Department of Defense (DoD) in a number of positions since she completed her academic studies. She is currently a senior policy analyst with responsibility for developing and implementing policies that promote the use of good engineering practices within the DoD.

Rodríguez was born on March 18, 1953, in San Benito, Texas, to Ignacia and Manuel Rodríguez, of Mexican descent. After her marriage, she began to use the hyphenated name of Rodríguez-Johnson. She attended the University of New Mexico, from which she earned her B.S. in mathematics in 1975, her M.A. in 1976, and her Ph.D. in program management and development and experimental statistics in 1980.

After completing her doctoral studies, Rodríguez-Johnson was hired as a mathematician and program manager at the Pacific Missile Test Center (PMTC) at Point Mugu, California. Between 1981 and 1984, Rodríguez-Johnson was also a part-time mathematics instructor at Oxnard Community College in Oxnard, California. In 1988, she left PMTC to join the Office of the

Secretary of Defense as research analyst. Over the next decade, Rodríguez-Johnson served in a number of positions with the DoD and other agencies, including assignments at the DoD's Office of Defense Research and Engineering and the Office of Operational Test and Evaluation, the Naval Research Laboratory, the White House Office of Science and Technology Policy, the Department of Transportation, and the Office of Management and Budget of the U.S. House of Representatives.

Between 1998 and 2000, Rodríguez-Johnson was director of the Y2K Management Office for the Undersecretary of Defense for Acquisitions, Technology, and Logistics (AT&L). In this position, she was responsible for ensuring the safe operation during the year 2000 transition of nearly 6,000 systems in seven areas: logistics, weapons systems, procurement, environmental security, science and engineering, facilities and installations, and the nuclear, chemistry, and biological areas. After completing this task, Rodríguez-Johnson became involved in AT&L interoperability issues, efforts to ensure that DoD programs and systems were able to mesh efficiently with those of other governmental and private programs and systems.

Rodríguez-Johnson is now senior policy analyst in the Developmental Test and Evaluation Systems Engineering Office of the Undersecretary of Defense for AT&L. She also serves on a number of DoD committees and programs. For example, she has been the DoD's program manager for the Value Engineering Program, the Reduction in Total Ownership Costs program, and the Lean Aerospace Initiative.

Further Reading

"Elizabeth Rodríguez." In *The Hispanic American Almanac,* 3d ed., edited by Sonia G. Benson, 782. Farmington Hills, Mich.: Thomson Gale, 2003.
PEO/SYSCOM. "Dr. Elizabeth Rodríguez-Johnson." 2004 PEO/SYSCOM Proceedings. Available online. URL: http://www.peosyscom.com/biographies/rodriguez.html. Downloaded on March 12, 2005.
"Rodríguez, Elizabeth." In *Who's Who among Hispanic Americans, 1994–95,* 3d ed., edited by Amy Unterburger, 694. Detroit: Gale Research, 1995.

Rodriguez-Sierra, Jorge F.
(Jorge Fernando Rodriguez-Sierra)
(1945–   ) *medical researcher*

Jorge Fernando Rodriguez-Sierra has made important discoveries in a number of fields of research but primarily in neuroendocrinology. Neuroendocrinology is the study of the interaction between the nervous system and the endocrine system, especially the role of hormones on brain development and the role played by the brain in the release and use of hormones. He is also interested in the role that various chemicals in the body play in the development of brain abnormalities and in the development of contraceptive materials.

Rodriguez-Sierra was born in Havana, Cuba, on September 18, 1945, the son of Odilia M. and Fernando F. Rodriguez-Sierra. He attended Pasadena City College, in Pasadena, California, where he received his A.A. in social science in 1968. He continued his studies at California State College, in Los Angeles, from which he earned his B.A. in psychology in 1970 and his M.A. in psychology in 1972. His doctoral studies were completed at Rutgers University, in Newark, New Jersey, where he earned his Ph.D. in psychobiology in 1976. Rodriguez-Sierra completed two postdoctoral programs, one at the Neuroendocrinology and Neurochemistry Units of the Wisconsin Regional Primate Research Center, in Madison (1976–78), and another in the department of anatomy of the University of Nebraska Medical Center (UNMC), in Omaha (1978).

In September 1978, Rodriguez-Sierra was appointed assistant professor of anatomy at the UNMC, beginning a relationship that continues to this day. He has since been promoted to associate professor and adjunct associate professor of psychology (1982) and to professor of cell biology and anatomy and adjunct professor of psychology at UNMC (1989), posts he continues to hold. He has also been director of the Behavior Laboratory at the Nebraska Center for Neurovirology and Neurodegenerative Disorders, UNMC (1999–present); adjunct professor of pharmacology, physiology, and therapeutics at the University of North Dakota College of Medicine, in Grand Forks (1999–present); and adjunct professor of pathology and microbiology at UNMC.

Rodriguez-Sierra's current research focuses on attempts to identify certain common biochemical, neural, and behavioral changes that may be associated with a number of apparently unrelated brain disorders such as Alzheimer's disease and Parkinson's disease. He has developed models that can be used with experimental animals to look for changes that may be early indicators of these and related disorders. Rodriguez-Sierra has published more than 75 articles in peer-reviewed journals and taught courses on a wide array of subjects, including behavioral endocrinology, electron microscopy, endocrinology, histology, neuroanatomy, neurochemistry, neuroendocrinology, neuroimmunology, neuropharmacology, psychopharmacology, and statistics.

Further Reading

"Rodriguez-Sierra, Jorge F." In *American Men & Women of Science,* 21st ed., edited by Pamela M. Kalte and Katherine H. Nemeh, vol. 6, 261. Detroit: Thomson Gale, 2003.

"Rodriguez-Sierra, Jorge Fernando." In *Who's Who among Hispanic Americans, 1994–95,* 3d ed., edited by Amy Unterburger, 711. Detroit: Gale Research, 1995.

Rodriguez-Trias, Helen
(1929–2001) *physician, health care advocate*

Helen Rodriguez-Trias was a highly respected advocate for the expansion of health care for women, children, minorities, and the poor. She was the first Latina president of the American Public Health Association, the world's largest organization of public health workers, and recipient in 2001 of the Presidential Citizens Medal in recognition of her work on behalf of minorities and the disadvantaged.

Rodriguez-Trias was born in New York City on July 7, 1929. While still a young child, she returned with her family to Puerto Rico, where her parents had grown up on a coffee plantation in Cayey. Her grandparents had come to Puerto Rico in the 1850s from Venezuela in an effort to escape the revolutionary movement then sweeping South America. At the age of 10, Rodriguez-Trias and her family went back to New York City, where she completed elementary and high school. She again returned to Puerto Rico in 1948 to attend the University of Puerto Rico (UPR) in San Juan. She arrived on campus at the height of a student protest movement launched in support of Puerto Rican independence. Already interested in political causes such as the free speech movement and Puerto Rican independence, Rodriguez-Trias became part of the campus protests. That act proved to have dire consequences, however, when her brother, who was supporting her financially at the university, threatened to withdraw his support if she continued to take part in protests. The threat became moot, however, when conditions on campus became so unsettled that the president of the university closed down the school for two months. Apparently defeated in her efforts to continue her education, Rodriguez-Trias returned to New York City, where she remained politically active. One campaign in which she was involved was an effort to register Puerto Ricans to vote. While working on this cam-

Helen Rodriguez-Trias was the first Latina president of the American Public Health Association and a widely respected advocate for improved health care for women, children, and minorities. *(Courtesy Dr. Jo Ellen Brainin-Rodriguez)*

paign, she met David R. Brainin, a labor organizer, whom she later married. In a short period of time, they had three children, to whom she gave her full attention.

In 1955, Rodriguez-Trias decided to return to UPR, where she majored in premedicine. She earned her B.S. in 1957 and then remained at UPR to complete her M.D. in 1960 and her residency in pediatrics in 1963. While still a student, Rodriguez-Trias founded the island's first neonatal care unit, a facility of which she was later to become director.

After serving as a physician in San Juan for seven years, Rodriguez-Trias moved back to New York City once again, this time becoming director of the department of pediatrics at Lincoln Hospital in the South Bronx, a New York City neighborhood that had more than its share of economic, social, and political problems. She later described her years at Lincoln as the most difficult of her professional career. Still, the assignment forced her to confront the problems faced by women, minorities, and children attempting to obtain even the most basic forms of health care. When she moved to St. Luke's-Roosevelt Hospital Center in upper Manhattan four years later, this experience was even more strongly reinforced.

After a year at St. Luke's-Roosevelt, Rodriguez-Trias took a teaching position in the Biomedical Program at the City College of New York. Over the next dozen years, she held a variety of teaching positions at Columbia University, Yeshiva University, and Albert Einstein College, all in New York City, and at Rutgers University in New Brunswick, New Jersey. She also became very active in a number of public health campaigns relating to the medical needs of women and minorities. In 1975, she was a founding member of the Committee to End Sterilization Abuse, an organization whose purpose was to reduce the number of forced sterilizations carried out on poor women and women of minority groups. Three years later, she helped found another organization, the Committee for Abortion Rights and Against Sterilization Abuse, with similar goals.

In 1987, Rodriguez-Trias was appointed chair of the New York State AIDS Institute, one of the first research and educational organizations formed to deal with the newly discovered disease caused by human immunodeficiency virus (HIV) infection. She was one of the first experts to point out the dangers that HIV/AIDS poses to women, children, poor people, and people of minorities, in contrast to the greater emphasis then being placed on the risks to gay men. In 1993, Rodriguez-Trias was elected president of the American Public Health Association, the first Latina to be chosen for this post. She also served as president of the board of the National Women's Health Network, an organization founded in 1975 to provide women with a stronger voice in the health care system. She retired from teaching and most advocacy work in 1990 in order to spend more time with her family.

Rodriguez-Trias was awarded the Presidential Citizens Medal on January 8, 2001, by President Bill Clinton for her work as "a dedicated pediatrician, outstanding educator, and dynamic leader in public health." She died later that year, on December 27, 2001, in Brookdale, California, of lung cancer. She had quit smoking 35 years earlier and become an outspoken opponent of cigarette advertising by tobacco companies, especially ads aimed at young and minority groups. Toward the end of her life, she continued to campaign against a practice—cigarette smoking—that she viewed as terribly harmful to human health but that continued to be sold to Americans by corporate interests.

Further Reading

Bonilla-Santiago, Gloria. "Helen Rodriguez." In *Notable Hispanic American Women,* edited by Diane Telgen, Jim Kamp, and Joseph M. Palmisano, 348–349. Detroit: Gale Research, 1998.

National Library of Medicine. Changing the Face of Medicine. "Dr. Helen Rodriguez-Trias." Available online. URL: http://www.nlm.nih.gov/changingthefaceofmedicine/physicians/biography_273.html. Downloaded on December 31, 2004.

Wilcox, Joyce. "The Face of Women's Health: Helen Rodriguez-Trias." *American Journal of Public Health* 92 (April 1, 2002): 566–569.

Romero, Juan Carlos
(1937–   ) *physiologist*

Juan Carlos Romero is an authority on the physiology and pathophysiology (changes in physiology due to disease or damage) of the kidney, on the mechanisms by which the kidneys are involved in hypertension (high blood pressure), and on the use of computerized tomography for the study of renal (kidney) function.

Romero was born in Mendoza, Argentina, on September 15, 1937, the son of Graciela Vizcaya and Juan Romero. He attended San José College in Mendoza, from which he received his B.A. in 1955, before entering the University of Cuyo School of Medicine, also in Mendoza. After two years of study, he left school to serve in the Argentine army and then returned to Cuyo and earned his M.D. in 1964. Upon completing his medical studies, Romero took a job as research assistant at the Institute of Pathological Physiology in

Mendoza for one year before becoming fellow at the Consejo Nacional de Investigaciones, also in Mendoza.

In 1967, Romero entered and won a competition sponsored by the Eli Lilly International Program for Development of Biological Sciences that allowed him to continue his studies at the University of Michigan in Ann Arbor. He served as a research fellow there for one year before being hired as a research associate in hypertension in the department of internal medicine, a post he held from 1968 to 1973. In 1973, he was offered a position as assistant professor at the Mayo Clinic in Rochester, Minnesota. He was later promoted to associate professor (1979) and full professor of physiology and biophysics (1981). He now holds the titles of professor of physiology and biomedical engineering and associate professor of internal medicine, as well as serving as director of Mayo's Hypertension Research Laboratory. In 1995, Romero was also honored with an appointment to the (nonresident) Arthur C. Guyton Honorary Chair of Physiology by the University of Mississippi at Oxford.

Romero has been responsible for some important breakthroughs in renal studies. For example, he has discovered the roles played by nitric oxide, by a group of compounds known as the prostaglandins, and by a collection of structures known as the renin angiotensin system in the circulation of fluids through the kidney. He has also developed methods by which computerized tomography (the use of X-rays to created cross-sectional images of parts of the body) can be used to observe and measure kidney function, thus providing evidence on the health and possible disorders of the kidney.

Romero has published more than 230 scholarly papers on the kidneys and has written more than 25 book chapters on the subject. He is also the author of two books, one about the heart (*El corazon: Anatomía clínica y funcional del cuerpo humano*) and the other about the larynx (*La laringe: Anatomía clínica y funcional del cuerpo humano*), published in Spanish in 1997. Romero has been honored with the Teacher of the Year Award of the Mayo School of Medicine (1984), the Cum Laude Research award of the American Society of Computed Body Tomography (1991), the Lewis K. Dahl Memorial lectureship of the American Heart Association (1991), and the Alejo Zuloaga award of the University of Venezuela (2001).

Further Reading

Bleifeld, Maurice. "Juan Carlos Romero." In *Notable Twentieth-Century Scientists,* edited by Emily J. McMurray, 1,707–1,708. Detroit: Gale Research, 1995.

Mayo Clinic. "Juan Carlos Romero, M.D." Mayo Graduate School—Biomedical Engineering Program. Available online. URL: http://www.mayo.edu/bme/faculty/Romero.htm. Downloaded on March 13, 2005.

"Romero, Juan Carlos." In *Who's Who among Hispanic Americans, 1994–95,* 3d ed., edited by Amy Unterburger, 716. Detroit: Gale Research, 1995.

Ruiz, Joaquin
(1951–) *geochemist*

Joaquin Ruiz is a geochemist, a chemist who studies the composition and evolution of materials found on Earth, with a special interest in the evolution of Earth's crust and mantle, the origin of ore deposits, the ancient history of the Earth's surface, and a variety of environmental and archaeological problems.

Ruiz was born in Mexico City on November 18, 1951, the son of Deany and Angel Ruiz Collantes. His mother was from New York City, but was of Austrian descent, while his father was originally from Spain. Ruiz attended two private bilingual schools in Mexico City and then a Jesuit high school, from which he graduated in 1969. He then took a year off from his studies and worked as a truck driver in his father's business because he was uncertain as to what he wanted to do next in his life. By 1970, he had decided to continue his studies and enrolled at the Universidad Nacional Autónoma de México in Mexico City, where he majored in chemical engineering. Before long, he changed his major to chemistry and received his B.S. in that subject in 1974.

Still uncertain as to what he would do with his life, Ruiz took a job teaching high school in Mexico City. He then had an experience that changed his life. His cousin asked him to assist her in a project that involved dating some very

Joaquin Ruiz has served in the department of geosciences at the University of Arizona since 1983, where his special areas of interest include the composition and evolution of materials found in the Earth's crust. *(Jeff Smith/FOTOSMITH)*

old pyramids in Mexico using carbon 14. Carbon 14 is a radioactive isotope, that is, a form of the element carbon that spontaneously decays (breaks down) into another element (nitrogen) at a very precise rate. One can estimate the age of an object by measuring the amount of carbon 14 it contains compared to the amount of carbon 12, another form of carbon that is not radioactive. Carbon 14 is only one of many radioactive isotopes that can be used to find the age of very old materials and objects.

The excitement that Ruiz experienced in working on this project convinced him that he should continue his studies in chemistry. He moved to the United States and attended the University of Miami, where he earned a B.S. in chemistry and a B.Sc. in geology simultaneously, receiving them in 1977. He next moved to the University of Michigan in Ann Arbor for his graduate studies, receiving his M.S. and Ph.D., both in geology, in 1980 and 1983, respectively. Upon his graduation, Ruiz was offered a job as assistant professor of geosciences at the University of Arizona in Tucson, beginning an affiliation that continues today. He has served as associate professor (1989–93), full professor (1993–present), head of the department of geosciences (1995–2000), and dean of the College of Science (2000–present) at Arizona.

An important part of Ruiz's research involves the use of radioactive (and, in some cases, non-radioactive) isotopes to date geological materials. One of the isotopes he uses most commonly is rhenium 187, which decays to produce the isotope osmium 187 over very long periods of time. By measuring the amounts of these two isotopes in a material, Ruiz is able to estimate with considerable accuracy the age of the material. Ruiz is also interested in why elements are concentrated in some areas. For example, he tries to find out why deposits of gold, silver, copper, and other metals are usually concentrated in seams from which they can be mined rather than being distributed more uniformly throughout the Earth's crust.

Ruiz has published more than 75 scholarly articles and 18 chapters in books and encyclopedias. In 2004, he was awarded the Medal of Merit by the Mining Foundation of the Southwest.

Further Reading

Mining Foundation of the Southwest. "Dr. Joaquin Ruiz." American Mining Hall of Fame. Available online. URL: http://www.miningfoundationsw. org/htm/Ruiz_2004.html. Downloaded on March 13, 2005.

"Ruiz, Joaquin." In *Who's Who among Hispanic Americans, 1994–95,* 3d ed., edited by Amy Unterburger, 727. Detroit: Gale Research, 1995.

Society for Advancement of Chicanos and Native Americans in Science. "Dr. Joaquin Ruiz—Geochemist." SACNAS Biography Project. Available online. URL: http://64.171.10.183/biography/ Biography.asp?mem=80&type=2. Downloaded on March 13, 2005.

S

Sabatini, David Domingo
(1931–) *cell biologist*

David Domingo Sabatini's most important contribution to cell biology may be his research on the signal hypothesis, an explanation of the mechanism by which newly made proteins find the way to their proper location within cells. Sabatini's collaborator in this work, Günter Blobel, was awarded the 1999 Nobel Prize in physiology or medicine for this discovery. Sabatini has also contributed significantly to scientists' understanding of the composition of cells and the way that proteins are moved about within the cell.

Sabatini was born in Bolívar, Argentina, on May 10, 1931. He attended Rosario National College, in Rosario, from which he received his bachelor's degree, and the National University of the Litoral, also in Rosario, where he received his M.D. in 1954. In 1957, Sabatini was awarded a United Nations Education, Scientific, and Cultural Organization fellowship to study at the Biophysics Institute in Rio de Janeiro, Brazil. In the same year, he was appointed to the post of instructor in the Institute of General Anatomy and Embryology and director of admissions at the University of Buenos Aires Medical School. He was later promoted to lecturer and associate professor at the institute.

Sabatini remained at Buenos Aires until 1960, when he was offered a Rockefeller Foundation postdoctoral fellowship at Yale University School of Medicine in New Haven, Connecticut, and Rockefeller University, in New York City, for the period of 1961–63. Concurrently, he was appointed research associate and assistant professor of cell biology in the Cell Biology Laboratory at Rockefeller University. While serving in these posts, he also began studies toward his Ph.D. in cell biology, which he received from Rockefeller in 1966. He was promoted to associate professor at Rockefeller, where he remained until 1972. He then moved to the New York University School of Medicine as full professor and chair of the department of cell biology. Two years later, he was named Frederick L. Ehrman Professor of Cell Biology, a post he continues to hold.

Sabatini is the author of more than 175 papers in peer-reviewed journals. His work has been recognized with a number of awards, including the Wendell Griffith Memorial Lectureship at St. Louis University, in St. Louis, Missouri (1977); the Mary Peterman Memorial Lectureship of the Sloan Kettering Institute of New York City (1977); the 25th Robert J. Terry Lectureship at Washington University, in St. Louis (1978); the Samuel Roberts Nobel Research Recognition Award of the Samuel Roberts Nobel Foundation (1980); the E. B. Wilson Award of the American Society of Cell Biology (1986); the Seventh Annual Kenneth F. Naidorf Memorial Lectureship at Columbia University, in New York City (1989); and the

Charles Leopold Meyer Grand Prix of the French Academy of Sciences (1989). He has been elected a member of the National Academy of Sciences, a Foreign Associate member of the French Academy of Sciences, and a member of the Argentine Medical Association.

Further Reading

Interscientia. "David D. Sabatini, M.D., Ph.D." Available online. URL: http://www.uottawa.ca/publications/interscientia/biographies/sababio.html. Downloaded on April 27, 2005.

"Sabatini, David Domingo." In *American Men & Women of Science,* 21st ed., edited by Pamela M. Kalte and Katherine H. Nemeh, vol. 6, 409. Detroit: Thomson Gale, 2003.

"Sabatini, David Domingo." In *Who's Who in America—2005,* edited by Karen Chassie, 4,051. New Providence, N.J.: Marquis Who's Who, 2004.

Sadosky, Cora

(1940–) *mathematician*

Cora Sadosky's special fields of interest are harmonic analysis (the analysis of the way in which a periodic function can be analyzed into its components), partial differential equations, and operator theory.

Sadosky was born in Buenos Aires, Argentina, on May 23, 1940. Her early education took place in Europe, where her parents, both of whom were mathematicians, were completing their postdoctoral studies. When they returned to Argentina, she studied with private tutors and eventually entered the University of Buenos Aires, from which she received her Licenciatura en Ciencias Matemáticas (equivalent to a master's degree in mathematics) in 1960. She came to the United States in 1962 for her graduate studies at the University of Chicago, earning her Ph.D. in 1965. Sadosky then returned to Argentina for two years before accepting a position as visiting assistant professor at Johns Hopkins University, in Baltimore, Maryland, in 1967. After completing this assignment, she went back to Argentina once again until she immigrated to the United States permanently in 1980 to take a position in the department of mathematics at Howard University, in Washington, D.C., where she now serves as professor of mathematics.

In addition to her assignment at Howard, Sadosky has been visiting professor at a number of institutions, including the University of Buenos Aires (1984–85), the University of California at Santa Cruz (1990), and the University of California at Berkeley (1995–96). She has also made short-term visits to a number of other institutions, including the Center for Pure and Applied Mathematics, in Nice, France; the University of Bari and the University of Catania, in Italy; the National University of Córdoba, in Argentina; the Autonomous University of Barcelona, in Spain; the Mittag-Leffler Institut, in Stockholm, Sweden; the Center for Research in Mathematics, in Barcelona; the University of Leipzig, in Germany; the International Centre for Mathematics, in Edinburgh, Scotland; the Massachusetts Institute of Technology, in Cambridge; the Argentine Institute of Mathematics, in Buenos Aires; and the University of Paris, France.

Sadosky is the author of more than 60 refereed papers and one book, *Interpolation of Operators and Singular Integrals: An Introduction to Harmonic Analysis* (1978). She is the editor of two other books, *Harmonic Analysis and Partial Differential Equations: Essays in Honor of Alberto P. Calderon* (2000) and *Analysis and Partial Differential Equations: A Collection of Papers Dedicated to Mischa Cotlar* (1990).

Further Reading

Canadian Mathematical Society. "Affirmative Action: What Is It and What Should It Be." Women in Today's Mathematical World. Available online. URL: http://camel.math.ca/Women/BOOK/cora.txt. Downloaded on April 29, 2005.

Mathematical Association of America, Texas Section. "Information on Speakers." MAA Meeting. Available online. URL: http://orgs.tamu-commerce.edu/maa/pnotes05.html. Downloaded on April 29, 2005.

Samora, Julián
(1920–1996) *sociologist*

Julián Samora was the first Hispanic American to receive a doctorate in sociology and anthropology. For more than 40 years, he was a leader in efforts to bring more Latinos and Latinas into the field of sociology and to develop an objective basis for understanding the characteristics of minority populations in general and of Latino populations in particular.

Samora was born in Pagosa Springs, Colorado, on March 1, 1920, to a family of Mexican descent. He attended Adams State College, in Alamosa, Colorado, from which he received his B.A. in 1942. Samora then took a teaching job at Huerfano County High School for one year before beginning his graduate studies. He earned his M.S. at Colorado State University in 1947 and his Ph.D. in sociology and anthropology at Washington University in St. Louis in 1953. His doctoral dissertation was about "Minority Leadership in a Bi-Cultural Community." While working on his master's degree and doctorate, Samora held a variety of teaching positions: research fellow at Colorado State (1943–44), assistant professor at Adams State (1944–45), teaching assistant at the University of Wisconsin (1948–49), and teaching assistant at Washington University (1949–50).

In 1955, Samora was appointed assistant professor at the University of Colorado Medical School, in Boulder. He remained at Colorado until 1957, when he accepted a position as associate professor of sociology at Michigan State University in East Lansing. Two years later, he left Michigan State to join the faculty at Notre Dame University, in South Bend, Indiana, as professor of sociology. When he retired from Notre Dame in 1985, he was made professor emeritus. While at Notre Dame, Samora served as head of the sociology department from 1963 to 1966, director of the Mexican-American Graduate Studies Program from 1971 to 1985, and director of the Graduate Studies Program from 1981 to 1984. He also served as visiting professor at a number of other institutions, including the University of New Mexico (1954), the Universidad Nacional de Colombia (1963), the University of California at Los Angeles (1964), the University of Texas at Austin (1971), and the University of Michigan (1987).

Samora experienced discrimination because of his Latino background throughout the early years of his life and decided early on that he would do whatever he could to ensure that others of his background would not have similar experiences. He decided that the best way to battle discrimination was to obtain factual information about Hispanic culture and to make that information available to the general public. In that way, he felt, people would come to understand how much they have in common, regardless of their ethnic backgrounds.

The primary focus of Samora's research, then, was not abstract theory but the analysis of practical problems from everyday life. This emphasis is reflected in the types of books he published, including *La Raza: Forgotten Americans* (1966), *Mexican Americans in a Midwest Metropolis: A Study of East Chicago* (1967), *Mexican Americans in the Southwest* (1969), *Los Mojados: The Wetback Story* (1971), *A History of the Mexican American People* (1977), and *Gunpowder Justice: A Reassessment of the Texas Rangers* (1979).

Samora's expertise and experience were respected not only within the academic community but also throughout the wider political and social society. Among the committees on which he was asked to serve were the President's Commission on Rural Poverty, the President's Commission on Income Maintenance Programs, National Upward

Bound, the Indiana Civil Rights Commission, the Mexican American Legal Defense and Education Fund, and the National Assessment of Education Progress. He also served as a consultant to the U.S. Commission on Civil Rights, the U.S. Public Health Service, the Rosenburg Foundation, the Ford Foundation, the John Hay Whitney Foundation, the National Endowment for the Humanities, the National Institutes for Mental Health, the U.S. Bureau of the Census, the National Science Foundation, the W. K. Kellogg Foundation, and the Smithsonian Institution.

Samora was very active within the Latino community. In the 1960s, he was among the early founders of the National Council of La Raza. He and two other researchers, Herman Gallegos and Ernesto Galarza, traveled throughout the Southwest attempting to learn more about the needs of the Latino community and the type of organization that might be formed to meet those needs. Later in life, he often pointed out that the achievement of which he was most proud was his mentoring of more than 50 graduate students in sociology who would go on to extend and refine his own work. In 1989, the Julián Samora Research Institute was founded at Michigan State for the purpose of developing a database of information that can be used to serve the economic, educational, and community needs of the Hispanic population.

Samora's contributions to sociology and the general community were recognized on a number of occasions. He was honored with the La Raza Award of the National Council of La Raza in 1979; the Honorary Alumni Award of Colorado State University in 1981; the Emily M. Schossberger Award from Notre Dame University in 1981; the White House Hispanic Heritage Award in 1985; the National Hispanic University of San Jose, California, Medal of Honor in 1985; the Midwest Latin Council on Higher Education Award in 1985; and the government of Mexico's Order of Aguila Azteca (Aztec Eagle) in 1991.

Samora died on February 2, 1996, in Albuquerque, New Mexico, from progressive nuclear palsy, a rare disorder of the nervous system.

Further Reading

Gawenda, Mary J. "Scholar in Chicano Studies Dies at 75." State News. Available online. URL: http://www.jsri.msu.edu/collection/personal/statenews96txt.html. Downloaded on March 14, 2005.

"Julián Samora." In The Hispanic American Almanac, 3d ed., edited by Sonia G. Benson, 789. Farmington Hills, Mich.: Thomson Gale, 2003.

Lamanna, Richard. "A Tribute to Julian Samora." Notre Dame Sociology. Available online. URL: http://www.nd.edu/&soc/samora/lamanna.html. Downloaded on March 14, 2005.

Rochin, Refugio I. "Dear Friends and Colleagues." Julián Samora Research Institute. Available online. URL: http://web.jsri.msu.edu/jsamora/. Downloaded on March 14, 2005.

Sanchez, Isaac C.
(Isaac Cornelius Sanchez)
(1941–) *physical chemist*

Isaac Cornelius Sanchez's research covers a range of topics related to polymer science and engineering, including the thermodynamic properties of polymers, the solubility of fluids in polymers, the permeability of gases in polymers, and computer models of polymer properties.

Sanchez was born in San Antonio, Texas, on August 11, 1941, the son of Marce and Isaac Sanchez, of Mexican ancestry. He earned his B.S. from St. Mary's College, in San Antonio, and his Ph.D. in physical chemistry at the University of Delaware in Newark, in 1969. He continued his studies with a postdoctoral grant from the National Research Council of the National Academy of Sciences at the National Bureau of Standards (now the National Institute of Standards and Technology), in Washington, D.C., from 1969 to 1971. He then took a job as associate scientist at Xerox Laboratories from 1971 to 1972 before moving to the University of Massachusetts at Amherst as assistant professor of polymer science and engineering, a post he filled from 1972 to 1977. He then returned to the National Bureau of Standards as research chemist at the Institute of Materials Science and Engineering from 1977 to 1986. Sanchez next spent two years as research fellow at Alcoa Research Laboratories, in New Kensington, Pennsylvania.

In 1988, Sanchez was offered the Matthew Van Winkle Regents Chair of Chemical Engineering at the University of Texas at Austin. He has remained at Austin ever since, where he is now William J. (Bill) Murray, Jr., Endowed Chair of Engineering and associate chair of the department of engineering. In 1995, he was on leave from Texas, serving as Harold A. Morton Distinguished Visiting Professor at the University of Akron, in Akron, Ohio.

Sanchez has been honored with the Bronze Medal (1980) and Silver Medal (1983) of the U.S. Department of Commerce, the Edward U. Condon Award of the National Bureau of Standards (1983), the Engineering Foundation Faculty Excellence Award of the College of Engineering of the University of Texas at Austin (1994), and a Society of Plastics Engineers International Research Award (1996). He was elected to the National Academy of Engineering in 1997 and made a fellow of the American Physical Society in 1979. He is the editor of the book *Physics of Polymer Surfaces and Interfaces* (1992).

Further Reading

"Sanchez, Isaac C." In *Who's Who among Hispanic Americans, 1994–95,* 3d ed., edited by Amy Unterburger, 748. Detroit: Gale Research, 1995.

"Sanchez, Isaac Cornelius." In *American Men & Women of Science,* 21st ed., edited by Pamela M. Kalte and Katherine H. Nemeh, vol. 6, 451. Detroit: Thomson Gale, 2003.

Sánchez, Pedro
(Pedro Antonio Sánchez)
(1940–) *agronomist*

Pedro Antonio Sánchez has traveled to and worked in more than 60 countries around the world with the goal of improving soil, forest, and agricultural practices that will allow communities to develop more efficient and more environmentally friendly methods of growing food and maintaining forest and other natural resources. He is perhaps best known for his 20-year project on soil and crop research, development, and management in the jungles of Peru.

Sánchez was born in Havana, Cuba, on October 7, 1940, to Georgina and Pedro Antonio Sánchez. His mother was a high school teacher and a pharmacist, and his father, a manager of a family farm and a fertilizer salesman. As a child, Sánchez was introduced to agricultural problems related to the wise use and conservation of natural resources by traveling with his father in the Cuban countryside. By the time he had graduated from the Colegio (high school) de la Salle in Havana in 1958, Sánchez knew that he wanted to make agronomy—the science of crop production and soil management—his life's work. He chose to immigrate to the United States and enroll at Cornell University, in Ithaca, New York, partly because it has one of the finest schools of agriculture in the world and partly because both of his parents had graduated from Cornell.

Sánchez eventually earned his B.S. in agronomy in 1962, his M.S. in soil science in 1964, and his Ph.D. in soil science in 1968, all from Cornell. During the last three years of his doctoral studies, Sánchez was a graduate assistant in soil science at the University of the Philippines–Cornell Graduate Education Program in Los Baños, Philippines. At the same time, he also carried out his Ph.D. research at the International Rice Research Institute at Los Baños.

After completing his studies at Cornell, Sánchez accepted an appointment as assistant professor of soil science at North Carolina State University

(NCSU), in Raleigh. He has maintained an affiliation with NCSU ever since, serving as associate professor (1973–79), professor (1979–91), and professor emeritus (1991–present). Although he long held academic appointments at NCSU, Sánchez has spent much of his time doing fieldwork at locations far from Raleigh. From 1968 to 1971, for example, he was coleader of NCSU's Agricultural Mission to Peru/National Rice Program of Peru, in Lambayeque, a program designed to help rural Peruvians develop self-sufficiency in rice production. From 1971 to 1976, he was leader of the Tropical Soils Program of NCSU's soil science department, with soil research projects in the Brazilian Cerrado, the Amazon regions of Peru, and various parts of Central America. In 1982, Sánchez accepted a joint appointment as chief of NCSU's Mission to Peru, technical chief of the Instituto Nacional de Investigación y Promoción Agropecuaria (INIPA), and senior adviser to the World Bank, a combined effort to improve Peru's agricultural research, educational, and extension system.

After his retirement from NCSU in 1991, Sánchez was appointed director general of the International Centre for Research in Agroforestry (ICRA), in Nairobi, Kenya. ICRA is an international agency devoted to the reduction of poverty, land degradation, and tropical deforestation by improving agricultural and forestry systems throughout the world, particularly in developing countries. After 10 years with ICRA, Sánchez spent a year as visiting professor of tropical resources in the department of environmental science, policy, and management and senior research fellow at the Center for Sustainable Resource Development at the University of California at Berkeley. He then accepted a trio of appointments as director of tropical agriculture at the Earth Institute at Columbia University, in New York City, senior research scholar at the International Research Institute on Climate Prediction, and cochair of the Hunger Task Force of the United Nations' Millennium Project. He continues to hold these three positions.

Sánchez has garnered a host of awards and honors during his life, including a National Plant Food Institute Agronomy Achievement Award (1960), the Diploma de Mérito of the Ministerio de Agricultura del Perú (1971), the Diploma de Honor of the Instituto Colombiano Agropecuario (1979), the Orden de Mérito Agrícola from the government of Peru (1984), the International Soil Science Award of the Soil Science Society of America (1993), and the International Service in Agronomy Award of the American Society of Agronomy (1993). In 2002, he was named the World Food Prize laureate by the foundation of the same name. He has also been appointed honorary professor at the Universidad Nacional de la Amazonia Peruana, in Iquitos, Peru (1987), adjunct professor of tropical conservation by Duke University (1990), and professor emeritus of soil science and forestry at North Carolina State University (1991). Sánchez was given an honorary doctorate by the Katholieke Universiteit Leuven of Belgium in 2001 and in the same year, was anointed Luo Elder with the name of Odera Kang'o by the Luo community of western Kenya.

Further Reading

Fedunkiw, Marianne. "Pedro A. Sanchez." In *Notable Twentieth-Century Scientists,* edited by Emily J. McMurray, 1,774–1,775. Detroit: Gale Research, 1995.

"Pedro Antonio Sánchez." In *The Hispanic American Almanac,* 3d ed., edited by Sonia G. Benson, 790. Farmington Hills, Mich.: Thomson Gale, 2003.

"Sanchez, Pedro Antonio." In *Who's Who among Hispanic Americans, 1994–95,* 3d ed., edited by Amy Unterburger, 752. Detroit: Gale Research, 1995.

Serrano, Alberto C.
(Alberto Carlos Serrano)
(1931–) *psychiatrist*

Alberto Carlos Serrano is a widely respected specialist in child, adolescent, and family psychiatry. He is especially interested in issues involving family therapy, group psychotherapy, culture and ethnicity, divorce and stepfamilies, and systems of care for children and adolescents.

Serrano was born in Buenos Aires, Argentina, on April 7, 1931, the son of Regina Robredo and Alberto Pedro Serrano. He received his B.A. in 1948 from the Colegio Nacional Mariano Moreno in Buenos Aires and his M.D. from the University of Buenos Aires School of Medicine in 1956. He did his internship in psychiatry at the Clínica Córdoba of the National Institute of Mental Health in Buenos Aires from 1955 to 1957. In 1957, Serrano moved to the United States, where he became a resident in psychiatry and neurology in the department of neurology and psychiatry at the University of Texas Medical Branch at Galveston until 1960. He then continued there as resident in child psychiatry until 1962.

Upon completion of his residency, Serrano accepted an appointment at the Galveston medical branch, first as instructor and later as assistant professor of psychiatry. In 1966, he was named medical director and chief executive officer of the Community Guidance Center of Bexar County (where San Antonio is located), Texas, a post he held until 1986. During his tenure at Bexar County, Serrano also held other appointments. In 1969, he was appointed director of child and adolescent psychiatry at the University of Texas Health Science Center in San Antonio, and four years later, he was named clinical professor of psychiatry and pediatrics at the center. He also retained both of these jobs until 1986, when he moved to the University of Pennsylvania School of Medicine, in Philadelphia, where he became professor of psychiatry and director of the Division of Child and Adolescent Psychiatry. At Pennsylvania, he also later served as medical director of the Philadelphia Child Guidance Center and psychiatrist in chief and director of the Psychiatry Division at the Children's Hospital of Philadelphia.

In 1997, Serrano left Pennsylvania to become professor of psychiatry at the University of Hawaii School of Medicine and director of the University of Hawaii Consortium of Education and Training in Child and Adolescent Mental Health, posts that he held until his retirement in 2003. Serrano has written extensively in the literature of his profession and is the author of two chapters, "A Child-Centered Family Diagnostic Interview" and "The Chicano Child and His Family," in one of the primary references for his field, *Basic Handbook of Child Psychiatry.*

Further Reading

"Albert Serrano." In *The Hispanic American Almanac,* 3d ed., edited by Sonia G. Benson, 793. Farmington Hills, Mich.: Thomson Gale, 2003.

"Serrano, Alberto Carlos." In *Who's Who among Hispanic Americans, 1994–95,* 3d ed., edited by Amy Unterburger, 775. Detroit: Gale Research, 1995.

Sposito, Garrison
(1939–) *soil scientist*

Garrison Sposito's research deals with the chemical composition and behavior of soils, especially with regard to the ways in which minerals, aqueous (water) solutions, and microorganisms contribute to the development of particular types of soils in particular locations. His current areas of research include studies on coordination chemistry (the ways in which certain metals react with organic compounds), surface chemistry (chemical changes that take place on the surface of materials), colloidal behavior, mathematical models of the way materials are transported through soils, and the computer simulation of natural aqueous systems.

Sposito was born in Los Angeles, California, on July 29, 1939, the son of Geraldine Virginia Hanks and Jesús Gabriel Navarro, of Mexican ancestry. He changed his name in 1952 after his mother had been divorced and remarried to

Albert Cono Sposito. He attended the University of Arizona, where he earned his B.S. in agriculture in 1961 and his M.S. in soil physics in 1963. He received his Ph.D. in soil science from the University of California at Berkeley in 1965. After completing his studies at Berkeley, Sposito took a job as assistant professor of physics at Sonoma State College, in Sonoma, California, where he eventually rose to the rank of professor before leaving in 1974. He then moved to the University of California at Riverside as assistant professor of soil science, where he again reached the position of professor before his departure in 1988. At that point, Sposito took his current job at the University of California at Berkeley, where he is professor of ecosystem sciences and environmental engineering.

In addition to his teaching and research assignments at Sonoma State, Riverside, and Berkeley, Sposito has been senior Fulbright fellow at the University of Córdoba, in Spain; Guggenheim Fellow at the University of Oxford, in England; a fellow of the American Geophysical Union, American Society of Agronomy, European Association of Geochemistry, Geochemical Society, International Union of Pure and Applied Chemistry, and Soil Science Society of America; Miller Research Professor at the University of California at Berkeley; and Walter J. Weber, Jr., Distinguished Lecturer in Environmental Sciences and Engineering at the University of Michigan in Ann Arbor. He has been awarded the Soil Science Research Award of the Soil Science Society of America, the Hydrology Section Research Award of the American Geophysical Union, a Distinguished Teaching Award from Sonoma State University, a Distinguished Teaching Award from the University of California at Riverside, and a "Landmark" Paper Award by the Association of Environmental Engineering and Science Professors. In 2004, he received the Robert E. Horton Medal of the American Geophysical Union for outstanding contributions to hydrology.

Further Reading

"Sposito, Garrison." In *American Men & Women of Science,* 21st ed., edited by Pamela M. Kalte and Katherine H. Nemeh, vol. 6, 926. Detroit: Thomson Gale, 2003.

"Sposito, Garrison." In *Who's Who among Hispanic Americans, 1994–95,* 3d ed., edited by Amy Unterburger, 793. Detroit: Gale Research, 1995.

"Sposito Receives 2004 Robert E. Horton Medal." *Eos* 86 (February 1, 2005): 50.

Suárez-Orozco, Marcelo
(1956–) *psychologist, anthropologist*

Marcelo Suárez-Orozco is author or editor of 20 books dealing primarily with the education of Latino, Afro-Caribbean, and Asian immigrant children in the United States. From 1997 to 2004, he was cochair of the Harvard Immigration Projects at the Harvard Graduate School of Education (HGSE), in Cambridge, Massachusetts.

Suárez-Orozco was born in Buenos Aires, Argentina, on September 21, 1956. He studied at the University of California at Berkeley, where he received his A.B. in psychology and his M.A. and Ph.D. in anthropology in 1980, 1981, and 1986, respectively. While studying at Berkeley, he held a number of positions, including teaching assistant and associate and research assistant in the department of anthropology. Upon receiving his doctorate, Suárez-Orozco held a series of visiting professorships at the University of California at Santa Cruz (1986 and 1987), the University of California at Santa Barbara (1986 and 1987), and the Centrum voor Sociale en Culturele Antropolgie at the Katholieke Universiteit te Leuven, in Belgium (1989). He also served as lecturer in the department of anthropology at the University of California at San Diego (1987 and 1988).

In 1988, Suárez-Orozco was appointed assistant professor in the department of anthropology at the University of California at San Diego, eventually receiving a promotion to associate professor in 1992, a post he held until 1995. During his seven years at San Diego, Suárez-Orozco was also fellow at the Center for Advanced Study in the Behavioral Sciences at Stanford University, in Stanford, California (1992–93); visiting associate professor in the Faculty of Psychology at the University of Barcelona, Spain (1993); and visiting associate professor in the department of human development and psychology at HGSE (1994–95). After leaving San Diego in 1995, Suárez-Orozco was hired as professor of human development and psychology at HGSE. Two years later, he was also named faculty associate at the Weatherhead Center for International Affairs at Harvard and in 2001 was made Victor S. Thomas Professor at HGSE.

One of Suárez-Orozco's primary responsibilities at HGSE was the Harvard Immigration Projects, the largest research program ever funded by the National Science Foundation's division of cultural anthropology. The Harvard Immigration Projects was an effort to understand how children of immigrant parents adapted to the American educational system and how, in turn, they impacted the educational system. While still a faculty member at Harvard, Suárez-Orozco also spent a year (1996–97) in Europe, where he was Norbert Elias Lecturer at the Amsterdam School for Social Sciences, in the Netherlands; director of associated studies at the École des Hautes Études en Sciences Sociales, in Paris; and scholar in residence at the Ross Institute, in New York City.

In 2004, Suárez-Orozco resigned from HGSE to become university professor and Courtney Sale Ross University Professor of Globalization and Education at New York University, in New York City. His research there deals primarily with immigration and globalization, cultural psychology, psychological anthropology, and culture and education.

Further Reading

Mandel, Andrew K. "Suarez-Orozco to Leave Harvard for NYU." *The Appian* (May 3, 2004). Available online. URL: http://gseacademic.harvard.edu/~theappian/articles/spring04/suarezorozco0504.htm. Downloaded on April 20, 2005.

Steinhardt School of Education, New York University. "Marcelo Suárez-Orozco—The Courtney Sale Ross University Professor of Globalization and Education." Available online. URL: http://education.nyu.edu/education/steinhardt/db/faculty/1380/Dept_design/0. Downloaded on April 20, 2005.

T

Taboada, John
(1943–) *physicist, inventor*

John Taboada spent most of his professional career at the U.S. Air Force School of Aerospace Medicine, at Brooks Air Force Base, Texas. His research there involved problems in applied physics and biophysics (physical problems related to living organisms), such as the effects of radioactive isotopes on human populations, infrared sensing in biological systems (the use of infrared radiation for studying populations of organisms), and the effects of radio frequency and ultrashort laser radiation on organisms. He has registered a number of patents related to the products of his research, probably the best known of which deals with laser treatment of eye disorders.

Taboada was born in Tampico, Mexico, on September 8, 1943, the second of seven children. He grew up in San Antonio, Texas, spending much of his spare time in his father's radio and television repair shop, discovering early on that he wanted to pursue a career in science. He attended Briscoe Elementary School and Fox Technical High School in San Antonio before going on to college at Trinity University, in San Antonio, where he earned his B.A. in physics in 1966. He continued his graduate studies at Texas A&M University, in College Station, receiving his M.S. and Ph.D., both in physics, in 1968 and 1973, respectively.

Upon his graduation from Texas A&M in 1968, Taboada took a job as a research physicist with the Aerospace Medical Division of the Air Force School of Aerospace Medicine at Brooks Air Force Base, where he remained until 1997. He was appointed chief of the Applied Optics Laboratory of the Ophthalmology Branch and senior research physicist of the Optical Radiation Branch in the Directed Energy Bioeffects Division of the Human Effectiveness Directorate of the Air Force Research Laboratory at Brooks. He remained in those posts until his retirement in 2002. In 1999, Taboada also cofounded with his son Taboada Research Instruments, Inc., a company that researches and develops laser tools and instruments for a variety of client needs. He continued to operate the company after his retirement from Brooks.

Of his many discoveries and inventions, the one for which Taboada will probably best be remembered is the process of the photorefractive keratotomy process, used to correct myopia (nearsightedness) by means of a laser beam. The process has largely replaced the riskier and more expensive process of radial keratotomy, in which a diamond knife is used to correct the shape of the cornea of the eye. All told, Taboada has been granted 20 patents on inventions such as laser imaging and ranging systems, an optical system for topographic mapping, a system for using gamma rays as a camera, and a method for detecting biological aerosol particles.

Further Reading

Purifactor, Rudy. "Former Brooks Scientist Inducted into Science Hall of Fame." *Discovery* (November 19, 2004), 4. Available online. URL: http://www.brooks.af.mil/HSW/PA/discovery/2004%20Discovery%20Issues/Nov19web.pdf. Posted on November 19, 2004.

"Taboada, John." In *American Men & Women of Science,* 21st ed., edited by Pamela M. Kalte and Katherine H. Nemeh, vol. 7, 3. Detroit: Thomson Gale, 2003.

Talamantes, Frank
(1943–) *endocrinologist*

Frank Talamantes is an internationally recognized authority in endocrinology, the study of hormones that occur within the body and the organs that produce those hormones and respond to them.

Frank Talamantes joined the El Paso School of Medicine of Texas Tech University as professor and head of the research division for the department of pathology in 2004, after more than 30 years at the University of California at Santa Cruz. *(Photo by Nati Perez)*

His special areas of expertise concern the role that the placenta plays in hormonal function, the role of hormones in the development of breast cancer, and the mechanism by which the growth hormone functions in the body.

Talamantes was born in Los Angeles, California, on July 8, 1943, into a family of Mexican heritage. He grew up in El Paso, Texas, where he attended Catholic schools, graduating from Cathedral High School in 1962. Talamantes praises his Catholic education because it lacked the type of prejudice and discrimination that many Latinos experienced in public schools at the time. After graduation from high school, he thought it only natural to continue his studies at a Catholic college and enrolled at the University of St. Thomas in Houston, Texas, where he originally planned to follow a predental curriculum. However, the influence of a faculty member, Dr. Henry Browning, an endocrinologist, was so strong on Talamantes that Talamantes decided to change his major and study to become an endocrinologist also. After this change of heart, Talamantes graduated from St. Thomas in 1966 with a B.A. in biology. He then continued his studies at Sam Houston State University, in Huntsville, Texas, earning his M.A. in biology in 1970, and at the University of California at Berkeley, from which he received his Ph.D. in endocrinology in 1974.

Upon completion of his doctoral studies, Talamantes was offered a job as assistant professor at the University of California at Santa Cruz. He accepted the offer, beginning an affiliation with Santa Cruz that was to last 30 years. He was eventually promoted to associate professor (1980) and then professor (1984). In 2000, Talamantes was appointed vice provost and dean of graduate studies at Santa Cruz. Talamantes ended his long association with Santa Cruz in 2004 to join the El Paso School of Medicine of Texas Tech University as professor and head of the research division for the department of pathology. Less than a year later, he was promoted to assistant dean for research of the school.

Talamantes was named the Transatlantic Medal Lecturer by the British Society for Endocrinology in 1991 and the Solomon A. Berson Lecturer by the American Physiological Society Division of Endocrinology and Metabolism in 2001. He was awarded the Society for the Study of Reproduction Research Award in 1993, the Endocrine Society's Sidney H. Ingbar Distinguished Service Award for 2000, and the E. E. Just Award of the American Society of Cell Biology in 2002. Talamantes is the author of more than 160 scholarly papers and 13 book chapters.

Further Reading

"Frank Talamantes." In *The Hispanic-American Almanac,* 3d ed., edited by Sonia G. Benson, 799. Farmington Hills, Mich.: Thomson Gale, 2003.

Stephens, Tim. "Biologist Frank Talamantes Named Vice Provost and Dean of Graduate Studies." UC Santa Cruz Press Release. Available online. URL: http://www.ucsc.edu/news_events/press_releases/archive/00-01/07-00/talamantes.htm. Posted on July 28, 2000.

Society for Advancement of Chicanos and Native Americans in Science. "Dr. Frank Talamantes—Endocrinologist." SACNAS Biography Project. Available online. URL: http://64.171.10.183/biography/Biography.asp?mem=81&type=2. Downloaded on March 14, 2005.

Texas Tech University Health Sciences Center. "New Research Dean Appointed at Texas Tech El Paso School of Medicine." Campus News. Available online. URL: http://www.ttuhsc.edu/elpaso/NewsEvents/frankTalamantes.aspx. Downloaded on March 14, 2005.

Tapia, Richard A.
(Richard Alfred Tapia)
(1939–) *mathematician*

Richard Alfred Tapia is an internationally recognized scholar in the fields of computational and mathematical sciences. He is at least as famous for his work to increase opportunities for members of minorities in the mathematical sciences. Tapia has received well over 30 honors and awards in recognition of his service to the mathematical profession and to minorities.

Tapia was born in Santa Monica, California, on March 25, 1939, the son of Magda and Amado Tapia. Although there is some uncertainty, he believes that his family roots can be traced to the Tarahumara tribe in Chihuahua, Mexico. He has written that he learned a number of important values from his family, including "good work habits, belief in yourself, pride in who you are, respect for others, and sensitivity to their needs." When he was in high school, Tapia gave little or no thought to getting a college education, so he enrolled in Harbor Junior College, in Los Angeles. At Harbor, however, his mathematical skills were recognized, and he was encouraged to continue his education at the University of California at Los Angeles (UCLA). He did so, eventually earning his B.A., M.A., and Ph.D., all in mathematics, there in 1961, 1966, and 1967, respectively. He then spent one year as instructor of mathematics at UCLA and two years as assistant professor at the Mathematics Research Center of the University of Wisconsin, at Madison.

In 1970, Tapia was offered the position of assistant professor of mathematical sciences at Rice University, in Houston, Texas. He accepted the offer, beginning a relationship that has lasted to the present day. He was promoted to associate professor in 1972 and to professor in 1976 and in 1991, was named Noah Harding Professor of Computational and Applied Mathematics at Rice. He has also held a number of other positions at Rice, including chair of the department (1978–83), director of education and outreach programs at the Center for Research on Parallel Computation (1989–2000), associate director of graduate studies (1989–present), and director of the Center for Excellence and Equity in Education (1999–present). In addition,

Richard A. Tapia is an internationally recognized scholar in the fields of computational and mathematical sciences and a strong advocate for improving opportunities for members of minorities in the mathematical sciences. *(Photo by Tommy LaVergne)*

Year by *Hispanic Engineer* magazine (1990); the George R. Brown Award for Superior Teaching at Rice (1991); first recipient of the A. Nico Habermann Award of the Computer Research Association (1994); selection as Hispanic Engineer of the Year by *Hispanic Engineer* magazine (1996); recipient of the Presidential Award for Excellence in Science, Mathematics, and Engineering Mentoring of the National Science Foundation (1996); induction to the Hall of Fame of the Houston Hispanic Forum (1997); selection as a 1999 Giant in Science Award of the Quality Education for Minorities Network (1999); 2000 Peace Award for Education of the Spiritual Assembly of the Baha' of Houston; Reginald H. Jones Distinguished Service Award of the National Action Council for Minorities in Education (2001); Distinguished Public Service Award of the American Mathematical Society (2004); and Society for Industrial and Applied Mathematics Prize for Distinguished Service to the Profession (2004). Tapia has received honorary doctorates from the Colorado School of Mines and Carnegie Mellon University. He has also been honored by the Association for Computing Machinery by having an annual symposium and a special award—the Richard A. Tapia Achievement Award for Scientific Scholarship, Civic Science, and Diversifying Computing—named after him.

Further Reading

Neyra, Linda S. "Richard Alfred Tapia." Mathematical Association of America Online. Available online. URL: http://www.maa.org/summa/archive/tapia. htm. Downloaded on April 20, 2005.

Rice University, Department of Computational and Applied Mathematics. "Dr. Richard A. Tapia." Available online. URL: http://www.caam.rice. edu/~rat/. Downloaded on April 20, 2005.

"Tapia, Richard." In *American Men & Women of Science,* 21st ed., edited by Pamela M. Kalte and Katherine H. Nemeh, vol. 7, 19. Detroit: Thomson Gale, 2003.

Tapia has held appointments at a number of other institutions, including visiting associate professor of operations research at Stanford University, in Stanford, California (1976–77); adjunct professor at the Texas Institute of Rehabilitation and Research of the Baylor College of Medicine, in Waco, Texas (1978–83); and adjunct professor in the College of Natural Sciences and Mathematics at the University of Houston (2000–present).

The honors Tapia has received reflect the contributions he has made in a variety of fields. They include selection as College Level Educator of the

U

Urquilla, Pedro R.
(Pedro Ramón Urquilla)
(1939–) *pharmacologist*

Pedro Ramón Urquilla has worked most of his life in the pharmaceutical industry, where he has been interested in the development, testing, and registration of drugs for the treatment of a variety of diseases and disorders, including coronary disease, atherosclerosis, myocardial infarction, stroke, cancer, autoimmune disorders, and age-related macular degeneration, a chronic disease of the eyes caused by the deterioration of the central portion of the retina.

Urquilla was born in San Miguel, El Salvador, on July 28, 1939. He attended high school at the Instituto Católico de Oriente, in San Miguel, from which he graduated in 1957. He enrolled at the University of El Salvador's School of Medicine, where he was awarded his B.S. in premedical studies in 1961 and his M.D. in 1965. He was then hired as instructor in pharmacology at the University of El Salvador, in San Salvador, for one year before receiving a fellowship from the Pan American Health Organization and a postdoctoral fellowship in pharmacology from the U.S. Public Health Service. He returned to the University of El Salvador to serve as associate professor in the department of physiology and pharmacology from 1969 to 1972, during which time he was also acting chair of the department from 1969 to 1971.

Urquilla continued his academic career as associate professor in the department of physiological sciences in the Faculty of Medicine at the Universidad Autónoma, in Madrid, Spain, from 1972 to 1973, and at West Virginia University, in Morgantown, where he was assistant professor (1973–76) and associate professor (1976–79) in the department of pharmacology.

In 1979, Urquilla left academia to take a position in the pharmaceutical industry as associate director of medical research at Miles Pharmaceutical, in West Haven, Connecticut. He then moved to other positions within the industry: associate and then senior associate director in the department of clinical research at Pfizer, Inc., from 1981 to 1987; director of cardiovascular clinical research at Bristol-Myers, from 1987 to 1989; senior associate director of the department of clinical research at Pfizer, Inc., from 1989 to 1992; director of cardiology in the department of clinical research at Toehringer Ingelheim Pharmaceuticals, in Ridgefield, Connecticut, from 1992 to 1996; and director of clinical services in the department of medical affairs, from 1996 to 1998, then director of clinical pharmacology, from 1998 to 2000, at Genetech, in South San Francisco, California.

Between 2000 and 2002, Urquilla was a consultant to Cell Genesys, in South San Francisco; XOMA Ltd., in Berkeley, California; GenVec, in Gaithersburg, Maryland; and SRI International, in

Menlo Park, California. In 2002, he was named vice president for medical affairs at FibroGen, a biotechnology company in South San Francisco.

Further Reading

FibroGen. "Pedro R. Urquilla, M.D., Named Vice President, Medical Affairs, FibroGen, Inc." News Release. Available online. URL: http://www.fibrogen.com/news/fg20020423.html. Posted on April 23, 2002.

"Pedro Ramón Urquilla." In *The Hispanic American Almanac,* 3d ed., edited by Sonia G. Benson, 805. Farmington Hills, Mich.: Thomson Gale, 2003.

V

Valdés, James J.
(James John Valdés)
(1951–) *biotechnologist*

James John Valdés is chief scientist of biological sciences and scientific adviser for biotechnology at the U.S. Army's Edgewood Chemical Biological Center (ECBC). He is an expert on the development of countermeasures that can be used against attacks with biological weapons.

Valdés was born in San Antonio, Texas, on April 5, 1951, the son of Barbara and Fernando Valdés, of Spanish heritage. He earned his B.S. in psychology and biological sciences from Loyola University of Chicago in 1973, his M.S. in physiological psychology from Trinity University in San Antonio in 1976, and his Ph.D. in neuroscience from Texas Christian University, in Fort Worth, in 1979. From 1979 to 1982, Valdés was a postdoctoral researcher in neurotoxicology (the study of the effects of certain types of chemicals on the nervous system) at Johns Hopkins University, in Baltimore, Maryland.

In 1982, Valdés began work as a physical scientist at the U.S. Army's ECBC at the Aberdeen Proving Ground in Maryland. He later served as pharmacologist (1984–88) and biotechnologist (1988–present) at ECBC. Valdés is the author of more than 100 research papers and has spoken and presented papers at meetings and conferences on biological weapons and related issues throughout the world. His special area of expertise is the development of systems for the detection of biological weapons and the study of long-term effects of such weapons.

Valdés was distinguished visiting professor to the Republic of Korea in 1987. His work has been recognized by the U.S. Army Materiel (USAM) Command Ten Best Personnel Award in 1988, the USAM Research and Development Achievement Award in 1984 and 1987, and a 2003 Presidential Rank award, one of the highest honors given to career government personnel.

Further Reading

Edgewood Chemical Biological Center. "Army Scientific Advisor Dr. James Valdes Wins Presidential Rank Award." News Release. Available online. URL: www.edgewood.army.mil/pr/download/pr04–02_valdes_james_dr.pdf. Posted on March 24, 2004.

"James J. Valdés." In *The Hispanic American Almanac,* 3d ed., edited by Sonia G. Benson, 805. Farmington Hills, Mich.: Thomson Gale, 2003.

"Valdes, James John." In *Who's Who among Hispanic Americans, 1994–95,* 3d ed., edited by Amy Unterburger, 834. Detroit: Gale Research, 1995.

Vallbona, Carlos
(1927–   ) *pediatrician, medical researcher*

Carlos Vallbona is a highly respected authority in a number of medical fields, including cardiorespiratory problems of disabled persons, the control of hypertension and diabetes, physical exercise, pediatric rehabilitation, applications of data processing equipment and systems in medical care, and special problems encountered in newborn babies. He was a member of the medical crew that studied cardiac functions in astronauts who participated in the first spaceflights as part of the Gemini program in the mid-1960s.

Vallbona was born in Barcelona, Spain, on July 29, 1927. He attended the University of Barcelona, from which he received both his B.S. and B.A. in 1944 and his M.D. in 1950. He served for one year in Spain as a physician specializing in the health of schoolchildren and then began his residency in pediatrics at the Children's International Center of the University of Paris, France. He did a second residency and his internship at the University of Louisville School of Medicine, in Louisville, Kentucky, and a third residency at the Baylor College of Medicine, in Houston, Texas. He has maintained an affiliation with Baylor ever since that time.

In 1956, Vallbona was appointed an instructor of pediatrics and physiology and, concurrently, instructor of rehabilitation at the Community Health Program of the Harris County Hospital District (HCHD), in Houston. He was later promoted to associate professor in both departments. In 1967, Vallbona was named professor of rehabilitation at the Baylor College of Medicine, and two years later, he was appointed professor and chairman of the department of community medicine at HCHD and chief of community medical services at HCHD. He now holds the title of distinguished service professor of the departments of community medicine and physical medicine and rehabilitation at Baylor while also serving as adjunct professor of preventive medicine with the Center for Health Promotion Research at the University of Texas Health Science Center at Houston.

Vallbona has been honored with a long list of awards, including selection as an outstanding faculty member by students at Baylor on five different occasions; the Cross of Officer of the Order of Civilian Merit, from King Juan Carlos I of Spain; Barbara & Corbin Robertson Award for excellence in education at Baylor; the Narcís Monturiol Medal of the government of Catalonia; the Heart of the Year award of the Catalan Association of Cardiology; and honorary doctorates from the Autonomous University of Barcelona and the University of Las Palmas, Gran Canaria, Spain.

Further Reading
"Carlos Vallbona." In *The Hispanic American Almanac,* edited by Nicolás Kanellos, 695. Detroit: Gale Research, 1997.

"Vallbona, Carlos." In *American Men & Women of Science,* 21st ed., edited by Pamela M. Kalte and Katherine H. Nemeh, vol. 7, 215. Detroit: Thomson Gale, 2003.

Valverde, Rodrigo A.
(Rodrigo Alberto Valverde)
(1952–   ) *botanist*

Rodrigo Alberto Valverde specializes in the study of plant viruses, microscopic agents responsible for a host of diseases in a great variety of plants. He is especially interested in viral diseases affecting sweet potatoes, peppers, and related plants and in the use of recombinant DNA for the development of transgenic plants with resistance to viral diseases. Transgenic plants are plants that contain genes from two or more organisms, produced by recombinant processes in which the genes from one organism are transplanted into a second organism.

Valverde was born in Puerto Limón, Costa Rica, on February 13, 1952, the son of Argentina

Rodrigo A. Valverde is professor in the department of plant pathology and crop physiology at Louisiana State University. His area of research is viral diseases that affect food plants, such as sweet potatoes and peppers. *(Photo by LSU Agricultural Center)*

Rivas Arroyo and Alberto Valverde Rarahona. He received his undergraduate degree with a major in agronomy from the University of Costa Rica, in San José, in 1978. He then immigrated to the United States, where he continued his studies at the University of Arkansas, in Fayetteville, earning his M.S. and Ph.D. in 1980 and 1984, respectively. Valverde then completed two postdoctoral programs, one at the University of California at Riverside, from 1984 to 1986, and the other at the University of California at Davis, from 1986 to 1987, after which he joined the Ball PanAm Plant Company as a plant pathologist for one year.

In 1988, Valverde accepted an offer from Louisiana State University, in Baton Rouge, to become assistant professor in the department of plant pathology and crop physiology. He has since been promoted first to associate professor and then to full professor, a title he currently holds. In 1995, Valverde received a Fulbright grant to spend a year at the Institute of Plant Molecular Biology at the Université Louis Pasteur, in Strasbourg, France. From 2000 to 2002, Valverde worked with scientists at the Phytovirology and Biotechnology Laboratory of the National Agricultural University, in Kiev, Ukraine, to develop a program on plant virology that involved the development of methods for the detection and identification of plant viruses and for methods of developing plants with greater resistance to viral diseases.

Further Reading

"Valverde, Rodrigo Alberto." In *American Men & Women of Science,* 21st ed., edited by Pamela M. Kalte and Katherine H. Nemeh, vol. 7, 216. Detroit: Thomson Gale, 2003.

"Valverde, Rodrigo Alberto." In *Who's Who among Hispanic Americans, 1992–93,* 2d ed., edited by Amy Unterburger, 705. Detroit: Gale Research, 1992.

Vega, Fernando E.
(1962–) *entomologist*

Fernando E. Vega is a research entomologist at the U.S. Department of Agriculture's Agricultural Research Service (ARS). His special area of interest is in the biological control of insect pests that attack commercial crops, causing very significant economic damage to the agricultural industry throughout the world. His current field of research is focused on the coffee berry borer, an insect that attacks and destroys coffee plants, making it one of the coffee industry's most serious economic problems.

Vega was born in Santurce, Puerto Rico, on January 29, 1962. He attended the Academia Immaculada Concepción high school in Mayagüez from 1975 to 1979 and earned his B.S. in agriculture at the University of Puerto Rico in 1983. He continued his studies at the University of Maryland at College Park, where he was awarded his M.S. in horticulture in 1986 and his Ph.D. in entomology in 1992. During this period, Vega also worked as a technical information specialist for the U.S.

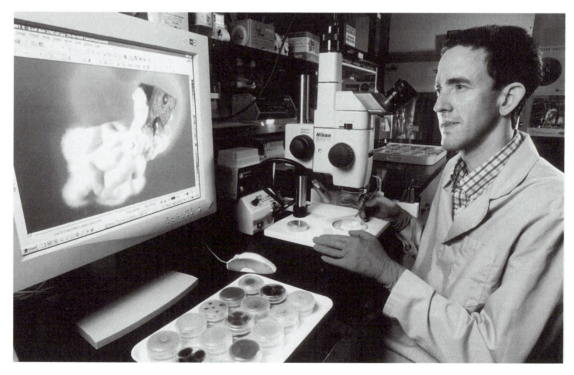

Fernando E. Vega is an entomologist with the U.S. Department of Agriculture's Agricultural Research Service with research interests in pest damage to economically important crops grown around the world. *(USDA/ARS: Photo by Peggy Greb)*

Agency for International Development's Pesticide Information Program from 1983 to 1986.

After receiving his doctorate from Maryland, Vega took a position with the ARS in Peoria, Illinois, as a research entomologist in the agency's mycotoxin research unit. Mycotoxins are poisons produced by fungi that can affect plants and animals, including humans. Vega was then assigned to a variety of other positions as a research entomologist within the ARS, including appointments at the subtropical insects research unit in Orlando, Florida (1994), the bioactive agents research unit in Peoria (1995–96), the European Biological Control Laboratory at Montpellier, France (1996–99), and the insect biocontrol laboratory at Beltsville, Maryland (1999–present). In addition to these research assignments, Vega has served as an adjunct faculty member at Valencia Community College in Orlando and at the University of Central Florida in Orlando.

Vega's research and consultancy work has taken him to a number of countries around the world, including Austria, Bulgaria, Costa Rica, Dominican Republic, Ecuador, France, Germany, Guatemala, Honduras, Italy, Jamaica, Mexico, Nicaragua, Portugal, Republic of Georgia, Spain, Switzerland, Uganda, and the United Kingdom. He is the author of more than 80 scholarly papers and 30 abstracts and coeditor of a well-reviewed text, *Insect-Fungal Associations: Ecology and Evolution* (with Meredith Blackwell, 2005).

Further Reading

Durham, Sharon. "Stopping the Coffee Berry Borer from Boring into Profits." *Agricultural Research* (November 2004). Available online. URL: http://www.ars.usda.gov/is/AR/archive/nov04/coffee1104.htm. Downloaded on August 12, 2005.

U.S. Department of Agriculture, Agricultural Research Service. "People and Places: Fernando E. Vega." Available online. URL: http://www.ars.usda.gov/pandp/people/people.htm?personid=5818. Downloaded on August 12, 2004.

Vélez, William Yslas
(1947–) *mathematician*

William Yslas Vélez specializes in number theory, group theory, communication theory, and signal processing. He has also worked on a number of committees and programs designed to interest a larger number of Latino students in mathematics and science.

Vélez was born in Tucson, Arizona, on January 15, 1947, to Julia and Emilio Vélez. Both of his parents originally came from the state of Sonora in Mexico. His father died when Vélez was nine years old, and his mother was forced to take three jobs to earn enough to keep the family together. In spite of the family's difficult economic conditions, Vélez worked hard in school and graduated from Salpointe Catholic High School in Tucson in 1964 with a good academic record. He then decided to major in chemical engineering in college, he later wrote, because a chemical engineer who had visited his high school had revealed that he made the astounding salary of $11,000 per year.

That decision turned out not to be a wise one for a number of reasons. Among those reasons was Vélez's problems working in the laboratory, where almost anything he tried to do seemed to come out wrong. His grades were so bad for his first semester at the University of Arizona that he decided to change his major. Fortunately, he found a substitute quickly: mathematics. Although he had not done well in his first math course, he took calculus in his second semester, found that he loved the subject, and earned an A in the course. The direction of his career had been set, and he eventually earned his B.S. in mathematics at Arizona in 1968.

After completing his undergraduate studies, Vélez, a member of the U.S. Naval Reserves since 1965, was called to active duty. He served from March 1968 to September 1969 on the aircraft carriers USS *Yorktown* and USS *Kearsarge* as a weather observer. At the completion of his active duty, he returned to the University of Arizona, where he

William Yslas Vélez is a mathematician with special interest in number theory, group theory, communication theory, and signal processing, as well in extending opportunities for minorities in the field of mathematics. *(Courtesy of SACNAS)*

was awarded his M.S. and Ph.D. in mathematics in 1972 and 1975, respectively. He then accepted an offer to work as a member of the technical staff at Sandia National Laboratories, in Albuquerque, New Mexico. In 1977, he left Sandia to become assistant professor of mathematics at the University of Arizona. He was promoted to associate professor in 1981 and to full professor in 1989, a post he continues to hold.

In addition to his long tenure at Arizona, Vélez has held a number of other academic appointments, including visiting professor at the Mathematics Institute of the University of Heidelberg, in Germany (1983–84); consultant at the Naval Ocean Systems Center, in San Diego, Cali-

fornia (summers of 1989, 1990, and 1991); and program director for the Algebra and Number Theory Program of the National Science Foundation (1992–93). He has also served as president of the Society for the Advancement of Chicanos and Native Americans in Science (1994–96) and director of the Southwest Regional Institute in the Mathematical Sciences (1994–99). Vélez has received the Outstanding Student Advisor awards from various departments at Arizona in 1989, 1990, 1991, 1992, 1994, and 1996. In 1997, he was given the President's Award for Excellence in Science, Mathematics, and Engineering Mentoring Program, and in 2005, he received the QEM/MSE (Quality Education for Minorities/Mathematics, Science, and Engineering) Network Giants in Science Award.

Further Reading

Society for Advancement of Chicanos and Native Americans in Science. "Dr. William Vélez—Mathematician." SACNAS Biography Project. Available online. URL: http://64.171.10.183/biography/Biography.asp?mem=83&type=2. Downloaded on March 15, 2005.

"Vélez, William Yslas." In *Who's Who among Hispanic Americans, 1994–95,* 3d ed., edited by Amy Unterburger, 858. Detroit: Gale Research, 1995.

Vigil, Eugene L.
(Eugene Leon Vigil)
(1941–) *botanist*

Eugene Leon Vigil is best known for his research that identified a new class of organelles in plants known as peroxisomes, structures that contain about 40 enzymes involved in the oxidation of organic molecules and other essential functions. He also spent many years in administrative positions that supported the advancement of women and minorities in science.

Vigil was born in Chicago on March 14, 1941. His father, of mixed Navajo and Mexican heritage, owned his own electrical repair business; his mother, from the Ukraine, kept house for her husband and their eight children. Vigil's parents believed strongly in the value of a good education, and most of the children achieved significant academic success in their lives. His oldest brother became an electrical engineer and patent attorney, his younger brother graduated from college with a degree in physics, and three sisters became teachers. Vigil's mother encouraged him to consider a career in medicine, but he decided instead on botany after having taken his first course in the subject as a junior at Loyola University, in Chicago. He eventually earned his B.S. in the subject in 1963 and went on to receive an M.S. and Ph.D. in botany at the University of Iowa, in Iowa City, in 1965 and 1967, respectively.

After graduation from Iowa, Vigil completed a two-year postdoctoral program at the University of Wisconsin at Madison. It was during this period that Vigil began his groundbreaking studies of peroxisomes, for which he became famous. He found that these structures occur not only in plants but also in mammalian cells. Later studies have found that abnormalities in peroxisomes are related to a variety of human diseases. Vigil continued his studies of peroxisomes and related biological problems in a second postdoctoral program at the University of Chicago, where he studied from 1969 to 1971. He then took a job as assistant professor of cell biology at Marquette University, in Milwaukee, Wisconsin, where he remained until 1979. Next, he moved to the University of Maryland in College Park, where he was assistant professor of botany until 1981, when he took the post of research associate in the university's department of horticulture.

In 1988, Vigil left the academic world to take a job as plant physiologist in the Climate Stress Laboratory of the U.S. Department of Agriculture in Beltsville, Maryland. At Beltsville, he attacked a problem that had plagued the cotton industry for decades and cost it huge financial losses. The problem was that cotton fibers that had been dyed sometimes developed white specks that spoiled the appearance of any material made of the fibers. Vigil found that the problem resulted from the fact that drought affected the rate at which cotton seeds germinated and developed, causing them to develop a resistance to dyes that showed up as white specks in fibers.

In 1995, Vigil made another career change, accepting an opportunity to become program director in the Minority Biomedical Research Support (MBRS) Program at the National Institute of General Medical Sciences, in Bethesda,

Maryland. MBRS is designed to increase the number of researchers from underrepresented minority groups in the biomedical sciences. The new job provided Vigil with a way of pursuing a goal that he had set for himself early in his academic career, helping other members of minorities achieve success in their pursuit of science as a career. Three years later, Vigil changed positions once more, becoming a scientific review administrator at the Center for Scientific Review of the National Institutes of Health, in Bethesda, a post he held until his retirement in 2001.

Further Reading

American Society for Cell Biology. "Eugene Vigil." Member Profiles. Available online. URL: http://www.ascb.org/profiles/9607.html. Downloaded on April 19, 2005.

Society for Advancement of Chicanos and Native Americans in Science. "Dr. Eugene Vigil—Plant Biologist." SACNAS Biography Project. Available online. URL: http://64.171.10.183/biography/Biography.asp?mem=85&type=2. Downloaded on April 19, 2005.

"Vigil, Eugene Leon." In *American Men & Women of Science,* 21st ed., edited by Pamela M. Kalte and Katherine H. Nemeh, vol. 7, 284–285. Detroit: Thomson Gale, 2003.

Villablanca, Jaime R.
(Jaime Rolando Villablanca)
(1929–) *neurobiologist*

Jaime Rolando Villablanca's research deals with the ways in which a brain recovers from damage that occurs to it following some type of injury. His studies focus in particular on changes in the physical, chemical, and biological characteristics of the brain that has been damaged shortly after birth or before birth. Villablanca's research is expected to have important applications to an understanding of neurological disorders such as cerebral palsy in children, strokes in adults, and a variety of psychiatric conditions seen in childhood.

Villablanca was born in Chillán, Chile, on February 28, 1929, the son of Teresa Hernández V. and Ernesto Villablanca. He attended the National Institute of Chile, in Santiago, earning his bachelor's degree in biology in 1946, and the University of Chile, in Santiago, where he received his licentiate in medicine in 1953 and his doctor of medicine in 1954. Upon completion of his graduate studies, Villablanca was hired as instructor of pathological physiology at the University of Chile's School of Medicine, where he was eventually promoted to full professor. During this period, he also held academic appointments in the United States, including a Rockefeller Foundation postdoctoral fellow in physiology at Johns Hopkins University, in Baltimore, Maryland (1959–61); a fellow in the Neurological Unit of the Harvard Medical School, in Boston (1961); and an NIH (National Institutes of Health) Fogarty international research fellow in anatomy at the University of California at Los Angeles (UCLA, 1966–68).

In 1971, Villablanca left Chile to take a position as associate researcher in anatomy and psychiatry at the UCLA School of Medicine, after which he became associate professor (1972) and professor (1977) of psychiatry and biobehavioral sciences. He is now professor of neurobiology and of psychiatry and biobehavioral sciences at UCLA's Brain Research Institute. Among the honors he has received are the Decorated Order of Francisco de Miranda of the government of Venezuela (1988), the Queen Sofia Award of the government of Spain (1990), and the Lifetime Achievement Award of the UCLA School of Medicine (2001).

Further Reading

"Villablanca, Jaime Rolando." In *American Men & Women of Science,* 21st ed., edited by Pamela M. Kalte and Katherine H. Nemeh, vol. 7, 287. Detroit: Thomson Gale, 2003.

"Villablanca, Jaime Rolando." In *Who's Who in America—2005,* edited by Karen Chassie, 4,822. New Providence, N.J.: Marquis Who's Who, 2004.

Villa-Komaroff, Lydia
(Lydia Villa)
(1947–) *molecular biologist, scientific administrator*

Lydia Villa-Komaroff is an internationally recognized authority in cell and molecular biology, with special interest in cell development, protein synthesis, and recombinant DNA studies. Since 1998, she has devoted most of her time to administrative responsibilities, serving first as vice president for research at Northwestern University, in Chicago, and later as vice president of research and chief executive officer of the Whitehead Institute, a biomedical research and teaching institution founded in 1982 in Boston to recognize and support some of the best researchers in science.

Born Lydia Villa in Las Vegas, New Mexico, on August 7, 1947, she was the oldest of six children. Her mother was a social worker and teacher, and her father, a musician and teacher. She came from a family of strong, self-sufficient women. Her paternal grandmother had been a *curandera,* or healer, and her maternal grandmother had survived by selling chemical toilets on horseback to mountain dwellers. The Villa family had come originally from Spain, lived in Mexico for many generations, and moved to the United States in the early 20th century.

Villa-Komaroff credits much of her later academic success to the encouragement she received from her parents. For example, when she was only five years old, her father bought her the multivolume *Encyclopaedia Britannica,* a considerable financial investment for a family of modest means. By the time she was nine, Villa had decided to become a scientist and, while still in high school, was awarded a scholarship that allowed her to attend a summer research program in Texas sponsored by the National Science Foundation (NSF).

After graduating from high school in 1965, Villa entered the University of Washington, in Seattle, with plans to major in chemistry. Her first year at Washington was something of an academic disaster, however, capped by a counselor's advice to her that "women didn't belong in chemistry." Having had greater success in her freshman biology classes than her chemistry courses, she decided to change her major to biology with plans to become a physiologist.

In 1967, Villa left Seattle to follow her future husband, Tony Komaroff, to the Washington, D.C., area, hoping to continue her studies at Johns Hopkins University, in Baltimore, Maryland. Again, however, the specter of sexism reared its ugly head when she found that women were not being admitted to Johns Hopkins. Instead, she enrolled at nearby Goucher College, in Towson, Maryland, from which she received her B.A. in 1970. That same year she married Tony Komaroff and moved to Boston, where she began her graduate studies in biology at the Massachusetts Institute of Technology (MIT), in Cambridge. There, she worked with two of the great names of modern biology, David Baltimore and Harvey Lodish. With Baltimore, she studied the virus that causes poliomyelitis (polio), and with Lodish, she studied the mechanisms by which proteins are produced in cells. Her own doctoral thesis, for which she earned her Ph.D. in 1975, was a synthesis of these two lines of research: a study of the way in which polio virus proteins are synthesized in cells.

After completing her doctoral studies, Villa-Komaroff decided to continue her research at nearby Harvard University in one of the newest and most exciting fields of biological research, recombinant DNA. The term *recombinant DNA* (rDNA) refers to the process by which pieces of natural and/or synthetic DNA (deoxyribonucleic) molecules are cut apart and recombined in various ways, producing new types of organisms. One of the applications of DNA research is cloning, a process by which exact copies of some organisms are produced synthetically.

Villa-Komaroff's first research project at Harvard, an attempt to clone the American silkmoth, was thwarted, however, when in 1976 the city of Cambridge (where both MIT and Harvard are located) decided to place severe restrictions on the conduct of rDNA research within its boundaries. Along with a number of other researchers, Villa-Komaroff moved her research to facilities at Cold Spring Harbor, on Long Island, New York, where no such ban existed. She continued her work there until Cambridge modified its restrictions on rDNA research about a year later, allowing her to return to Harvard. Back in Cambridge, she worked on a research team led by Nobel Prize laureate Walter Gilbert, attempting to find a way of using bacteria to synthesize insulin. The team was successful in 1978, announcing a method for the production of insulin by bacteria and making one of the historic breakthroughs in modern biotechnology.

By the end of 1978, Villa-Komaroff had completed her studies at Harvard and had accepted a position as assistant professor of microbiology at the University of Massachusetts Medical School, in Worcester. There, she continued her research on insulinlike molecules but also spent more and more time teaching and on administrative responsibilities. Eventually, she came to feel that she was stretching herself too thin and in 1985, accepted a job in the Neurosciences Division at Children's Hospital in Boston that allowed her to focus more on research and less on teaching and administration. She remained at Children's Hospital for 10 years, where she studied problems in cell biology and endocrinology.

Throughout her decade at Children's, Villa-Komaroff found herself once more drawn to administration tasks, both at the national and local levels, and enjoying those responsibilities more and more. Thus, Northwestern University's offer of the post of associate vice president for research in 1995 seemed to be the ideal opportunity for her to make a career change. The greatest challenge, other than leaving research, was having to live in Chicago, 1,000 miles away from her husband, who still held a job in Boston. They decided to take a chance, however, and she moved to Chicago and Northwestern in 1996. Two years later, she became vice president for research at Northwestern, serving also as professor of neurology at the university's medical school. At Northwestern, Villa-Komaroff was in charge of research at all nine of the university's schools and director of its 17 research centers (nine of which were founded under her tenure).

In 2002, Villa-Komaroff received an offer from the Whitehead Institute to return to Boston and become vice president of research and chief executive officer with responsibility for establishing and defining the goals of the institute and managing the interaction between its research and administrative divisions. She accepted the offer with little hesitation, at least partly because it allowed her to return to her husband. She officially joined the institute on January 1, 2003.

For someone with as many job-related responsibilities as she has, it is somewhat surprising to learn that Villa-Komaroff also has a number of hobbies. Foremost among these is singing. While living in Chicago, she studied voice and performed as Lady Tiang in the Rodgers and Hammerstein musical play *The King and I.* She is also a strong advocate for greater participation by minorities in the sciences and mathematics and was a founding member of the Society for the Advancement of Chicanos and Native Americans in Science. In 1992, she was given a Hispanic Engineer National Achievement Award.

Further Reading

Meier, Matt S., with Conchita Franco Serri and Richard A. Garcia. "Villa-Komaroff, Lydia." In *Notable Latino Americans,* 288–289. Westport, Conn.: Greenwood Press, 1997.

Society for Advancement of Chicanos and Native Americans in Science. "Dr. Lydia Villa-Komaroff—Biologist." SACNAS Biography Project. Available online. URL: http://64.171.10.183/biography/Biography.asp?mem=86&type=2. Downloaded on March 21, 2005.

Whitehead Institute. "Whitehead Welcomes Lydia Villa-Komaroff." Available online. URL: http://www.wi.mit.edu/nap/features/nap_feature_lvk.html. Downloaded on March 21, 2005.

Worhach, Denise. "Lydia Villa-Komaroff." In *Notable Hispanic American Women,* book II. Detroit: Gale Biography Resource Center, 1998. Available online. URL: http://www.gale.com/free_resources/chh/bio/villa_l.htm. Downloaded on March 21, 2005.

Villarreal, Luis P.

(1949–) *virologist*

Luis P. Villarreal is interested in the chemical structure of viruses and the way they may have been involved in the early evolution of eukaryotic cells (cells that contain a nucleus enclosed within a membrane) and, hence, many forms of life that exist on Earth today. He also studies a number of other topics related to viruses, including the ways in which they can be "engineered" to perform new and different functions, such as the treatment of genetic disorders; the role played by viruses in cancer; and mechanisms by which the body defends against viral attacks.

Villarreal was born in East Los Angeles, California, on July 6, 1949, into a family of Mexican heritage. His father was involved in the real estate business, and the family moved frequently. Villarreal eventually attended 11 different grammar schools, three junior high schools, and five high schools. That experience, he later wrote, made him "very adaptable." Although he had little difficulty with his work in high school, he had few role models to whom he could look for guidance as to what he was to do with his life. In fact, he said that he never thought about pursuing graduate studies until he was a senior at California State University of Los Angeles (CSULA). Then, one of his teachers suggested that he pursue a doctoral program rather than going directly to work after leaving CSULA. After completing his B.S. in biochemistry at CSULA in 1971, Villarreal went on to the University of California at San Diego, where he earned his Ph.D. in biology in 1976.

Villarreal continued his studies in a postdoctoral program at Stanford University, in Stanford, California (1976–78), before taking a job as assistant professor at the University of Colorado School of Medicine, in Boulder, where he was later promoted to associate professor in 1984. A year later, he left Colorado to take a similar position at the University of California at Irvine, where he has remained ever since. In 1989, he was promoted to full professor. Villarreal has also been director of the university's Minority Science Program (1994–present), director of the Viral Vector Design Facility (1997–present), director of the Irvine Research Unit on Animal Viruses (1998–99), and director of the Center for Virus Research Organized Research Unit (1999–present).

Villarreal is the author of more than 90 papers in peer-reviewed journals and the book *Viruses and the Evolution of Life* (2005) and the coauthor of two other books, *Biology of AIDS* (2000) and *AIDS: Science and Society* (1998), both with Hung Fan and Ross F. Conner. He has been honored with the Distinguished Scientist Award from the Society for Advancement of Chicanos and Native Americans in Science (1997), a Distinguished Alumnus Award from CSULA (1997), and a Presidential Award for Excellence in Science, Mathematics and Engineering Mentoring in 2000.

Further Reading

College of Natural and Social Sciences, California State University at Los Angeles. "1997 Distinguished Alumnus." Newsletter, Director of Development. Available online. URL: http://www.calstatela.edu/

academic/nssd/nssoffice/Newsletter.htm. Downloaded on April 20, 2005.

Society for Advancement of Chicanos and Native Americans in Science. "Dr. Luis P. Villarreal—Virologist." SACNAS Biography Project. Available online. URL: http://64.171.10.183/biography/Biography.asp?mem=88&type=2. Downloaded on April 20, 2005.

"Villarreal, Luis Perez." In *American Men and Women of Science,* 21st ed., edited by Pamela M. Kalte and Katherine H. Nemeh, vol. 7, 288. Detroit: Thomson Gale, 2003.

Vivó, Juana Luisa Acrivos.   *See* ACRIVOS, JUANA LUISA VIVÓ

Z

Zavala, Maria Elena
(1950–) *botanist*

Maria Elena Zavala's area of expertise is in root development of plants. Her research is aimed at developing a better understanding of the way plant genes turn on and off in an orderly sequence that results in the regular growth of roots.

Zavala was born in Pomona, California, on January 9, 1950. At the time of her birth, her Mexican-American parents were migrant farmworkers who traveled around the state picking lemons. She grew up in a tightly knit community of Mexican Americans in Laverne, California. Her great-grandmother was a *curandera* (healer) whose large garden of herbs and other plants fascinated the young Zavala, perhaps inspiring her to consider botany as a life's work.

Zavala has written that she was regarded as a bit "weird" in high school because she did well in academic subjects and played in the school band. Most teachers and counselors at the time had low expectations for Latino students and wondered why someone like Zavala would consider going to college. They encouraged her to pursue a business course in high school so that she would have some skills "to fall back on" if she did not succeed in college.

Zavala never had to face that problem. She attended Pomona College, in Claremont, California, a highly respected private college, and earned her A.B. in botany in 1972. She then continued her studies at the University of California at Berkeley, receiving her Ph.D. in 1978. At the time, she thought that she might want to become a physician and took a number of premed courses, but she changed her mind after graduating from Berkeley and decided to pursue a career of research and teaching in botany.

After completing her doctoral program, Zavala moved to Indiana University, in Bloomington, for her postdoctoral studies. She then completed two more postdoctoral programs, one at the U.S. Department of Agriculture's Western Region Research Center in Albany, California, and one at Yale University, in New Haven, Connecticut. In 1986, she was offered a Rosa Parks/Cesar Chavez Visiting Professorship at Michigan State University, in East Lansing.

In 1988, Zavala was offered the post of assistant professor of botany at California State University at Northridge (CSUN). She has since been promoted to associate and full professor at Northridge. In addition to her teaching and research responsibilities there, Zavala is director of the Minority Access to Research Careers (MARC) program at Northridge, a program that was created in 1975 by the National Institute of General Medical Sciences to increase the number of biomedical and behavioral scientists from minority groups. In January 2001, Zavala was honored with the Presidential Award for Excellence in Science,

Mathematics, and Engineering by President Bill Clinton and in the same year, received a Wang Family Excellence Award from CSUN. In 2003, she was featured in a special series honoring Latino and Latina heroes by Los Angeles television station KCET.

Further Reading

American Society for Cell Biology. "ASCB Profile: Maria Elena Zavala." *ASCB Newsletter* 42 (October 2001): 18–20.

Society for Advancement of Chicanos and Native Americans in Science. "Dr. Maria Elena Zavala—Plant Biologist." SACNAS Biography Project. Available online. URL: http://64.171.10.183/biography/Biography.asp?mem=91&type=2. Downloaded on March 15, 2005.

Justgarciahill.org: A Virtual Community for Minorities in Science. "Zavala, Maria Elena, Ph.D." Available online. URL: http://justgarciahill.org/jghdocs/webbiographydtl.asp. Downloaded on March 15, 2005.

Zuñiga, Martha C.
(Martha Cecilia Zuñiga)
(1950–   ) *biologist*

Martha Cecilia Zuñiga's major research interest is the molecules that make up the major histocompatibility complex (MCH). These molecules alert the immune system when viruses invade the body or when foreign tissue is introduced into the body, as when grafts are made. A better understanding of MHC molecules is essential, therefore, in developing methods for treating viral diseases and for improving physicians' ability to make tissue grafts for the treatment of diseases and disorders.

Zuñiga was born in Laredo, Texas, on December 28, 1950, the second of 10 children born to Gloria Novoa and Guillermo Zuñiga, of Mexican ancestry. She grew up in an extended family, including more than 80 cousins, that held educational accomplishments in high regard. She developed an interest in mathematics and science early in life, although she often did not receive much encouragement from her schoolteachers. Still, as she later wrote, "there was never any doubt" that she would attend college, and her interest in a career in science was encouraged by a handful of teachers and counselors who made a special effort to encourage her.

Upon graduation from high school, Zuñiga enrolled at the University of St. Thomas, in Houston, Texas, before transferring to the University of Texas at Austin, from which she received her B.A. in zoology in 1971. At the time, she was considering a career in medicine, but by the time she began her graduate studies at Yale University, in New Haven, Connecticut, she had decided instead to pursue a career in research. She was awarded her M.Phil. and Ph.D. in biology from Yale in 1975 and 1977, respectively. She then remained at Yale to pursue her postdoctoral studies from 1978 to 1981.

In 1981, Zuñiga accepted an appointment as visiting research fellow at the California Institute of Technology in Pasadena, after which she was appointed postdoctoral fellow from 1982 to 1985 and then senior research fellow from 1985 to 1986. At the completion of that assignment, Zuñiga took a job as assistant professor of biology at the University of Texas at Austin. In 1990, she moved to the University of California at Santa Cruz, where she is now associate professor of molecular, cell, and developmental biology.

Zuñiga's research on MHC molecules may have a number of important applications in medicine. In the first place, it may help scientists better understand the changes that occur in cells and tissues when they are invaded by viruses, thus suggesting methods by which viral diseases may be treated. The research may also provide a better understanding of the mechanisms by which the body's immune system recognizes and rejects tissue grafts (such as skin grafts), thus improving the chance of survival of patients who depend on such grafts. There is some reason to believe that MHC molecules may also play a role in helping the body to destroy and reject tumors that begin to grow in the body, thus providing a possible treatment for at least some forms of cancer.

Further Reading

Society for Advancement of Chicanos and Native Americans in Science. "Dr. Martha Zuniga—Biologist." SACNAS Biography Project. Available online. URL: http://64.171.10.183/biography/Biography.asp?mem=92&type=2. Downloaded on March 16, 2005.

"Zuñiga, Marta Cecilia (Martha)." In *Who's Who among Hispanic Americans, 1994–95,* 3d ed., edited by Amy Unterburger, 886. Detroit: Gale Research, 1995.

BIBLIOGRAPHY

Benson, Sonia G., ed. *The Hispanic American Almanac.* 3d ed. Farmington Hills, Mich.: Thomson Gale, 2003.

Bernstein, Leonard, Alan Winkler, and Linda Zierdt-Warshaw. *Latino Women of Science.* Maywood, N.J.: Peoples Publishing Group, 1998.

Chassie, Karen, managing ed. *Who's Who in America–2005.* New Providence, N.J.: Marquis Who's Who, 2004.

Henderson, Ashyia N., ed. *Contemporary Hispanic Biography.* Farmington Hills, Mich.: Thomson Gale, 2003.

Hispanic Employment Program. "Featured Hispanics—NASA News Releases." Available online. URL: http://oeop.larc.nasa.gov/hep/hep-newsrelease.html. Downloaded on May 11, 2005.

———. "Hispanics@NASA LaRC." Available online. URL: http://oeop.larc.nasa.gov/hep/hep-bios.html. Downloaded on May 11, 2005.

———. "Latina Women of NASA." Available online. URL: http://oeop.larc.nasa.gov/hep/lwon/. Downloaded on May 11, 2005.

———. "NASA Hispanic Astronauts." Available online. URL: http://oeop.larc.nasa.gov/hep/hep-astronauts.html. Downloaded on May 11, 2005.

Kalte, Pamela M., and Katherine H. Nemeh, eds. *American Men & Women of Science.* 21st ed. Detroit: Thomson Gale, 2003.

McMurray, Emily J., ed. *Notable Twentieth-Century Scientists.* Detroit: Gale Research, 1995.

Meier, Matt S., with Conchita Franco Serri and Richard A. Garcia. *Notable Latino Americans.* Westport, Conn.: Greenwood Press, 1997.

Meyer, Nicholas E. *Biographical Dictionary of Hispanic Americans.* 2d ed. New York: Checkmark Books, 2001.

Olesky, Walter. *Hispanic-American Scientists.* New York: Facts On File, 1998.

Society for Advancement of Chicanos and Native Americans in Science. SACNAS Biography Project. Available online. URL: http://64.171.10.183/biography/listsscientist.asp. Downloaded on February 4, 2005.

Telgen, Diane, Jim Kamp, and Joseph M. Palmisano, eds. *Notable Hispanic American Women.* Detroit: Gale Research, 1998.

Unterburger, Amy, ed. *Who's Who among Hispanic Americans, 1994–95.* 3d ed. Detroit: Gale Research, 1995.

ENTRIES BY AREA OF ACTIVITY

Agronomy
Sánchez, Pedro

Anatomy
Alcalá, José Ramón

Anesthesiology
Garcia, Catalina Esperanza

Anthropology
Suárez-Orozco, Marcelo

Astrophysics
Córdova, France Anne

Atmospheric Chemistry
Molina, Mario

Biochemistry
Gutierrez, Peter L.
Ochoa, Severo
Rodríguez, Eloy

Biology
Avila, Vernon L.
Ayala, Francisco J.
Macagno, Eduardo R.
Zuñiga, Martha C.

Biomathematics
Cardús, David

Biophysics
Morales, Manuel F.

Biotechnology
Valdés, James J.

Botany
del Moral, Roger
Gómez-Pompa, Arturo
Macagno, Eduardo R.
Valverde, Rodrigo A.
Vigil, Eugene L.
Zavala, Maria Elena

Cardiology
Cardús, David
Cintron, Guillermo B.

Cell Biology
Gomez-Cambronero, Julian
González, Elma
Sabatini, David Domingo

Chemical Engineering
Estévez, L. Antonio

Chemistry
Abel, Carlos A.
Bernal, Ivan
Gomez, Frank A.
Ortiz de Montellano, Paul R.

Computer Science
García, Oscar N.
Noriega, Carlos

Dermatology
Diaz, Luis A.
Gigli, Irma

Ecology
Castro, Gonzalo
Lugo, Ariel E.
Mora, Miguel A.
Pérez, Francisco L.
Rodón-Naveira, Miriam

Economics
Mesa-Lago, Carmelo
Ricardo-Campbell, Rita
Robles, Bárbara J.

Educational Administration
Avila, Vernon L.
Castro, George
Córdova, France Anne
Cota-Robles, Eugene
Fernandez, Louis Anthony
Macagno, Eduardo R.
Maidique, Modesto A.

Endocrinology
Talamantes, Frank

Engineering

Alvarado, Raul, Jr.
Cubero, Linda Garcia
Foyo, George
Garcia, Marcelo H.
García, Oscar N.
Garcia-Luna-Aceves, J. J.
Gonzalez, Rafael C.
Gutiérrez, Ana Sol
Gutierrez, Orlando A.
Gutiérrez, Sidney
Hernández, John W.
Macari, Emir Jose
Maidique, Modesto A.
Medina, Miguel A., Jr.
Ochoa, Ellen
Peralta, Richard C.
Renteria, Hermelinda
Rodriguez-Iturbe, Ignacio

Entomology

Barbosa, Pedro
Rodriguez, Juan G.
Vega, Fernando E.

Environmental Science

Gonzalez, Paula
Hernández, John W.
López, Ann

Ethnology

Cabrera, Lydia

Geochemistry

Ruiz, Joaquin

Geology

Fernandez, Louis Anthony

Government

Carmona, Richard H.
Cavazos, Lauro F.
Diaz, Nils J.

Gutiérrez, Ana Sol
Novello, Antonia

Health Administration

Delgado, Jane L.
Novello, Antonia
Ramírez, Mario E.
Rodriguez-Trias, Helen
Villa-Komaroff, Lydia

Health Sciences

Cavazos, Lauro F.
Delgado, Jane L.
Novello, Antonia

Home Economics

Gilbert, Fabiola Cabeza de Baca

Immunology

Abel, Carlos A.
Aguilera, Renato J.
Benacerraf, Baruj

Invention

Alvarez, Luis Walter
Fernández-Pol, José A.
García, Oscar N.
Garcia-Luna-Aceves, J. J.
Gonzalez, Rafael C.
Maidique, Modesto A.
Marquez, Victor E.
Martinez, Richard I.
Ochoa, Ellen
Ondetti, Miguel A.
Rael, Eppie D.
Taboada, John

Mammology

Mares, Michael A.

Marine Biology

Alvariño, Angeles
Castro, Peter

Díaz, Robert J.
Ortega, Sonia

Mathematics

Bañuelos, Rodrigo
Berriozábal, Manuel
Calderón, Alberto P.
Calderón, Calixto P.
Ferreyra, Guillermo S.
Martínez, Cleopatria
Quesada, Antonio R.
Rodríguez-Johnson, Elizabeth
Sadosky, Cora
Tapia, Richard A.
Vélez, William Yslas

Mathematics Education

Escalante, Jaime
Quesada, Antonio R.

Mechanical Engineering

de la Mora, Juan Fernández
Figueroa, Orlando
Garcia, Carlos Ernesto

Medical Practice

Carmona, Richard H.
Finlay, Carlos Juan
Garcìa, Héctor P.
Hernández, Enrique
Novello, Antonia
Ramírez, Mario E.
Rodriguez-Trias, Helen

Medical Research

Cintron, Guillermo B.
Fernández-Pol, José A.
Finlay, Carlos Juan
García, Celso-Ramón
Gigli, Irma
Hernández, Enrique
Perez, Edith A.
Rodriguez-Sierra, Jorge F.
Vallbona, Carlos

Medicinal/Pharmaceutical Chemistry
Catalano, Carlos
Marquez, Victor E.
Ondetti, Miguel A.

Meteorology
Cortinas, John V., Jr.
Díaz, Henry F.
Kalnay, Eugenia

Microbiology
Alderete, John F.
Barrera, Cecilio
Cota-Robles, Eugene
Rael, Eppie D.

Molecular Biology
Alvarez-González, Rafael
Bustamante, Carlos J.
Gutierrez, Peter L.
Márquez-Magaña, Leticia
Villa-Komaroff, Lydia

Natural History
Mexía, Ynés

Neurosciences and Neurosurgery
Díaz, Fernando G.
García, Julio H.
Gonzalez-Lima, Francisco
Martinez, Joe L., Jr.
Villablanca, Jaime R.

Nuclear Physics
Diaz, Nils J.
Fernández-Baca, Jaime A.
Reyes, José N., Jr.

Nursing
Amaya, Maria
Calvillo, Evelyn R.

Oceanography
Garzoli, Silvia L.

Ophthalmology
Candia, Oscar A.
Fischbarg, Jorge

Parasitology
Guerrero, Jorge

Pediatrics
Novello, Antonia
Vallbona, Carlos

Pharmacology
Cuatrecasas, Pedro
Urquilla, Pedro R.

Physical Chemistry
Acrivos, Juana Luisa Vivó
Castro, George
Martínez, Richard I.
Sanchez, Isaac C.

Physics
Alvarez, Luis Walter
Baez, Albert V.
Cardona, Manuel
Chang-Díaz, Franklin
Garcia, Jose Dolores, Jr.
José, Jorge V.
Llamas, Vicente J.
López, Jorge A.
Macagno, Eduardo R.
Rios, Miguel, Jr.
Taboada, John

Physiology
Cavazos, Lauro F.
Ochoa, Severo
Romero, Juan Carlos

Planetary Geology
Ocampo, Adriana C.

Psychiatry
Escobar, Javier I.
Serrano, Alberto C.

Psychology
Arredondo, Patricia M.
Barona, Andrés, Jr.
Bernal, Martha
De La Cancela, Victor
Delgado, Jane L.
Gómez, Cynthia A.
Padilla, Amado M.
Suárez-Orozco, Marcelo

Research/Policy Analysis
Rodríguez-Johnson, Elizabeth

Scientific Administration
Niebla, Elvia
Ortega, Sonia
Rodón-Naveira, Miriam
Villa-Komaroff, Lydia

Science Education
Baez, Albert V.
Cifuentes, Inés
Llamas, Vicente J.

Seismology
Cifuentes, Inés

Sociology
Alvarez, Rodolfo
Baca Zinn, Maxine
Castro, Max
Hernández, José
Ortiz, Vilma
Rodríguez, Clara E.
Samora, Julián

Soil Science
Niebla, Elvia
Sposito, Garrison

Space Sciences

Acuna, Mario
Chang-Díaz, Franklin
Figueroa, Orlando
Gutiérrez, Sidney
Lopez, Ramon E.
Noriega, Carlos
Ochoa, Ellen

Statistics

Duran, Benjamin S.

Telecommunications

Foyo, George

Virology

Casals-Ariet, Jordi
Villareal, Luis P.

Wildlife Administration

Castro, Gonzalo

Wildlife Biology

Dallmeier, Francisco

Writing

Avila, Vernon L.
Baez, Albert V.
Castro, Max

Zoology

Rivero, Juan A.

ENTRIES BY YEAR OF BIRTH

1833
Finlay, Carlos Juan

1870
Mexía, Ynés

1894
Gilbert, Fabiola Cabeza
de Baca

1899/1900
Cabrera, Lydia

1905
Ochoa, Severo

1911
Alvarez, Luis Walter
Casals-Ariet, Jordi

1912
Baez, Albert V.

1914
García, Héctor P.

1916
Alvariño, Angeles

1919
Morales, Manuel F.

1920
Benacerraf, Baruj
Calderón, Alberto P.
Ricardo-Campbell, Rita
Rodriguez, Juan G.
Samora, Julián

1921
García, Celso-Ramón

1922
Cardús, David

1923
Rivero, Juan A.

1926
Cota-Robles, Eugene
Ramírez, Mario E.

1927
Cavazos, Lauro F.
Vallbona, Carlos

1928
Acrivos, Juana Luisa Vivó
Gutierrez, Orlando A.

1929
Hernández, John W.
Rodriguez-Trias, Helen
Villablanca, Jaime R.

1930
Abel, Carlos A.
Escalante, Jaime
Ondetti, Miguel A.

1931
Bernal, Ivan
Bernal, Martha
Berriozábal, Manuel
Gigli, Irma
Sabatini, David Domingo
Serrano, Alberto C.

1932
Gonzalez, Paula

1933
García, Julio H.

1934
Ayala, Francisco J.
Cardona, Manuel
Gómez-Pompa, Arturo
Mesa-Lago, Carmelo

1935
Candia, Oscar A.
Fischbarg, Jorge
Hernández, José

1936
Alvarez, Rodolfo

Cuatrecasas, Pedro
Garcia, Carlos Ernesto
Garcia, Jose Dolores, Jr.
García, Oscar N.

1937
Romero, Juan Carlos

1938
Diaz, Nils J.

1939
Calderón, Calixto P.
Castro, George
Duran, Benjamin S.
Fernandez, Louis Anthony
Gutierrez, Peter L.
Sposito, Garrison
Tapia, Richard A.
Urquilla, Pedro R.

1940
Acuna, Mario
Alcalá, José Ramón
Maidique, Modesto A.
Sadosky, Cora
Sánchez, Pedro

1941
Avila, Vernon L.
Garzoli, Silvia L.
Rios, Miguel, Jr.
Sanchez, Isaac C.
Vigil, Eugene L.

1942
Baca Zinn, Maxine
Barrera, Cecilio
Cintron, Guillermo B.
Diaz, Luis A.
González, Elma
Gonzalez, Rafael C.
Guerrero, Jorge

Gutiérrez, Ana Sol
Kalnay, Eugenia
Ortiz de Montellano, Paul R.
Padilla, Amado M.
Rodriguez-Iturbe, Ignacio

1943
Calvillo, Evelyn R.
Castro, Peter
del Moral, Roger
Escobar, Javier I.
Fernandez-Pol, José A.
Lugo, Ariel E.
Macagno, Eduardo R.
Marquez, Victor E.
Mesa-Lago, Carmelo
Molina, Mario
Rael, Eppie D.
Taboada, John
Talamantes, Frank

1944
Barbosa, Pedro
Llamas, Vicente J.
Martinez, Joe L., Jr.
Martinez, Richard I.
Novello, Antonia
Rodríguez, Clara E.

1945
Arredondo, Patricia M.
Barona, Andrés, Jr.
López, Ann
Mares, Michael A.
Niebla, Elvia
Rodriguez-Sierra, Jorge F.

1946
Alvarado, Raul, Jr.
Díaz, Fernando G.
Díaz, Robert J.
Foyo, George
Medina, Miguel A., Jr.

1947
Córdova, France Anne
Garcia, Catalina Esperanza
Rodríguez, Eloy
Vélez, William Yslas
Villa-Komaroff, Lydia

1948
Díaz, Henry F.
Martínez, Cleopatria
Quesada, Antonio R.

1949
Carmona, Richard H.
José, Jorge V.
Peralta, Richard C.
Villareal, Luis P.

1950
Alderete, John F.
Chang-Díaz, Franklin
Estévez, L. Antonio
Pérez, Francisco L.
Zavala, Maria Elena
Zuñiga, Martha C.

1951
Bustamante, Carlos J.
Castro, Max
Gutiérrez, Sidney
Hernández, Enrique
Ruiz, Joaquin
Valdés, James J.

1952
De La Cancela, Victor
de la Mora, Juan Fernández
Valverde, Rodrigo A.

1953
Dallmeier, Francisco
Delgado, Jane L.
Ferreyra, Guillermo S.

ENTRIES BY ETHNICITY OR COUNTRY OF ORIGIN

Argentina
Abel, Carlos A.
Acuna, Mario
Calderón, Alberto P.
Calderón, Calixto P.
Candia, Oscar A.
Fernandez-Pol, José A.
Ferreyra, Guillermo S.
Fischbarg, Jorge
Garcia, Marcelo H.
Garzoli, Silvia L.
Gigli, Irma
Kalnay, Eugenia
Macagno, Eduardo R.
Ondetti, Miguel A.
Romero, Juan Carlos
Sabatini, David Domingo
Sadosky, Cora
Serrano, Alberto C.
Suárez-Orozco, Marcelo

Bolivia
Escalante, Jaime

Chile
Estévez, L. Antonio
Peralta, Richard C.
Villablanca, Jaime R.

Colombia
Bernal, Ivan

Costa Rica
Chang-Díaz, Franklin
Valverde, Rodrigo A.

Escobar, Javier I.
García, Julio H.
Gutierrez, Peter L.
Ocampo, Adriana C.

Cuba
Acrivos, Juana Luisa Vivó
Cabrera, Lydia
Castro, Max
Delgado, Jane L.
Díaz, Henry F.
Diaz, Nils J.
Finlay, Carlos Juan
Foyo, George
García, Oscar N.
Gonzalez, Rafael C.
Gonzalez-Lima, Francisco
Gutierrez, Orlando A.
Maidique, Modesto A.
Martínez, Richard I.
Medina, Miguel A., Jr.
Mesa-Lago, Carmelo
Rodriguez-Sierra, Jorge F.
Sánchez, Pedro

Dominican Republic
Reyes, José N., Jr.

Ecuador
Cifuentes, Inés

El Salvador
Gutiérrez, Ana Sol
Urquilla, Pedro R.

Honduras
Morales, Manuel F.

Mexico
Aguilera, Renato J.
Alderete, John F.
Alvarado, Raul, Jr.
Alvarez, Rodolfo
Alvarez-González, Rafael
Amaya, Maria
Arredondo, Patricia M.
Avila, Vernon L.
Baca Zinn, Maxine
Baez, Albert V.
Bañuelos, Rodrigo
Barona, Andrés, Jr.
Barrera, Cecilio
Bernal, Martha
Berriozábal, Manuel
Calvillo, Evelyn R.
Castro, George
Catalano, Carlos
Cavazos, Lauro F.
Córdova, France Anne

Cortinas, John V., Jr.
Cota-Robles, Eugene
Díaz, Fernando G.
Duran, Benjamin S.
Garcia, Carlos Ernesto
Garcia, Catalina Esperanza
García, Héctor P.
Garcia, Jose Dolores, Jr.
Garcia-Luna-Aceves, J. J.
Gilbert, Fabiola Cabeza de Baca
Gómez, Cynthia A.
Gomez, Frank A.
Gómez-Pompa, Arturo
González, Elma
Gonzalez, Paula
Gutiérrez, Sidney
Hernández, John W.
José, Jorge V.
Llamas, Vicente J.
López, Ann
López, Jorge A.
Macari, Emir Jose
Mares, Michael A.
Márquez-Magaña, Leticia
Martínez, Cleopatria
Martinez, Joe L., Jr.
Mexía, Ynés
Molina, Mario
Niebla, Elvia
Ochoa, Ellen
Ortiz de Montellano, Paul R.
Padilla, Amado M.
Rael, Eppie D.
Ramírez, Mario E.
Renteria, Hermelinda
Rios, Miguel, Jr.
Robles, Bárbara J.
Rodríguez, Eloy

Rodriguez, Juan G.
Rodríguez-Johnson, Elizabeth
Ruiz, Joaquin
Samora, Julián
Sanchez, Isaac C.
Sposito, Garrison
Taboada, John
Talamantes, Frank
Tapia, Richard A.
Vélez, William Yslas
Vigil, Eugene L.
Villa-Komaroff, Lydia
Villareal, Luis P.
Zavala, Maria Elena
Zuñiga, Martha C.

Nicaragua
Ortega, Sonia

Peru
Bustamante, Carlos J.
Castro, Gonzalo
Diaz, Luis A.
Fernández-Baca, Jaime A.
Guerrero, Jorge
Noriega, Carlos

Puerto Rico
Alcalá, José Ramón
Barbosa, Pedro
Carmona, Richard H.
Castro, Peter
Cintron, Guillermo B.
Cubero, Linda Garcia
De La Cancela, Victor
Fernandez, Louis Anthony
Figueroa, Orlando

Hernández, Enrique
Hernández, José
Lopez, Ramon E.
Lugo, Ariel E.
Novello, Antonia
Ortiz, Vilma
Perez, Edith A.
Rivero, Juan A.
Rodón-Naveira, Miriam
Rodríguez, Clara E.
Rodriguez-Trias, Helen
Vega, Fernando E.

Spain
Alvarez, Luis Walter
Alvariño, Angeles
Ayala, Francisco J.
Cardona, Manuel
Cardús, David
Casals-Ariet, Jordi
Cuatrecasas, Pedro
de la Mora, Juan Fernández
del Moral, Roger
Díaz, Robert J.
García, Celso-Ramón
Gomez-Cambronero, Julian
Ochoa, Severo
Pérez, Francisco L.
Quesada, Antonio R.
Ricardo-Campbell, Rita
Valdés, James J.
Vallbona, Carlos

Venezuela
Benacerraf, Baruj
Dallmeier, Francisco
Marquez, Victor E.
Rodriguez-Iturbe, Ignacio

INDEX

Boldface locators indicate main entries. *Italic* locators indicate photographs.